TRAVEL COMPANION

INDREK ROHTMETS

A CULTURAL GUIDE TO ESTONIA

Translated by
Marika Liivamägi
Tiina Randviir

CONTENTS

Foreword 5
Hiiumaa 7
Saaremaa 25
Pärnumaa 45
Läänemaa 61
Raplamaa 77
Harjumaa 95
Lääne-Virumaa 121
Ida-Virumaa 151
Jõgevamaa 173
Tartumaa 193
Põlvamaa 217
Võrumaa 239
Valgamaa 259
Viljandimaa 281
Järvamaa 319
Indexes 349

TRAVEL COMPANION

Original Title:
Indrek Rohtmets
Kultuurilooline Eestimaa. Teekaaslane
Varrak, 2004

The publication of this book was supported
by Estonian Ministry of Culture

Translated by Marika Liivamägi and Tiina Randviir
Edited by Neil Taylor
Designed by Kersti Tormis

© Translation. Marika Liivamägi and Tiina Randviir, 2006
© Foreword. Neil Taylor, 2006
© Kirjastus Varrak, 2004, 2006
ISBN 9985-3-1044-6

Kirjastus Varrak
Tallinn, 2006
www.varrak.ee

Printed by OÜ Greif

Even 15 years after independence was restored to Estonia, far too many visitors see Tallinn and Estonia as synonymous. In Soviet times, this was understandable since most of the country was closed to foreigners. As a result, the myth arose that there was little else to visit in Estonia and the vast majority of tourists still spend just a day or two in Tallinn before racing on to Riga. With this book, the truth should finally come out and probably many foreign residents in Tallinn will be surprised at how little they know of Estonia. Even if they only venture to Harjumaa, they will see the diversity of what Estonia beyond its capital has to offer, in nature and in buildings that may be modern or which have a history stretching back several centuries. Having written an English-lanugage guidebook myself to this country, I thought I knew the country well. Reading "The Cultural Guide to Estonia" was in some ways a shock, as the limits of my knowledge were brought home to me. On the other hand, I was glad to see how much more there is to discover, even though I spend several weeks each year exploring the country.

Indrek Rohtmets has been very courageous in ignoring Tallinn and Tartu in this book, but it is a sensible move. We do not need further descriptions of Toompea, St Olav's or Jaani Kirik. What foreigners do need, and now have with this book, is comprehensive coverage of every county, with their churches, castles and national parks. The author has not however just parked his car for a few minutes at each location and written a bland description of what he happens to notice. If an item worthy of note requires a long walk to reach it, this does not deter him. He has tracked down artistic gravestones, recent archaeological discoveries and individual houses worthy of note. We learn where Estonia's artists, writers and politicians were born, where they lived, where they died and where they are now buried. We learn of the difficulties even the rich Baltic-German landlords had in completing their manor-houses, but we are equally made aware of all the destruction caused by the warfare during Estonia's first struggle for independence in 1918-20 and then the neglect of so many buildings during the forty-five years of the Soviet occupation. Fifteen years is hardly long enough to remedy the horrors of the preceding eighty years, but the author conscientiously tells us of the work that has been carried out during that time and what we can expect to see in the near future from his continuation.

Conscientious authors such as Indrek Rohtmets are always eager to hear from readers who may have made further discoveries or who might even have found a mistake. I am sure however that the greatest compliment to this book will be the close similarity the second edition will have with this first one. A few updates will of course be necessary as restoration continues around the country, but the bulk of his scholarship will be valid for decades to come and it is hard to think of this book ever being replaced.

Neil Taylor

HIIUMAA

The first settlers of Hiiumaa were supposedly the seal hunters from Scandinavia who burned their campfires on Kõpu Peninsula as early as 7600 years ago. It took over 2000 years before the hunters began establishing the first permanent settlements on the island. In Kõpu, the first villages were inhabited about 5000 years ago. In 1228, the Emperor of the Holy Roman Empire gave the island to Bishop Gottfried, calling it Dageida, an isolated and deserted island (*insula deserta*). Such thoughtlessness is certainly not to the liking of any Hiiumaa inhabitant, and the archaeologists object as well. True, the island has never been densely populated, a fact that is not unpleasant in our modern over-populated world.

Hiiumaa has sometimes been regarded as the back yard of its bigger southern neighbour, Saaremaa. This might have been true in olden times. However, according to historians, the history of the two islands went their separate ways from the beginning of the Livonian War (1558–1583), and later the people of Hiiumaa have rather looked towards the Western coast and the capital city Tallinn. Dialectal languages of the two islands still manifest traces of similar origin. Some West-Hiiumaa settlements probably originate from West-Saaremaa, and the same goes for several eastern settlements. The Swedes who once inhabited Northern Hiiumaa were, on the orders of Catharine II, largely deported to Southern Ukraine in the 18th century, and in 1810 the local manor lords Ungern-Sternbergs forced the remaining population to Vormsi Island and Noarootsi Peninsula.

Hiiumaa still has a lot of wild nature, forests and miles of sandy beaches. It also has many historical and architectural monuments that speak of the island's fascinating and even dramatic past.

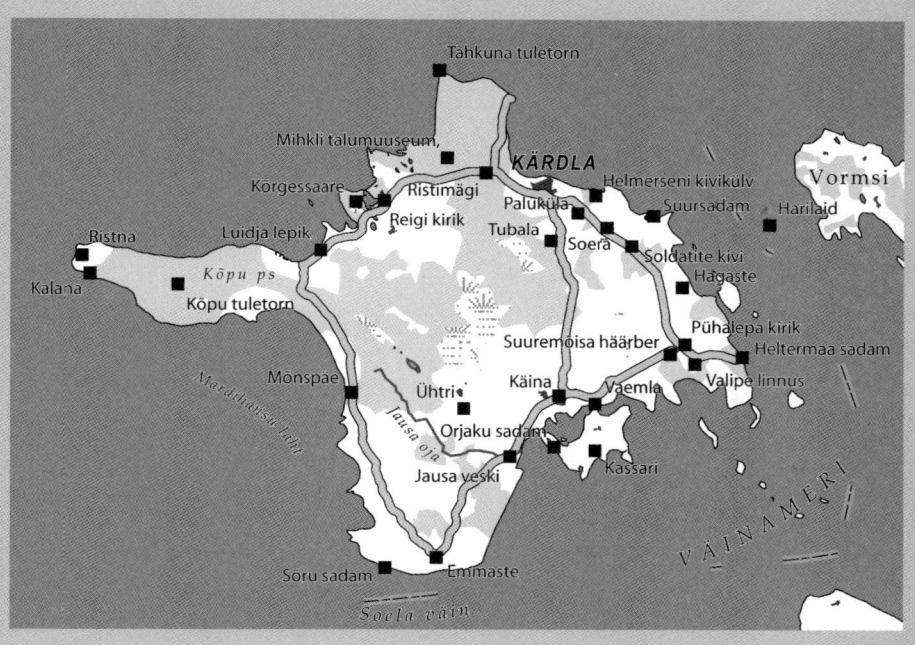

PÜHALEPA

Although it is possible to fly to Hiiumaa from Tallinn, the most important connection between the island and the mainland is the Rohuküla – Heltermaa ferry. On a clear day, Hiiumaa is visible from the mainland. After the 22-km, 90-minute journey the visitor steps on firm ground in Heltermaa, the biggest port of the island. Weather permitting, the voyage offers spectacular views of the islets of Väinameri in the south and Hari kurk in the north.

Heltermaa harbour was established in the second half of the 19th century. The first steamer, grandly called "Progress", started regular traffic to Haapsalu in 1870. Over the years, the harbour has been expanded and modernised.

In 2000 Aulin Rimm's sculpture "Woman in the Wind" was set up at the harbour.

Valipe stronghold. About 5 km from Heltermaa towards Kärdla, a signpost points to a hill with a pine-grove about 2 km off the road. This is thought to be the site of the stronghold belonging to both the Ösel-Wiek bishop and the Livonian Order, although the stronghold was never actually completed.

Another assumption is that there was a harbour near Valipe about 700 years ago (the sea was much higher then, or to be more precise, the land was lower). The survived wall remains, stairs and the well-site date from a later period.
Archaeological excavations confirm that these are the ruins of a modest fortified manor house or stronghold from the 15th–17th centuries.

Suuremõisa mansion. At the point where the Käina Road turns off the Heltermaa-Kärdla Road, stands one of the grandest buildings in Hiiumaa, also considered one of the most remarkable and beautiful examples of a Baroque manorial complex in Estonia. The history of Suuremõisa dates back to the 16th century; the Baroque castle was built in 1755–1760 and wings were added in 1772. At that time the manor belonged to Ebba Margaretha Stenbock (*nee* De la Gardie). When the castle was being completed, the Russian empress Yelizaveta Petrovna visited Suuremõisa.

Suuremõisa mansion and territory is associated with one of the most famous, or rather notorious, Hiiumaa inhabitants of all time – the Ungru Count or Baron Otto Reinhold Ludwig von Ungern-Sternberg. He had seen the world, served various rulers and studied at Leipzig University. In 1781 he bought the Kõrgessaare manor in Hiiumaa and settled there. The owner of Suuremõisa at the time, Count Jakob Pontus Stenbock, lived a lavish life and always ran into debt, so von Ungern-Sternberg began buying up his debentures. As a result, the new owner of Suuremõisa in 1796 was the Ungru Count.

The Count was a man of contradictions, on the one hand being deeply religious, educated and enterprising, but on the other also extremely greedy and scheming. He was an expert businessman and farmer, set up workshops, distilled spirits and built ships. His house contained an excellent collection of literature and his rye was sold in the markets of Amsterdam. At the same time he was involved in rescuing shipwrecks, which was a paid activity at that time. As Kõrgessaare manor was responsible for the Kõpu light-

The mid-18th century Suuremõisa Baroque mansion imitates the style of Swedish royal castles.

house, the baron managed to get considerable sums of money out of the state, but it was still not enough. However, he was no pirate. He was primarily accused of putting enormous price tags on his rescue services, hiding the saved treasures and doing business with goods on which he had paid no duty.

The fatal moment arrived on 19 October 1802 when the Count, in the course of a fierce argument in his office with Karl Johann Malm, captain of "Brig Moranian", knifed him dead. The Stenbocks who had never managed to accept the loss of Suuremõisa, now arranged for the Baron to be put on trial and sentenced to hard labour. The Count of Ungru died in 1811 in the town of Tobolsk in Siberia, where he suffered no deprivation of any kind as his family sent him 20,000 roubles a year.

Suuremõisa Manor originally had 64 rooms. Remarkable details include a carved oak main door, ceiling painting in the dining room with an inscription, "God will lay the table for those who stay sober and pious at work", stairs, smoke hoods and the double ceilings in the attic where the baron allegedly kept his loot. The castle is surrounded by the two hundred years old English-style park.

Alleys offer a great sight as well. They were planted around two hundred years ago in the best traditions of German alley culture. Chestnut, oak and maple alleys run towards Heltermaa; those in the direction of Kärdla consist of horse chestnuts, maples and oaks, whereas Käina Road is lined by a 5-km long alley of 150-year-old common alders.

An alley of deciduous trees in Suuremõisa is several hundred years old.

Today, the mansion accommodates a school and Suuremõisa Technical College, where among other things, young people can also study seafaring.

Pühalepa Church. Pühalepa village lies near Suuremõisa in the direction of Kärdla. In the middle of the village stands Pühalepa Church, reputedly the oldest surviving building in Hiiumaa, which originates from the mid-13th century. Similarly to other places of worship, the church has been destroyed and rebuilt many times over the centuries.

Pühalepa Church acquired the appearance it has today in the last quarter of the 19th century. The beautiful interior offers various sights to the visitor, e.g. the Baroque stone pulpit, which is unique in the whole country. The walls are decorated with the Knights of Malta Crosses, an indication that the Baron belonged in the Order of Malta. There is also a sign of cross resembling swastika near a staircase, the only example in the churches of the Baltic countries. The famous carved altar is today displayed at the Museum of Estonian Art in Tallinn.

The churchyard in spring delights the visitor with a carpet of naturalised wild tulips.

Stones of covenant. Turning from Pühalepa towards Kerema, we soon come upon a pile of stones a few metres high and a few dozen metres wide, called Otimäe stones. There are several theories as of the origin of this huge heap. The first is an ancient custom of Hiiumaa by which every man who returned from the sea added a stone as a protection

The Baroque stone pulpit in Pühalepa Church is the only of its kind in Estonian rural churches.

In spring the Pühalepa Church is surrounded by red tulips.

An offering place for seamen, grave of the Viking king or a reminder of manorial serfdom?

against misfortune. The other legend claims this to be the burial place of Ingvar, king of the Vikings who was allegedly killed in battle around the year 600. According to sagas he was buried where he fell, and one of the possible places is Otimäe. At the same time there is a place in Läänemaa with another 'grave' of Ingvar.

The reason for amassing such a heap of stones could in fact be much simpler. There exists, for example, a legend about a cruel bailiff at Suuremõisa who forced people to gather stones there in order to set up a monument to himself. Exegi monumentum!

Kallaste cliff is hidden in the forest.

Turning from the Heltermaa-Kärdla Road at the Vahtrepa crossroad to the lane running along the coast, we pass the 10 m high and 400 m long Kallaste cliff.

The first Estonian ship that sailed the South Seas was built at Suursadam.

Suursadam (Big Harbour). Turning from the Heltermaa-Kärdla Road towards Sääre we reach the former most important harbour in Hiiumaa. In the Middle Ages people burnt lime and built ships here. Lime has always been a significant export article.

The most famous ship built at the harbour was the barque 'Hioma', completed in 1848 that belonged to Heinrich Georg Eduard von Ungern-Sternberg. 'Hioma' was most likely the first Estonian boat and crew who sailed on the seas of southern hemisphere, turned around Cape Horn and reached the Pacific Ocean.

Some old harbour buildings have survived; one of them accommodates a small museum of local maritime history. Anchors standing by the entrance gate belonged to the ships of Carl XII (1682–1718). Today, Suursadam functions as a shipyard and a fish-collecting centre.

Another interesting phenomenon is connected with the harbour. In various places around Hiiumaa, stone labyrinths have been found under the turf. One lies near Suursadam by the road leading to Sääre. It is 2.5 km long and has 54 circular passages.

The villagers gave the two men from Siberia a proper burial place.

Memorial to Russian soldiers. Near the old Partsi crossroad stands a memorial stone to two unknown Russian soldiers who were captured by the Germans in 1917 and executed at the manor. The locals buried the two Siberian men and set up a stone in their memory.

Soera farm museum. From Palade crossroads towards the coast and Kukka, is the Palade schoolhouse, and a few hundred metres further we see Soera Farm Museum. The museum gives an idea what a typical Hiiumaa farm looked like a few hundred years ago. The old houses display various agricultural tools, from a threshing machine to querns. Those who would like to see the really huge Kukka boulder – the size of a house – must drive on to Kukka village.

Paluküla Church is also a seamark.

Soera Farm Museum shows the everyday life of Hiiumaa inhabitants a few hundred years ago.

Paluküla Church has also served the inhabitants as a seamark for as long as a century and a half. The church was built by the sons of the Ungru Count in 1820.

Kärdla meteorite crater. Estonia ranks first in the world for the number of meteorite craters per one area unit, boasting 400 times more craters on a unit than the world average. No wonder then that Hiiumaa has its own crater. Never mind that it happened 445 million years ago when today's Estonia acted as seabed somewhere in the South Pole.

The celestial stone had a diameter of about 22 m, causing a 500-m-deep hole with a perimeter of 4 km. The crater gradually filled with sediments and mud, the explosion walls crumbled as well, so that the real nature of the crater emerged only in 1980. Besides layers of rock, the holes bored into the crater revealed mineral water that was bottled and sold under the name 'Kärdla' until 1933.

Today the outline of the crater can barely be guessed. For a better view a platform has been built nearby.

Helmersen boulders. These magnificent boulders can be found in Hausma village near Kärdla. Gregor Helmersen, a Baltic German academic in St Petersburg, named them the most typical of their kind in the entire Baltic region. The boulders are scattered on an area of half a hectare.

Tubala village and Hiiumaa anchor. The village (5 km south along Käina Road) is worthy of mention for quite a peculiar reason. It has an oblong esker that according to a legend was once amassed around the stake which keeps Hiiumaa anchored to the bottom of the sea.

KÄRDLA

The former Hiiu-Swedish coastal village (one of many Swedish names was Kärr Dale) began to develop fast when in 1829 the sons of the notorious Ungru Count transferred their broadcloth factory there from Suuremõisa. The factory was well equipped, and most of the machinery worked on steam. Soon a new wharf was completed and comfortable houses for the workers were under way. Various facts nevertheless darken the seeming idyll created by the Ungern-Sternbergs.

The Swedes in Hiiumaa had been free men as long as anyone could remember and had no wish to stoop to the power of the Baltic German aristocracy. In 1781 over one thousand Swedes were deported to the Ukraine to 'secure' the empire's borders. In 1810 the Ungern-Sternbergs raised all taxes so much that most Swedes moved to Vormsi Island, Haapsalu and Noarootsi. Having got rid of the Swedes the barons could shape a submissive and dutiful workforce. The number of workers rose quickly. In order to prevent them from leaving the owners paid them with 'factory' money that was valid in factory shops. These, naturally, again belonged to the Ungern-Sternbergs.

The broadcloth factory expanded, the population of Kärdla increased and culture flourished. In 1860 the factory developed into a branch of heavy industry that operated for a few dozen years, producing various agricultural tools. The new factory buildings were completed after the fire in 1870.

The broadcloth factory operated until 1941 when the Soviet army burnt it down. Because of competition, the last dozen or so years were not very successful.

Kärdla today still has a lot that recalls the old broadcloth factory. The latter's residential houses had once won awards at world fairs.

The most important of the surviving buildings is the so-called Pikk (long) house that accommodates the **Hiiumaa Museum**. Only a century ago this house was home to the factory's administration. The museum offers a thorough overview of Hiiumaa's history.

Monument to Kärdla broadcloth factory burnt down by the Soviet army.

Monument to the song festival in Kärdla Park.

A monument in the courtyard of the former factory remembers the once flourishing enterprise. The copper plate on the pediment shows a bas-relief of the factory that was completed in 1873. Turning from there to Vabaduse Square we soon reach the crossroad of Kalda Street, the site of the first residential workers' house with a chimney.

Rannapark and 'the last Swede'. The park lies behind the museum. It was previously called Paruniaed (Baron's Garden) because baron R. E. von Ungern-Sternberg had it established in the place of a Swedish cemetery. An iron cross in the western side of the park is the one surviving element of the old cemetery. This was the grave of Karel Tarning, the last person to be buried in that cemetery about one hundred years ago.

The local choir stand is in the **Kärdla Linnapark (Town Park)**. The first song festival in Kärdla took place here in 1926 and a monument is dedicated to this event. The first song festival in Hiiumaa, however, was organised as early as 1867 in Leigri village in the courtyard of the pub in Murru.

Kivi-Jüri (Stone-Jüri). On the most important Kärdla crossroad where the Heltermaa-Käina-Kõrgessaare roads start, stands a granite column with a head of a soldier on it. This is quite likely the biggest granite bust in Estonia, made by sculptor Endel Taniloo and architect Ülo Sibul.

Stone-Jüri remembers all who perished in the war.

The 10-tonne stone head, commemorating everybody who fell in the Second World War, is familiarly known as Kivi-Jüri.

KÕRGESSAARE

Ristimägi (Cross Hill). The hill is located about 6 km from Kärdla towards Kõrgessaare, in Risti village. It offers a memorable sight – an entire hill full of crosses and cross-shaped objects.

There are quite a few legends about wedding processions who met face to face here at the hill and soon quarrelled as neither wanted to give way to the other. In the ensuing fighting some people were killed, including the bride on one side and the bridegroom on the other. The surviving reputedly later married. According to another legend, the first crosses were put there by local Swedes who were deported from their homes in 1781.

In 1991, 210 years after the forceful deportation, a cross of two stone hand mills was placed on the hill to remember the deported Swedes. Why or who put the very first cross here, is not known. Locals, however, seem certain of one thing – you can hope for happiness in marriage only after putting your own cross on Ristimägi!

Mihkli Farm Museum. 1.5 km from Kõrgessaare Road towards Malvaste (Tahkuna road) is the Museum, a bit right from the road. The open-air branch of Hiiumaa Museum consists of eight buildings, including the farmer's house, barns, sauna, stables and cellar.

Like Saaremaa, Hiiumaa has its Mihkli Farm Museum as well.

Tahkuna Peninsula can be regarded as the gatepost of the Gulf of Finland. No wonder then that this gatepost was closely guarded by both the tsarist and Soviet armies. The woods near the coast still contain various firing positions, shelters and cast iron foundations for cannons. A narrow-gauge railway was established before WW I for transporting military equipment. Only the causeway remains of it today. Although the reach of the powerful 300-mm cannons was 26 km, they did not play a great part in the battles of WW I.

After the so-called August 1939 treaty of military bases, the Soviet Union set up a battery of four

Ristimägi has become a legend itself.

The lighthouse was brought from Paris

The bell ringing in the wind remembers those who died on the ferry Estonia.

130-mm cannons and numerous other defence constructions. This battery did not play any great part in the battles either. In October 1941 fierce fighting broke out between the marines of the Baltic navy and the Estonian battalion supported by German troops. This battle is remembered on a memorial plaque at the foot of a mighty lighthouse at the end of the Tahkuna cape. The cast iron lighthouse was made in Paris and set up here in 1875. It is 42.6 m high casting light over a distance of 33 km.

Right behind the lighthouse stands a memorial to the Stockholm-Tallinn ferry "Estonia" that sank on 28 September 1994. The sculpture, made by Mati Karmin, has a cross and a bell, both of which swing in high winds.

There is another stone labyrinth near the lighthouse, similar to that at Suursadam. Since 1995 the first wind-generator has operated in Tahkuna.

Reigi village and church. The village on the Kärdla-Kõrgessaare Road used to be the centre for Swedish inhabitants in Hiiumaa. Under the pressure of Count Stenbock the Swedes of Reigi parish were outlawed and deported to the Ukraine in 1781 according to the ukase issued by Catherine II. Even before the Swedes had left, Stenbock sold his manor to count Ungern-Sternberg who thus began his conquest of Hiiumaa.

Reigi Church is located a bit further from the village, by the road and in fact belongs to Pihla village.

The existing church was built

Reigi Church was built by the Ungru Count in memory of his son who committed suicide.

by Baron Otto Reinhold Ludwig von Ungern-Sternberg or the notorious Ungru count in memory of his son Gustav Dietrich Otto who committed suicide. The latter served in the St Petersburg Guards, lived a life of luxury and ended up with huge debts. His strict father refused to help him out. Gustav is buried in the Reigi cemetery.

Coat of arms of the Ungern-Sternbergs.

It is a one-aisle simple church, with beautiful altar paintings and an unusual, lily-shaped weathervane that refers to the Ungern-Sternberg coat of arms.

About 200 m from the church on the other side of the road is the vicarage, a modest late-18th century Baroque building.

In 1627-1665 the pastor at Reigi was P. A. Lempelius who is immortalised in a novel by Aino Kallas. The tragic love affair between the pastor's wife and the curate also inspired an opera and a film.

Kõrgessaare village emerged around a former heart of the manor. The most famous manor lord was the count of Ungru who bought it from his schoolmate Stenbock for 55 000 silver roubles.

The wooden main building has not survived. The old distillery, now a restaurant, is the most remarkable of the buildings still standing. A memorial stands by the pond to an Estonian lightship 'Hiiumadal'. On 22 June 1941 a German torpedo boat attacked and sunk it without any apparent reason. Ships equipped with blinking lights and fog sirens had been patrolling the waters for over 40 years.

A peculiar sight is the huge boulder called Ungrukivi standing southwest from the manor on Ninametsa Peninsula. There are three big holes in the stone where the Ungru count allegedly fastened a powerful lantern and thus lured ships to shallow water. Shipwrecks were certainly a nice source of income for the owner of the seashore.

Legendary Ungrukivi.

Right in the heart of the Kõrgessaare manor we find a place with a weird name – **Viskoosa**. This is associated with an ambitious undertaking last century.

In 1911 some Jewish businessmen bought 470 hectares of land nearby in order to set up a modern factory producing artificial silk that was supposed to give work to 1200 people. New big buildings appeared, the harbour was expanded and even a man-made lake was dug, but then the First

World War cancelled all further plans. The new buildings were blown up in 1917 and the equipment taken to Moscow.

Nature, forests and clean water of Hiiumaa were saved from a certain catastrophe. Today, Viskoosa accommodates a fish-processing plant.

The Kõrgessaare harbour has a long history. This was the start of the first regular boat traffic in the 17th century that transported goods to the Stockholm market and also took passengers. An important export article was the glassware made in 1628-1664 at the first Estonian glass factory at Hüti south of Kõrgessaare. The products included bottles, windows, laboratory and chemist's glassware, etc.

Distillery at Kõrgessaare Manor.

Luidja. Luidja village is located at the point where Kõrgessaare-Kõpu Road reaches Emmaste crossroads.

About a hundred years ago this village experienced a most unusual danger. A few immense dunes moved from the shore towards the nearby farmhouses. People planted pine trees in an effort to stop the dunes but to no avail. Finally the local forester suggested planting common alders. Today, the sea is separated from the road by a 2.2 km long alder wood that once saved the villagers from the fate of desert people.

A memorial stands there to the clever forester Karl Ahrens.

The road from Luidja to Kõpu is remarkably sinuous and as far as Hiiumaa people are concerned, this is how it is going to stay.

Kõpu. Here is the highest point of the West-Estonian islands. Today's 68-m high Tornimäe area emerged from the Baltic ice reservoir about 11 000 years ago. No wonder then that the oldest traces of human habitation can be found in Kõpu. In the mid-1990s the archaeologists discovered the oldest settlement on the island in Ülendi village near Kõpu cemetery. It is approximately 7500 years old. The settlement belonged to the seal hunters who lived on the coast, probably only from time to time.

At the edge of the Kõpu village starts the 1.5 km long Rebastemäe nature track that offers a chance to admire the surroundings from a viewing platform. The other track runs along the Linnaru dunes and leads to Kaplimäe Hill where a chapel once stood. A pastor had allegedly set fire to it as he did not fancy climbing the hill every day. Kaplimäe hill is also the place where the gold of ancient Swedish kings is reputedly hidden.

In Mägipea village on top of the hill stands the Kõpu lighthouse, the first lighthouse on the Baltic Sea and the greatest tourist attraction in Hiiumaa.

It is generally thought that the building of **Kõpu lighthouse** began in 1504, a mere dozen years after Columbus discovered America for Europeans. At first about a twenty-metre high foundation was set up upon which fire was built, but only in the mid-17th century. By that time the tower was much higher. Firewood was hoisted up by a winch that must have been endlessly busy as the fire needed incredible quantities of wood in order to be a fathom high.

Instead of outside stairs, a staircase was cut into the tower in 1810, and a room for the maintenance crew was built as well. The light of the oil lamps was directed by mirrors. The lamps consumed over three tonnes of oil each year. The lantern room we see today came from the 1900 Paris World Fair. The lighthouse is 37 m high and reached 104.6 m above sea level.

Today, Kõpu is one of the oldest working lighthouses in the world.

In Ristna, the westernmost corner of Hiiumaa, one can perceive a weird 'end-of-the-world' feeling – the pine trees bending in the wind, high foamy waves and the sea vanishing beyond the curve of the Earth. There is hardly another place in Estonia with similar genius loci.

Kõpu Peninsula ends in two capes – North and South Capes. At the tip of the northern cape stands **Ristna lighthouse**, bought in Paris at the same time as the Tahkuna lighthouse. According to a legend the lighthouses were mixed up en route, and the lower construction, meant for Tahkuna, ended up at Ristna. Ristna is 29.5 m high, 37 m above sea level, and the light is visible at the distance of 31.5 km.

Kalana harbour, almost hidden in a quiet bay, forms the sea gate for Kõpu. In the 1930s a peculiar chapel was still standing there. A very long time ago, survivors of shipwrecks had built it in gratitude for their lucky escape. The chapel had two metal fish figures, and where their noses pointed, a good catch was guaranteed. Ristna was said to be well off just because of these fish figures. In order to improve their own fishing, the envious Saaremaa inhabitants stole the figures. One of the fish is now kept at the Estonian National Museum.

In Soviet times, the chapel found itself on the military territory and was slowly crumbling. Today, only the foundation still stands.

Kõpu lighthouse was built at approximately the same time as Columbus discovered America.

EMMASTE

Half way from Kõpu to Emmaste we arrive in **Mõnspäe** village with its old chapel and chapel yard. According to a legend this chapel was also built by grateful survivors from shipwrecks. A big stone in the chapel yard commemorates 14 local farmers, killed by the retreating Soviet troops in autumn 1941.

Memorial to the murdered farmers in the Mõnspäe chapel yard.

3 km before Emmaste, a path turns off the Kõrgessaare-Emmaste Road and heads towards the coast to **Sõru harbour**. Water at this 19th-century harbour is not deep and it has not been extensively used. However, since 1996 the Saaremaa-Hiiumaa ferry operates from there.

Sõru has a 5-year-old museum where the most important exhibit is the boat 'Alar'. The wooden engine yacht was completed before WW II, miraculously survived the turmoil of war and sailed with the retreating Germans to Hamburg. One of the boat's previous owners, Arnold Türi, saw it there and thanks to him the boat finally found its way back home in 1998.

Driving through Emmaste towards Käina the traveller sees right by the road a post mill that is one of a few of its kind in Hiiumaa.

Turning from the Emmaste-Käina Road at Utu village towards Männamaa, we arrive in **Ühtri village**, the birthplace of modernist painter Ülo Sooster (1924–1970). A memorial called 'Stone Juniper' stands in his native farm, as junipers were among the favourite objects of the artist. Sooster lived the second part of his life in Moscow.

Turning from the Emmaste-Käina Road towards Orjaku we actually leave Hiiumaa and come to the neighbouring island of Kassari. It is almost impossible to notice the change of island as the road runs along a solid causeway. A few hundred years ago water was much deeper between the two islands, and the western part of Kassari, Orjaku, was a separate island in the Middle Ages. Käina bay today is shallow, muddy and largely overgrown with reed – an ideal place for numerous species of birds. A tower has been set up on Orjaku for bird-watchers. Mud in the southern part of the bay has remarkable healing properties.

If we regard **Kassari** an island, it is the fifth largest in Estonia, emerging from the sea about 3000 years ago. There used to be a wooden manor house in the centre of the island, but now only the park and the bailiff's house have remained. The house accommodates the Kassari branch of Hiiumaa Museum.

The cultural life of Kassari is largely rotating around a small red house with a thatched roof that stands on the southern slope of the central elevation called Veskimäe. It was originally built by a manor bailiff Villem Tamm (1836–1915), also known as Handsome Villem. One of the most prominent Estonian painters, Johann Köler, used him as the model for his paintings of Christ. Tamm rented the house to the border guards, and the building is still known as the old cordon house.

In the 1920s and 1930s it was used as a summer resort by various Estonian artists and writers. In 1964 a small **Aino Kallas Museum** opened there and is privately owned at present. Kallas was a Finnish-Estonian writer who, inspired by local legends, wrote many stories about Hiiumaa and Kassari in particular. She later lived in London as wife of the Estonian ambassador there, Oskar Kallas.

Sculpture of Leiger stands at the most important crossroad in Kassari.

Aino Kallas Museum in the old guard station in Kassari.

From central Kassari, the road takes the visitor to Orjaku that will soon narrow down to **Sääretirp**. At the beginning of the 3-km path stands a 3.5-m high bronze statue of Leiger, hero of many Hiiumaa legends (sculptor Kalju Reitel, 1991).

Leiger and his son supposedly built that path as they were waiting for Leiger's brother from Saaremaa and wanted to ease his journey.

Kassari Chapel is located in the north-eastern part of the island. Many well-known Estonian cultural people rest in the nearby graveyard.

The eastern causeway connecting Kassari with Hiiumaa, Vaemla or Laisna, was started by the Kassari manor lord Eduard Heinrich August Stackelberg. Before that people either crossed the sea or used various wooden bridges.

The centre of southern Hiiumaa is **Käina**, second largest settlement on the island. There is a church which has been standing in ruin since WW II.

Ants Eskola, one of the best actors in Estonia, rests here.

Käina Church has stood in ruin for sixty years.

About 1 km from central Käina towards Emmaste, in the former house of the local pastor and schoolmaster, is a small **Rudolf Tobias Museum**. The composer's father and grandfather were both clergymen. Tobias (1873-1918) wrote the first Estonian symphony.

Vaemla village, the former heart of the manorial complex, is located at Kassari crossroads on the Käina-Suuremõisa Road. The manor house stands in ruin; the old park has a memorial to painter Johann Köler. It was during his visit to Vaemla in 1863 that the famous academic at the St Petersburg Academy of Art created many of his well-known works.

Vaemla wool factory at the Kassari crossroad functions more like a museum, although the one hundred years old wool-manufacturing machinery is in perfect working order.

Vaemla can also be called the 'oil capital' of Hiiumaa, because one of the Baltic German landlords, Gustav Wilhelm Gotthard von der Pahlen, hoped to find oil here. A few years before WW I numerous bores were drilled in the vicinity of Vaemla, but nothing was found. Some were still trying in the early 1920s but finally gave up hope. A popular legend says that local men who were hired to carry out this well-paid job, sometimes poured a bit of oil into the holes to keep the paymaster hopeful.

SAAREMAA

Ten and a half millennia ago the first tiny islets emerged from the sea – two near Viidumäe and two at Kõpu. The land kept rising, the sea retreated, more islands appeared until they blended together and Saaremaa acquired its now familiar shape.

About six thousand years ago the first seal hunters and fishermen settled here. By 1000 BC Saaremaa was well known to the western Viking peoples and to the inhabitants of the mainland. The island's strongholds and fierce fighters posed a serious problem to the Teutonic order during its conquests. Saaremaa surrendered only in 1227 when the enemy had assembled an enormous army and attacked with all flags flying.

A new religion and way of life were thus enforced upon the local population. A few centuries later, it seemed as if the Saaremaa mythical hero Suur Tõll (Big Tõll) had become Christian as well; why else was he busy erecting churches in so many legends.

The key words associated with Saaremaa and its people always tend to be the same: juniper, stone fences, windmills, stubbornness, stamina, sense of humour, beer and smoked eels. These are promoted by songs, tourists and the people themselves. Juniper is indeed a significant symbol of Saaremaa nature, there are plenty of stone fences, and more are restored every year, there is quite a few windmills of which one even operates.

However, it is possible to approach Saaremaa without any clichés. The history, ancient hill forts, medieval churches and the Order castles offer much fascinating information. The local nature includes high limestone cliffs, meadows with rare plants, marshland and coastal pine forests, to say nothing of idyllic villages. Various museums around the island introduce its folk culture.

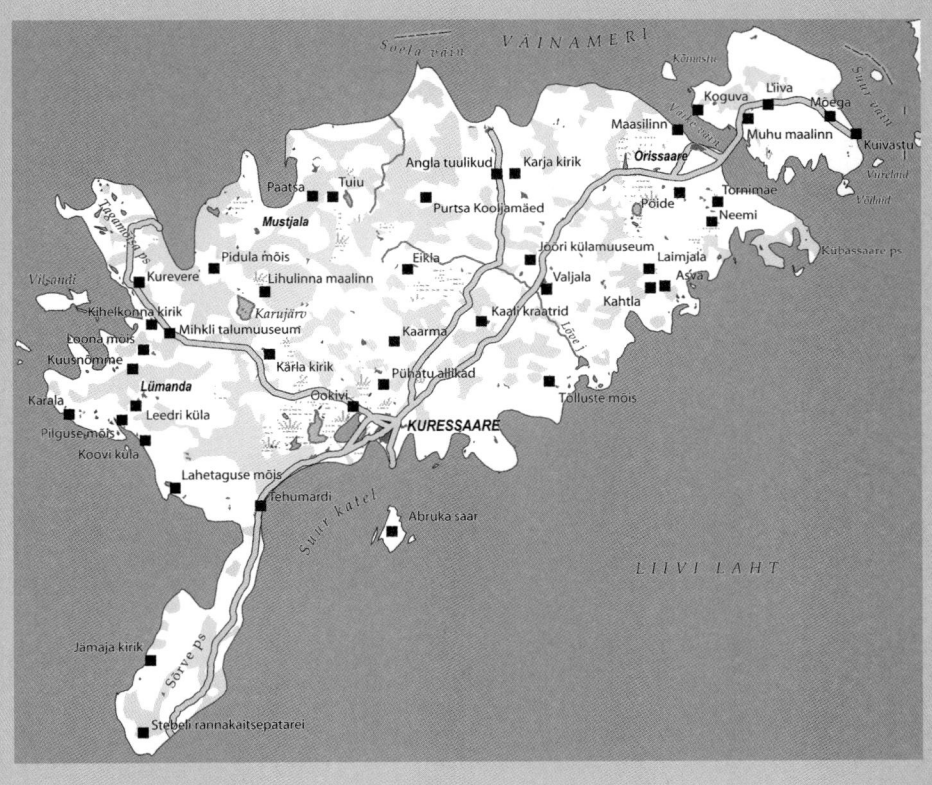

ACROSS THE SEA

The visitor gets the first glimpse of the Saare county during the 7-km and 30-minute journey across the Suur väin (Big Strait). Several small islands have lighthouses to guide the ships to Väinameri.

MUHUMAA

Kuivastu is an ancient harbour where traffic between the islands and the mainland has proceeded for centuries. In olden times, the local pub used to serve as a waiting room for passengers. The pub was quite famous, and not only around the Baltic Sea. Many a story began with the words, "This happened in Kuivastu pub...".

In 1885 an Estonian linguist and poet Villem Grünthal-Ridala was born here. He is called the poet of Estonian coasts and it is clear where he got his inspiration for his beautiful nature poems and ballads. He also wrote textbooks for schools and researched Estonian dialects.

The pub was restored in the 1980s but is in a very bad shape today.

There is a 4.1 km long cobblestone road running along the coast towards Võiküla.

About 4 km from Kuivastu towards Kuressaare, capital of Saaremaa, we arrive in Mõega village and the **Tammisaare Farm Museum**. The museum displays items connected with navigation, and boasts impressive stone fences.

The heart of Muhu is the Liiva village with **Muhu Church**. The church was probably built in late 13th century as a replacement of the previous wooden building and

Kuivastu pub was known to everybody sailing the Baltic Sea.

initially also served as a fortification. The one-aisle church has no spire, thus resembling Karja and Püha churches on Saaremaa and Pühalepa church on Hiiumaa. The walls have fragments of medieval paintings, and the 17th century altar is one of the oldest on the islands. The nearby vicarage built in 1832 has survived as well.

In 1941 the church caught fire. Restoration work, supported by former Muhu residents, was completed in 1993. As church and pub have always been seen together in Estonia, Aki pub was restored as well.

Muhu Church used to be a fortification.

Turning off the Kuivastu-Kuressaare Road after Piiri village and driving for about 6 km, the visitor reaches **Koguva village**. The village is certainly one of the best surviving and most picturesque complexes in the whole of Estonia.

The stone fences are at least two hundred years old, the history of the village itself reaches back at least five hundred years. In olden days the villagers, mostly free peasants, had the duty to deliver the post and to transport passengers across Väike väin (Little Strait) to Maasilinn. They managed to get rid of this duty only in the 19th century, after long and persistent litigation.

The farm buildings seen today mostly date from the early 19th century and are all listed, including the sauna, stables, barns and the summer kitchen. The more barns a farm had the wealthier it was.

Water permitting, it is sometimes possible to walk through the sea to Kõinastu islet that used to be a pasture for the bailiff's horses.

Tooma farm in the village is the birthplace of the writer Juhan Smuul (1922–1971) who made the village famous in his numerous novels and travelogues.

Muhu stronghold is located about a kilometre away from the damway of Väike väin, on the left when you come from Kuivastu.

The stronghold was once surrounded by a huge ring wall, which has almost disappeared today.

Muhu played a significant part in the ancient struggle for freedom, resisting the invasion of the Order until winter 1227 when the invading army of twenty thousand men attacked the stronghold and managed to capture it after a week of fierce fighting. The fall of

The stone fences in Koguva village are a few hundred years old.

The fall of the Muhu stronghold in 1227 marked the surrender of the whole of Saaremaa.

The unique Eemu windmill is still grinding flour today.

the Muhu stronghold decided the entire fate of Saaremaa.

A granite monument in memory of our courageous ancestors stands in the middle of the former stronghold courtyard.

Nearby at the Kuivastu Road is **Eemu windmill** that has become one of the symbols of Muhu Island. The post mill sits on the site of previous windmills but is in fact only a quarter of a century old. It is one of the few working mills in Estonia.

The 3-km long **Väike väin dam** dates back to the tsarist period, 1894-97, whereas work was started at both sides at the same time. The damway was initially quite narrow so that vehicles could pass one another only at road extensions after each half kilometre. The crossing was not free; a carriage for example cost 80 kopecks and a goat or a dog 3 kopecks. The dam was later made much higher and wider. The road was asphalted in 1960. As the dam prevented the fish access to their traditional spawning places, a canal was dug in the dam in the late 1940s. The monument at Muhu side commemorates the first centenary of the dam.

ORISSAARE

The 550-year-old Orissaare had always been one of the sea gates of Saaremaa. Before the dam a small ship travelled between Oris-

Maasilinn used to guard the traffic on the sea and between Muhu and Saaremaa.

saare and Muhu, often called the skate of the strait. Besides people and goods it could also transport a carriage with horses.

About 4 km from Orissaare towards Leisi we reach the ruins of **Maasilinn** (Maasi castle, also known as Soneburg). The castle was built in 1345 after the whole Saaremaa was conquered by the Teutonic Knights. The castle was constantly expanded and fortified. During the Livonian War (1558–1583) the Danes owned the castle but blew it up in 1576.

Maasilinn has stood in ruin ever since, and today we only see a hill, bits of wall and cellar. The oldest shipwreck in Estonia was found nearby in 1985. The 16-m long and 3-m wide wreck was taken to a temporary shed on Illiku islet where it still waits restoration work. The ship was probably built in Saaremaa around 1550. A model is displayed at the Marine Museum in Tallinn. A peculiar sight in central Orissaare is the football field with a huge magnificent oak tree growing in the middle. The ground around the tree is well trodden.

AROUND PÖIDE

Turning off the Kuivastu-Kuressaare Road towards Laimjala we soon see the **Pöide Church** on the left. It is connected with the rebellion in 1343 against the Teutonic Order. The islanders demolished the castle and also the church. The present church was probably built on the site of the castle. It has a powerful tower that was supposed to offer protection against possible attackers. The spire was struck by lightning in 1940 and perished. In subsequent years the Soviet soldiers totally wrecked the church. The

Pöide Church is the biggest place of worship in Saaremaa. In the Soviet period it was used as stables.

collective farm even used it as stables. The church is now being restored.

The church is the largest place of worship on Saaremaa. The most valuable items that have survived include a grand portal, epitaph of Baron von Üxküll with his coat of arms from 1666 and carved figures of peasants in national costume on the consoles. 2.5 km west from Pöide Church, in the middle of empty fields, stands Pöide or Kahutsi stronghold, one of Saaremaa's mightiest ancient castles.

Oti manor house, probably the oldest in Saaremaa, is situated near Pöide Church, by the road leading to Tornimäe. The manor was first mentioned in historical records in 1309. The last owner was the Aderkas family who pro-

Oti Manor has been carefully restored.

duced many philanthropists and educational figures. Today the manor is privately owned.

The Aderkas Chapel in the cemetery near Pöide Church is well worth a visit. This is a joint chapel of three Baltic German families and a remarkable example of what can be accomplished with Saaremaa dolomite.

Proceeding from Oti towards Tornimäe we see a pretty Orthodox church with six towers, a mark of the widespread conversion of the islanders to Orthodox church in the hope of getting land in return during the second half of the 19th century. There is another sight at Tornimäe – a 100-m long and 10-m wide former pier way off the coast. This proves that Saaremaa is slowly rising from water as in the 17th century ships still landed at that pier.

Neemi village south of Tornimäe boasts an impressive dendrological park, the result of 34-year long work by the local blacksmith **Mihkel Rand**. The park contains several hundred species of trees and shrubs and offers a welcome chance to rest your tired feet on a bench.

IN LAIMJALA

a visitor should see the stone lions guarding the local government building. The animals, perhaps a bit simple, but certainly dignified, were carved a century ago by a well-known Saaremaa sculptor **Jüri Veller**.

Stone lions guarding the Laimjala rural municipality.

The area around Laimjala has several Bronze Age settlements, the most famous of which is the **Asva fortified settlement**. It lies at 1 km from the Laimjala-Kuressaare Road behind a village of the same name. Asva is considered the oldest castle in Saaremaa. A stone and wood fence surrounded the settlement already in the 7th-8th centuries BC.

Research has proven that the castle perished in fire several times. One of the fires occurred 2600-2700 years ago and supports the popular legend that Asva and some other Saaremaa castles were destroyed in the explosion of

Well in Laimjala park.

Valjala Church is probably the oldest stone church in Estonia.

the Kaali meteorite. However, geologists think the celestial stone crashed down much earlier.

Numerous finds have been unearthed at Asva, such as tens of thousands pottery shards, stone tools, bone and bronze objects and bones. Various other fortified settlements have been discovered in the neighbourhood.

AROUND VALJALA

The most important sights are the church and ancient castle. **Valjala Church** is reportedly the oldest stone church in Estonia founded upon the underground cemetery of our ancestors. The building probably started after the fateful year 1227 when Saaremaa surrendered to the invaders. In any case, parts of the church walls were up before 1261 when the islanders' rebellion temporarily halted the work. As a result of the rebellion, the church was turned into a fortification as well. The church only got a steeple in the 17th century. Like other buildings, the Valjala church has been expanded, restored and repaired.

The **Valjala stronghold**, one of the largest in Estonia and the mightiest in Saaremaa, lies a bit south. Its ringwall castle stood on a hill. The site is a wealth of archaeological finds. Today, the limestone castle well has survived.

This was the last foothold of ancient Estonians before they surrendered to the Christian faith.

Valjala stronghold used to be the most formidable in Saaremaa.

Jõõri Village Museum is near the Kuivastu-Kuressaare Road, a few kilometres from Valjala towards Kuivastu. It contains an old smithy, barn, agricultural machinery and plenty of household utensils. The visitors can try some farming and even have a go in the smithy.

PIHTLA

11 km from the Valjala crossroad towards Kuressaare a sign points to the famous island sight – **Kaali meteorite field**. These craters are supposed to be 2400 to 7500 years old.

The diameter of the largest, the Kaali Lake, is 110 m and the depth is 22 m; the other eight craters, within a walking distance, are much smaller. The biggest iron meteorite was about 5 m in diameter and travelled at the speed of 20 km a second.

The Kaali craters are quite unique in the whole world, and numerous old stories and legends are associated with them, the

Tõlluste is reputedly the birthplace of the legendary hero Suur Tõll.

more so that a veil of mystery till hangs above their origin and age.

In the southern part of Pihtla rural municipality are the **Tõlluste** village and manor. Here is the supposed birthplace of the ancient hero of Saaremaa, Suur Tõll (Big Tõll). One of the nicest buildings is the summerhouse with its thatched roof and columns.

KAARMA area in central Saaremaa was one of the first places where people settled. Kaarma rose from the sea about 8000

Kaali crater is still surrounded by a veil of mystery.

years ago. In the heart of the settlement stands a church and a bit further off an ancient stronghold. **Kaarma stronghold** was among the most powerful fortifications on the island. It was probably also a large trading centre. The last battle was fought here in winter 1261 against the overpowering Teutonic Order.

Kaarma Church was completed in late 13th century. One side of the tower bears a plaque with the words: "This church was completed on the day of Peter 1407", which is considered the oldest written sentence in Estonian.

Near the Pähkla village between Kaarma and Kuressaare we find the **Pühatu (Põhjatu) spring** that was considered sacred. People used to bring offerings here.

On the 5th km on the Kuressaare-Kihelkonna Road lies a peculiar hollow boulder called the **Oo stone**. A Suur Tõll legend is connected with this boulder. The Old Devil who had turned himself into a horse ('oos' in local dialect) once tried to kidnap a young girl. Tõll managed to rescue the girl by cutting off the head of the animal from Hell. At that moment morning dawned and the horse turned into stone.

The oldest known sentence in Estonian on the wall of Kaarma Church.

Fragments of medieval paintings have survived in the church.

Kaarma stronghold used to be a trading centre as well.

Oo stone shows the stick marks of Suur Tõll.

KURESSAARE, CAPITAL OF SAAREMAA,

emerged around an **Episcopal castle** in the 14th century. The settlement received the rights of town in 1563 from Duke Magnus, brother of the Danish King. The charming Baroque town that developed by the late 17th century, has largely survived. One of the best-survived buildings is the bishop's castle of dolomite blocks, erected in the second half of the 13th century.

In early 19th century Arensburg, as it then was, was turning into a popular summer resort. The first healing mud and bathing establishment were completed in 1840. During the Crimean War (1853–1856) the prominent Russian surgeon Nikolai Pirogov, professor at Tartu University, sent the wounded to Kuressaare to convalesce, which increased the resort's fame in Riga, St Petersburg and elsewhere in Russia. A steamer began cruising between Riga and Kuressaare in 1858 and the number of holidaymakers increased rapidly.

' The largest enterprise before WW I was the leather factory that was destroyed in 1915. A marine school was opened in Kuressaare in the late 19th century.

After Estonia became independent (1918) the traffic between Riga and Kuressaare diminished and the number of visitors dropped. Over the last decade, however, the ever-growing demand for quality holidays has again made Kuressaare very popular.

Since 1952 until independence the town was called Kingissepp after the active communist and revolutionary Viktor Kingissepp who was born there.

The predecessor of the Episcopal castle was a ringwall castle

In the medieval period Kuressaare stronghold was called Kotkalinnus (Eagle's castle).

with a watchtower built on the site in the 1260s. The tower was surrounded by a 20-m wide moat filled with seawater. After the islanders conquered the Pöide stronghold in 1343, the Ösel-Wiek bishops decided to construct a castle that could not be defeated. It took a long time, until early in the 15th century. The castle contained rooms for the bishop and his attendants, all the necessary auxiliary rooms, a chapel and a prison.

The massive rectangular castle with one gate and two towers was surrounded by a ring wall, to which another wall was later added and fortified with cannon towers. The Ösel-Wiek bishops surrendered the castle to Danes; later it was owned by the Swedes.

Kuursaal (assembly hall) is near the moat.

In the Great Northern War (1700–1721) the Swedish garrison capitulated to the Russians. The Russians blew up some of the fortifications, but most of the building survived. In the course of the following centuries the castle was repeatedly repaired and restored.

In the Middle Ages the castle was called *arx aquila* (eagle's castle) whence comes Kuressaare's German name Arensburg. The eagle was an attribute of John the Baptist, patron saint of the castle, and later appeared on the Kuressaare coat of arms.

Today the castle accommodates the **Saaremaa Museum** and is a good place for concerts. The castle is surrounded by the 150 years old well-kept park with magnificent beech trees.

Several historical buildings are located near the central square. The 18th century **Knighthood House**, now accommodating the Saare local government, stands at the beginning of Lossi Street.

In Tallinn Street, the **town hall** and the old **weighing house** stand facing each other. Both date from the mid–17th century and represent the so-called northern baroque. The weighing house is the only of its kind still surviving in Estonia. The town hall has the Tourist Information offices and an art gallery. In the first floor reception room the visitor can admire the largest ceiling painting on canvas in the country, the origin of which is unfortunately not known.

Two museums are worth a visit – the **Citizen's Museum** in the castle courtyard and the **Aaviks' House Museum** at Vallimaa 7. The latter belonged to the promi-

The weighing house represents Nordic Baroque.

The Town Hall has the largest painting on canvas in Estonia.

A charming house with a tower and a clock stands in the centre of Kuressaare.

Kudjape cemetery also offers a resting place to the German soldiers killed in WW II.

nent Estonian language reformer Johannes Aavik (1880–1973). He innovated the language structure and introduced many new words. His cousin Joosep Aavik later lived there who was a well-known music teacher and organist.

Another sight is a hundred years old stone **Dutch windmill** in the heart of town that today operates as a café-bar.

Driving out of town towards Kihelkonna we reach the stone bridge built in 1820 called **Suur-**

Suursild is gradually being repaired.

sild (Big Bridge), one of the biggest, longest and oldest stone bridges in the country, currently under repair.

Kudjape cemetery is by the Kuivastu Road at the border of the town. It has several beautiful classicist chapels. A German military cemetery with dolomite crosses lies next to the last resting place of Soviet soldiers.

SÕRVE PENINSULA

Sõrve Peninsula, 30 km long and 10 km wide, looks like the back of a gigantic whale as the central part of the peninsula rises 40 m above sea level. The border is Salme River, the remainder of a strait that separated Sõrve from the big island a few thousand years ago.

A bit before the river, 16 km from Kuressaare, stands a tall dolomite monument in the shape of a sword. Here, on the night of 9 October 1944, the brutal Tehumardi battle took place between the Estonian battalion within the Red Army and the German troops. As there were many Estonians also on the German side, the battle fought in the autumn darkness could easily set brother against brother.

The two world wars have left many traces in Sõrve. The peninsula is a place of a number of mass graves and monuments. Sõrve people have been deported, conscripted into alien armies, arrested and murdered.
The tip of the peninsula still has concrete cannon foundations from WW I, and fortifications from WW II. The most powerful of them was **Stebel's coast battery**, named after the Soviet officer Alexander Stebel. The under-

Tehumardi – monument recalling a brutal killing.

A concrete-iron lighthouse stands at the tip of the peninsula.

ground battery is now under water. It was blown up in October 1941 before the Germans arrived. Several attempts have been made to explore the 16-m deep rooms of the battery, now filled with water, but with no success.

Another blown-up building was the late 18th century stone lighthouse, destroyed by the Germans in 1944. At the start of the long sinuous **Sõrve säär** that proceeds into the sea stands a concrete Soviet lighthouse.

Driving back to Saaremaa along the western coast of the peninsula we pass the **Jämaja Church** and cemetery with a monument to the hospital ship 'Moero', sunk by a Soviet plane in 1944. Over 3000 people drowned.

AROUND LÜMANDA

A beautiful coastal road leads to Koovi village, birthplace of the famous Estonian writer **August Mälk** (1900–1987) who depicted the life of coastal people in many of his novels. Mälk was educated in Saaremaa and Tartu and worked as schoolmaster in Sõrve and Lümanda. He was also member of the Estonian parliament. When the state elder Konstantin Päts gave him Lagle farm near Tallinn as a present, he moved there. In 1944 he escaped to Sweden where he was chairman of the exile Estonian Writers Union for many years.

August Mälk was one of the best to describe the life of coastal people.

Lümanda is connected with another prominent person, **F. G. B von Bellingshausen** (1778–1852) who sailed around the world and was one of the first to explore the Antarctic. In the 18th century the Bellingshausens had two manor houses – Lahetaguse and Pilguse. The latter where the explorer was born, already belonged to another family in the early 19th century. Bellingshausen first travelled around the world in 1803–1806 when he accompanied his compatriot **A. J. von Krusenstern** who owned the Kiltsi manor on Virumaa.

The later owner of Pilguse manor was J. W. L. von Luce from Germany. He studied both medicine and theology and worked as pastor in Saaremaa. Von Luce was keen on the history of the island, the local language and encouraged cultural activities. He wrote a history book about Saaremaa in German and several Estonian-language books for local people about health, education and household matters.

Pilguse manor stands on the way from Lümanda to Sõrve. Turn off after 2 km towards Karala. The manor, surrounded by well-preserved stone fences, is privately owned. A memorial plaque on a big stone is dedicated to Bellingshausen. Travelling towards Karala we see a lighthouse a bit further from the sea and a huge oak cross in memory of all who perished in the sea.

Kuusnõmme village in Lümanda was home to two brothers who greatly influenced Estonian life. The writer **Aadu Hint** (1910–1989) was in fact born in Muhu but grew up here. He used his childhood memories in his later numerous novels, the most important of which is the tetralogy

The famous explorer von Bellingshausen was born in Pilguse Manor.

'The Windy Coast'.

His brother **Johannes Hint** (1914–1986) was an engineer and an inventor. He innovated the production of building materials for which he received many awards and honorary titles. Later Hint found himself in conflict with the Soviet authorities, he was stripped of all his titles and medals until he finally died in prison.

One of the prettiest and most typical villages in Saaremaa is **Leedri village**. In addition to the stone fences the village has retained old farm buildings and ancient trees.

AROUND KÄRLA

On the 17th km on the Kuressaare-Kihelkonna Road the visitor can turn right towards Kärla. The local church has one of the most beautiful renaissance wooden sculptures in the country – memorial plaque to Otto von Buxhoevden. The author is thought to be a woodcarver from Lübeck. Going towards Mustjala we pass the oldest and largest lake on the island that also has the purest water – **Karujärv** (Bear's Lake). North-east from the lake, in the midst of forests and marshlands, is the site of a mighty stronghold – Kärla Lihulinn. The courtyard itself was almost 2 hectares.

KIHELKONNA

Kihelkonna is an ancient centre and harbour settlement. The church, first built in 1270, is among the oldest on the island. A peculiar feature is that the belfry stands near the church on a low hill. The belfry is about 250 years older than the present steeple.

Kihelkonna Church is also famous for its organ, one of the most valuable in Estonia. It came from Germany and has a beautiful sound. An organ music week is organised in the church every summer. The pulpit dating from 1604 in the oldest in Saaremaa and the steeple, which has been an important seamark, is the highest (72 m). In the cemetery we can see stone steps that help people across the fence. Building such steps instead of a gate was quite common on the island.

4 km after leaving Kihelkonna for Lümanda comes the **Loona Manor**. Today it houses the centre of Vilsandi National Park and a guesthouse. The small manor has been repeatedly rebuilt; in medieval times it was probably a vassal castle.

The best-known Saaremaa **farm museum** called **Mihkli** is located on the 3rd kilometre on the Kihelkonna-Kuressaare Road in Viki village. Most of the buildings date from the mid–19th century and nearly all items have been made by the farm people in the course of two centuries. It is thus a unique museum as no exhibits have been collected from elsewhere. The last owner, Jakob Reht (1886–1969), donated everything to the state, and the museum opened in 1959.

Most of what is seen at the Mihkli Museum was made on the site.

The former belfry of Kihelkonna Church stands apart from the church.

Kurevere burial places have revealed a richly ornamented sword.

In about 5 km going from Kihelkonna towards Tagamõisa we arrive in the **Kurevere village** where there are numerous stone burial places and cup-marked stones. Some burial places date back to the first millennium BC, although most are much younger. These places and stones are scattered in the meadow covered with junipers so it is not easy to spot them. Many fine archaeological finds have been unearthed at Kurevere, including a sword with a silver-ornamented hilt and various pieces of jewellery.

The rocky and beautiful **Vilsandi Island** is the heart of Vilsandi National Park, although the park covers a wide coastal area and over 160 islands and islets. Vilsandi only reaches 4.5 m from sea level and has been inhabited in the last three hundred years. Nowadays only a dozen or so people live here all year round. Vilsandi is the westernmost inhabited piece of land in Estonia.

The most important building is the white lighthouse. A large quite dilapidated shed stands nearby. In the 1920–1930s rescue boats were kept here. The most famous Vilsandi person is the lighthouse keeper **Artur Toom** (1884–1942) who initiated bird protection and rented several small islets in order to keep the birds from harm. Artur Toom protected his bird kingdom until the start of WW II when he was arrested and executed in Siberia.

To get to Vilsandi the visitor should contact the head office of the National Park at Loona manor. Boats leave from Papisaare port, reached by a several kilometres long old cobblestone road. However, there is another way to Vilsandi. A huge van with very high

The centre of Vilsandi National Park is located at Loona Manor.

Pidula Manor was probably named after a medieval hospital.

Shed for rescue boats and lighthouse in Vilsandi.

Vikat harbour is the sea gate of Vilsandi.

wheels drives people to the island from the tip of Kuusnõmme peninsula via Käkisilma shallow.

The mid-18th century Baroque **Pidula manor** is located on the 11th kilometre of the Kihelkonna-Mustjala Road. It is thought that around 1240 the Teutonic Knights ran a hospital here. In the first millennium a stronghold stood on the site of the present park.

MUSTJALA AREA

Visitors to Mustjala area usually aim to get to the 21-m high Panga cliff. This is the highest point for enjoying a sea view on any coast of Saaremaa. En route to the cliff it is worth making a few stops to see some interesting places.

The largest ancient and medieval iron manufacture in Estonia was found at **Tuiu**. Heaps of iron slag on the dunes at Järise Lake attracted the attention of the Baltic German researchers, although a more serious investigation started only in the 1960s.

Various remains of furnaces and forges have been found. Between the 11th and the 14th centuries about 1000 tons of iron was smelted at Tuiu. High-quality iron was produced from bog ore. 100 kg of iron required 600-700 kg of ore and 1.5 tonnes of charcoal.

Some enterprising archaeologists tried the same method, naturally on a far smaller scale, and successfully produced a few kilos of iron.

AROUND LEISI

The famous **Angla windmills** stand by the 6th km stone on the Leisi-Kuressaare Road. There are four post mills and one Dutch-

The group of Angla windmills is one of the symbols of Saaremaa.

Karja Church has hardly been rebuilt.

Karja Church abound in sculptures.

type mill. Angla village once had 12 windmills and the entire Saaremaa had 800. Only a few have survived, of which one, the Eemu mill, still works.

The Angla windmills offer a spectacular sight albeit a rather desolate one, as they represent a part of village way of life that has as good as disappeared. Like any other ancient work, grinding flour was an art in itself. The best flour was reputedly produced when the wind blew from the west or the north.

2 km from Angla towards Pärsama stands the small **Karja Church**. It has no tower but is beautifully proportioned, having survived almost unchanged from the first half of the 14th century. Karja is unanimously regarded as one of the most remarkable rural churches in the country. It has numerous limestone allegorical sculptures and medieval murals. No other church in the Baltic countries has quite so many. Various magical signs such as pentagrams and triskelia have given rise to many theories.

From Pamma village west of Karja village a signpost points to **Purtsa stronghold**. It is located in the middle of the pine forest in the dunes known as Kooljamäed (Hills of the Dead). In 1344 the final bloody stage of the peasant uprising took place there. The Order sent thousands against the islanders who were sheltering in the stronghold.

PÄRNUMAA

SIIN SÜNDIS 24. XII 1843
JA ELAS 1850. AASTANI
Lydia Koidula

PÄRNUMAA

Pärnumaa is rich in sea and forest, marshland and meadow. The southern coast has high dunes whereas in the north the seaside is stonier. The area also has a fair number of rivers, such as Pärnu, Halliste, Navesti and Reiu. The Stone Age settlements at the mouth of Pärnu River are the oldest and richest in finds in Estonia.

Pärnumaa has been ruled by bishops and the Teutonic Order, Polish and Swedish kings and Russian tsars, like the rest of Estonia. During the period of national awakening Pärnu and Vändra became important cultural centres. The poet Lydia Koidula (1843–1886), also known as the Nightingale of Emajõgi River, was born in Vändra. Her father Johann Voldemar Jannsen founded an influential newspaper 'Perno Postimees' that during its heyday had about 2000 subscribers, a huge number at that time.

For many, today's Pärnumaa is associated with the town of Pärnu, a well-known summer resort.

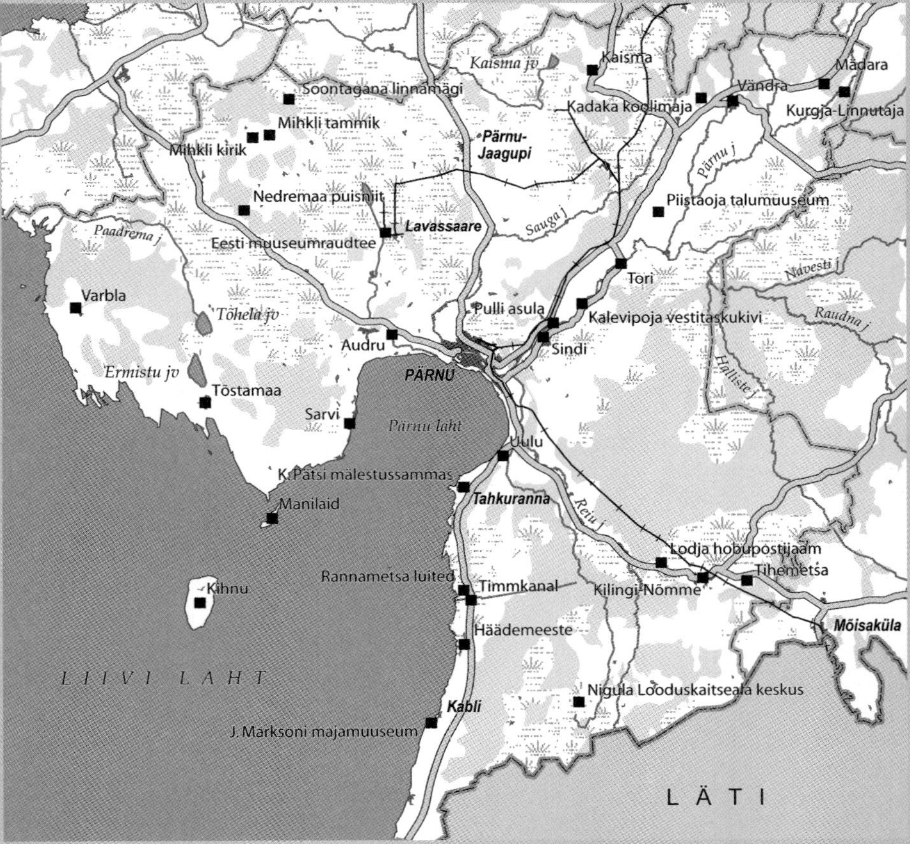
Kaisma jv
Kaisma
Mädara
Soontagana linnamägi
Vändra
Kadaka koolimaja
Kurgja-Linnutaja
Mihkli tammik
Mihkli kirik
Pärnu-
Jaagupi
Pärnu j
Nedremaa puisniit
Piistaoja talumuuseum
Paadrema j
Lavassaare
Sauga j
Eesti muuseumraudtee
Tori
Navesti j
Varbla
Pulli asula
Tõhela jv
Kalevipoja vestitaskukivi
Raudna j
Audru
Sindi
Halliste j
Ermistu jv
PÄRNU
Tõstamaa
Sarvi
Pärnu laht
Uulu
K. Pätsi mälestussammas
Tahkuranna
Reiu j
Manilaid
Lodja hobupostijaam
Tihemetsa
Rannametsa luited
Timmkanal
Kilingi-Nõmme
Kihnu
Mõisaküla
Häädemeeste
LIIVI LAHT
Nigula Looduskaitseala keskus
Kabli
J. Marksoni majamuuseum
LÄTI

SOUTH FROM PÄRNU

Travelling from Pärnu towards Riga we arrive in **Uulu**. In the second half of the 19th century the manor there belonged to Baron von Holstein who was popularly known as an iron baron or simple Old Rein. The baron had excellent connections with the St Petersburg court. He was a very enterprising man and did not shrink from any farm work himself. His manor flourished. In the 1860s a grand limestone mansion was built at Uulu, resembling Windsor castle, which entertained various powerful people from St Petersburg. The future tsar Alexander III visited Uulu in 1879 or 1880. He had reputedly shot a roebuck where today stands a plaque to his memory, although the inscription on it is hardly legible. For Estonians, Alexander III is associated with harsh Russification policy and is certainly not regarded kindly.

Nothing is left of Uulu mansion now, only the park is still there. The house was looted and burnt down in 1918, and the stones were used as building material elsewhere. The burial chamber is the only thing to remember von Holstein.

Tahkuranna is primarily associated with the name of **Konstantin Päts**, the first president of the Republic of Estonia. He was born on 23 February 1874. Two years previously an Orthodox church had been built at Tahkuranna, and the child was baptised there. Already in his lifetime, a monument was put up here, destroyed by the communists in August 1940 after Estonia had 'voluntarily' joined the Soviet Union. Päts died in 1956 after 16 years of suffering in various prisons.

The monument was restored in

The monument to President Konstantin Päts was put up during his lifetime.

1989. The inscription reads: "We are not free because of the mercy of others, we fought for it."

Going from Tahkuranna towards Häädemeeste, the Pärnu-Riga Road crosses the **Timmkanal** channel. It was dug on the initiative of Alexander Thimm (1808–1862) who rented the state-owned Häädemeeste manor. Thimm hoped to halt the spread of marshland. The digging started in 1858. At first about 7–8 km were dug and a few dozen kilometres added later so the channel could be used for transporting logs.

North of the Timmkanal channel bridge are the **highest dunes in the Baltic countries** that reach

Timmkanal was dug by human hands.

The dunes, now under forest, were regarded as sacred places in Rannametsa.

up to 34 m. The dunes, now covered with a pine forest, are called hills. Some have names such as Robbers' Hill or the Hill of Oath. The latter was thought to have been a sacrificial place where people took their offering.

Häädemeeste is about half way between Pärnu and Ikla, the village on the border with Latvia. Here it is possible to turn off the busy Via Baltica and take the beautiful coastal path, the old Pärnu-Riga Road. There are many legends why the place is called Häädemeeste (Good Men). Either there lived two kind brothers, or some really good men, or it is a story about shipwrecked people who were saved by kind-hearted locals.

Häädemeeste was once famous for its sailboats. Every fifth boat built in Estonia between 1858 and 1910 was built here. Most of the builders came from Saaremaa; they had never had any formal instruction, learning the craft in the course of work and passing their skills on to the next generation. Most important was to put a gold coin under every mast to make the boat work well and move fast. The sailboats were

Häädemeeste Museum introduces the life of the coastal people and the history of shipbuilding.

slender but at the same time quite bulky, because building was expensive and they had to earn the money back as quickly as possible. Especially profitable was transporting salt during the Russian-Turkish war (1877–1878). The first large sailboat was completed in 1861 and called 'Julie'. In 1986 a monument to 'Julie' was set up in Häädemeeste. The boat perished in a storm either in 1865 or 1866 on its way to Sweden.

The shipbuilding boom naturally required qualified people. Some Häädemeeste shipowners thus decided to establish a maritime school to train both Estonian and Latvian seamen. The Heinaste School opened in 1864 and taught 3760 sailors in 50 years. Today the school has a museum but in order to visit it one has to cross over to Latvia as the schoolhouse is in Ainazhi.

There is another museum in Häädemeeste, offering an overview of local history, nature and culture.

Driving from Häädemeeste along the old Pärnu-Riga Road we come to **Kabli** that used to be a village of seamen and ship-builders. Several grand wooden mansions are still standing. In the **house of Jakob Markson** (1840–1930) is his museum, introducing local history and shipbuilding. Kabli is also known as the centre of bird-ringing where since 1969 over 600 000 birds have been ringed.

Nigula Nature Reserve area can be found after turning towards Massiaru from the new Pärnu-Kabli Road. The specially made paths and viewing towers enable the visitor to get a good overview of a typical Estonian marshland. Besides marshland research, cranberries are cultivated and grown here.

Markson was one of the best-known shipowners in Kabli. His home is now a museum.

Kabli people honour the memory of their captains and shipowners.

From the Pärnu-Riga Road at the Reiu crossroads it is possible to turn towards Kilingi-Nõmme. A few kilometres before this small town in the middle of forest stands the **Lodja stagecoach station** dating from the early 19th century. It is well preserved.

Kilingi-Nõmme got its name from the former Kilingi Manor and Nõmme pub. There are two churches: the crumbling Russian Orthodox church and Saarde parish church. The settlement developed here because of the spread of the so-called tsarist faith – the farmers who accepted the Orthodox church was given some land.

The entrance to the Voltvet Mansion is guarded by lions.

In the cemetery half a kilometre from Saarde church (left) stands a monument to schoolchildren who perished in 1937. The celluloid film that was used back then somehow caught fire in cinema and the ensuing chaos ended in the tragic death of the children.

Underground water formed the caves at Allikukivi. A spring flows there to this day.

3.5 km from Kilingi-Nõmme towards Valga is **Tihemetsa**, centre in Soviet times of a state farm technical college. The future mechanics and bookkeepers were taught in the former Voltvet (the name comes from one of the previous owners, the Wolffeldts) Manor. The mansion has been largely reconstructed. Today it houses a centre for vocational education.

Half a kilometre towards Valga is the former **Voltvet pub** that, with its 85 metres, is the longest in Estonia. The caves of Allikukivi between Tihemetsa and Kilingi-Nõmme are worth a visit. The spring water has bored three caves into the sandstone, with a total length of 30 metres.

NORTH OF PÄRNU

A drive towards Lihula takes us to **Audru** where a big part of the heart of the former manor complex has survived, except the wooden mansion that burnt down during WW II. The spectacular servants' house with a bell tower and the stone distillery still stand. A nice walk in the park takes you along the bridges to the islands in the Audru river. The museum in the former bailiff's house describes the local heritage.

Another building worth mentioning is the **Kuldlõvi** (Golden Lion) pub that has been operating since the first half of the 19th century. The middle section used to have the pub and living quarters and the ends were stables. Audru Church of 1680 is considered one of the oldest Lutheran churches in Estonia. The steeple was added a few dozen years later.

Towards Tõstamaa, left after Lindi, is the Sarvi village. An iron cross marks the site of the medieval St Martin's chapel. It is presumed that the chapel, like many other places of worship built by the Germans, was established on the site of an ancient Estonian place of offering.

In order to get to **Manilaid** and **Kihnu**, one should turn off the Pärnu-Tõstamaa Road and find Munalaiu harbour, which is fairly new, completed only a dozen years ago. Kihnu is the biggest island in the Livonian Bay: 7 km long and 3.3 km wide, with an area of 16.4 sq km. The oldest data about the island originate in 1518. The population was at its highest in the 1930 (1200); not about 500 people live on the island.

A peculiar bell tower catches the eye near the servants' house at Audru manor.

The former distillery building is adorned by a medieval wall pillar.

"Kuldlõvi" pub is over 150 years old.

Kihnu has been famous for its culture and language for ages. Every Estonian recognises the colourful national costumes of Kihnu. The skills of making these costumes are being taught at school. Several documentary films have been made about the inhabitants of Kihnu. It is an island of shipbuilders, seafarers, seal hunters and fishermen.

A good overview of the island's history can be obtained at the **Kihnu Museum** in the old schoolhouse opposite the church.

After the widespread conversion that began in the 1840s, the local Lutheran church was converted into an Orthodox church. People who accepted the Orthodox faith were promised some land in return. **Kihnu Church** then got an onion-shaped dome instead of its former steeple.

The cemetery is just as sacred to the islanders as the church. People go there quietly and always during the day so as not to disturb the dead. The famous captain **Enn Uuetoa** or **Kihnu Jõnn** is buried near the main gates. When his ship sank in 1913 near the coast of Denmark, the survivors buried their captain there. His remains were brought home only in 1992. The captain was made famous by Juhan Smuul, a writer from Muhu. There is no other man in Estonian navigation history who learned every skill and trick in the trade without attending any maritime school, and who later managed to persuade the navigation academy to issue him captain's papers.

Before the nationalisation by the Republic of Estonia in 1919, **Tõstamaa Manor** belonged to the Stael von Holsteins. The most prominent of them was Baron A. W. Stael von Holstein (1876–1936) who taught Sanskrit and Tibetan at Beijing University and advised the Chinese government. A monument was set up to him in the park.

Tõstamaa Mansion is today a schoolhouse. Going north towards Männikuste we pass the Ermistu and Tõhela lakes and come to Tõhela village where the attic of the local community centre has been turned into a museum.

The next rural community centre is **Varbla** with its early classicist manor house, old stables and park. The writer Karl Ristikivi (1912–1977) and the wrestler Kristjan Palusalu (1908–1987), gold medallist at the Berlin Olympic Games, were born nearby. Both have a monument in Varbla. Ristikivi lived the other half of his life in Sweden and mostly wrote historical novels and short stories. Palusalu won in heavyweight wrestling both in freestyle and graeco-roman wrestling. In his heyday in the 1930s he worked as a prison guard in Tallinn Central Prison; he later defected from the Red Army and was deported to a prison camp.

Nedrema wooded meadow stretches on both sides of the road towards Koonga. Over the

Enn Uuetoa alias Kihnu Jõnn reached home ground only 69 years after his death.

Estonia's most primeval landscape, wooden meadow, at Nedrema.

past few years the 90-hectare meadow has been regularly looked after

In the Middle Ages the Koonga manor in the Koonga village belonged to a bishop and was an important regional centre. The house was later considerably rebuilt to accommodate a school. According to a legend, the pastor serving in the **Mihkli (St Michael's) Church**, 6 km from Koonga, was no other than the famous chronicler Henry of Livonia (Henrici Cronicon Lyvoniae) who described life in Latvia and Estonia between 1180 and 1227. The present church dates from the 14th century, but has been rebuilt many times. The 400 years old church bell, cast in Sweden, disappeared mysteriously during the Second World War. It was found by chance in an underground shelter in 1971 and put up again.

The **oak grove** near Mihkli is one of the most beautiful in Estonia. 2 km north lies the Salumägi hill that with fine weather offers a spectacular view of the surroundings.

Soontagana hill-fort on a bog island in the southern part of Avaste marshland is among the

The famous chronicler Henry of Livonia reputedly preached at Mihkli church.

Mihkli oak forest used to be a sacred place, but is today more interesting to naturalists. The oaks are mostly over 200 years old.

most significant ancient monuments in Pärnumaa, used in the 11th–13th centuries. The 3500 sq m area was surrounded by a ringwall.

The fort-hill was the centre of the ancient parish and various bloody battles were waged at it. In 1216 it surrendered to the cru-

A corduroy path used to lead to Soontagana stronghold.

Lavassaare introduces the history of Estonian narrow-gauge railway.

saders and had to accept the Christian faith. At that time reputedly only a secret corduroy road led to the fort. Excavations have revealed remains of an ancient gate tower and an iron ploughshare.

Among the largest Estonian peat bogs at Lavassaare is a museum with unusually bulky exhibits – the **Estonian Railway Museum** and its 64 locomotives and carriages that once travelled on the narrow-gauge railway. A small section still operates.

UPSTREAM ALONG PÄRNU RIVER

Staring in Raeküla in Pärnu, going along the road towards **Sindi**, we soon come to the mouth of Reiu River. Numerous bone and stone items have been unearthed here. The most important settlement site is near Sindi in Pulli village on the northern shore of Pärnu River.

Pulli settlement was discovered in 1967 under a 3-m deep sand and clay layer. The finds included remnants of various tools, animal bones, arrow- and spearheads. It is thought that these ancient people were some Europeans who spoke Proto-European language.

The emergence of the **town of Sindi** is connected with the broadcloth factory established there in 1832 by the Riga merchant and industrialist J. C. Wöhrmann (1784–1843). Soon after the factory started work a new residential area for workers was developed. In 1840 around one thousand people worked at the factory. Huge barrack-type houses were built for the workers. One enormous room, separated by wooden partitions, often accommodated 70 families. Big barrels stood by the wall of the barrack where urine was gathered. This

House of the factory owner Wöhrmann.

Sindi Museum introduces the history of the broadcloth factory.

Sindi dam is 150 m long.

An example of the 19th century industrial architecture.

Sindi factory had its own power plant.

was needed at the factory for washing the broadcloth and producing a certain blue dye.

In the 19th century, a foundry, gas plant, brickyard and a brewery were built near the broadcloth factory; in mid-century the latter was equipped with mechanical looms which was quite innovative at the time. The old sawmill was renovated as well. The Sindi town hall was completed in 1938.

Here is one of the longest dams in Estonia, 150 m long and 4.5 m high, established in the 1930s for the Sindi hydroelectric power plant. The town museum includes a living-room of a factory worker about one hundred years ago.

Travelling towards Tori, a stop could be made at an ancient sacrificial stone lying in water near the northern shore of the Pärnu River. The stone reaches 4 m above the surface and is known as the epic hero **Kalevipoeg's waistcoat pocket stone**. According to a legend the mighty man intended to hurl the stone at the town of Võnnu (today's Cesis), but the stone failed to reach that far. It is also known as Võnnukivi (stone of Võnnu).

For most Estonians, the village of **Tori** on both shores of the Pärnu River, is associated with the famous breed of Tori horse. The more so that the coat of arms of the Tori rural municipality is adorned by a horseshoe. However, Tori is known by other things as well, such as the **Tori Hell** – a cave hollowed by spring waters in the sandstone near the southern bank of the Pärnu River.

The history of the **Tori horse** starts in 1856 when the Estonian knighthood set up the Tori manor and a stud farm in order to improve the local breed. The first head of the establishment was the famous naturalist Alexander von Middendorf (1815–1894). The most important animal in the history of Tori horse-breeding was the Polish stud called Hermann who was used between 1892 and 1912. He was brought to Tori by the Sangaste manor lord F. G. Magnus von Berg (1845–1938). Between 1892 and 1912 the work was supervised by the vet and scientist Mihkel Ilmjärv in whose memory a monument now stands in the park. The Tori breed met diverse requirements: the animals had to be useful in the field and for transport, i.e. had to be both strong and quick.

As the whole breeding process is something that is never totally completed, the Tori horse is still being 'perfected'. The emphasis today seems to lie more on the speed of the animal so that these beautiful creatures could be used in sport.

The Tori Mansion is a simple wooden building, whereas the stable complex and the 1856 stone gate are remarkably grand.

The **Tori pub** dates from 1845. It is a large, 70-m long house with ten columns, considered one of the most impressive of its kind in all the Baltic countries. It used to be a stagecoach station as well, as the pub was situated by a fairly busy road. In olden days, pubs and coach stops could be found at every thirty km along a road, as this was supposed to be the distance a horse could cover in a day. More refined travellers slept in better rooms whereas peasants spent the night on simple wooden plank beds. Even the horses of the different customers were placed in different stables.

The Tori pub near the church was set up by Baranov, leaseholder of the local state-owned manor. His business thrived because the Tori farmers, like all the others in

The Devil reputedly appeared from Tori Hell to make mischief on earth.

One of the symbols of Tori – the gate of the stud farm.

Tori pub used to stand at a busy road.

the country, were only too eager to proceed to the pub after getting their spiritual nourishment in church.

The **stone church in Tori** dates from mid-19th century. After WW II it stood neglected for decades but has now been restored. The re-born church is dedicated to all Estonian soldiers and displays the bust of Julius Kuperyanov (1894–1919), legendary guerrilla leader during the War of Inde-

Tori Church stood in ruins for a long time, but has now been restored.

Behind the church, St George is fighting the dragon.

70 years ago, Piistaoja was the model farm in the whole country.

pendence. Mati Karmin's sculpture of St George and the dragon stands in the churchyard.

On the southern shore of Pärnu River, beyond Tori bridge, lies a half-kilometre long and about 400 million years old strip of Devon sandstone where the slope is occasionally 10 m sheep. Spring water has dug a high and deep cave in the soft sandstone.

Over the last century the cave has partly collapsed several times. The first instance occurred in 1908 when a farmer was ploughing the field right above the 'Hell'. He crashed into the cave but his horses managed to drag him out. In 1974 the entire mouth of the cave collapsed.

There are many legends about the Tori 'Hell', a place where the Devil appeared on earth to carry out his evil deeds.

Turning left from Pärnu-Paide Road at Mannare, we come to **Piistaoja farm** where some rooms now function as a farm museum. The farm was founded in 1925 by **Theodor Johann Pool**, a well-known agriculturist and statesman. He initiated the land reform of 1919–1921 that divided the manorial lands between farmers. In the 1930s Piistaoja was seen as the most innovative farm in the country, with its milking machines and an electric guard to watch over cattle. Pool also bred Estonian black-and-white oxen and published the magazine 'New Farm'. Pool died in a Siberian prison camp.

In Kaisma manor park by the Järvakandi-Pärnu Road stands a monument to the naturalist **C. F. Schmidt** (1832–1908) who was born in the manor. He was a prominent botanist and geologist, and the long-time director of the Mineralogy Museum in St Petersburg.

Vändra's 'totem animal' is the bear, at least partly because of the vast forests in the area. However, the main reason was probably the publication of the hugely popular poem about a bear hunt in the paper published by Otto Wilhelm Masing in the 1820s. Masing was a man of letters, a significant figure in Estonian enlightenment who first employed the letter õ. It is not known where he got inspiration for his little poem that is still sung today.

In 1872 **Carl Robert Jakobson** settled in Vändra. Another important year is 1819 when **Johann Voldemar Jannsen** was born in Vana-Vändra. The editors of two essential newspapers in the period of enlightenment were thus both connected with Vändra. A daughter was born to Jannsen in 1843 who later became known as one of the best poets of all times, **Lydia Koidula**. The pictures of Koidula and Jakobson (still) adorn two Estonian bank notes.

Lydia Koidula's birthplace is marked with a monument by the Vändra-Suurejõe Road in a park where the house once stood. In a schoolhouse near Vändra, writer **Ernst Särgava** was born in 1868 to the family of the local teacher. He taught in Vändra for a few years as well. Särgava is mostly known for his skilful depictions of life in the countryside and in city slums. Some of his fairy tales belong among the classics of Estonian children's literature.

Jannsen was the talented son of a miller. Besides working as a schoolteacher and assistant to the local pastor, he managed to publish some issues of a small paper which mostly contained light-natured short stories. In 1850 the family moved to Pärnu where Jannsen founded Estonian journalism. The first 'Perno Postimees' appeared in 1857.

A **monument to Jannsen** stands in the town park.

Among the cultural figures of Vändra, mention should also be made of **Lilli (Caroline) Suburg** (1841–1923) who is thought to be the first Estonian feminist. She was the daughter of an employee at the manor house and grew up

The name Vändra has changed a lot over 500 years.

Monument to Johann Voldemar Jannsen in Vändra.

Monument to Lydia Koidula.

together with the children from the 'big house'. She studied at the Pärnu German-language school for girls at the same time with Koidula. When her parents bought a large farm she returned home and set up school. In Vändra she met Jakobson who encouraged the talented woman to try her hand in writing.

Her first short story was about a young Estonian girl in a German school who managed to remain faithful to her language and nationality. Later Suburg edited a newspaper and published a magazine for women called 'Linda' that she had established herself. She was the first female member of the Learned Estonian Society.

Suburg is buried in Vändra cemetery where her grave is marked by a monument from Estonian women.

Another fascinating person in Vändra was **Mats Tõnisson** (1853–1915) who published calendars. His calendars were so popular that at one point the print run reached 150 000. He also published equally popular ABC books. Unfortunately his constant criticism of the authorities caused him much trouble and he ended his days in a St Petersburg prison, accused of insulting priests. Tõnisson is buried in Türi cemetery.

Between 1860 and 1891 the Vändra pastor was **Ernst Sokolovski** who founded the first school for the deaf-mutes. The money was raised locally.

The activities of **Carl Robert Jakobson** are connected with the **farm museum at Kurgja-Linnutaja** (as he called his farm), one of the major tourist attractions in Vändra region. The road to the farm turns off from Vändra-Paide Road about a dozen km from Vändra.

Carl Robert Jakobson lived in this sauna at Kurgja, and there he died as well.

In 1874 Jakobson bought the place determined to set up a model farm to all Estonian farmers, in aadition to editing the paper 'Sakala' in Viljandi. He first built the sauna, also used as domicile, stables and a barn for keeping honey. The big two-storey residence was started in 1879 but was abandoned after the owner's death in 1882. The house was completed as late as in the 1950s when Kurgja had become a museum.

The 1880s were certainly most unfortunate for the farm. After Jakobson's death the farm was sold on auction to pay the debts. The joint effort of his friends managed to save the place for the family in 1886. Jakobson's widow with her two daughters ran the farm for fifty years until her death in 1940. The elderly daughters had to face all the subsequent horrors of war and forced collectivisation. Despite that the museum was opened in 1950.

A bit before Kurgja crossroads, south of the road, is **Mädara hillfort**. The steep bank by the river offers a splendid view of the surroundings. An ancient stronghold in the same site used to protect locals during the second half of the first millennium.

LÄÄNEMAA

LÄÄNEMAA

The coastal Läänemaa with its two deep bays and the island of Vormsi has remarkably beautiful nature and a fascinating history. A large part of that history is associated with coastal Swedes whose ancestors, fishermen and seal hunters, arrived in the area approximately eight hundred years ago. Läänemaa was fought over by the Danes, Swedes and Germans. Local people fought with all of them, but had to surrender in the end. The German conquest introduced to Läänemaa bishops and the Episcopal castles in Lihula and Haapsalu. Lihula even had two monasteries in medieval times.

In the turmoil of the Livonian War (1558-1583), Haapsalu and its surroundings were sold, given as a present and conquered umpteen times. Sweden took over later. After the Great Northern War (1700-1721), plagues and anarchy, the iron rule of Russia was established, carried out by local manor lords, just like everywhere in Estonia.

Throughout centuries Läänemaa has controlled the traffic and trade routes between the mainland and the islands. Behind the dilapidated industrial buildings on Virtsu Peninsula we can see the ruins of a mighty ancient stronghold. Five hundred years ago, one of the most influential families in Läänemaa, the von Uexkülls, reigned here, keeping an eagle eye on all trading, or in other words, were engaged in piracy.

The main attraction of Haapsalu has been mud with all its healing qualities. In the late 19th century it even attracted St Petersburg royalty, to say nothing of other nobility and various persons of significance. They arrived in a special steamboat and later by train.

Läänemaa also contains Matsalu bird sanctuary, a fascinating world of its own.

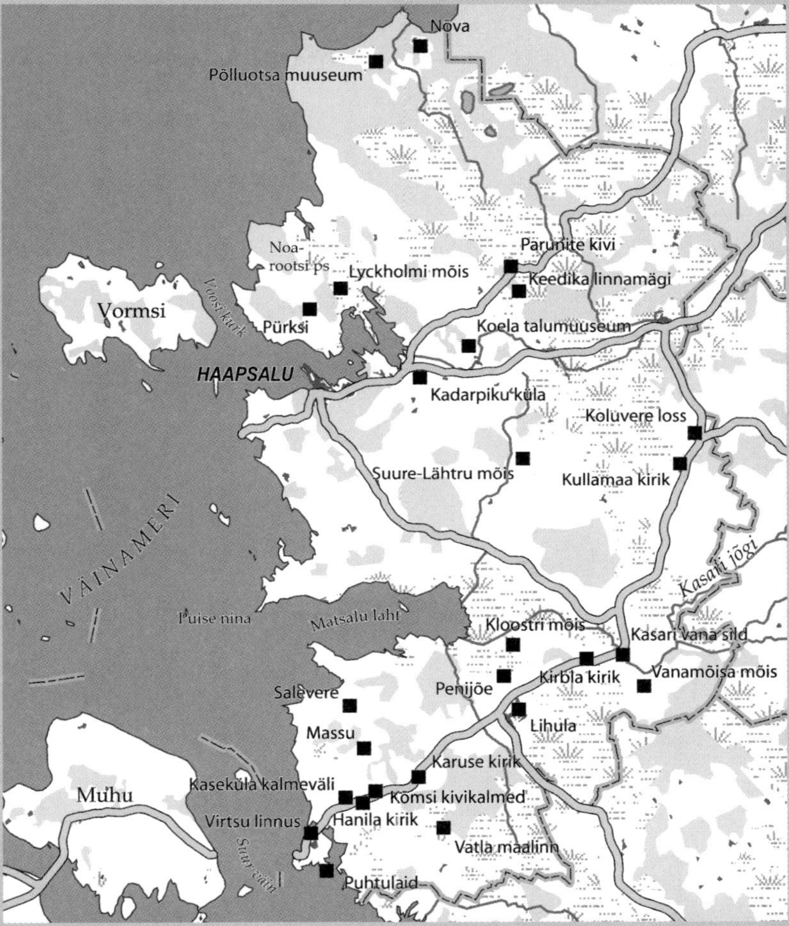
Nõva
Põlluotsa muuseum
Noa-
rootsi ps
Lyckholmi mõis
Pürksi
Vormsi
Voosi kurk
Parunite kivi
Keedika linnamägi
Koela talumuuseum
HAAPSALU
Kadarpiku küla
Koluvere loss
Suure-Lähtru mõis
Kullamaa kirik
VÄINAMERI
Kasari jõgi
Puise nina
Matsalu laht
Kloostri mõis
Kasari vana sild
Kirbla kirik
Vanamõisa mõis
Penijõe
Salevere
Lihula
Massu
Karuse kirik
Kasekula kalmeväli
Kõmsi kivikalmed
Muhu
Virtsu linnus
Hanila kirik
Vatla maalinn
Suur väin
Puhtulaid

AROUND NÕVA

Nõva is primarily known for its landscape: its marshlands, forests full of berries and clear lakes are a delight to every friend of nature. The simple greyish blue **wooden church** in **Nõva** village almost blends into the landscape as well. With its modest size, it represents one of the few surviving examples of coastal churches. Inside, the visitor sees differently shaped seats for men and women, and a wooden circle cross. Men's seats have a back, those designated for the opposite sex do not – apparently women had to just sit straight! In the nearby cemetery is a grave of the lady of the manor, Josephine von Baggehufwudt who designed the cross herself. She was highly skilled in handicraft, as the pulpit and altar are decorated by wooden lace carved by her. The lady was also known as a cobbler and sometimes made shoes for the village children.

Peräküla village north-west of Nõva has a **farm museum**, displaying various agricultural tools. It was founded on private initiative. The farm consists of eight buildings and additionally introduces trees prevalent in Estonia and teaches how to distinguish between them.

Noarootsi churchyard contains ancient ring crosses.

Josephine von Baggehufwudt designed the cross herself.

NOAROOTSI

Noarootsi became a peninsula only a few hundred years ago when several islands merged. The Swedes who arrived there in the 13th century therefore settled on many islands that finally, with the rising of the land, joined the mainland. The "Swedish period" in that region lasted about eight hundred years and ended only with the onslaught of the Soviet army in 1944 when the locals fled across the sea. Many Swedish place names are still used today, such as Gutanäs, Birkas and Österby.

The centre of Noarootsi lies in **Pürksi** with its church dating from around 1500 and a nicely restored manor house. In the early 18th century, the manor was owned by Johann Karl Emmanuel von Ungern-Sternberg who had studied at Dresden Art Academy.

Lyckholm Manor again belongs to the former owners, the von Rosens.

He painted the portraits of many Tartu university professors, plus villages and landscapes in Livonia. Today the manor houses the Noarootsi School.

Turning from Pürksi towards Saare, the visitor arrives 4 km later in **Lyckholm Manor** that used to belong to the von Rosen family for several centuries. Today the manor again belongs to the Rosens and has been beautifully restored. The former stables accommodate a museum about the history of Noarootsi.

Lyckholm is also the centre of the Silma Nature Reserve that mostly protects rare wooded meadows and birds whose number can reach 100,000 during their migration period. Two watchtowers and nature paths have been established for people interested in bird life.

The tallest building on Vormsi, the Saxby lighthouse.

The church stone on the north-eastern coast of Vormsi is 5.6 m high.

VORMSI

Those wishing to visit Vormsi Island should find Rohuküla harbour where ferries to Hiiumaa also set off. The island's most important harbour Sviby is on the southern coast. Vormsi is the fourth biggest island in Estonia. As in Noarootsi, the inhabitants of Vormsi were Swedish who arrived in the late 13th century. During the tsarist Russian rule, the Swedes were free peasants and lived according to Swedish law. They spoke an old-fashioned dialect and followed ancient traditions.

The Swedish name for Vormsi is Ormsö, meaning an island of

snakes. The land here is even, with many wooded meadows and idyllic beaches. Best known sights include the 14th century stone St Olof's church in the "capital" Hullo and an old cemetery. It is thought that a wooden church once stood on the same site and that the year 1219 above the door of the present building marks the year of the older one. The highest construction on Vormsi is the Saxby lighthouse in the north-western corner of the island.

Today's Vormsi increasingly relies on holiday-makers.

AROUND RISTI AND TAEBLA

8 km from Linnamäe towards Keila lies Keedika village. At the site of the former manor house, a peculiar stone with names stands by the road. It is known as the **Stone of the Barons**, because the names and dates of Keedika manor lords, the von Knorrings, are carved into it.

A few kilometres towards Palivere by the road, stands the **Keedika hill-fort**, the site of a 1st-millennium stronghold.

On the 4th km of the road from Linnamäe to Nigula, the visitor can see what is on offer in **Koela Farm Museum** that was established in 1987. Besides the usual agricultural tools, machinery and farm buildings the museum also includes a collection of toys.

Kadarpiku village is situated 12 km from Haapsalu near the Haapsalu-Tallinn Road. The village was home to one of the founders of Estonian painting, **Ants Laikmaa** (1866–1942). His home is quite interesting architecturally and houses a museum, offering an overview of the artist's life and work, and exhibiting numerous items brought from various exotic foreign travels. Laikmaa chose and designed his own resting place, a few hundred metres from the house under tall spruce trees. Juhan Raudsepp's monument to the artist stands on his grave.

The park around the museum has, among other trees, nine oaks dedicated to nine Estonian writers who often visited the artist.

Laikmaa studied at Düsseldorf and mostly painted landscapes and portraits of Estonian intellectuals and local peasants. He also worked as an art teacher, founding the first studio-school, and was actively involved in Estonian art and social life.

AROUND KULLAMAA

By the road from Risti to Virtsu, at Märjamaa crossroads, stands **Koluvere Castle** with its menacing towers and moats. Today it houses a home for the elderly.

The history of Koluvere stronghold dates back to the 1430s when a knight called Lode built a tower-stronghold. Quite soon, however, it was taken over by the bishops of Öesel-Wiek who established a convent-type castle around the original tower and dug the moats.

Koluvere castle used to belong to Prince Grigori Orlov, one of the

The home of painter Ants Laikmaa is a striking building.

Koluvere Castle has its own ghost.

Koluvere belonged for a long time to the Buxhoevden family. Their coat of arms still adorns the castle.

favourites of the Russian empress Catherine II. He bought the castle in 1771 and lived there for some time after falling out of favour with the empress.

After Orlov's death Catherine II bought the manor from his heirs and left it to her daughter who was married to Orlov's one-time adjutant, count Buxhoevden. Perhaps it should be further noted that the daughter's father was none other than Prince Orlov. The manor was thus owned by one of the oldest Baltic German noble families. The Buxhoevdens carried out extensive reconstruction work, partly necessitated by two big fires.

Koluvere castle has its own ghost – Augusta Caroline, Princess of Württenberg, who was exiled to Koluvere during the reign of Catherine II and died there under suspicious circumstances. The Princess is buried in Kullamaa church.

Kullamaa church, a few km from Koluvere, offers the final resting place also to Heinrich Göseken Sen (1612–1681) who in 1660 published an Estonian grammar and compiled a 10, 000 word German-Latin-Estonian dictionary. He reputedly translated the New Testament and numerous religious songs, but these have not survived. A fine baroque epitaph

The cannon tower was built in the 16th century when firearms became common.

Kullamaa Church resembles the former Haapsalu castle church.

adorns the church wall to this day. The church cemetery contains a number of rare 18th century ring crosses on the graves of local peasants.

LÄÄNEMAA

A ring cross at the Kullamaa church cemetery.

Turning off the Haapsalu-Tallinn Road at Palivere towards Martna, we arrive in **Suure-Lähtru manor**, a fine example of late baroque where summer visitors can examine the display about the history of the manor in a small museum. The manor is privately owned.

HAAPSALU

The town was built on small islands that emerged from the sea, and today the oldest part of Haapsalu stretches into the bay in two narrow peninsulas. Land continues to rise and the sea retreats, which makes the western edge of Estonia bigger and bigger. The heart of the town is the bishop's castle, now sadly in ruins.

The Bishop of Ösel-Wiek allegedly started to build a stronghold in the 1260s on the sacred hill of the conquered people. In 1265 bishop Hermann I transferred his residence to Haapsalu when the Lithuanians had destroyed his previous headquarters. The cathedral with its auxiliary buildings progressed rapidly and attracted many artisans and merchants to settle in the vicinity. After all, this was an excellent harbour. As early as in 1279 Bishop Hermann I granted Haapsalu the Riga town rights. This date marks the birth of Haapsalu.

The castle has been rebuilt several times. The walls were made

Haapsalu Episcopal Castle has stood in ruins for three hundred years.

higher and wider, and more towers were added, the mightiest of which was the 38-m high watchtower that presented an excellent view of the whole bay. The watchtower is still standing and open to visitors. In the 16th century the castle was surrounded by 10-m high walls, altogether 800 m long, and protected by cannon towers. During the Livonian War (1558–1583) the castle changed hands eight times and was seriously damaged. Postwar Läänemaa belonged to the Swedes and post-Northern War Läänemaa to the Russians. The latter, afraid of the next Swedish invasion, blew up the castle walls in 1715. The ruins have thus reached the respectable age of 300!

The western wing houses a **museum** that introduces medieval weapons found in the castle, and the life and even the appearance of people at that time, such as the lord of the castle, a bishop, simple clergy, monks and citizens.

It is also possible to visit the **cathedral** that embraces the entire southern wing. This used to be the biggest single-nave place of worship in the Baltic region, much valued for its acoustics. The vaults rise 15.5 m from the floor. Numerous paintings and tombstones were destroyed in frequent lootings, fires and reconstructions. Only some plant ornaments of wall capitals are still visible.

An interesting building is the round baptistery added to the church in the 15th century. The baptismal font, now in the Haapsalu museum, used to stand in the middle of the chapel.

The famous legend about the White Lady of Haapsalu is connected with the cathedral. In the moonlit nights of August, a pale woman's figure appears in the middle window of the baptistery. According to a legend, the mistress of a canon was walled in there, and has not found peace ever since. There is another more realistic explanation. The moonshine enters through the eastern Gothic window of the baptistery and casts a bright patch on the opposite wall that is visible from the middle window.

It is impossible not to wonder whether the ancient builders had done this on purpose as the chapel was dedicated to Virgin Mary, or whether the apparition is accidental.

Opposite the bishop's castle by the former market place stands a house that used to be the town hall. It was completed in the 1770s thanks to the lavish donation of count Magnus Gabriel De la Gardie. During the last fifty years this pretty late baroque building accommodates the **Läänemaa Museum**, which introduced the history of the county and of Haapsalu.

The façade of the Haapsalu Cathedral is decorated by a fine rosette window.

Kooli Street that begins near the museum is one of the oldest in town. The first school opened doors here in the 16th century. The wooden house on the corner is birthplace (1887) of **Anna Hedvig Büll** (Bühl). As a missionary she travelled to Armenia to help women and children who suffered in the Turkish genocide there. She set up sanctuaries for the orphans and the sick and even opened an Armenian-language school. Grateful Armenians placed a plaque on her house in Haapsalu. Büll died in Germany in 1981.

A monument to Rudolf Tobias (1873–1918), one of the founders of the Estonian national music culture, was unveiled in the Tobias Park in 1929. Rudolf Tobias was born in Käina, Hiiumaa, and learned to play the piano at six. He went to school in Haapsalu. Tobias was our first university-educated man of music, attending two classes at St Petersburg Conservatory – organ and composition. After graduation, Tobias worked in St Petersburg, mainly as an organist. During his entire life he was unable to attain financial security. In search of a better life he moved to Berlin where he died at 45. The composer was buried there, but in 1992 his remains were brought to Estonia to his family burial place in Kullamaa cemetery. His most famous work is "The Mission of Jonah".

The visit to this town should include a nice stroll along the Great Promenade by the 'African' coast. Haapsalu is, after all, a summer resort. As such, its history is connected with the Baltic German doctor **Carl Abraham Hunnius** (1797–1851). After graduating from Tartu University he took up a job in Haapsalu and having examined the mud in the bay, discovered its healing properties. He founded the first mud establishment in 1825 and the second in 1845. A monument near the sanatorium marks his life and work.

In the mid-19th century Haapsalu was a popular summer destination for the St Petersburg aristocracy. In 1845 regular steamboat traffic with St Petersburg was opened. Russia's last four sovereigns Nicholas I, Alexander II, Alexander III and Nicholas II all came to Haapsalu. At the turn of the 19-20th centuries, about 4000 holidaymakers visited Haapsalu every year. Numbers were similar in the 1930s and even in Soviet times. Today's Haapsalu with its cosy old town, pretty alleys, historical castle and varied cultural life remains a highly popular place in Estonia.

Composer Rudolf Tobias is one of the most famous citizens of Haapsalu.

Haapsalu Kuursaal is the centre of the holiday resort.

The grandest of all buildings by the seaside is the late 19th century **Kuursaal** (German Kurhaus). The author of the project was Rudolf Otto von Knüpffer. The Kuursaal was an important meeting place where the orchestra played twice each day, with concerts and dancing in the evening. The building has been superbly restored and continues very much as before.

Besides various crowned heads, one of the most prominent persons to have spent holidays in Haapsalu was the famous Russian composer Pjotr Tchaikovski (1840–1893). He spent time in Haapsalu together with his brothers and some other relatives after he had become professor at the Moscow Conservatory. He depicted Haapsalu in a few of his piano pieces.

The famous composer's visit is remembered by a dolomite bench by the bay – the so-called **Tchaikovski bench**. The notes carved into it are part of his 6th Symphony where he used the Estonian folk song "Darling Mari".

The early 20th century railway station stood out for its length – the platform under the roof was

The monumental stone bench is dedicated to the summer visit of the famous composer Pjotr Tchaikovski.

the longest in Europe. The wooden station building, together with the platform, is listed and today houses a **railway museum** that introduces the history of Estonian wide-gauge railway.

Communications museum is located at 21a Tamme Street where the visitor gets an overview of the development of the post, telegraph, telephone and radio in Western Estonia. It is known, for example, that the first radio programmes were transmitted in Haapsalu in 1924. Haapsalu was later an important receiver of communications between Finland and Western Europe.

The **Museum of Coastal Swedes** is located on the northern shore of a peninsula. Founded in 1990, it introduces the history and culture of coastal Swedes who lived on Estonian coastal areas and islands for over 800 years. The current King of Sweden, Karl XVI Gustav, visited the museum during his official visit to Estonia.

Haapsalu railway station.

Composer Cyrillus Kreek lived in Haapsalu for twenty years.

A few years ago the composer **Cyrillus Kreek apartment-museum** was opened in Väike-Viigi Street. Kreek (1889–1962) lived there for more than 20 years and most of his works – he was famous for his choral songs – were written there.

The colourful history of Haapsalu also includes the notorious 19th century Russian statesman and diplomat, Prince **Aleksandr Gorchakov** (1798–1883). He was Russian foreign minister for 26 years. Today's children's library at Wiedemanni Street bears a plaque which claims that he was born in that house. This fact is much disputed. In late 18th century, the Prince's father was commandant of the cuirassier regiment in Haapsalu. Whatever the theories, the only mention of Haapsalu in the Encyclopaedia Britannica refers to it as the town where Prince Gorchakov was born.

One of the centres of the town's art life is the **Evald Okas Museum**, opened in 2003 on the initiative of his family and supported by the city council. Its location at 24 Karja Street displays art on two floors. Besides the permanent display dedicated to the work of Okas (born 1915), the museum often has other exhibitions as well.

Even the King of Sweden has visited the Museum of Coastal Swedes.

AROUND LIHULA

7 km from Lihula, on the Risti-Virtsu Road, stands Kirbla Church, unanimously considered to be the smallest medieval church in the country. It is 29 m long and 11 m wide and dates from the early 1500s.

A few kilometres before Kirbla the road crosses the Kasari River. Upstream from the new bridge where the old Virtsu road crosses the **Kasari**, stands the **old bridge**. In 1904 when it was completed, its 308 metres made it the longest reinforced concrete bridge in the world. It has now been restored and is nicely illuminated.

Another remarkable 64-m long bridge is in Vanamõisa, about 5 km from the Risti-Virtsu Road. The **Vanamõisa bridge** was built in the mid-19th century and has been nicely restored. The local manor house stands in ruins. At some point it belonged to Otto von Budberg (1850–1907), head of the Estonian Knighthood. The baron developed road construction in the country and supported the building of several hospitals. In 1907 he was murdered by local villagers who were after his money.

The **history of Lihula** resembles a many-layered cake where all the significant parts of Estonian history are clearly represented. In the 2nd millennium BC Lihula was probably situated on an islet and was first inhabited at that time. By the early 13th century, however, Lihula with its mighty stronghold, called Leale, had become the most important centre of Läänemaa. No wonder then that Bishop Albert planned to establish his headquarters there. But in 1220 the Swedes decided to participate in the sharing of Estonia and chose to attack Lihula first.

The recently opened Evald Okas Museum has become a cultural centre.

The old bridge over the Kassari River was at one time the longest concrete iron bridge in the world.

They took the stronghold and left their men to guard it. All of a sudden, however, a large army of Estonians turned up at the stronghold and conquered it.

The stone stronghold was built between 1238 and 1242. From

the second half of the 13th century until 1561, **Lihula stronghold** was jointly owned by Ösel-Wiek bishops and the Livonian Order. Like the entire Lihula, the stronghold suffered extensive damage in the Livonian War and was never restored.

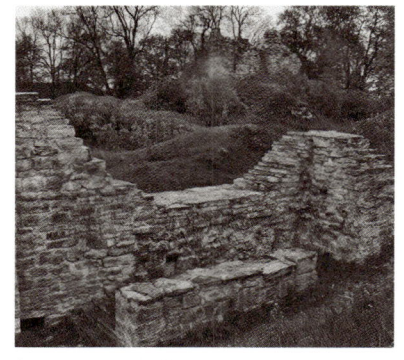

Lihula stronghold used to be one of the mightiest in Western Estonia. It also had a Cistercian nunnery.

Memorial to the island and Läänemaa people who won the stronghold back from the Swedes in August 1220.

In medieval times a settlement of artisans and merchants sprang up near the stone stronghold. The walls of these buildings were found in recent archaeological excavations. A **Cistercian nunnery** was founded in the late 13th century. The pious ladies also owned **Kloostri Manor** with its extensive lands. The Swedes closed down the nunnery of which nothing has survived to this day. Since 1939–40 the Kloostri manor stands in ruins.

Another proof of brisk business and trading in medieval Lihula was the founding of another **monastery** – this time by the **Franciscans**. The pretty classicist **Lihula mansion** on Lihula Lossimägi was built in 1824. After innumerable owners, the mansion currently belongs to the foundation "Medieval Lihula" that has opened a museum there, introducing the history of Southern Läänemaa.

The **Penijõe Manor** near Lihula houses the centre of **Matsalu Nature Reserve**. The manor was recently restored and has a museum about the history of nature protection, the plants and various species of birds and animals. The 486-sq km Reserve was established in 1957. Around 350, 000 migratory birds stop there every year.

HANILA

Two churches stand by the road to Virtsu, **Karuse** and **Hanila**, both dating from the mid-13th century and started as fortified churches. The towers were added later. The former school in Hanila has a local museum.

Kõmsi lies between Karuse and Hanila. Near the Orthodox church we find Kõmsi stone-cist graves. This burial ground was discovered

Lihula Church is located a few hundred metres from the castle towards Virtsu.

Lihula classicist mansion houses a museum.

The former Hanila school now has a museum.

Over two thousand years old Kõmsi tarand graves have yielded tools and jewellery.

early in the 20th century when peasants found various items and bits and pieces of burnt bones. The burials by fire took place in the 11–13th centuries. In addition, the so-called tarand graves that are one thousand years older, have been discovered in Kõmsi. The area is marked and open to visitors.

An ancient stronghold site has been uncovered in **Massu village** north of Kõmsi. The circular wall is about 60–70 cm high. Another theory suggests that similar constructions dating from I millennium, found in Saaremaa and other places in Western Estonia, were in fact cult centres.

Half a km from Massu on the road to Mõisaküla stands the **Massu Liukivi** (Slide Stone) with its numerous small cult hollows and three grooves. According to a legend people used to slide down the grooves and make a wish. When the person managed to stay upright after the slide, the wish was fulfilled. The stone was especially popular amongst young girls and women who wanted to find a suitable husband or have children.

In **Kaseküla** north of Hanila, 16 stone-cist and tarand graves, plus two settlement sites have been discovered. Archaeologists have established that the settlers arrived over two thousand years ago, which makes Kaseküla one of the oldest villages in the country.

A little bit after Karuse Church it is possible to turn off the Risti-Virtsu Road towards Vatla. In 5 kilometres and 1 km to the left, lies the **Vatla (Linnuse) stronghold**. It was surrounded by a 2–3 m high wall that was in turn surrounded by a wide moat. The stronghold used to be the centre of Karuse parish.

Virtsu stronghold was destroyed in the battles for the bishopric in 1530.

VIRTSU

Virtsu Peninsula, the current "gate" to Saaremaa, was an island only one and a half centuries ago. In the 15–16th centuries, the south-western corner of the island had a mighty stronghold that belonged to the influential family of von Uexkülls. The stronghold was probably built in the 1430s as a fortification, rather than as a residence for people. Controlling the traffic between Saaremaa and the mainland, it sat on a small island and was surrounded by water on all four sides.

The life of the **Virtsu stronghold** was cut short. Between 1532 and 1536 a bloody war raged for the Öesel-Wiek bishopric. The vassals refused to accept the new bishop Reinhold von Buxhövden and wanted the Brandenburg margrave Wilhelm who was in the end forced to retreat.

Puhtulaid with its beautiful woody landscape has also only recently become a peninsula. For centuries, Puhtu has been connected with the manor of Virtsu. The place was made famous by the biologist and founder of biosemiotics, **Jakob Johann von Uexküll** (1864–1944) who spent his summers there in the 1930s. His summer cottage was later turned into an ornithology station that is used by nature researchers to this day. The last owner of Puhtu before the Soviet regime was another world famous scientist and philosopher, count **Hermann Alexander von Keyserling** (1880–1946).

The owner of the Virtsu manor, Dorothea Augusta von Rosen (née Helvig) set a monument to the German writer Friedrich Schiller (1759–1805). The simple monument suffered badly in the world wars. Today the original, diligently assembled from the pieces, is displayed in the Haapsalu museum. Its exact copy stands under the shade of tall trees where the original was once placed.

RAPLAMAA

RAPLAMAA

Raplamaa is a relatively flat area on thick limestone layers. Limestone alternates with low hills and some marshland. The county has the least number of lakes in Estonia.

There are several remarkable strongholds and castles of which Varbola is the best known. Catapults, a siege tower and ram help the visitor imagine the past. How would it feel like to attack the stronghold or to resist the enemy from inside? Keava hill fort offers more surprises. Who laid the birch bark path 7000 years ago?

According to historical sources, Estonians destroyed most of the manors in Raplamaa twice - in 1343 and 1905 when people rebelled against their oppressors. The interval was long enough for many new manors to be built. One of the best examples today is the Raikküla Mansion, home to the world famous naturalist Count A. F. von Keyserling whom Charles Darwin considered his predecessor, and to his philosopher son Count Hermann A. von Keyserling. The latter sought to bring different cultures together, something that is increasingly important in our world today (see later in the chapter).

Raplamaa is usually associated with the so-called Mahtra War (see Around Juuru), the best known amongst all peasants' uprisings in the country.

Raplamaa is part of the heart of Estonia; it is full of historical and cultural places and was the birthplace of many people who played an important role in Estonia's history.

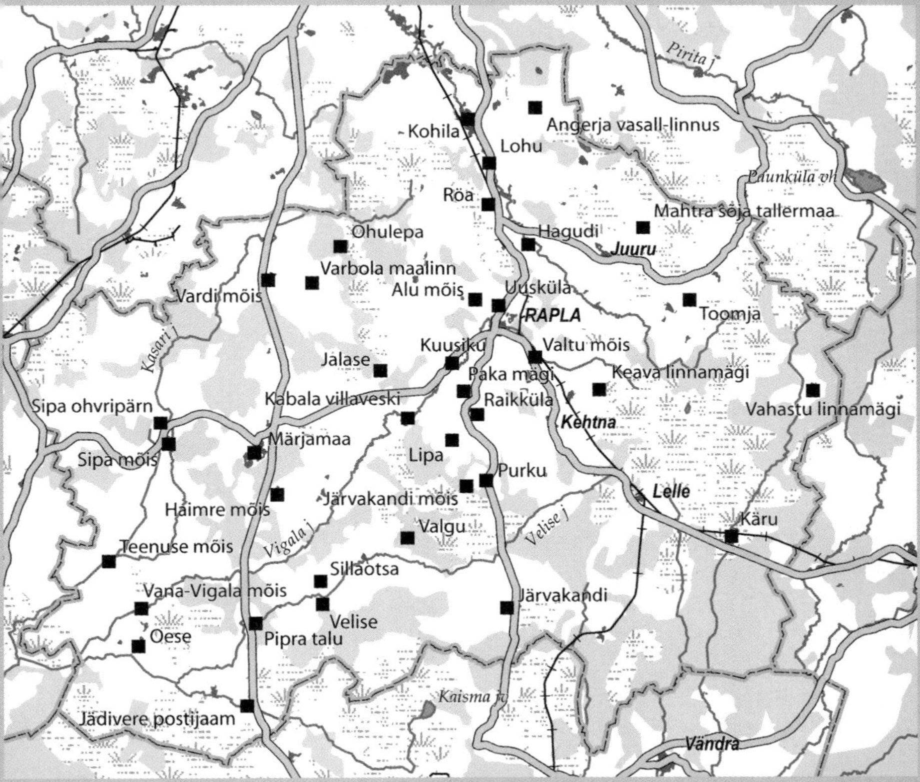

Pirita j
Angerja vasall-linnus
Kohila
Lohu
Paunküla vh
Röa
Mahtra sõja tallermaa
Ohulepa
Hagudi
Juuru
Varbola maalinn
Alu mõis
Uusküla
Vardi mõis
RAPLA
Toomja
Kasari
Kuusiku
Valtu mõis
Jalase
Paka mägi
Keava linnamägi
Kabala villaveski
Raikküla
Vahastu linnamägi
Sipa ohvripärn
Kehtna
Märjamaa
Sipa mõis
Lipa
Purku
Lelle
Haimre mõis
Järvakandi mõis
Käru
Velise j
Valgu
Teenuse mõis
Vigala j
Sillaotsa
Vana-Vigala mõis
Järvakandi
Velise
Oese
Pipra talu
Kaisma j
Jädivere postijaam
Vändra

AROUND KOHILA

3 km beyond Kohila, beside the Tallinn-Rapla Road, stands **Lohu Jaanilinn** (St John's town), one of the mightiest of its time. The ancient stronghold site is located in the bend of the Keila river on a 3–4 m hill and is surrounded by a horseshoe-shaped rampart. The yard is about 6500 square metres. The stronghold was probably used in the 12–13th centuries. Archaeological excavations have revealed a large number of pottery shards, a buckle and an axe.

Traces of a smaller and a few hundred years younger stronghold site were found south of Jaanilinn. 1 km south of Lohu stronghold is the Lohu Manor, once famous for its pictorial wallpapers that are now displayed at the Maarjamäe Museum in Tallinn. The privately owned mansion has been restored.

The former Kapa-Kohila was a modest little village until the building of the narrow-gauge railway and a paper factory in the late 19th century. Paper manufacturing was initiated by the local landlord Karl von Lueder.

Kohila has two manor houses: **Kohila Manor** in private possession and **Tohisoo Manor** that used to belong to the von Wrangells. In the 1920s Benita von Wrangell married the Swedish journalist Carl Mothander who later published a fascinating overview about the life of Baltic Germans in Estonia, Barons, Estonians and the Bolsheviks. Today Tohisoo houses an educational and recreational centre.

Beside the road west of Kohila, at the Urge crossroads at the Tallinn-Rapla Road, lie the ruins of **Angerja vassal castle**. The castle was established by the Teutonic Knights. The main building had two storeys and was surrounded by a circular wall and a moat. It

Another floor to the Tohisoo Manor was added later.

The development of Kohila is directly connected with the hundred-year-old paper industry.

Kohila Manor used to belong to the von Lueders who established the paper industry.

The medieval Angerja inhabitants were protected by a fortified manor.

has been standing in ruins since the Livonian War that began in 1558.

In the 13th century the area around Angerja belonged to the nobleman of Estonian origin, Haenrich van Angern whose descendants were the vassals of the Danish king. At that time this area used to be densely inhabited, shown by numerous sacrificial stones, sacred groves and springs, ancient fields, graves and various bits of jewellery, mostly silver brooches and necklaces.

AROUND JUURU

Mahtra is certainly one of the best known Estonian place names because of the events that took place there in 1858. The whole of North-Estonia was seething – after passing the 1856 law regulating the rights of the peasantry, people did not think the manors had any right to demand unpaid labour in addition to innumerable tasks they had to carry out for the manors anyway.

Unfortunately, the paragraph concerning unpaid labour in the new law was rather vague and thus open to different interpretations.

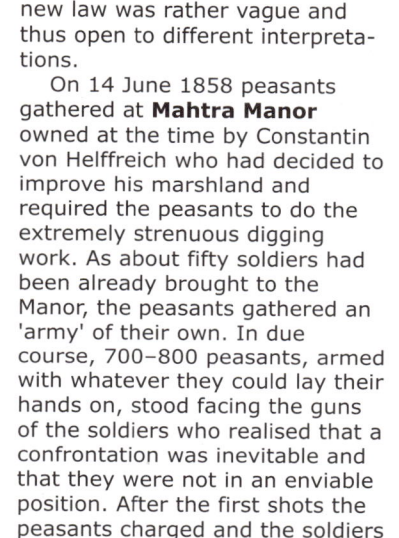

On 14 June 1858 peasants gathered at **Mahtra Manor** owned at the time by Constantin von Helffreich who had decided to improve his marshland and required the peasants to do the extremely strenuous digging work. As about fifty soldiers had been already brought to the Manor, the peasants gathered an 'army' of their own. In due course, 700–800 peasants, armed with whatever they could lay their hands on, stood facing the guns of the soldiers who realised that a confrontation was inevitable and that they were not in an enviable position. After the first shots the peasants charged and the soldiers fled. The simple wooden manor house was burnt down.

The next stage in the story of Mahtra Uprising took place on 22 February 1859. No less than 900 soldiers gathered in the nearby field in order to mete out punishment to 41 peasants. Two of them received the maximum penalty – they had to run the gauntlet with 1000 strokes. And that was not all – should the men survive they faced twenty years of hard labour. Six men received 600 strokes and four 400.

Atla-Eeru pub was where the peasants hatched their war plans.

On the field of blood, dozens of peasants were almost beaten to death.

A dolomite monument stands in the courtyard of the former Mahtra Manor commemorating people who demanded their rights.

Mahtra Farm Museum is the Rapla County Museum.

The events of Mahtra are remembered in several memorial stones and a dolomite monument in the former manor courtyard. A boulder stands where the beatings took place, known as the Field of Blood.

The best overview of Mahtra is available at the **Mahtra Peasant Museum** at Juuru, which also serves as the county museum. It introduces the life of Estonian peasantry in the 19th century, displaying various items, such as petroleum lamps, clocks, pipes, old books, etc.

There is a branch of Mahtra Museum, at the **Atla Eeru pub**, the oldest surviving peasant pub in the country. This was the place where people hatched their battle plans in 1858. One room is dedicated to the Mahtra uprising.

WESTERN RAPLAMAA

Follow the signpost on the 51st km on the Tallinn-Pärnu road. By the Varbola-Rapla Road lies one of the mightiest ancient Estonian fortifications, the **Varbola stronghold (Jaanilinn)**. It was mentioned in the Chronicles of Henry of Livonia and in the 1212 Novgorod Chronicle when Prince Mstislav raided Harjumaa. It is thought that the enemy failed to conquer the stronghold because of its 10-m stone walls, and had to reach an agreement with the local elders.

The stronghold yard was about 2 hectares, with a well and various wooden buildings. Archaeological excavations at Varbola have revealed over 4500 finds (ceramics, jewellery, spearheads, arrowheads, knives, etc.).

The stronghold was used from the 11th century. The yard later served as the village cemetery and afterwards belonged to a

The restored gates of Varbola stronghold.

farm so that part of it was ploughed. Today, part of the ancient gateway has been restored and visitors can see the models of a ballista, battering ram and siege tower.

Opposite Varbola across the road lies an irregularly shaped boulder that is considered a sacrificial stone. According to a legend, ghosts move around it at night.

The former **Vardi Manor** near Varbola by the Märjamaa-Tallinn Road belonged in 1807–1813 to the playwright **August von Kotzebue** (1761–1819). Born in Weimar, he was ennobled in 1785 upon becoming president of Estonian regional government. Since he had been involved in the theatre in Germany and influenced by no less a person than Goethe, he actively participated in the founding of the first theatre in Tallinn, Revaler Liebhaber-Theater which opened with one of his own comedies. His plays became so popular that he took up writing full time, and in the late 18th century he enjoyed great success also in Europe. Kotzebue wrote 211 plays in all, and Beethoven commissioned him to write librettos to two short operas (Overture

Ancient siege machinery is on display at Varbola.

to King Stephen, Op 117 and The Ruins of Athens, Op 113).

Between 1798 and 1800 he was head of the court theatres in Vienna, Weimar and Jena. When he lived at Vardi he edited the anti-Napoleon satirical magazines Die Biene and Die Grille that were published in Königsberg. Kotzebue was understandably dismayed and worried when Napoleon arrived in Russia. He reputedly had a two-horse carriage ready to make his escape at any time.

Kotzebue was also an enthusiastic promoter of potatoes. According to a popular story he had his potato fields rigorously

The mansion has not survived, only a barn and a bird-house (above) have done so.

guarded in daytime but removed the guards at night so that local peasant could steal the potatoes and plant them in their own fields. August von Kotzebue had numerous children from his three marriages. Otto von Kotzebue (1788–1846) from his first marriage was a famous navigator and explorer who took part in three Russian round-the-world voyages, two under his own leadership. Alexander von Kotzebue (1815–1889) from the third marriage achieved great renown as a painter of many battles. His best works depict the events of the Great Northern War, military campaigns of the Field Marshal Alexander Suvorov (1729–1800) and other battles that brought glory to Russian armies.

During his time at Vardi August Kotzebue employed August von Hagen (1786–1877) and painter Carl Walther (1783–1867) to teach his children. The first later became a well-know figure in Estonian music. Other teachers were J. C. Petri who wrote several books, the most important of which is the 3-volume Ehstland und die Esten, published in Gotha in 1802, and botanist G.A. Pahnsch (1842–1880) who collected plants and compiled an extensive herbarium, now kept in the Estonian Natural Museum.

There is a bird house in the heart of the manor. One of its walls has a sentence on it: *Omnia ab ovo* (everything starts from the egg).

By the Koluvere-Märjamaa Road, north of Sipa village, grows one of the most famous big trees in Estonia – **Sipa sacrificial lime**. It is difficult to measure its real size as its branches stretch in all directions. At 0.5 m from the ground the lime's diameter is 9 m. The Sipa lime is growing around a sacrificial stone.

Sipa Manor in Sipa village used to be the centre of Loodna rural municipality. After the two municipalities joined, the manor became a kindergarten and an elementary school. The 18th century manor was burnt down during extensive unrest in the coun-

People used to bring offerings to the Sipa linden tree.

try in 1905, but was later rebuilt.
During the Livonian War in 1566 a fierce battle was waged nearby between the Swedish and Polish armies. The Swedes won, and the head of the Poles, Kasper (Jasper) von Oldenbockum, who was called the last knight of Livonia, was badly wounded and soon died.

Friedrich Brandt (1830–1880), former Sipa schoolmaster, son of the manor's tailor, has a notable place in Estonian cultural history. He wrote and published no less than 95 books, mostly romantic stories. His song books became most popular of all, and were printed in large numbers. He also enthusiastically promoted the standard Estonian language.

Teenuse Manor by Loodna-Vana-Vigala Road used to belong to the von Maydells. The well-known Baltic German painter and sculptor **Friedrich Ludwig von Maydell** (1795–1846) was born there. Among other things he illustrated many Estonian-language publications. He was prolific in many fields of art, for example, painting and designing altars and he founded the art of woodcutting in Estonia. His copper engravings depict the history of the Baltic provinces within the Russian empire.

Vana-Vigala Manor between Tallinn-Pärnu and Tallinn-Virtsu Roads, 9 km from Kivi-Vigala, belonged to the von Uexkülls for nearly 500 years. The original heart of the manor was located in Kivi-Vigala, south-east of the present site, where a mighty vassal castle stood in the 15th century. The latter was destroyed in the Livonian War and the new manor was built in Vana-Vigala.

According to an old legend, Vana-Vigala Manor sunk into the

According to ancient legends, the Vana-Vigala Manor had sunk to the bottom of a lake.

bottom of a river in one night. This is hardly likely, but the building that was started in 1762 was actually stopped for quite some time because the house on the soft clay soil began to sink a bit. The grand mansion was finally completed in 1775.

The park has trees which are several hundred years old and cascading ponds. The **burial ground of the von Uexkülls** lies in the farther corner of the park, alongside the ruins of a former chapel. A tall limestone wall lines the park in the north, laid in the late 1860s by peasants during a crop failure in return for the grain given by the manor lord. The 222-m long wall is therefore called the **Hunger Wall**. The recently completed choir stand is in the heart of the park. The park has trees of

The trees in the park offer shade to the last resting place of the von Uexkülls.

The Hunger Wall was made during the years of failed crops.

Marble plaques at Vana-Vigala, about 2,500 years old.

various types and the added labels help recognise the most exotic of them.

Spectacular **larch alleys** adorn the front of the Vana-Vigala Mansion, also lining the road leading to the manor. The biggest larch in Estonia with a diameter of 4.24 m grows in the park.

Today the mansion houses a school. Two relief marble tablets hang on the walls of the entrance hall. These originate from the Italian town of Pompei that was buried under the ashes of Vesuvius. Boris von Uexküll brought the tablets, estimated to be about 2500 years old, from his extensive travels in the early 19th century.

During the revolt of December 1905 the mansion was burnt down. The house was reputedly on fire for three days. As a result, one of the most valuable manorial archives in the Baltic region, a large art collection and a library were destroyed. The main building was restored by the then lord of the manor before the First World War.

Another sight nearby is the so-called **Vigala Deer Park** at the Vigala River. It was established over two hundred years ago. Similarly to the park at the manor, this park has also numerous foreign trees, and several attempts were made to settle the deer there. The animals lived within a large enclosure. On a river island in the western part of the park stands a peculiar column that consists of 13 millstones laid one upon the other. The column was supposed to keep off a haunting lady of the manor. One Vigala manor lord was rumoured to have practised all sort of witchcraft.

Oese village south of Vana-Vigala is the birthplace of **Matthias Johann Eisen** (1857–1934). About one hundred metres from the Oese bus stop, towards Kivi-Vigala, a small path turns right and leads to the former Oese schoolhouse, home of the great folklorist. Although Eisen studied theology, he devoted his life to Estonian folk poetry, especially mythology and ancient beliefs. He also translated the Finnish national epic Kalevala and taught at Tartu University.

West of the Tallinn-Pärnu Road near the Kivi-Vigala crossroads stands **Jädivere stagecoach** station, which was used as early as the 18th century. The classicist stone house was built in 1821–1822. Today, the stagecoach station is privately owned.

Märjamaa village is located in the middle of a large karst area where spring floods are frequent. Hence the name – **Märjamaa** means 'wet land'. The mid-14th century **church** has few windows and thick walls like a fortress. It was indeed a medieval fortified church, one of the mightiest in Western Estonia. It suffered considerable damage in various battles, including those of the Second World War. Its current facade in

Eisen was one of the most prominent scholars of Estonian mythology.

fact dates from only 1989. An interesting gate stands near the church commemorating the War of Independence (1918–1920) and all those from Märjamaa parish killed in battle. There are some temporary karst lakes called järtas to the east of the village. Two of them are under protection. They are filled with water only in spring, whereas in summer people make hay in them.

A few km after Märjamaa by the Tallinn-Pärnu Road, the road turns east towards **Haimre Manor**. The house has been standing in ruins since it was burnt down during the unrest in 1905. Ruins of a building with high arches can be seen in the grand park that is under protection.

Locals call this building 'the mosque'. According to a legend, the local manor lord had married a Turkish woman and built a mosque for her in the park. The building was probably never used as a place of worship, although its facade does suggest that it could have been. The crescent on it was still visible in the 1960s, enhancing the popular legends about the Turkish lady.

In the Middle Ages, Märjamaa Church was both a church and a fortification.

Only ruins are left of the Haimre mosque.

A monument commemorates the founders of the Velise Republic.

Tallinn arrived in the neighbourhood, and altogether twelve manor houses were looted and burnt down. On 19 December the rebels were attacked by rapidly formed troops of manor lords and tsarist soldiers, and were forced to withdraw. In January 1906 General Bezobrazov's guards arranged a public punishment session in front of the local community centre in Purku, where 54 men were brutally beaten and four were shot.

To remember the 'Velise Republic' and its bloody ending, local people started collecting donations and in 1936 a monument was set up in front of the Orthodox church.

At the Valgu-Rapla Road, 3.5 km from Valgu and north of the road, stands a dolomite monument to the Finnish pilots killed in 1941. It shows a broken wing of an aeroplane and was commissioned by the Finns.

Turning north from the Päärdu-Valgu Road at Velise crossroads, we come to **Sillaotsa Farm Museum**, east of the road. The museum was founded in 1982 by the local enthusiast Aleksei Parnabas. The central building is the 1914 barn-dwelling house, displaying various household items and agricultural tools. One of the most remarkable exhibits is the threshing machine, built by a local man. There is also a small dendrological park and a bronze bas-relief of Aleksei Parnabas.

Velise on the Päärdu-Valgu Road was one of the Raplamaa headquarters of the rebels during the 1905 unrest. The locals even managed to form a revolutionary government, the so-called Velise Republic.

In the course of the unrest, groups of armed workers from

AROUND RAPLA

Driving towards Rapla from Märjamaa, **Jalase Nature Reserve** is located north of the road. Its centre is a village of the same name, near the important ancient stronghold of Varbola. The village has a compact plan, the paths

A dolomite aeroplane wing commemorates the perished Finnish pilots.

The Sillaotsa Farm Museum was founded by Aleksei Parnabas.

Jalase tries to maintain the old way of village life.

leading as rays to former springs. In 1990 a nature protection area was established here.

Turning south from the Märjamaa-Rapla Road at Jalase crossroads we arrive at Tamme and can visit the **Kabala Wool Mill-Museum**. The display includes early 20th century machinery for the wool industry. The most remarkable item is the still operating spinning machine which dates from 1896. The Museum got its name from the nearby Kabala Manor, which houses the Raikküla local government.

North of Raikküla, west of the Rapla Road, is a hill covered with spruce trees that is known as **Paka Hill**. The western side of the hill ends with a 10-m high terrace. This area is under protection in order to maintain the coastal formations of the ancient Baltic Ice Lake. The local limestone and dolomite layers appeared here 440 million years ago. They have good technical qualities and are much appreciated as building materials. The limestone bed is 10–25 m wide and about half of Estonia lies on that; the layer here is fifty metres thick.

Folk legends describe Paka Hill as an ancient meeting place for different tribes where essential issues were discussed. There was probably also a sacrificial grove and a large sacrificial stone on the hill.

Röa village lies before Hagudi by the Tallinn-Rapla Road. This is the birthplace of the sculptor **Anton Starkopf** (1889–1966). A monument to him lies west of the road, between the road and the railway. A path from the Kärneri bus stop leads to it.

Starkopf studied in Munich and Paris. After Estonia became independent in 1918, he took part in founding the school of art called Pallas in Tartu. Starkopf's work is highly diverse, encompassing portraits, female figures and monuments. One of his favourite materials was granite, but he also made wooden sculptures.

An alley leads to **Hagudi Manor** from the Tallinn-Rapla Road. The manor belonged to the von Krusenstern family for nearly 250 years, and it is the birthplace of the most famous family member, the explorer Adam Johann von Krusenstern (1770–1846), who sailed around the world. The manor is being restored and a monument to the explorer has been set up in front of it (about Krusernstern see Lääne-Virumaa, Kiltsi).

Otto Tief is commemorated by a monument built from the chimney of his home.

Hagudi Manor is the birthplace of the famous explorer Adam Johann Krusenstern.

Turning towards Ohulepa from the Hageri-Kodila Road at Kodila-Uusküla, we come to **Ohulepa village**. Friedrich Reinhold Kreutzwald, folklorist and creator of the Estonian national epic, spent five summers here as a young man. The house bears a plaque to commemorate him.

In **Uusküla** near Rapla, an old chimney has been designed into a memorial to **Otto Tief** (1889–1976) to mark his birthplace.

Tief studied law in St Petersburg and later fought in the War of Independence (1918–1920). Between 1920 and 1930 he worked as a lawyer, was an MP and minister of justice. During WW II he was among those who tried to maintain Estonia as an independent republic, but their efforts failed. Tief was arrested in 1944 and sentenced to ten years of hard labour in Siberia. After that he lived in the Ukraine and Latvia.

The first professional Estonian musician, **Johannes Kappel** (1855–1907) was also born in Uusküla. He graduated from St Petersburg Conservatory as an organist and composer, worked in St Petersburg and organised several song festivals in Estonia. Kappel died in Germany.

The most remarkable sights in **Rapla** include the **church** with two towers and a late 19th century stone bridge across the Vigala River. About a hundred years ago the previous church became dan-

Rapla Church is the only rural church in Estonia with two towers.

gerously unstable and had to be demolished. A new capacious church was built in its place. No other rural church in Estonia has two towers. Several items in the church come from the previous one, such as the 800-years-old baptismal font and a beautiful baroque altar.

The neo-Gothic **Alu Manor** near Rapla was built in 1875 according

Alu Manor houses the study centre of the Estonian Defence League.

the project of Paul Friedrich Wilhelm Alisch. It has three storeys, with high arched windows and a square corner tower. Since 1999, the building belongs to the Estonian Defence Guard.

Kuusiku lies 6 km south-west of Rapla and is primarily known for its meteorological station. The recorded winter temperatures here are often the lowest in the country. Kuusiku has a long tradition of plant breeding. Among its best known achievements is breeding the Swedish turnip that was later grown all over the Soviet Union. Today, the testing and experimenting with various plants continues.

The wooden mansion now accommodates a kindergarten.

The classicist **Raikküla Mansion** with its six columns has been slowly decaying over the last twenty or so years, and is waiting for renovation. On a small hill in the far corner of the green area in front of the mansion stands a modest monument to the former owners, the Keyserlings. This family boasts famous scientists, philosophers and politicians. The most prominent is perhaps Count **Alexander Friedrich von Keyserling** (1815–1891) who settled in Raikküla in 1847. The grand mansion had been completed in 1820 and the Count acquired it after marrying Zenaida, daughter of the Russian minister of finance, Count Georg von Cancrin (Jegor Kankrin). The manor was part of her dowry.

On his scientific expeditions, Alexander Keyserling explored the Ural Mountains, the Pyrenees and the Carpathian Mountains. He was keenly interested in geology, zoology and botany. He compiled handbooks about birds and plants, wrote thorough geological overviews, tackled biological problems and earned the recognition of Charles Darwin. He was elected as a member of the St Petersburg Academy of Sciences and as the head of the Estonian Knighthood.

Besides all that, he found time to run the manor and improve the life of the peasants. He began charging money instead of forced labour for the rent of the peasant cottages. The villagers knew how to appreciate what he did for them. For example, when the other local landlords had to find shelter in towns after the Mahtra Uprising in 1858, Count Keyserling could calmly stay at home without any fear of revenge attacks. As head of the Knighthood, he had to negotiate between other landlords, the peasants and the authorities in St Petersburg.

Alexander Keyserling is considered to be the founder of the first rock garden in Estonia in 1881. A mighty oak once grew near the manor, known as the Bismarck oak. The German chancellor was a friend of the Keyserlings and visited Raikküla on several occasions. The Count liked to entertain his guests under the oak tree, which was then named after the most prominent visitor. Another oak, the Count still exists, about one km south form the manor. The villagers used to celebrate St John's Eve there and the Count had beer made for the occasion and brought to the oak in barrels that contained five buckets of beer. Men then measured their strength; the strongest were able to lift the 80-kg barrel to their mouth and drink from it. The Count himself reputedly also managed this feat.

Alexander Keyserling is buried in Hauametsa (Grave Forest) cemetery about 1.5 km south-west of the manor. There is a signpost pointing the way.
The Count's grandson **Hermann Alexander von Keyserling** (1880–1946) also achieved international recognition. He was a philosopher, especially keen on the Orient. He attempted to blend different cultures and thus reach a different level of thinking. He founded the philosophical educational establishment 'The School of Wisdom' that started in Darmstadt in 1920. His son Arnold (born in 1922) is also a philosopher and cultural historian. He has visited Estonia several times.

To commemorate the Keyserlings, the plays of Eduard von Keyserling (1855–1918), nephew of Alexander, are staged each year at Raikküla. He was a prominent Baltic German writer whose works include those about the life of local nobility.

The Raikküla manor park contains various exotic trees.

Uku Masing's birthplace in Lipa village. Masing (1909–1985) was one of the most fascinating figures of Estonian culture of all times. He was a theologian and writer, an expert in Finno-Ugric mythology, translated the Old Testament from Hebrew, also literature form Latin, Greek, Japanese, Catalan and many other languages, wrote complicat-

Uku Masing was one of the most original thinkers in Estonia.

ed and sensitive poetry and prose. His works were prohibited in the Soviet period, although several were published in the West.

In 1989 a monument to Uku Masing was unveiled in the courtyard of his home farm in Lipa village. It stands under the tree that had reputedly been a great inspiration to the poet.

The Estonian painter **Johannes Võerahansu** (1902–1980) was born in Keo village near Raikküla. He studied art at the Pallas School in Tartu and later in Paris. Afterwards he taught young painters at Tartu Art School and Tartu State Art Institute and then in Tallinn. Most of Võerahansu's paintings depict landscapes, village scenes and portraits.

His home now houses the museum about his life and art.

Before Kehtna, a road turns east from the Rapla-Käru Road at Metsaääre, towards Keava. Driving from Keava towards Ingliste, we first pass the decaying heart of the Keava manor complex and reach the **Keava hill-fort**, west of the road. The ancient hill-fort lies on the southern part of a steep ridge. The Russians successfully attacked Keava as early as 1054. In the early 2000s the archaeologists discovered that the Linnaaluste village nearby was one of the largest Viking-period villages, founded in the 7th–8th centuries. However, according to pollen analysis, people cultivated land there already one thousand years before that. About one kilometre north of the hill-fort, once stood another one, which was even older.

Valtu Manor near Rapla by the Rapla-Türi Road is directly connected with the development of the town of Rapla. The brick factory established near the manor in the late 19th century greatly advanced local life.

Talking of Valtu, alas, one must use the past tense. The manor was among the most beautiful classicist mansions in Estonia, which was destroyed in the course of revolutionary unrest in 1905. Only a few auxiliary buildings have survived.

North-east of Kaiu, by the road at **Toomja**, stands a monument to local people who were deported to Siberia in March 1949.

AROUND JÄRVAKANDI

In **Purku** by the Rapla-Järvakandi Road there is a huge boulder in front of the schoolhouse. It commemorates the events of the 1905–1906 unrest. The notorious General Bezobrazov meted out cruel punishment to the peasants here.

At the start of the path leading to Lipa village (first mentioned in 1241) stands a monument to **four men of Jalase village** who avoided conscription to the Soviet army. They were caught and shot in July 1941. These Jalase men were the first war victims in Rapla parish. Next year the local people set up a monument, which in

The former Keava Manor stands by the road leading to the hill-fort.

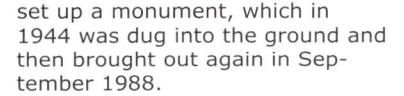

A secret passage was discovered at the hill-fort (below) and a 7000-year-old path paved with birch bark.

set up a monument, which in 1944 was dug into the ground and then brought out again in September 1988.

Järvakandi Manor is located about 10 km north of Järvakandi. The visitor must turn off from the Rapla-Järvakandi Road at the Purku crossroads towards Valli village. The manor lies in ruins and the burial chapel in the park has been looted.

The manor was closely connected with the development of Järvakandi hamlet and its famous glass-works. In 1879 the local landlord von Taube built a bottle factory on the manor land. The first bottles and jars were ready in September. In Soviet times also window glass was produced. Today the glass-works focuses on various glass containers. Glass is made of Piusa glass sand, Tamsalu limestone and imported soda.

AROUND KÄRU

In Käru by the Rapla-Türi Road we find both the heart of the manor and the church. The **Käru Mansion** has survived, but was reconstructed to accommodate a schoolhouse and suffered damage

mer historicist house with turrets has lost most of its grandeur. An interesting sight is the smithy that looks like a small fortress. Käru Church is rather modest, but a charming wooden building, dating from 1860.

By the Viljandi Road in Käru, a monument has been built to **commemorate the Baltic Chain** of 23 August 1989 when about 2 million inhabitants of Latvia, Lithuania and Estonia held hands to demand their freedom. The chain stretched from Tallinn to Vilnius and covered about 620 km (approximately the distance, for example, between Paris and Liverpool, or Los Angeles and San Francisco).

In Vahastu by the Kuimetsa-Türi Road stands the **Vahastu hill-fort** with a steep north side. Excavating gravel has greatly damaged the site.

HARJUMAA

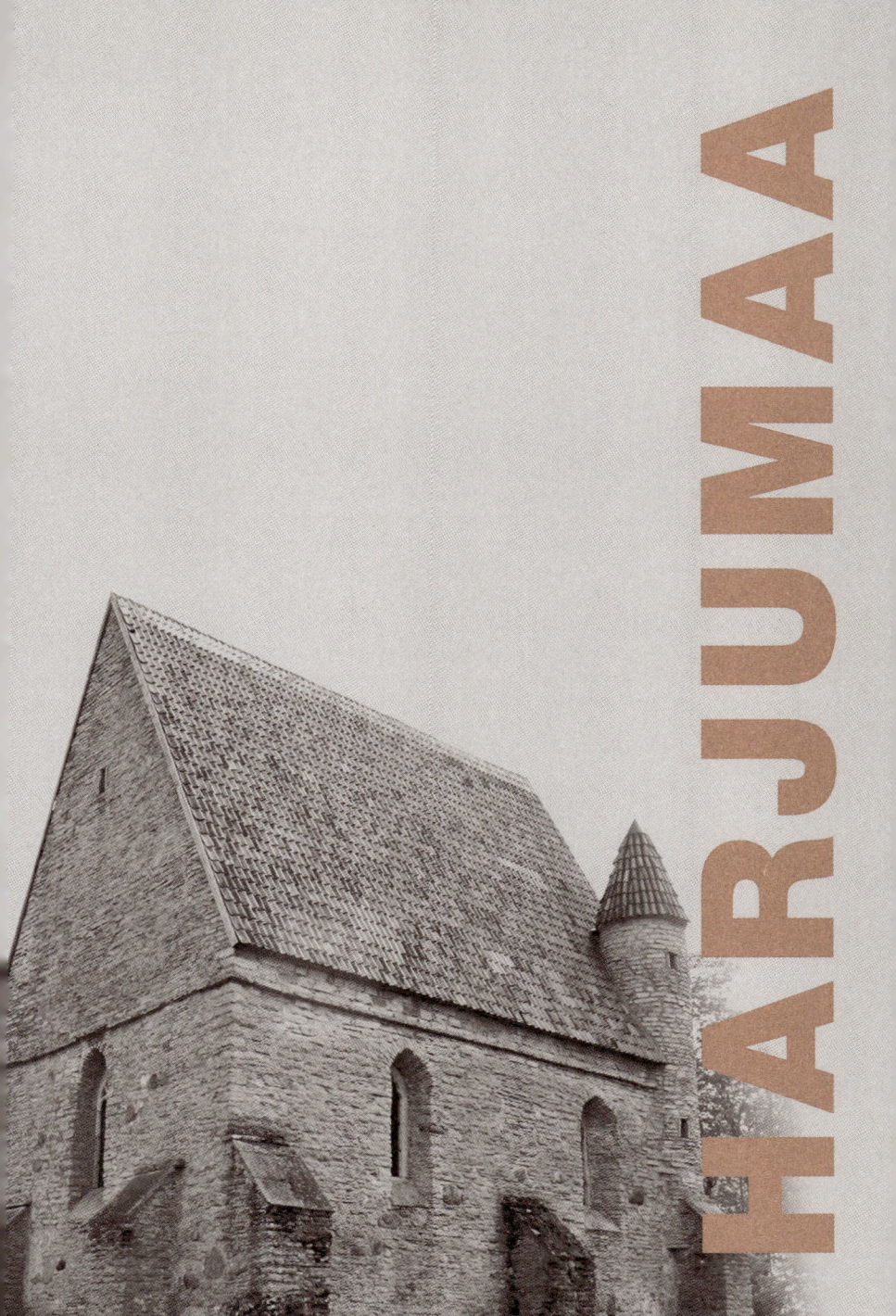

HARJUMAA

With the number of inhabitants reaching half a million, Harjumaa is the most populous county in Estonia. This is only to be expected as it constitutes the area around the capital city of Tallinn. Harju was densely populated for its time already three thousand years ago, when fields were ploughed and cattle pastured near today's Iru thermal station. Numerous burial grounds and sacrificial stones are witnesses of a considerable ancient population.

The lengthy limestone cliff running along the northern coast is certainly the mightiest amongst the natural phenomena in Harjumaa. In Türisalu and Rannamõisa, west of Tallinn, it rises above the sea, and hurls down rivers at Keila-Joa and Jägala.

Harjumaa, initially owned by the King of Denmark in 1219–1220, has been ravaged many a time, as all the major invading armies always ended up in Tallinn. The surroundings of the capital were therefore a battlefield for centuries, although luckily the town itself was always spared warfare, except in WW II when it was extensively bombed by the Russians.

In the twentieth century, the seeds of revolt growing in Tallinn have resulted in extensive burning of manor houses in Harjumaa and nearby counties as well. Today, when restoring the manors seems to be all the rage, Estonians find it difficult to identify with the pillagers of olden times.

Harjumaa is home to an exceptional figure in Estonian cultural history, Bengt Gottfried Forselius. As a young man, barely out of school himself, he started teaching the village children in the 1680s (see Risti Vicarage and Harju-Madise Church).

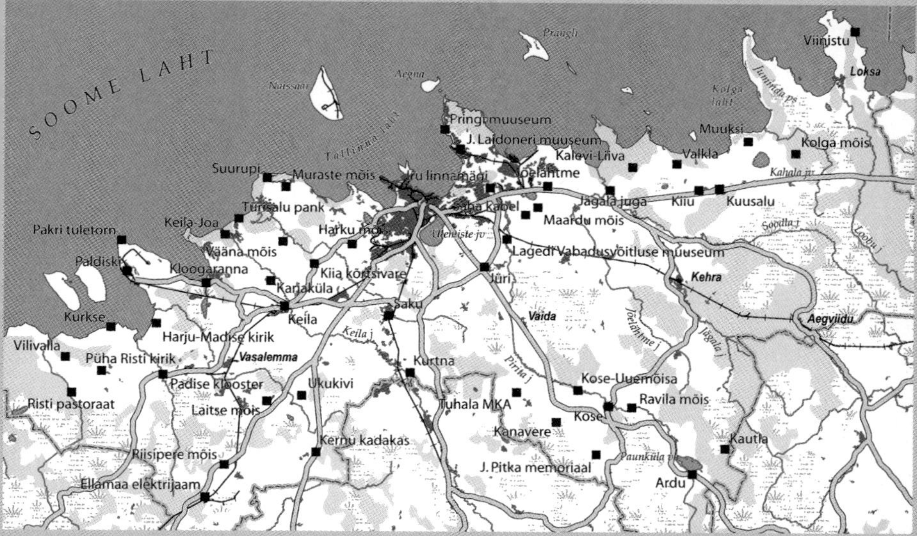
SOOME LAHT
Naissaar
Aegna
Prangli
Tallinna laht
Kolga laht
Juminda ps
Viinistu
Loksa
Pringi muuseum
J. Laidoneri muuseum
Kalevi-Liiva
Muuksi
Valkla
Kolga mõis
Kahala jv
Suurupi
Muraste mõis
Jõelähtme
Jägala juga
Kiiu
Kuusalu
Turisalu pank
Saha kabel
Maardu mõis
Keila-Joa
Pakri tuletorn
Harku mõis
Ülemiste jv
Soodla j
Loobu j
Vääna mõis
Lagedi Vabadusvõitluse muuseum
Paldiski
Kloogaranna
Kiia kõrtsivare
Jüri
Kehra
Keila
Saku
Vaida
Aegviidu
Kurkse
Harju-Madise kirik
Keila j
Jõelähtme j
Jägala j
Vilivalla
Püha Risti kirik
Vasalemma
Kurtna
Pirita j
Padise klooster
Ukukivi
Kose-Uuemõisa
Ravila mõis
Risti pastoraat
Laitse mõis
Tuhala MKA
Kose
Kanavere
Kautla
Kernu kadakas
Riisipere mõis
J. Pitka memoriaal
Ardu
Ellamaa elektrijaam

AROUND HARJU-RISTI AND PADISE

In the south by the road from Harju-Risti towards Vihterpalu lies **Vilivalla village cemetery** dating from the 13th century, with about one hundred graves of local Swedes who had lived on the islands and coasts of Western Estonia since the 13th century. There is also a small chapel.

Like most stone crosses in Harjumaa cemeteries, these too were cut from Vasalemma limestone that is often called Estonian marble. Limestone quarries were started in Vasalemma as early as in the 13th century and the material has been used as a finishing material both inside and outside buildings.

The best-known cross in the cemetery is a circle cross in memory of two men, executed by shooting in 1632. It is not known why such harsh punishment was carried out. One theory suggests these two millers were smugglers.

Harju-Risti Church of the Holy Cross was almost completed when the whole of North Estonia was involved in the turmoil caused by the St George's Night Uprising in 1343 when the peasantry decided to rebel against the landowners.

The church was completed in the early 15th century. Its tower is quite peculiar. The initially round tower began crumbling and needed supporting with buttresses. The crumbled part was not rebuilt in a round shape but was built up as a straight wall. Thus we see today a tower that starts as a cylinder and continues as a cylinder cut into half, crowned by a low spire.

Archaeologists discovered that one of its bronze bells was cast in the 14th century, and is therefore one of the oldest in Estonia.

Harju-Risti Church has one of the strangest-looking towers in Estonia.

The ruins of the **Risti vicarage** (former Aru church manor) lie south-west of Harju-Risti, by the road leading to Hatu, on a hill with tall trees. This was the place where the founder of Estonian rural schools, **Bengt Gottfried Forselius** (1660–1688) started his work. Having studied in Wittenberg, he tried to use European innovative educational ideas in teaching local children (see also Harju-Madise).

Near the ruins stands a monument to the school that started there in 1683.

Straight north from Harju-Risti by the sea is a small **Kurkse harbour village**. The first monument to soldiers of the re-independent Estonia stands there. On 11 September 1997, 14 young soldiers perished in the Kurkse bay when their commander made them cross the sea on foot carrying full equipment. The bay is 3.2 km wide and the wind that day was blowing at 12–17 metres per second.

The monument commemorates the fourteen young men who died.

The steeple of Harju-Madise Church is an important landmark.

Harju-Madise Church stands on the limestone cliff and is seen across the Paldiski Gulf. Its tower has been an important landmark. In the 17th century, fire was built on the flat platform of the tower. Today the church has a lighthouse, which makes it the only church-lighthouse on Estonian shores.

Besides Harju-Madise Church, a mighty boulder commemorates the educationalist Bengt Forselius who was born in Madise in the family of a Finnish pastor in 1660. His father, Johann Forselius (1607–1684), was also interested in local people, he gathered folklore and later published his observations about local customs and beliefs. Unfortunately his writing was not to the liking of the church and his books were destroyed. A copy was found, translated into Estonian and published in the 19th century.

Bength G. Forselius acquired an excellent education in Wittenberg, Germany, and upon his return to Risti started teaching local chil-

Forselius started educating future teachers.

dren. The year 1684 is significant in the history of Estonian schools, because Forselius opened the first school for teachers near Tartu, the Forselius Seminar. During four years he taught about 160 young people there, of whom one third later became teachers.

Forselius also innovated and simplified standard Estonian spelling. For example he began using the letter 'ä', and wrote a textbook. The still young enthusiast of popular education tragically perished in the stormy Baltic Sea in 1688 when he was on his way to Sweden to popularise his teaching methods.

The Harju-Madise cemetery has the burial chapel built in the 19th century to the most influential local manor lords, the von Ramm family.

The most famous landmark in Padise is the **Padise Monastery**, more precisely its ruins. The monastery was founded in the early 14th century when the inhabitants of the Cistercian monastery on the territory of today's Latvian Daugavgrîva (former Dünamünde) sold their monastery and moved to Padise.

The initially wooden house also acted as a fortification. Nevertheless, the Estonian rebels managed to conquer it during the St George's Night Uprising in 1343. 28 'sufficiently guilty' monks were murdered and the monastery was thoroughly ravaged. This is why very little of the original building is surviving today. The later convent-type fortification-monastery was a set of buildings gathered around a square courtyard.

During the 15th–16th centuries, new defence towers were added to keep up with the rapid spread of firearms. One of the towers has partially survived. An interesting archaeological find tells about the warring past of the monastery: about 500-litre huge riveted cauldron where food was cooked for hundreds of soldiers at one time.

Padise fortified monastery played a clear military role in the Livonian War (1558–1583). For a few years it belonged to the Russians who undertook major fortification work. Later during the Swedish time and after the Northern War (1700–1721) the monastery was used as their residence by the owners of the Padise Manor, the von Ramm family who received it as a gift from the Swedish King Gustav II Adolf. In 1766 the monastery caught fire and has stood in ruins ever since. The von Ramms built a new manor house near the ruins and lived there until their property was expropriated a few years after the

Nice arcades and some sculptured stones have survived in Padise monastery church.

In medieval times Padise was inhabited by Cistercian monks.

new Republic of Estonia had passed the agrarian law in 1919. Today they have bought back their ancestors' mansion.

A small museum near the ruins gives an overview of the history of the monastery. It is also worthwhile to climb to the north-eastern tower, first by a spiral staircase and then along boards placed over the vaults of the monastery church.

About one km south from the ruins in the bend of the Kloostri river, is an ancient hill-fort, known as **Vanalinn** (old town). It was used in the middle of the first millennium and later as well, and the remains of a wooden building dating back to about 1250 have been found there.

AROUND RIISIPERE

Riisipere is located in the vicinity of large bogs and marshes, and has provided people with peat for centuries. South-east of Riisipere is even a place called Turba (peat). The inhabitants of Turba have used peat for heating probably more than anywhere else in Estonia. In 1923–1966 the **Ellamaa Power Plant** operated there purely on peat. At first the energy was used to keep the peat industry going, but later electricity was also taken to Haapsalu and Tallinn. The former power plant now accommodates a boiler house, and the building is protected as an architectural monument.

By the Tallinn-Haapsalu Road, 2 km from Nissi crossroads stands one of the grandest classicist buildings in Estonia – **Riisipere Mansion**. Although it is empty and decaying, it is possible to see traces of its former glory. The facade has a powerful porch of six columns; the heart of the building is a remarkable cupola hall on the first floor, the ceiling of which was adorned with rosettes.

The mansion was completed at the time when the Estonian peasantry had just been liberated from slavery, in 1818–1821. The builder was Peter von Stackelberg. The family owned the manor until the land reform of the first Estonian Republic in 1919; afterwards, over a period of 60 years, the mansion was a home for orphans.

Turning left from the Tallinn-Haapsalu Road at Laitse crossroads we come to **Ruila**. The former Ruila manor house now accommodates a school, where the visitor can see a little display about local history and nearby sights. The 6-m tall **Ukukivi** near Ruila on the Kääbaste Hill is the biggest sacrificial stone in the country. The boulder turns up in many an old legend. It was reputedly hurled both by the Estonian national epic hero Kalevipoeg and by the Old Devil himself. Another legend tells about a silver plate placed on top of the stone. Water accumulating in the plate could heal various diseases.

Ellamaa power plant operated on peat.

Turning right from the Tallinn-Haapsalu Road at Laitse crossroads, we arrive after one kilometre at an eclectic building, the **Laitse manor** house. It was built in the late 19th century and displays a number of styles. In Soviet times it belonged to the military; today the manor is privately owned.

The symbol of Kernu area is a **juniper with seven twists** by the Tallinn-Pärnu Road near Kernu school in Kernu village. It was reputedly planted during the Northern War by Karl XII, King of Sweden. According to a legend the 'good old Swedish time' will return when the juniper withers. Only recently it was in perfectly good health and stretched to 4 metres.

AROUND KEILA

The Harjumaa Museum on an island of Keila River in the **town of Keila** is located in the former manor house. In 1976 the medieval vassal castle walls were discovered near the manor. Today the walls have been unearthed. The museum has thus medieval ruins in its courtyard, dating from the 15th–16th century. It was probably a small castle used as a residence. The walls were not very strong and were quite sloppily built. Numerous archaeological finds have been discovered nearby, such as coins, fragments of Dutch clay pipes and jewellery – these items can be seen in the museum.

The two-aisled **Keila Church** is situated by the central square of the town. The fortified church dating from the second half of the 14th century has been rebuilt several times. The tower acquired its present shape in 1851. Some Baltic German families have their burial chapels in the churchyard. Similar chapels were built after 1774 when the Russian empress Catherine II banned burying the dead inside churches, mainly motivated by the fear of disease from plague-ridden corpses.

In Karjaküla a few kilometres north from Keila, once stood a manor house connected with the life and work of the prominent Estonian writer **Eduard Vilde** (1865–1933).

The twisted Kernu juniper is associated with the Swedish King Karl XII.

Keila churchyard has several burial chapels of local manor lords.

At seventeen, he wrote his first short story that got published. The writer later often visited his father in Karjaküla who managed the local manor. Across the road from the crumbling manorial buildings is a monument to the writer who reputedly liked to rest on that spot under a big birch and ponder his next literary oeuvres. Instead of the so-called Vilde tree, a younger tree now grows there.

Karjaküla has also a far more exotic connection. In 1732 an Ethiopian nobleman **Abram Hannibal** (1696–1781) bought the manor and lived there until 1740, thus avoiding the political intrigues of St Petersburg. That dark-skinned gentleman, the so-called Peter the Great's Moor, was the ancestor of the famous poet Alexander Pushkin on his mother's side.

Hannibal was a military engineer and supervised the construction of fortifications in the town of Paldiski. He also taught mathematics and engineering at Pärnu military school and worked as artillery chief and commandant in Tallinn.

Opposite the museum (below) in the former Keila mansion stand the ruins of a small ancient castle (above).

Keila Church has two aisles.

PALDISKI

The birth and destiny of the town on the **Paldiski** Peninsula have largely been determined by military interests. The Swedes founded a modest stronghold there, called Ragövik (Rogerwiek) in the 17th century. In 1715 it attracted the attention of the Russian tsar Peter I. On his orders, the building of a new harbour, naval fortification and settlement started in 1716, and in 1723 the Tsar arrived there in person to lay the cornerstone for the new town. Later Paldiski saw such eminent visitors as empresses of Russia Elizaveta Petrovna and Catherine II. The latter changed the Swedish name into Baltiiskii Port (Baltic Port). Everything was built by convicts, widely used manpower in Russia. The plan to protect the harbour with very long piers was abandoned, but only after 40 years of fruitless effort. But the mighty fortification was completed, and offers quite a sight even today.

Among the convicts labouring in Paldiski were many participants of the Pugachov Rebellion. Yemeljan Pugachov (1742–1755) was a Cossack at River Don who declared himself Tsar Peter III and unleashed a massive peasant rebellion in 1773–1774. He ended on the scaffold and many of his fellow rebels as convicts. One of the Paldiski convicts was the Bashkir national hero and first poet, a commander in Pugachov's army, **Salavat Julajev** (ab 1752–1800) and his father Julai Aznalin. Together with Bashkir people, a monument has been put up to Salavat Julajev in the town centre.

The Baltic railway, running from Pakri Peninsula to St Petersburg opened in 1870 and connected Paldiski with the outside world. As the harbour was practically ice-free all year round it was advantageous

The convicts in Paldiski also included Salavat Julajev, national hero of the Bashkir people.

to start the goods train business. Various exotic fruits for tsarist Russia arrived in Paldiski, and the railway was sometimes called 'railway of oranges'. Today the two harbours service numerous cargo ships exporting among other things timber, scrap metal, peat and limestone.

During the First World War a coastal battery was established on Pakri Cape and Väike-Patarei, the concrete iron buildings have survived to this day. Besides the border guard cordon stands the highest lighthouse in Estonia. The 52-m high building was completed in 1889. The Pakri cliff (Pakerort) rises steeply above the sea at the tip of the cape where it is 25 m high.

Most of the old Paldiski was destroyed in 1944 when the Germans burnt the town. The Soviets installed their military navy there and the town and entire peninsula became a closed military zone. A base of nuclear submarines and a naval training centre were established in Paldiski, with a nuclear reactor. The huge training centre, several hundred metres long, known locally as 'Pentagon', is now standing empty and waiting for new users. The Russian troops left in 1994. After that the formerly

The Pakerorti lighthouse is the tallest in Estonia.

overwhelmingly Russian military town has started to integrate itself in the Republic of Estonia. Numerous crumbling military buildings in the midst of the beautiful landscape of Pakri Peninsula will probably remind the visitor of past times for a long time to come. As a town of contrasts where yesterday and today so clearly clash, it is certainly worth a visit.

Rätsepa farm on Uuga limestone cliff near Paldiski, was home to one of the most prominent sculptors in Estonia, **Amandus Adamson** (1855–1929). He studied art in St Petersburg and established a studio in Paldiski. He spent his last years in his house here. Among the numerous works produced by Adamson, is the Russalka monument in Tallinn, the monument to the poet Lydia Koidula in Pärnu and the monument to the creator of Estonian national epic, Friedrich Reinhold Kreutzwald, in Võru. A memorial museum used to operate in the former house of the sculptor, but is has now closed. The house is still there, with the plaque to his memory, and a monument to Amandus Adamson stands at the corner of Sadama Street.

The local Lutheran church is dedicated to the notorious Russian Tsar Nicholas I (1796–1855) who earned the title of the 'Gendarme of Europe', but nevertheless supported the building of a Lutheran church in a distant provincial town. In front of the church, a monument commemorates the Estonian soldiers, the so-called Finnish Boys, who arrived from Finland in 1944 to fight for the freedom of their country (see also Tartumaa, Pupastvere and Äksi).

COASTAL AREA WEST OF TALLINN

At Kloogaranna, after the railway crossing, a forest road turns south off the Tallinn-Paldiski Road. A concentration camp operated here during the Second World War. In 1944 the Germans who feared the approaching enemy, transported the mainly Jewish prisoners from another camp in Ida-Virumaa to

Memorial to Amandus Adamson, one of the most prominent Estonian sculptors, who lived and worked in Paldiski.

Monument to Estonians who arrived from Finland to fight the enemy in summer 1944.

Commemorating those killed in the Klooga death camp.

Klooga. On 19 September the Germans executed about 1800–2000 prisoners. The place is now marked by a monument.

The traveller can reach **Keila-Joa**, certainly one of the most beautiful spots of nature in the country, by driving out of Tallinn towards Keila and turning off at Kiia. The major attraction is the 6-m high and 60-70-m wide **Keila Waterfall**. A water mill once operated there and later a hydroelectric power plant. It is planned to start the latter again. The scientists have established that the waterfall eats into the soft limestone and retreats about a dozen metres in the course of a century.

The first mansion on the high bank of the primeval valley was built during the Swedish time. Considering the remarkable landscape, the owner of the local manor, Alexander von Benckendorff, decided in 1827 to replace the single-storey modest house with a far grander neo-Gothic castle. The house was completed in 1833. The housewarming party guests included the Russian emperor Nicholas I who valued von Benckendorff, the founder of his secret police, very highly and called him irreplaceable. The money for building the castle came from the state coffers. A magnificent view opened from the castle to the waterfall and the park.

After von Benckendorff's death in 1844 the Keila-Joa manor belonged to the aristocratic

Keila waterfall attracts visitors all year round.

Volkonski family through the middle Benckendorff daughter Maria. The last owner was Grigori Volkonski (1870–1940) who led a simple life, spoke Estonian and was much respected among local people.

The complex included various other buildings, bridges and pavilions in the park. Most of them have disintegrated or are decaying. The desolate general picture is made worse by the buildings set up by the Soviet military. Two suspension bridges have been restored. Newlyweds often tie a padlock to the bridge chains and throw the key into water as a symbol of their lasting life together. The mansion belongs to the state and is standing empty. A few years ago the Tallinn Drama Theatre gave a few performances there. The cast included Peeter Volkonski, a distant relative of the former owners.

Alexander von Benckendorff, Grigori Volkonski and many of their close relations rest in the family cemetery on the Meremõisa natural terrace near Joa park. The cemetery has been repeatedly pillaged.

East of Keila-Joa, at the crossroads of Rannamõisa Road, stands **Vääna Manor** where the most famous owner was Otto Magnus von Stackelberg (1787–1837). He was a highly educated man, keen on the antique and an artist as well. He had inherited an extensive collection of art and books that he continued to augment. The late 18th century late-baroque Vääna Manor with two round pavilions at both wings, is a remarkable building.

Driving towards Tallinn from Keila-Joa along the seaside Klooga Road, we arrive a few km later on the 30-m high **Türisalu Cliff.** This is a good place to admire the sea view, sunrise and sunset. Years ago this place was known as Hamlet's Hill because in 1964 Mosfilm Studios filmed a large part of the open-air episodes of their Hamlet on the cliff. A 'genuine' Danish royal castle of wood and cardboard was built for this purpose.

The road towards Tallinn runs along an even limestone plateau. Between the sea and the road the traveller can see huge weird houses with turrets.

In the newly independent Estonia these buildings have attracted quite a bit of attention. These private residences were built in the early 1990s as manifestations of

The formerly grand Keila-Joa castle today stands abandoned.

Türisalu cliff offers spectacular sights of the sea.

freedom, wealth and the brave new life. The set of houses is commonly known as the Village of Idiots.

Around **Suurupi** the high limestone plateau retreats from the sea. A bulky stone lighthouse dating from 1760 stands at the edge of the klint. The other Suurupi lighthouse is situated on the seashore and is thus invisible for anyone approaching from the land. It can be accessed on foot from the Suurupi beach. The lower, 15-m high building is the oldest wooden surviving lighthouse on the Estonian coast. The first light was lit in there in 1859 and it is still going strong.

A powerful coastal battery once stood here as well. In 1912 tsarist Russia decided to establish an extensive defence system that would run along the whole coast of the Gulf of Finland. The **naval fortification of Peter the Great** was constructed, consisting of numerous coastal batteries on the islands of Aegna and Naissaar, and in Suurupi, Kakumäe, Paljassaare, Miiduranna and near Paldiski.

The remains of these fortifications can be viewed today in Sõrve, Tahkuna, around Paldiski and Tallinn. Unfortunately the batteries and defence lines that cost Russia over one hundred million gold roubles failed to play a significant role in the First World War as they were not completed on time. The last batteries were blown up in 1918 before the onslaught of the German troops. The fortifications were partly restored for the Second World War but they were not much use then either. In 1941 the Red Army blew them up again before leaving Estonia.

The former grand neo-renaissance **Muraste Manor** stands in ruins by the Tallinn-Klooga Road. In Estonian cultural history, Muraste is known as the birthplace of the brothers Krusten (Krustein). Erni (Ernst, 1900–1984) became the People's Writer of Soviet Estonia and his brother Pedro (Peeter, 1897–1987) a well-known exile Estonian writer. The third brother Otto (1888–1937) was a caricaturist. The father of the three brothers worked as a gardener at Muraste Manor for many years.

The upper lighthouse of Suurupi has a thick outside wall.

In its heyday Muraste Manor was used as a summer resort.

The peace treaty signed in Harku Manor ended the Northern War on Estonian territory in 1710.

A few kilometres after Õismäe, near the Tallinn-Keila Road, is **Harku Manor**, today accommodating the Institute of Experimental Biology. The pretty neo-renaissance mansion was a witness of the end of the Swedish period in Estonia – the so-called Harku peace treaty was signed namely there, in the still unfinished building, in 1710. The Estonian Knighthood of Baltic Germans and the Swedish garrison in Tallinn surrendered to the Russian army. The local nobility nevertheless retained various privileges, e.g. the freedom of faith and the right to keep their own garrison.

The mansion acquired its current appearance in the 1870s.

For some time in the 19th century the Harku Manor belonged to Peter Ludwig Konstantin von Ungern-Sternberg (1779–1836), son of the notorious Ungru Count and the wealthiest manor lord in the country at the time. He was a shrewd businessman and owned huge lands. Among his many interests was the breeding of merino sheep, which encouraged the founding of Kärdla broadcloth factory in 1830 on Hiiumaa Island.

Driving towards Keila from Harku, by the road at Keila-Joa crossroads in **Kiia**, we see the **ruins of an old pub**, still quite a sight. This used to be the largest pub in the neighbourhood, called 'Golden Sun'. There are quite a few remains of the naval fortifications of Peter the Great nearby, bunkers and passages, some filled with water.

SAKU AND JÜRI

Driving out of Tallinn along Männiku Road we come to **Saku** settled locality. It would be no exaggeration to say that Saku owes its fame to beer. Saku beer is today also well known in Finland and Sweden. The brewing was started at Saku Manor by Count Carl Friedrich von Rehbinder (1764–1841). The enterprise really took off in 1876 when the new owner Valerian von Baggehufvudt established a new brewery that worked on steam power. Today, the von Baggehufvudt coat of arms can be seen for example on the label of *Saku Light*.

Saku Mansion was built during the Rehbinders' period and is one of the prettiest classicist man-

Owners of the Saku Manor successfully brewed beer, laying the foundation to the great industry today.

sions in Estonia. The park with its ponds and canals is also worth a visit.

Kurtna Motorcycle Museum is located at 1 Tagadi Road and displays over 30 German, American, Russian, English and other motorcycles. The 'biography' of each vehicle has been carefully recorded.

Along the Tallinn thoroughfare eastwards from Saku we come to **Jüri**. The surrounding area has numerous ancient sacrificial stones and settlement sites. The oldest smelting furnace of iron was found here, dating from the 1st–2nd centuries. A monument to the furnace stands in Jüri Park as an acknowledgement to our ancestors the metallurgists.

Jüri is connected with the sources of our written culture. In 1713–1748 Anton Thor Helle, linguist and theologian, worked there as pastor. He studied theology in Kiel and later supervised the translation of the Bible into Estonian. He probably translated the larger part of the Old Testament himself and revised the earlier translation of the New Testament. *Piibli Ramat* (*The Bible Book*) appeared in Tallinn in 1739. Helle also compiled an Estonian grammar and a dictionary. His Bible translation was considered excellent and it had an impact on the development of the written Estonian language.

Although the Bible was translated much earlier in Finland (1642), our advantage is that we understand the language even today, whereas the Finns cannot understand their first Bible without specialised help.

A monument to the first edition of the Bible in 1739 stands in the Jüri churchyard.

The nearby **Lehmja** oak forest is associated with a legend according to which the trees are not really

The oaks in the forest are allegedly people turned into trees.

Jüri pastor Anton Thor Helle arranged the translation of the Bible into Estonian.

trees but wedding party guests. Allegedly they behaved very badly, broke a lot of young oak trees and were turned into trees themselves. There are other versions of the story, but the oaks look quite peculiar indeed with their twisted trunks and wildly stretching branches.

Lehmja is probably an ancient sacred grove where some trees are over three hundred years old. Local people are still convinced that the oak forest must not in any way be damaged, because the wrong-doer will be punished. Sadly, this wise thought is not known in other parts of the country, and young trees seldom have a chance to grow up.

VIIMSI

The museum in Viimsi focuses on one of the most outstanding military men in the Estonian army, **General Johan Laidoner** (1884–1953; he died in a prison camp), who was commander in chief during the War of Independence (1918–1920) and later a statesman. The display includes his furniture, medals and numerous photographs.

The Museum also offers an overview of Estonian military history and introduces other remarkable people.

The Museum is located in the **Viimsi Manor**, presented to General Laidoner for his services in the War on Independence. By 1940 he managed to establish a well-functioning manor-farm (more about Laidoner, see Viljandimaa, his birthplace).

The Open-air Museum in **Pringi** village on Viimsi Peninsula consists of a set of old farm buildings, such as barn, threshing barn, stables, cellar and sheds for fishing nets. The buildings are furnished with genuine articles of the time.

EAST OF TALLINN

The surroundings of Tallinn boast a large number of various ancient relics: graves, cultic stones, sites of sacred groves and settlements. The ancient **Iru hill-fort** sits in the bend of the Pirita River in the grasp of the expanding city. The oldest settlement traces date from the second millennium BC. A fortified Bronze Age settlement existed there in the 7th–5th centuries BC. The strong limestone stronghold

The Johan Laidoner Museum is based in the former Viimsi Manor.

The open-air-museum in Viimsi introduces the life of coastal fishermen.

lasted until the 11th century. Iru has yielded many clay items, jewellery, tools and arrowheads of various periods. The reason why the stronghold was abandoned in the 11th century was probably the decreasing water level in the river, and the emergence of much stronger buildings in the nearby Tallinn.

An interesting sight is Juhan Raudsepp's (1896–1984) sculpture **Iru mother-in-law**, placed there instead of the former boulder of the same name.

In the vicinity of Muuga harbour in the seaside shrubbery lies the largest boulder in Estonia, **Muuga Kabelikivi** (Chapel Stone). Its perimeter is 58 m and height 6.4 m. The rest of the boulder, perhaps equally huge, might well be hidden underground.

The road to the **Maardu Manor** turns right off the Tallinn-Narva Road after the Maardu lake. The manor now belongs to the Bank of Estonia and is in an excellent condition. The central baroque part of the mansion deserves special attention as it was completed 350 years ago. Various auxiliary buildings and a nice park have survived as well. In the early 18th century the owner here was Hermann Jensen von Bohn who financially supported the translation and publication of the Bible by Anton Thor Helle (see Harjumaa, Jüri). Von Bohn was keen on the education of the peasantry and established 16 schools on his lands. The altruistic lord of the manor is remembered by a monument in the manor house courtyard.

At the end of the 19th century the owner of Maardu Manor, Otto von Brevern, decided to regulate the water level in the lake and dug a channel to the sea. He built a dike and water gates at the lake end of the channel. Alas, an accident soon happened that would have been more likely in Holland – someone opened the gates. Water rushed out, destroying everything on its way, even the bridge-guard's house, and gouged a tunnel, 10 m deep and 100 m wide. A few years later the lake was replaced by a meadow. The dike and the lake were restored in 1939.

By the Tallinn-Narva Road around **Jõelähtme** lies the **Rebala Heritage Reserve**. The settlement in

The predecessor of today's Iru mother-in-law was a boulder.

Muuga Kabelikivi is huge like a rock.

The former owner of Maardu Manor, Jensen von Bohn, established several schools.

that area emerged 3000 years ago and the fields are just as old. The ancient Rebala village probably gave name to the Revala county and to the later town of Reval. The Reserve extends from Maardu Manor to the lower course of Jägala River, and from Ülgase Hõbemägi to Kostivere. Over 200 stone graves, 80 cultic stones, several settlement sites and remains of ancient fields have been found here.

In Jõelähtme, by the Narva Road is a **museum** opened in 1994. It tells the visitor about the history of Rebala area and displays

Rebala displays numerous ancient settlement sites and fields.

various items found nearby. The burial mounds were discovered in 1985 in the course of a road extension and were taken some twenty metres out of the way. In that sense this is more an 'artificial' cemetery, but skilfully established.

Jõelähtme Church is visible from the Tallinn-Narva Road in the north. The Germans built the church, surrounded by several villages, in the middle of an ancient Repel parish in the early 14th century. The building acquired its current appearance in the early 20th century when a new neo-Gothic western tower was completed, replacing the previous tower destroyed by fire in 1910.

Mention should here be made of Jõelähtme pastor **Gustav Heinrich Schüdlöffel** (1798–1859) who wrote short stories and developed a new spelling for Estonian. He published a collection of folk legends about the Estonian national hero Kalevipoeg. He was buried in Jõelähtme cemetery, the resting place also for the von Brevern family.

We reach the **Saha Chapel** when turning off the Tallinn-Narva Road to the right, towards Loo. The chapel stands at the other end of the Loo village. The limestone building dates from the 15th century and has survived well, largely of course thanks to several restorations. It has a small turret in one corner so the church was probably used as a fortification as well.

According to a legend, a nobleman who escaped from certain death in the stormy seas decided to build a chapel in gratitude for his survival. Unfortunately he decided to establish his chapel right beside a sacred grove of rowan-trees. The locals were naturally against the plan and began

Saha Chapel is one of the most legendary Catholic places of worship in Estonia.

Jägala waterfall is the highest natural waterfall in Estonia.

demolishing the chapel walls at night. As a punishment and a warning to the others, the manor lord walled in three men by the chapel door. Nobody dared interfere with the building, but as people began avoiding it, the chapel soon fell into disuse and crumbled.

In the Külma park in Lagedi by the Pirita River, the **Estonian Liberation Movement Museum** was opened in 1994. It was founded by a local man, Johannes Tõrs, and is located in the house that once belonged to Voldermar Päts, younger brother of President Konstantin Päts (1874–1956), who died in a Soviet psychiatric hospital. The Museum records the fate of Estonian soldiers in both world wars and in the War of Independence (1918–1920). Anyone interested in weaponry can examine weapons from 23 countries.

After Jõelähtme along the Tallinn-Narva Road we come to a viaduct. The highest natural waterfall in Estonia, **Jägala waterfall**, can be reached by turning left towards Kaberneeme. After the 8-m waterfall the Jägala river forms a deep primeval valley. Downstream in the river bend is an ancient settlement site and hill-fort. There used to be a large stronghold, with the inner courtyard of 3 hectares. Before, in the 3rd and 2nd millennium BC, this place was home to hunters and fishermen.

Jägala water energy has been used for centuries. The oldest known water mill operated here in 1241.

Downstream in Jõesuu stands the recently renovated Linnamäe hydroelectric plant. It was established in the 1920s and was declared the most beautiful industrial enterprise in the country. A red viewing platform is now set up on the river.

By the road leading to Kaberneeme from Jägala-Joa is an area called **Kalevi-Liiva** that is associated with legends about the Estonian national hero Kalevipoeg (Kalev's Son). In 1942–1943 the Germans executed about 6000 people there, from different countries, mostly Jews. A memorial was established in 1961.

By the road 2 km from **Kiiu** in the direction of Valkla, by the road, stands a stone with the lettering: "Siiamaani ja mitte kaugemale." (So far and not a step further.)

This marks the place where the military unit, largely assembled of schoolteachers and students of the newly established Republic of Estonia, halted the onslaught of the Russian troops during the War of Independence (1918–1920). The situation was critical as this happened only 27 km from the capital Tallinn. The counterattack of Estonians that started a few days later changed the entire course of the war.

Kiiu village, known for its tower stronghold, is located by the Tallinn-Narva Road. Only two strongholds like that have survived to this day. The other one is Lääne-Virumaa in Vao. Both have been restored and are open to visitors.

The Kiiu tower castle was probably built in the early 16th century. The tower becomes thinner at the top and has modest dimensions – a diameter of 9 m at the bottom and a metre less at the top. Kiiu is one of the smallest castles in the Baltic countries. The ground floor had storage space, the first floor was living quarters and the two upper floors served defence purposes. It was built around 1520 by Fabian von Tiesenhausen.

After years of neglect, the building was restored in 1973. The tower now accommodates a café. Kiiu manor has been considerably rebuilt and is located near the tower.

A few hundred metres north off the Tallinn-Narva Road in Kuusalu, is a peculiar stronghold site – **Kuusalu Pajulinn** (Willow Town). The 11th century castle was built on a marshy land and archaeological excavations revealed a log foundation upon which the ramparts rested. In 1936 a large pot was found nearby with over 400 silver coins probably hidden there 900 years ago. At that time Kuusalu was a large settlement where people melted iron.

The late 13th century **Kuusalu Church** is one of the oldest in North Estonia, built by Cistercians. It has been rebuilt several times in the course of centuries. Although the church has St Lawrence, a saint connected with fire, as its patron saint, the church was struck

Here, the Estonians halted the attack of the Red Army.

Kiiu tower castle offered protection against the enemy.

by lightning twice in the 20th century. No major damage occurred in either case.

The founder of modern Estonian spelling, **Eduard Ahrens** (1803–1863) rests in Kuusalu churchyard. His idea to adapt orthography with pronunciation was approved and accepted by his contemporaries. Ahrens followed the example of the Finnish language, thus earning sharp criticism from his German colleagues.

Eduard Ahrens was pastor in Kuusalu since 1837 until his death. His research of the Estonian language soon attracted attention and he received the Demidov award issued by the St Petersburg Academy of Sciences. In 1844, the compiler of the Finnish national epic Kalevala, Elias Lönnrot visited him in Kuusalu.

Another famous person buried in the churchyard is **Gustav Vilbaste** (Vilberg, 1885–1967), an eminent biologist and nature protectionist. He was born in Haavakannu village where a monument now stands to commemorate him.

Vilbaste was also involved in gathering folklore and researching Estonian dialects. He published the results of his activities in several books. His special interest as a biologist was the fauna, and it is no wonder that Vilbaste was the one to publish the first serious guidebook about Estonian plants. He also published a popular magazine in the 1930s, called *The Observer of Nature*.

Travelling north-east of Kuusalu, towards the sea, we arrive in **Muuksi** village, known for its hill-fort and numerous stone-cist graves. The stronghold once stood on the 47-m high steep limestone cliff and probably acted as a lighthouse. The oldest finds date from the I millennium BC and the later from 11–13th centuries.

Kuusalu Church is one of the oldest in North Estonia.

South-west from Kahala lake lies a cemetery containing about one hundred stone cist graves. Such graves consist of a regular stone circle and a stone coffin built inside the circle. The coffin was made of limestone slabs. The diameter of the circles was between 4 and 10 metres, and the coffin was usually 2 m long and 0.8 m wide. This stone construction was then covered with earth.

Muuksi is the largest site of stone cist graves in Estonia. Its densest part (65 graves in one group) is called **Hundikangrud** (Wolves' Graves), which lie on the grounds of Toomanni farm. The hundred-year-old barn has a small museum displaying ancient tools, clothes and household items.

Gustav Vilbaste was the first professional nature protectionist in Estonia.

The high Tsitre limestone cliff near Muuksi has a cave, dug by water, which is popularly known as **Turje Cellar**. A nice waterfall can be seen there every spring. There is a legend about how the Devil turned the water into vodka. Everybody who once drank it was not able to live without it and had to bring all their money to the Devil who thus had a nice little business going.

Turning off the Tallinn-Narva Road towards Loksa, a few kilometres later on the left are the **Kolga village and manor**. The manor is one of the grandest classicist buildings in the country. The first mansion was completed in 1642 but was later thoroughly reconstructed. In its heyday the manor grounds were enormous – 50 000 hectares. The main building acquired its present appearance in 1820 and today accommodates a restaurant and the local shop. Several auxiliary buildings have also been restored, one is now a hotel and the other offers conference facilities. Kolga Manor used to belong to the Stenbock family who have bought it back again.

In the **Viinistu village** in the north-east part of Päripea peninsula, the former fishing factory has been rebuilt to house an art museum, a small concert hall and a hotel. The initiator of the whole undertaking is Jaan Manitski, an exile Estonian who returned to Estonia in the early 1990s and was briefly the Foreign Minister. His private expanding collection of Estonian art forms the permanent display at Viinistu.

AROUND KOSE, RAVILA AND ARDU

At the Kolu crossroads, a signpost points to the **Tuhala Nõiakaev (Witch's Well)** from the Tallinn-Tartu Road. In springs with plenty of waterfall, less frequently in winter and summer, the famous well in the Sulu farmyard 'boils over'. A dozen bucketfuls of water in a second gushes from the well, forming a small pond around it. The well feeds on the Tuhala river that runs underground for 1.5 km.

Tuhala Nature Reserve Centre operates near the well. There is a small museum introducing the surrounding karst area. A monument to our prominent geologist Ülo Heinsalu (1928–1994) stands nearby. He examined Estonian caves, compiled a book about Estonian primeval nature and was an enthusiast for nature protection.

The longest natural cave in Estonia, reaching to 54 m, is located in the south-west corner of Tuhala karst area. The cave fills at the time of flooding, because it is part of the underground river.

A gravel path from Kolu crossroads towards the south takes the visitor to **Kanavere battlefield** where in 1343 fierce fighting broke out between the Estonians and the troops of the Teutonic Order. The initial success of the Estonians soon abandoned them and they had to surrender. A memorial stone

Kolga Manor once boasted 50,000 hectares of land.

Water gushing out of Tuhala Witch's Well comes from the underground river.

Kanavere marshland was one of the places where the outcome of St George's Night Uprising was decided.

Tuhala Church stands in the protected karst area.

was set up on the 640th anniversary of the battle.

Going north at the Kuivajõe crossroads along the Tallinn-Tartu Road, we arrive after two km at **Kose-Uuemõisa**. The local manor is one of the oldest in Estonia, recorded in chronicles in 1340. In the 18th and the first half of the 19th centuries the manor belonged to the von Tiesenhausens who were notorious for their cruelty towards peasants. As violence creates violence, a revolt erupted in Kose-Uuemõisa in 1805. The peasants refused to work nightly at the manor. The lord of the manor asked soldiers to help, and a bloody conflict took place between 250 peasants armed with homemade weapons and professional soldiers. The battle lasted less than half an hour after which the peasants had to surrender. Many were harshly punished and 12 men were deported to Siberian prison camps. A memorial stone stands today in front of the local shop to commemorate the peasants who were killed.

In the mid-19th century Kose-Uuemõisa belonged to the von Uexkülls who completed the whole manor ensemble and also built a family funeral chapel in the park.

Kuivajõe pub by the Tallinn-Tartu Road at the Kose-Uuemõisa crossroads was connected with the rebellion. Here, the peasants who refused to do extra work for the manor gathered to hatch their plans for the rebellion. There is a plaque on the wall to commemorate their meetings.

39 kilometres along the Tallinn-Tartu Road the road turns from Kuivajõe towards **Kose** which, according to various archaeological finds, is an ancient settlement site. The largest treasure trove in the country, probably hidden there in the 12th century, was found in 1982 in Kose. It contained 1716 coins and fragments of silver items.

Kose Church dates from the 1370s, but has been substantially

Kose-Uuemõisa monument to the peasants' revolt.

Old circle crosses by the entrance of Kose Church.

rebuilt since. Today's appearance dates from the 19th century. The grave of Otto von **Kotzebue** (1787–1846) who sailed around the world twice is located in the churchyard and marked with a memorial stone. The same courtyard is the final resting place also for Peter August Friedrich von **Manteuffel** (1768–1842). The friendly Count learned the local language and published a collection of stories about the life and customs of the Estonian peasantry, *Aiawite peergo walgussel*. It was re-issued in 1967. Von **Manteuffel**, widely known as the 'Mad Count', ran his Ravila Manor for 63 years, participating in all farm jobs, constructing a flying machine, and was generally interested in everything in the wide world. He allegedly even had himself mildly whipped at his farm, just to know first-hand what this popular punishment at the time felt like.

Ravila Manor lies about 4 km east of Kose. Today the building houses a home for the mentally disabled.

An interesting monument stands in the centre of **Ardu** a few hundred metres from the Tallinn-Tartu Road. It presents our alleged ancient ancestor, the so-called **Ardu Man**

who lived about 5000 years ago and had a narrow face and nose. The story of the Ardu Man dates back to the 1930s when a grave was found there with two male

Owner of Ravila Manor Count Manteuffel was a very colourful man.

Ardu Man – a European from five thousand years ago?

skeletons, a stone axe, a clay vessel, a knife and a few small bone items inside. The skeletons revealed European features, and the Russian archaeologist Mikhail Gerassimov recreated the head of one of the Stone Age men. The Ardu Men were supposed to confirm the theory that although the majority of Estonian inhabitants came from the east, some arrived also from the south, i.e. Europe. The easterners had wide cheekbones and slightly mongoloid features and spoke old Finno-Ugric language. Many archaeologists, however, do not think that such massive movements of people took place – in their opinion, the Estonian population in this area has developed in the course of 11,000 years.

From Ardu, a forest road runs east along the southern bank of the Paunküla artificial lake, passes the Kautla lake and takes the visitor to the **Kautla Memorial** that commemorates the events of July-August 1941. A battle broke out here between the Red Army troops and a reconnaissance group of Estonians (called **Erna**) who had arrived from Finland, plus local anti-Soviet guerrillas known as forest brothers. The Erna group managed to break through the enemy lines. Their triumph was short-lived as the Russians were set on revenge: the entire village and most of Ardu were burnt down and many people killed.

The current monument remembering these events was made in 1999.

In memory of the Erna group, an international military-sporting event Erna has been organised since 1993. Groups in full military equipment compete in getting through a very difficult track through forests and marshland, where 'the enemy' most certainly lurks.

The **Aegviidu** settlement by the Piibe Road at the edge of Harjumaa emerged as a summer resort after the railway opened in 1870. Beautiful forests and pure lakes attract people for weekends and longer periods.

A few kilometres from Aegviidu towards Jäneda is **Nelijärve** village where the tsarist railway station has almost survived as it once was. It is now a listed building. The whole area is known for its diverse nature: numerous steep **eskers** and no less than five lakes.

Aegviidu railway station has survived from the late 19th century.

LÄÄNE-VIRUMAA

Lääne-Virumaa stretches between the northern coast and the Pandivere Uplands. The seaside and inland areas are naturally different, both with their own charm. Käsmu and Võsu used to exist on what the sea provided. Today the focus has shifted and these places rely on summer holiday-makers.

Ancient Virumaa included places such as Tarvanpea, Agelinde castle and Ebavere Hill, all mentioned in the Chronicles of Henry of Livonia (Heinrici Cronicon Lyvoniae, describing the history of Latvia and Estonia 1180-1227). The two largest strongholds of Lääne-Virumaa were Tarvanpea (Wesenberg; first mentioned in 1226)) in Rakvere and Toolse (completed around 1470) on the northern coast. Even older are the archaeological finds such as axes, spearheads, simple fishing equipment and other necessary tools, which date back 5, 000 - 10,000 years.

For centuries, Virumaa has been home to a large number of eminent people. Karl Ernst von Baer, a scientist and Friedrich Reinhold Kreutzwald, compiler of the Estonian national epic, were both Virumaa men. The long-time President of the St Petersburg Academy of Sciences, Friedrich B. Lütke, lived in Simuna. Ao Manor near Rakke was the birthplace of Friedrich Robert Faehlmann who was a keen folklorist, collecting and recording folk poetry and thus preserving the national heritage. These men are just a few of many other important figures in Estonian culture and science.

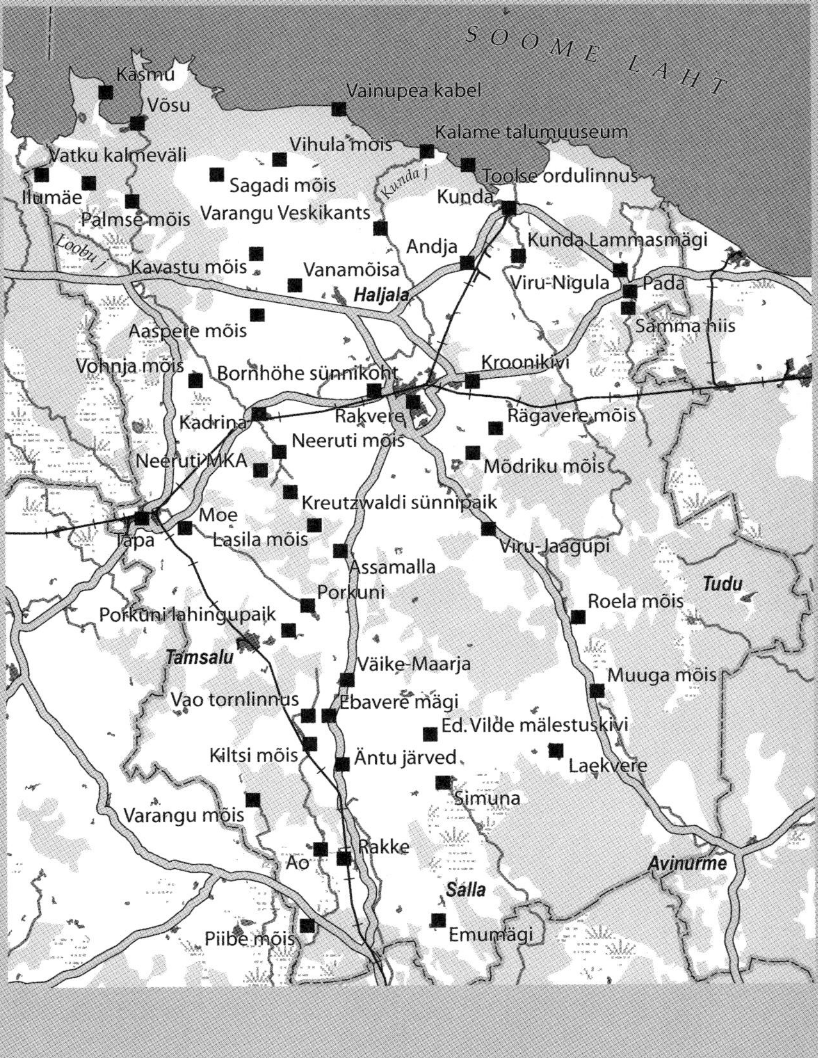

SOOME LAHT
Käsmu
Võsu
Vainupea kabel
Kalame talumuuseum
Vihula mõis
Vatku kalmeväli
Sagadi mõis
Toolse ordulinnus
Kunda j
Kunda
Ilumäe
Palmse mõis
Varangu Veskikants
Loobu j
Andja
Kunda Lammasmägi
Kavastu mõis
Vanamõisa
Viru-Nigula
Pada
Haljala
Samma hiis
Aaspere mõis
Vohnja mõis
Bornhöhe sünnikoht
Kroonikivi
Rakvere
Rägavere mõis
Kadrina
Neeruti mõis
Neeruti MKA
Mõdriku mõis
Kreutzwaldi sünnipaik
Moe
Tapa
Lasila mõis
Viru-Jaagupi
Assamalla
Tudu
Porkuni
Roela mõis
Porkuni lahingupaik
Tamsalu
Väike-Maarja
Muuga mõis
Vao tornlinnus
Ebavere mägi
Ed. Vilde mälestuskivi
Kiltsi mõis
Äntu järved
Laekvere
Simuna
Varangu mõis
Rakke
Ao
Avinurme
Salla
Piibe mõis
Emumägi

LÄÄNE-VIRUMAA

AROUND VÕSU, PALMSE AND VIHULA

Käsmu is a picturesque seaside village. Only about one hundred years ago it was one of the most important villages in Virumaa from the navigational point of view. Dozens of ships and boats of all sizes gathered there to winter; long-distance sailboats were built and captains were trained in Käsmu. An overview of all these activities can be seen at the local **Maritime Museum**.

Käsmu Museum is located in the former border guard station.

The wooden lighthouse was renovated on the initiative of Aarne Vaik.

The Maritime School operated in Käsmu between 1884 and 1931. The displays at the private museum, founded in 1993 by Aarne Vaik, reflect everything connected with the sea – navigation, fishing, moonshining, border guards, and also describe the sea itself as part of nature and a significant source of inspiration for photography and the applied arts.

The wooden lighthouse dating from 1892 has been restored as well. The lighthouse was built with donations instigated by the Maritime School. The seamen caught drunk at work had to pay a fine and that went straight to the lighthouse fund. A drunken captain had to pay a fine of one rouble and the shipowner, a fine of three roubles. The other surviving wooden lighthouse in Estonia is located in Suurupi near Tallinn.

The wooden chapel was built with donations from local people.

The villagers' donations paid for the wooden chapel in Käsmu too. It was completed in 1863. The chapel and cemetery are surrounded by a sturdy stone fence.

One of the prettiest tombstones was made by the sculptor Juhan Raudsepp and it depicts a kneeling maiden. The grave is that of Signe, daughter of the local captain Tiedemann.

Another site worth seeing is the **chapel of the von Dellingshausens**, Baltic German owners of Aaspere Manor who had a summer house in Käsmu. Baron von Dellingshausen was associated with the failed assassination attempt against Tsar Alexander II in 1861. Fearing punishment, the Baron vanished and had himself declared dead. A chapel was built where a coffin was laid, reputedly containing only a chunk of wood. When his deception was found out, the Baron fled to Germany. So it is believed that nobody was ever buried in the chapel at all.

Idyllic beach at Võsu.

Allegedly nobody has ever been buried in the Dellingshausens' chapel.

Käsmu is also famous for its numerous boulders, some of which are over 5 metres tall. Many boulders have names, such as Meremunk (Sea Monk), Maamunk (Land Monk), Vana-Jüri (Old Jüri), etc.

Võsu began a period of rapid growth and gentrification after 1879 when the owner of Palmse Manor turned into a property developer. The pretty surroundings soon attracted the attention of the St Petersburg aristocracy and lesser mortals. Local people were keen to rent out their cottages to the increasing number of holidaymakers. Today's Võsu is still a charming area where people can enjoy peace, fresh air, sea and the surrounding nature of the Lahemaa National Park.

The ancient road from Vihasoo along the klint edge towards Palmse has many villages on both sides. There are several burial grounds in the area, such as **Vatku** and **Tandemäe** with its **tarand-type graves**. The ancestors of today's Estonians were buried there more than 2500 years ago. Bronze jewellery and an iron axe have been found in the graves.

By the road between Ilumäe and Palmse grows a sacrificial linden-tree called **Hiieniinepuu**. People used to bring offerings to it and tie colourful ribbons to its branches in order to have their wishes fulfilled. **Ilumäe Church** was completed in 1843 thanks to the funding of the local landlords, the von der Pahlens. The church replaced an earlier wooden chapel that became too small for the congregations It is not known whether the grand Empire-style crystal chandelier (stolen from the church in 1979) adorned the wooden chapel or whether it was

Hiineniinepuu was thought to contain magical powers.

The pride of Ilumäe Church are the stained-glass windows.

brought from the manor.

The pride of Ilumäe Church is the stained-glass windows that depict coats of arms, dating back to the era of the wooden chapel in 1729. The arms are quite surprising as only two are genuine nobleman's coats of arms, whereas the others belong to simple folk. Six coats of arms show elements of peasant life: ploughing a field, tools of a carpenter, a windmill). Nobody knows how the peasants managed this, although it would certainly have been impossible without the consent and support of the lord of the manor. The present windows are copies, and the originals are kept in Rakvere Museum.

The von der Pahlen family rest in Ilumäe churchyard, which is also known for an old circular cross on the grave of the miller Jacob Muick who also had his coat of arms on the window.

West of Ilumäe by the road stands a **stone pillar** with a big stone orb on top. The monument was set up in 1863 by Alexander von der Pahlen in memory of his father Carl Magnus who died the same year.

A pretty pathway leads from Ilumäe to Palmse.

The stone monument commemorates the Palmse manor lord.

The Palmse manorial complex contains over twenty buildings and a grand park of 18 hectares. The 18th century Baroque mansion and the auxiliary buildings have been carefully restored. The mansion, built upon the ruins of the previous house that was destroyed in the Northern War, was completed in 1730 (it acquired today's appearance in 1785). Most of the stone household buildings date from the 19th century. The von der Pahlens owned the manor between 1676 and 1919. Walking around on the premises of Palmse, the visitor gets a good idea what a mighty family was able to achieve in the course of two and a half centuries. It is worthwhile to walk to the further end of the park where a pavilion called **Brest** stands on a high Oruveski slope, offering beautiful views of the surroundings. The southern part of the park has a large stone field known as Kloostrikivid (Monastery Stones).

Only one stool and a few stoves are surviving from the former contents of the mansion. The rest of the furniture has been purchased from various places and restored.

Palmse Manor Museum has also a collection of old vehicles, such as various horse-drawn carriages, bicycles and cars, all of which are displayed in the barn. The information centre of Lahemaa National Park and the local school are located near the mansion; the former distillery is now a hotel. On Thursdays, Fridays and Saturdays a blacksmith works in the smithy where those interested can try some forging.

West of the manor complex, on the other side of the Palmse-Vihasoo Road, are two large piles of stones, known as **Näljakangrud**

Palmse manor complex is beautifully set in the surrounding nature.

(Hunger Stones). Peasants reputedly gathered them in gratitude for the local manor lord's help during the difficult years of crop failure in 1695 and 1697. Another theory claims that these stones have been gathered over centuries which makes it unlikely that the gratitude stretched quite so long.

Sagadi Manor is situated 8 km north-east of Palmse, by the road towards Vihula. This estate has been nicely restored as well. The owners of Sagadi for a long time from the 17th century, were the von Focks who built the present mansion, which dates from 1795. The complex embraces various

A nice park stretches behind the Sagadi mansion.

The first thing that catches the eye is the grand gate tower.

About a dozen buildings belong to the Sagadi manor ensemble.

buildings, such as former stables, the manager's house, carriage shed and a grand gate tower, park and a pond with a small island. Today, Sagadi belongs to the Estonian Forest Industries Association. The Forestry Museum in the former stables introduces the past and present of forestry, hunting and wood handicraft. The mansion is open to visitors and also offers conference facilities and accommodation.

Various old and mighty trees grow by the pond in the park, including the tallest oak in Estonia that reaches to 33 m.

Vihula estate is located on the Sagadi-Karula Road beside a beautiful lake. Both the old and the new mansion have survived, together with various other buildings, including a water mill and a distillery. A peculiar building is the so-called coffee house by the main building that resembles a temple. Vihula is privately owned.

The picturesque **Vainupea Chapel** stands by the sea. It stood in ruins for a long time and was restored only in 1989. The wooden predecessor of today's stone chapel was built over two and a half centuries ago. One of Estonia's best-loved artists, **Richard Sagrits** (1910–1968) is buried in the churchyard. He was primarily known for his sensitive sea and landscape pictures.

The coffee house (left) at Vihula Manor resembles a small temple.

Vainupea Chapel stands by the sea.

AROUND KUNDA AND VIRU-NIGULA

Travelling from Vainupea along the coast towards Kunda we come to Rutja where we can see a peculiar monument on the territory of the local border guard station. The monument was set up to commemorate the **border guards' dog Djoma**. Although he spent most of his life 'serving' in the Soviet Army, he stayed behind when the Russian troops left in the early/mid-1990s and was looked after by local people. The letters on the stone say: "On the border until death".

East of Rutja on the shore of Selja river is Karepa, a popular summer resort. A farmhouse more than 100 years old is the birthplace of the painter **Richard Sagrits** (see Vainupea Chapel). It stands on the high eastern bank of the river. Now it operates as **Kalame Farm Museum** that introduces local history and the life and work of Sagrits. The Museum, a typical 19th century fisherman's farm, was founded by the widow of Sagrits in 1997.

Toolse Order Castle at the end of Toolse neem (cape) is situated between Karepa and Toolse. The castle was probably completed in

The border dog Djoma has his own monument.

Toolse stronghold was built for protection against pirates.

LÄÄNE-VIRUMAA

1471, replacing an earlier stronghold on the same site, and had to protect the harbour from pirates. The castle was constantly expanded and upgraded. The Swedes still used it in the 17th century until it was destroyed in the Great Northern War. The shifting land later helped demolish the structure further.

South of the ruins, between Kunda Road and the sea by the Toolse river grows a unique **oak grove**, one of the northernmost in Europe. Across the road from the grove, also by the river, stand two hill-forts – Toolse hill-fort and Toolse Ussimägi (Snake Hill). The latter is smaller and older and is situated about 1.5 km from the road. It was probably built to protect the harbour area. The walls of the ancient castle reached to 10 m. Archaeologists have found traces of various houses, built of clay and wicker mats.

A Dutch-type 19th century windmill, now in ruins, can be seen in **Andja village** west from the Põdruse-Kunda Road. An old stone bridge is about 30 m downstream from the new one.

Kunda became an industrial town largely thanks to the extension of the harbour that started in 1805. Soon a sawmill and a rope factory were established. The cement industry developed rapidly after the wealthy Tallinn merchant and owner of the Kunda manor, Johann Girard de Soucanton established the cement factory in the 1870s, using local blue clay and lake lime. The first hydroelectric power plant in the Baltic countries was built on the Kunda River in 1893 and provided energy for the factory.

Kunda cement was widely used during the period of Russian tsars, Estonian independence (1918–1940) and the subsequent Soviet era. The factory became really huge in the 1960s – the production increased and so did the pollution. The entire town was covered with a layer of cement dust. Today's technology, however, manages to keep the place clean.

The history of the cement industry is introduced in a museum (Jaama Street 1) in the office building of the old factory. The visitor can also see a typical work-

Kunda was covered with a layer of cement dust almost throughout the Soviet period.

The bottle chimney today belongs to the museum.

The manor that once belonged to the founder of the cement industry, Johann Girard de Soucanton, now stands in ruins.

er's apartment of the 1920s. The old factory now stands in ruins. The most remarkable sight there is the over one hundred year-old bottle stove, reputedly the only surviving of its kind in Europe.

The remains of the former **Kunda Manor** stand on the riverbank, a few kilometres south of the town. The manor was destroyed in the early days of the Second World War. Only some traces are still visible of the grand system of limestone dams and canals in the park.

Kunda Church certainly looks strange. Its bell is not located in a tower but instead hangs above the roof from a special console. The current church, famous for its excellent acoustics, was completed in the late 1920s. It replaced an earlier wooden church that burnt down during WW I.

In Letipea village 7 km northeast of Kunda, the second largest erratic boulder in Estonia stands in the shallow water. It has several names, the best known of which is **Ehalkivi (Sunset Stone)**, but it is also known as Suurkivi (Big Stone). The diameter is about 50 m and height 7.6 m. The boulder has served as a landmark for centuries.

The small bell of Kunda Church is suspended above the roof.

South of Kunda, by the road leading to Kohala and Uhtna, is Kunda **Lammasmägi (Sheep Hill)**, an ancient settlement inhabited already 11,000 years ago. This football-field-size area was a lake island where the hunters-gatherers found a safe place to live. Their only domestic animal was the dog, and most of their weapons were made of bone, smaller tools also of stone. Plenti-

Kunda Lammasmägi was once the site of Kunda Culture.

LÄÄNE-VIRUMAA

Stories about village life of Jüri Parijõgi are among the classics of Estonian literature.

The first church in Viru-Nigula was completed 750 years ago.

ful archaeological finds have given name to the whole human Stone Age culture by the eastern coast of the Baltic Sea – the Kunda Culture.

A well-known Estonian writer **Jüri Parijõgi** (1892–1941) was born in Siberi village near Lammasmägi. His birthplace is marked by a monument by sculptor Endel Taniloo that was set up there in 1971. Parijõgi vividly described his childhood and people's lives in Kunda in connection with the cement factory. Some of his works firmly belong among the classics of Estonian children's literature. Parijõgi was also a popular and respected schoolmaster. He was murdered by communists in Tartu prison in 1941.

Viru-Nigula village is located by the Kunda Road, 2 km from the Tallinn-Narva Road. A monument to those killed in the War of Independence (1918–1920) stands in the middle of the village on the square in front of the church. The church was completed in the second half of the 13th century, but has been repeatedly damaged and reconstructed. Another monument can be found behind the churchyard, in memory of **Kongla Anne** who was burnt at the stake in

The nameless grave of Kongla Anne behind the churchyard.

1640. She was a nanny in the local manor when one of her charges suddenly died. According to a paper of that time, Marahwa Näddala-Leht (Country People's Weekly), the nanny confessed to turning herself into a witch and a werewolf and thus causing a lot of damage in the neighbourhood. It is of course difficult to imagine that she confessed all this voluntarily.

Across the road from the church, under the leafy trees, stands the old vicarage. Between 1795 and 1815, the local pastor, a great enlightenment figure and a man of letters **Otto Wilhelm**

Otto Wilhelm Masing was pastor in Viru-Nigula for twenty years. His home is now a museum.

Masing (1763–1832) lived there. His father was Estonian, who was keen to give his son a good education. Masing's studies culminated at the liberal Halle University in Germany. He wrote several school textbooks and Bible studies, compiled useful handbooks for rural people, edited the weekly newspaper, reformed the Estonian language and introduced the letter 'õ' into the language.

A museum now operates in the old vicarage, presenting an overview of Masing's life and work and the history of Viru-Nigula parish.

Half a kilometre east from Viru-Nigula the visitor can see the ruins of the 13th century **Maarja (St Mary's) Chapel**, the oldest place of worship in Virumaa. It probably fell into ruins as early as the 16th–17th centuries. According to various chronicles from that time, the chapel was a place for pagan worshippers, much to the dismay of local pastors.

2 km south of Viru-Nigula, the Tallinn-Narva Road crosses the deep valley of the Pada River, called Padaorg. The former **Pada Manor** is located one kilometre south of the big road, by the road to Sonda. The once grand early classicist mansion was reputedly designed by one of the famous St Petersburg architects (de la Mothe or even the author of the Winter Palace, Bartolomeo Rastrelli). Unfortunately the building was destroyed during the revolutionary unrest in 1917. The windmill also stands in ruins.

There are **two hill-forts** on the eastern bank of the Pada River, near the Tallinn-Narva Road. The bigger is located between the old and the new Narva Road, the smaller one about one hundred metres west of the Sonda Road. A stronghold stood on the site of the first in the 7th–13th centuries and on the site of the latter, in the 5th–8th centuries. Archaeological excavations

The ruins of St Mary's chapel.

Pada mansion is now overrun by trees.

in Padaorg have revealed numerous tools and pieces of jewellery. The symbol of Padaorg is the **Pada** or **Vanaveski (Old Mill) pine** tree. Its diameter before it forks into two, is 3.6 m.

Turning south from the Tallinn-Narva Road at the Viru-Nigula crossroads we arrive in the ancient **Samma sacred grove** on a high bank of the Pada primeval valley. There are two sacrificial springs, 150 young oaks and a special gate where the visitor can enter the grove.

Picturesque ruins of the water mill in Pada primeval valley.

AROUND HALJALA

Aaspere Manor 1.5 km south of the Tallinn-Narva Road, is a classicist building with a six-pillared portico. The last owners were the von Dellingshausens. The manor also once had a nice park with bridges, ponds, alleys and a rotunda. The manor lords of Aaspere were among the first to start selling land to the peasants for good in the 1870s. (Although the von Stackelberg family in the Abja Manor in Viljandi did that already in the 1840s.)

Today, Aaspere is privately owned and is currently under renovation.

Only a staircase survives from the **Kavastu Manor** in Kavastu village north of Aaspere. There is, however, also a peculiar small limestone 6-m high building that at first sight resembles a medieval defence tower. In fact it was built in 1869 for pigeons.

The entrance to Samma sacrificial grove.

Travelling north-east of Haljala we arrive in Varangu in the south corner of the Selja river nature protection area, at the site of the so-called **Varangu Veskikants** (Mill Castle) where a stronghold stood in the 9th–13th centuries.

Aaspere mansion has the same number of pillars as the University of Tartu.

in Estonia. **Vanamõisa** with its 300 hectares and a distillery was one of the biggest manors owned by Germans in Estonia before WW II.

A prominent painter Karl Ludwig Maibach (1833–1889), mostly known for his landscapes, was born there in the family of the granary keeper at the manor. Maibach studied art in various places in Europe and travelled extensively.

RAKVERE AND ITS SURROUNDINGS

Turning north from the Kullaaru Road bus stop on the Rakvere-Kadrina Road, we come to Kullaaru village, **birthplace** of an eminent Estonian writer **Eduard Bornhöhe** (1862–1923). Bornhöhe was a man with a restless spirit – he travelled a lot in Europe and the Middle East, and had numerous jobs, from schoolteacher to magistrate. Besides popular short stories he was one of the first Estonian authors to write travelogues.

The symbol of the town of Rakvere is **Vallimägi Hill** where once stood an ancient stronghold called Tarvanpea. The German name for Tarvanpea, Wesenbergh, is thought to come from Low-German wesent that means aurochs. In 1220 it was conquered by the Danes who built a new stronghold, which was completed by 1252. During the next century, under the reign of the Livonian Order, the stronghold was extended and turned into a convent-type castle. In subsequent battles, however, the castle suffered major damage so that at some point it was decided not to restore it.

At first it was invaded by the Russians, then the Swedes and finally the Poles who completely destroyed it in 1605.

A monument commemorates the former Kavastu manor.

A castle? No, a bird-house.

Between Aaspere and Haljala, about 2 km north from the Tallinn-Narva Road, stands the **Vanamõisa Manor**, a two-storey historicist building. The owner, Hans von Brevern managed to keep the manor after the 1919 land reform

Three eminent figures of Estonian cultural life allegedly met on Vallimägi and swore to serve the nation. This pledge is known as Viru vanne (Viru pledge).

The huge sculpture by Tauno Kangro.

The later castle was built on the site of the ancient Tarvanpea stronghold.

After the Great Northern War in 1721 people broke off stones from the walls and used them to build the town. The first steps in preserving the remaining walls were taken in the late 1970s. Today, Vallimägi is a popular venue for parties and open-air performances. A museum tells the visitors about the history of the stronghold and displays various items found on the hill. There is also a special exhibition about medieval torturing devices.

In 2002 a huge bronze monument of an aurochs by the sculptor Tauno Kangro was set up on Vallimägi. Its golden horns can be seen from quite a distance.

The southern part of Vallimägi belongs to nature. A fascinating grove has been planted here of especially gnarled and thickset oak trees.

A manor house once stood on the northern slope of the hill that used to belong to the Tiesenhausens and the Rennenkampfs. In the 1920 it was decided to convert the mansion into a theatre house. The task was completed in 1940.

The building accommodating the **Exhibition House-Museum** at 3 Tallinn Street in Rakvere was built in 1789 and used to be a court, prison, shop, garrison, etc. The Museum mostly has temporary displays, but also an extensive permanent display of local archaeological finds.

The Citizens' Museum is located at 50 Pikk Street. It shows the living quarters of a late-19th century citizen, a tailor's workshop and a laundry room. The Museum also has a picture gallery of famous people from Rakvere.

In Kaarli near Sõmeru in the direction of Narva, **Friedrich**

Rakvere Theatre was built instead of the former manor house.

The museum presents various temporary exhibitions.

The Citizens' Museum describes the life of Rakvere inhabitants one hundred years ago.

Rägavere Manor was one of the first to be restored in the Soviet era.

This could be the stone where the future compiler of the national epic, Friedrich Reinhold Kreutzwald, liked to dream about his future.

Reinhold Kreutzwald, creator of the Estonian national epic Kalevipoeg (Kalev's Son) lived between 1804 and 1817. Behind the old wooden community centre stands a huge boulder with a concrete iron crown on top of it. It is therefore called **Kroonikivi** (Crown Stone). The diameter of the crown is one metre and it used to be of bronze. Alas, the bronze was stolen and in 2003 it was replaced by a concrete iron crown that shows characters from Kreutzwald's fairy tales.

Driving about 10 km out of Rakvere along the Rägavere Road we come to the **Rägavere Manor**. This was the first manor house restored during the Soviet period, in the early 1970s. Before that, the manor accommodated a schoolhouse. For twenty-odd years the late-18th century mansion functioned as a concert hall and a party venue. It is now privately owned.

Turning towards Vinni from the Rakvere-Rägavere Road, we arrive at **Mõdriku Manor** that today houses the Lääne-Virumaa vocational school. The wings of the mansion are of different styles and were built at different times. The Baroque eastern wing is one

A sculpture in the Mõdriku Park.

The Stallion's Pillar commemorates the Napoleonic Wars.

Monument to artist-brothers Raud.

and a half centuries older than the Classicist western wing and the section in between.

The visitor can see from afar a peculiar obelisk standing on the hill behind the manor park – a tall white pillar with a golden orb on top. Locals call it **Täkusammas** (Stallion's Pillar) because Reinhold August von Kaulbars, the manor lord, had set it up to commemorate his white stallion who brought his seriously wounded master out of the fierce battle in 1812. The grateful man probably also had in mind the victorious outcome of the war, conquering Paris and his own participation in these events.

Travelling from Rakvere towards Mustvee the next bigger settlement after Pajusti is **Viru-Jaagupi**. The famous seafarer and explorer **Ferdinand von Wrangell** (1796–1870) is buried at Viru-Jaagupi cemetery.

Viru-Jaagupi is the birthplace of the artists Kristjan (1865–1943) and Paul Raud (1865–1930). A **monument** commemorates the twin brothers who were both remarkable painters and Kristjan additionally a graphic artist. They received an excellent art education abroad and greatly encouraged art life in Estonia.

The parish museum is located at 7 Kooli Street in the former schoolhouse.

The former schoolhouse today accommodates a parish museum.

The pastor's grave in Viru-Jaagupi churchyard is right in front of the vestry door.

ROELA, LAEKVERE AND SIMUNA

The **Roela Manor** stands beside the Rakvere-Mustvee Road, about one kilometre east of the big road. The old baroque wooden mansion was built in the late 18th century. The new mansion was completed in the early 20th century and now belongs to the descendants of the von Wrangells. After the land reform of the Republic of Estonia in 1919 the then owner Hans Wrangell was allowed to keep, for services rendered, a smaller manor of 180 hectares. Before the reform, Roela Manor owned 10 000 ha of land, of which 900 were arable.

The most famous **von Wrangell** was the above-mentioned Ferdinand, whose name is recorded in the geography of Eurasia and America. A small Arctic island in the Chukchi Sea and a whole mountain range have been named after him. What is more – a spent volcano in the mountain range also bears his name – Mount Wrangell.

The mansion of the **Muuga Manor** beside the Rakvere-Mustvee Road between Roela and Paasvere was built between 1866 and 1873 by **Carl Timoleon von Neff** (1804–1877), academic at the St Petersburg Academy of Art. As is often the case in Estonia, the surroundings are ruined by a row of grey dilapidated stables, remains of the Soviet-time collective farming.

Von Neff's life was almost like a Cinderella story. He was born at Püssi Manor as an illegitimate child of a French governess and grew up at the Küti Manor near Viru-Jaagupi. A prominent painter of the time, Karl Ferdinand von Kügelgen (1772–1832), lived at Küti as well. Kügelgen taught painting to his own son and relatives and also to the young Karl Timoleon whom the local manor lord Heinrich Otto Zoege von Manteuffel had adopted. The adopted son showed great talent and was able to further his studies at the Dresden Art Academy. In 1844 he was ennobled and became the tsar's court painter. Von Neff produced pictures for the Winter Palace and St Isaac's Cathedral,

Roela Manor used to belong to the famous explorer Baron von Wrangell.

Von Neff who built the grand Muuga Manor, was born to a governess.

Beautiful caryatids support the Muuga portico.

Muuga now adorns the entrance hall of the Kadriorg Art Museum in Tallinn.

Turning west from the Rakvere-Mustvee Road at Paasvere crossroads, we reach **Laekvere** after 4 km. Looking back before arriving, we see Alutaguse, an area of woodland and marshes. Laekvere is a kind of border zone between the marshy and low Alutaguse and the higher and hilly Pandivere. Laekvere itself has several strong stone buildings, mostly 70–80 years old, such as the schoolhouse, dairy and the shop.

A few kilometres north-west of Laekvere is the 156-m Kellavere Hill, the second largest "mountain" in Pandivere.

The door of Laekvere school is lined with blue-black-white edge.

but he also painted Estonian peasants, although the latter were quite idealised. Von Neff's remarkable art collection is today displayed at the Museum of Estonian Art in Tallinn.

What strike the eye first while looking at the Muuga mansion, are the caryatids supporting the grand arcade. Inside the visitor can see a light grey marble staircase presented to von Neff by the Russian Tsar Alexander II. The marble copy of Venus de Milo that once stood in the grand hall of

Travelling 11 km west of Laekvere towards Väike-Maarja, we come to Simuna, centre of Avanduse rural municipality. The former manor now functions as the municipality office. **Avanduse Manor** was known primarily for one of its owners, Count Friedrich Benjamin Lütke (Russian: Litke) who lived from 1797 to 1882. Count Lütke was a famous explorer who took part in two round-the-world trips and mapped the coasts of the North Sea and Kamtchatka Peninsula. He was

The owner of Avanduse Manor, Count Lütke, was head of the St Petersburg Academy of Sciences.

among the founding members of the Russian Geographical Society and was its president for the last 18 years of his life. Count Lütke bought Avanduse Manor in 1845 and spent his summers there.

Between 1822 and 1827 the astronomer and geodesist Friedrich Struve (1793–1864) oranised a **large-scale experiment of measuring the meridian curve** in the Baltic area, with the aim of establishing the shape and diameter of Earth more precisely.

The late 15th century stone church in **Simuna** was repeatedly destroyed and rebuilt. The baroque pulpit and altar have survived. The owner of the Muuga Manor, Carl Timoleon von Neff, rests in the churchyard.

A large spring appears from underground in the park, which is the beginning of the Pedja River. As the surrounding area used to be called Katkuküla (Plague village), the spring is known as **Katkuallikas (Plague spring)**. In olden times, the word 'katk' (plague) denoted a wet area.

The Simuna-Käru Road runs across the Avanduse bog and the first village after Simuna is Metsaküla. This is the birthplace of a prominent Estonian painter and poet Aleksander Suuman (1927–2004) who has depicted his native landscapes both in his paintings and in his poems.

About 5 km north of Simuna, on the Määri-Äntu Road, is **Pudivere village**. One of the most important Estonian writers, **Eduard Vilde** (1865–1933) was born in the former manor. A **memorial plaque** to Vilde is about one kilometre from the very centre of the manor complex where houses for the manor employees once stood. The wooden mansion of Pudivere

A stone column commemorates the measuring of the meridian curve by Academician Struve.

The probable birthplace of the writer Eduard Vilde in a house on Pudivere Manor premises.

suffered damage in a fire and is now in ruins.

Eduard Vilde was a remarkably prolific writer and journalist. He produced jolly satirical stories but at the same time was a sharp and critical examiner of the wrongs of society at the time. His historical trilogy Mahtra sõda, Kui Anija mehed Tallinnas käisid, Prohvet Maltsvet (The Peasant War at Mahtra, When the Men of Anija Went to Tallinn, Propher Maltsvet) etc had a great impact on the Estonian society and the mentality of people.

Vilde travelled extensively in Europe and in America as a journalist. After Estonia became independent in 1918 he briefly worked in the diplomatic field.

AROUND TAPA

The birth and development of the town of Tapa is directly connected with the railway. In 1870, after the completion of the Tallinn-St Petersburg railway, the first rather modest railway station was built on the territory of the Tapa manor. Six years later, Tapa became a junction and started growing quickly. It became a town in the 1920s.

In August 1941 the Soviet troops destroyed a large part of the town centre, and what remained was heavily bombed and flattened in 1944. After WW II Tapa became a military and a railway town where the Russian language dominated. An airfield and a tank depot were built nearby. When the Soviet army finally left in 1994, Tapa attracted attention for its 'burning wells' – the soil was so immersed with fuel that it seeped to people's wells and made them inflammable. Extensive cleaning has greatly improved the situation and Tapa no longer looks quite so desolate. The museum at Mai 32, opened in summer 1994, gives an overview of the history of Tapa and the importance of the railway system to it.

Armoured trains built in Estonia played a crucial role in the War of Independence.

Driving out of Tapa along the Rakvere Road, the traveller soon notices tall industrial buildings in the east. It is the **Moe Distillery**, descendent of the old distillery that operated there already 200 years ago. Production was greatly increased by Jakob Kurberg who bought the manor in 1886.

In 1971 a Distillery Museum opened at Moe, in the rooms of the old, 19th century distillery. The exhibits include 18th century wooden distillery equipment and more modern tools of the 19th century that operated on steam,

The town of Tapa emerged thanks to the railway.

Moe Distillery introduced the history of vodka production in Estonia.

old bottles and labels, various models, etc.

Vohnja Manor can be reached by turning east off the Loobu-Tapa Road onto the road to Kadrina (the manor is about 3 km from the crossroads). The early 19th century classicist mansion is nicely restored and accommodates a school and a library. Various auxiliary buildings have survived as well. The park has ponds both in front and behind the mansion.

Vohnja Manor is associated with a notorious trial. In the early 18th century, the miller Ants and his son Jaan sued their manor lord who demanded excess work from local peasants. The trial dragged on for 17 years until it was referred to the higher court of Livonia and Estonia. In 1739 the court issued their verdict, known as Rosen's declaration as it was signed by Landrat Otto Fabian von Rosen.

Rosen declared that peasants had been slaves from the 13th century, and that all their possessions belong to the manor lord who can make the peasants work as much as he thinks necessary. The manor lord is even entitled to sell his peasants, although a line was drawn at actually murdering them. The miller's son Jaan was deported to Siberia and his possessions given to the manor lord.

AROUND KADRINA

Kadrina is located about 15 km west of Rakvere by railway. It is the centre of the rural municipality. In 1994 a monument to **Mother Tongue** was set up in front of the local school with just two words on it: Sona seob (word unites).

The Estonian language was well looked after in Kadrina already several centuries ago. In 1633–1638 Kadrina's pastor **Heinrich Stahl** (1600–1657), founder of the older standard Estonian language, wrote his main opus, the 4-volume Kasi- ja koduraamat Eesti vürstkonna jaoks Liivimaal (Handbook for the Estonian principality in Livonia) in German. The books contained religious songs, the catechism and the edifying stories, also the first Estonian-language textbook with a dictionary. Stahl's works are especially important

Monument to mother tongue.

from the point of view of analysing the development of the Estonian language (see also Jarvamaa, Jarva-Madise).

After Stahl, the next Kadrina pastor was **Reiner Brocmann** (1609–1647) who worked there until his death. He was the first to cultivate non-religious poetry in Estonian. He wrote poems in other languages as well, including Latin and Greek. According to the European custom of the time, Brocmann wrote his poems in a lofty style.

Brocmann is buried in Kadrina Church.

Arnold Freidrich Johann Knüpffer (1777–1843) was pastor in Kadrina in the early 19th century. He was an enthusiastic folklorist. In his grammar Stahl relied on Latin, whereas Knupffer advised taking Finnish as a model for Estonian.

Neeruti Manor is located by the Kadrina-Assamalla Road. It is one of the few Jugendstil manors in Estonia, built in 1903–1906 by a wealthy St Petersburg merchant Eduard Heinrich von Kirschten.

The most spectacular element of the building is the 30-metre high viewing tower. The cobblestone courtyard is surrounded by numerous auxiliary buildings. The 300 m long maple alley was established at the manor, and the owner began transforming the Neeruti hills into a wooded park. Today the grand Neeruti Manor is privately owned and is slowly disintegrating.

Neeruti Nature Reserve consists of many elevations and lakes, most of them associated with various folk legends and fairy tales.

The monument marking the birthplace of **Friedrich Reinhold Kreutzwald** (1803–1882) stands in Ristimetsa near Jõepere village by the Kadrina-Assamalla Road. Access is made easy by signposts. Ristimetsa, by the way, is Kreutzwald in German.

The writer's house has not survived.

Lasila Manor by the Kadrina-Assamalla Road is the place where a famous German-Estonian natu-

Neeruti Manor is adorned by a 30-m tower.

Monument to Friedrich Reinhold Kreutzwald.

Karl Ernst von Baer grew up at Lasila Manor.

ralist **Karl Ernst von Baer** (1792–1876) spent his childhood. At that time Lasila belonged to the future scientist's uncle. A memorial stone to Baer stands in front of the mansion by the small lake. The historicist mansion decorated with turrets today accommodates a schoolhouse. Besides other scientific interests, Baer was also keen on local culture. His graduation thesis, in the German language, at Tartu University was about the endemic diseases of Estonians. The booklet is available in Estonian as well, published in 1976. Baer's contribution to science is remarkable. We could name some of his discoveries and areas of research: he discovered the mammalian ovum, studied the embryonal development of animals, established an extensive skull collection at St Petersburg, contributed to studies in entomology, co-founded the Russian Entomological Society, took an interest in the Northern part of Russia and explored Novaya Zemlya in 1837 collecting biological specimens. Other travels led him to the Caspian Sea, the North Cape, and Lapland. He was a founder and the first president of the Russian Geographical Society.

AROUND VÄIKE-MAARJA

Porkuni battlefield. In Sauevälja by the Tamsalu-Väike-Maarja Road stands a mighty boulder with a memorial plaque. It commemorates a bloody battle that took place on 21 September 1944. The battle lasted no more than two hours. Retreating troops of the Estonian Legion, altogether about 1500 men, were attacked by a regiment of Estonian Rifle Brigade who were part of the Red Army. The legionnaires suffered a heavy defeat with 600 killed and 700 taken prisoner. The dead were buried in common graves that were marked with crosses only in 1998. Signposts pointing to the graves stand by the Sauevalja-Porkuni Road.

The Bishop of Tallinn, Simon von der Borch established a castle in Porkuni by the road from Tamsalu to Kullenga (Rakvere-Vageva

Porkuni Lake can disappear completely during the dry season.

Porkuni Manor was built near the former castle.

Road) as early as in 1479. The castle had corner towers and a small chapel in the courtyard. The castle was badly damaged in the Livonian War, and today only a gate tower and a piece of wall are still standing.

Porkuni Manor was initially located around the castle. The new grand neo-Gothic mansion was built in the second half of the 19th century when Porkuni belonged to the von Rennenkampfs. In 1924, the school for the deaf mute children moved there from Vandra and is still operating. A new building opposite the mansion was completed for the school in the 1950s.

There is a memorial stone to Ernst Sokolovski who started teaching the deaf mutes and founded a school for them.

The gate tower of the episcopal castle has been nicely restored and today houses the **Limestone Museum**, exhibiting the different types of limestone and what can be made from them. Another section of the museum tells about the history of educating deaf mute children in Estonia.

The name of Porkuni is widely known in Estonia thanks to an ancient legend about Barbara Tiesenhausen, daughter of the lord of the manor. About 450 years ago, her brothers allegedly pushed her through a hole in the ice-covered lake and drowned her because she had fallen in love with an unsuitable man. Afterwards people have seen a faint fluttering light under the ice, the soul of the unfortunate young woman. A number of writers have told her story in their poems and stories, and Eduard Tubin wrote an opera Barbara von Tisenhusen.

Porkuni Lake in the deep valley is famous for its floating islands, 17 altogether that are pushed along water by wind.

The 62-m high tower of **Väike-Maarja Church** is one of the highest in Estonia. The church was completed in the early 15th century and stands out for its thick walls and well preserved original shape. The churchyard contains the burial place of the world-famous explorers the von Krusensterns: the son and grandson of Adam Johann von Krusen-

The Limestone Museum in the medieval castle tower introduces the Estonian national stone.

The Krusenstern family resting place in front of the church.

Väike-Maarja Museum offers information about Anton Hansen Tammsaare and Jakob Liiv, as well as the wrestler Georg Lurich.

stern who was the first to sail around the world in Russia, respectively vice admiral Paul Theodor von Krusenstern (1809–1881) and lieutenant captain Paul von Krusenstern (1834–1871).

The name of Väike-Maarja is associated with a legend about the time when the church was built. A girl called Maria (Maarja) was allegedly walled in so that the building would stand safely. Hence the place name Klein-Marien or Väike-Maarja (Little Maarja).

The first parish school was founded in 1723 although it started regular work 150 years later. Various writers and poets lived and worked in Väike-Maarja in the late 19th century, e.g. Jakob Liiv (1859–1938), brother of one of Estonia's most beloved poets Juhan Liiv. Jakob was a schoolteacher and later opened a bookshop. The school has been restored and today houses a museum. The museum is unique as it is the only one in Estonia to cover exclusively the Soviet period and to write positively about a collective farm. **A monument to Jakob Liiv** stands in the park nearby.

One of the great men of Väike-Maarja was certainly the famous wrestler and weightlifter **Georg Lurich** (1876–1920). Lurich was one of the best in his fields of sport and travelled extensively in the world.

Jakob Liiv taught children and ran a bookshop in Väike-Maarja.

Travelling south along the Vägeva Road from Väike-Maarja, we see **Ebavere Hill** on the west by the road. Ebavere was the sacred grove of ancient Estonians, associated with many legends. Today, people ski there in winter and cycle and run in summer. With its 146 metres, Ebavere is the third tallest hill in Pandivere area.

Turning towards Koeru from Väike-Maarja, we come to the crossroads before Kiltsi. West from that is the **Vao tower castle** and in the east the Kiltsi Manor that used to belong to the Krusensterns.

Vao castle is in fact part of the former manor complex. The old wooden mansion caught fire in 1918 and burned to the ground. The 15th century tower castle has survived remarkably well. The 4-storey building houses a museum. For the most part of the 19th century, the **Kiltsi Manor** belonged to the von Krusensterns. In the late 18th century the medieval castle tower was united with the baroque mansion. Facing the mansion, the tower is to the left. Two long arcades stretch on either side of the mansion that today has a schoolhouse and a room dedicated to the explorer **Adam Johann von Krusenstern** (1770–1846) became a corresponding member of the St Petersburg Academy of Sciences when he was 33, and at once initiated the first Russian round-the-world trip which he led. The voyage took three years. Afterwards Krusenstern compiled an atlas of the South Seas that was considered one of the best at the time. He also developed the system of training marines in Russia. The famous explorer died at Kiltsi and was buried in the Tallinn Cathedral. His son and grandson rest in Väike-Maarja churchyard.

The pride of Kiltsi Manor is the arcade.

In the Prillapatsi area by the Väike-Maarja-Rakke Road there are seven beautiful lakes in the forest that feed on springs. They are called **Äntu Lakes**. The clearest and purest of them is Sinijärv.

Near Pikevere by the road from Väike-Maarja to Järva-Jaani via Ebavere, stands **Varangu Manor**. In Estonian cultural life this place is special as a childhood home of Eduard Viiralt (1898–1919), one

Vao tower castle gives an idea about the life of medieval vassal.

One of the Antu lakes has the most transparent water of all the lakes in Estonia.

of our best graphic artists ever. Viiralt's father was a bailiff at the manor and the family lived in a wooden house nearby. The house is still standing.

A path leads from the manor to Varangu springs in the forest.

The beautiful Varangu springs are located near the manor.

The bailiff's house was the birthplace of Eduard Viiralt.

AROUND RAKKE

Rakke village is known for its lime factory that started work in 1891. Right beside the village is an oblong fort-hill, an ancient stronghold site. Today, it is a venue for theatre and other open-air performances.

Marta Sillaots (1887–1969), a well-known translator and children's writer and her brother **Heinrich Riikoja** (1891–1988), an eminent hydrobiologist, were born in the former stagecoach station. The place bears a commemorative plaque. **Ernst Birnbaum** (1894–1965), another Rakke man, became famous for his hot-air balloon trips. He managed to rise as high as 19 km, which was the world record at the time.

Ernst Birnbaum managed to rise higher in his hot-air balloon than anyone before him.

One of the most significant figures in the Estonian National Awakening was **Friedrich Robert Faehlmann** (1798–1850), born in Ao village by the Rakke-Liigvalla Road. His father was a bailiff at the manor, and the son got a good education which enabled him to continue at the University of Tartu and study medicine. He had diverse interests: Faehlmann laid the foundation for cardiology in Estonia, was a founding member of the Estonian Learned Society, and he encouraged the gathering of folk tales that later evolved into the national epic Kalevipoeg (Kalev's Son). He wrote short stories and poems, and was a central figure at the birth of Estonian literature.

A memorial stone marks his birthplace.

At Piibe, by the road from Vageva to Koeru, about 1.5 km south from the crossroads, is the **Piibe Manor**, birthplace of the famous naturalist **Karl Ernst von Baer (see** Lasila Manor in Lääne-Virumaa).

Piibe belonged to the von Baers for nearly a century and a half. The former mansion is demolished, with only a few auxiliary buildings surviving. In 1960 a memorial stone to Baer was placed in the centre of the manor complex.

East of the Olju crossroads on the Rakke-Vägeva Road is the **Emumägi Nature Reserve**. Here is the 'ceiling' of Pandivere Uplands – the 166.5 m high Emumägi. The new viewing tower is 21.5 m high. A peculiar hut made of the roots of pine trees can be seen near the tower.

A hut of pine tree roots stands near Emumägi viewing tower.

IDA-VIRUMAA

IDA-VIRUMAA

As a strange inheritance from the Soviet era, Ida-Virumaa sometimes seems to be an alien in its own land. Fortunately, the industrial landscapes and settlements do not determine its essence; there is much more to it than what can be seen through a car window from a main road.

The primeval limestone cliffs – klint – have survived the Ice Age; the Alutaguse forests have always been among the symbols of Estonia. When we talk about our northern coast, we usually mean Virumaa.

If we leave aside the ground water, which we take for granted until the time we run out of it, oil shale is the second most important raw material that is found in Estonia. The Alutaguse bogs and mires are the huge reservoirs of clean water and the reserves of unspoilt nature. Ida-Virumaa is the area where primeval nature and modern industry, which helps our country to function, come into conflict. Our country's future can well be determined in Ida-Virumaa, since all engines need energy, and the energy supply for at least one more generation can be found in the bowels of Ida-Virumaa. We shall see what will come after that.

As a travel destination, Ida-Virumaa offers many surprises. Why not drop in to Sillamäe and walk towards the sea down the steps that remind us of Odessa; or climb the sightseeing tower on Tärivere hill in Iisaku to see whether the mountains of ashes, er ... sorry, the semi-coke heaps, can be seen far in the north. Or, go to Tudulinna and see the two churches, built by two quarrelling congregations, which glare at each other.

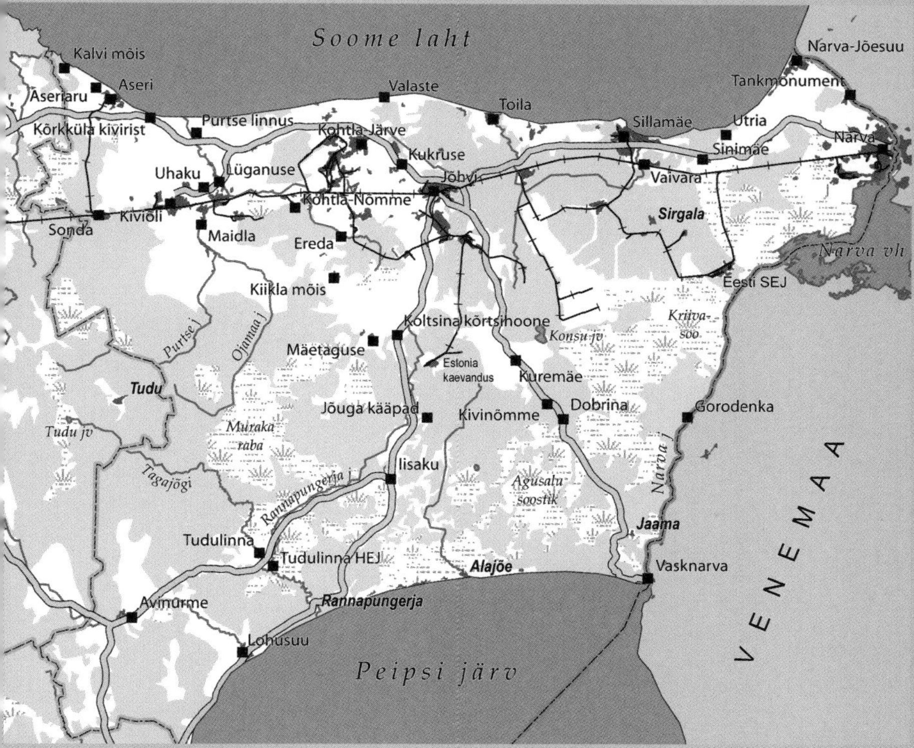

Soome laht
Kalvi mõis
Aseri
Aseriaru
Valaste
Toila
Narva-Jõesuu
Tankmonument
Kõrkküla kivirist
Purtse linnus
Kohtla-Järve
Sillamäe
Utria
Sinimäe
Narva
Kukruse
Uhaku
Lüganuse
Jõhvi
Vaivara
Kohtla-Nõmme
Sirgala
Sonda
Kiviõli
Maidla
Ereda
Narva vh
Eesti SEJ
Kiikla mõis
Purtse j
Ojamaa j
Koltsina kõrtsihoone
Konsu jv
Kriiva-soo
Mäetaguse
Estonia kaevandus
Kuremäe
Tudu
Jõuga kääpad
Kivinõmme
Dobrina
Gorodenka
Tudu jv
Muraka raba
Iisaku
Tagajõgi
Rannapungerja j
Agusalu soostik
Narva j
Jaama
Tudulinna
Tudulinna HEJ
Alajõe
Vasknarva
Avinurme
Rannapungerja
Lohusuu
Peipsi järv
VENEMAA

AROUND KIVIÕLI AND PÜSSI

The first records about **Kalvi Manor**, located on the northwestern shore of Ida-Virumaa, date back to the late 15th century. The von Kalff family, after whom the manor was named, obtained it in 1512.

The present Neo-gothic mansion was built by Nicolai von Stackelberg in 1913, who positioned it away from the site of the former manor house, which had been destroyed in a fire in 1911. During the Soviet era, the mansion housed a sanatorium for tuberculosis patients; now it has been restored and an elegant hotel opened there in 2002.

An old and time-worn **stone cross in memory of a Russian nobleman Vasili Rosladen** stands by the Tallinn-Narva Road in Kõrkküla, between Rannu and Purtse. The cross commemorates the Russian nobleman who died in a battle during the Russian-Swedish War near Narva in 1590. Rosladen who had initially fought with the Russians, had changed sides during the battle and joined the Swedes. He met his brother during the battle and fought with him. The cross was erected by the Swedes.

Near Aseri, by a smaller road that leads to the village of Aseriaru, stands a memorial stone to mark the site of one of the many WWII concentration camps in Ida-Virumaa. **The memorial stone to the victims of fascism**, imprisoned and killed there, was put up in 1967. The site of the camp is located deep in the forest and it is difficult to find (it is at the end of the village, quite near the road to Viivikonna). Other sites in Vaivara, Kiviõli and Ereda have also been marked.

The production of cement from the local Cambrian blue clay was started in **Aseri** at the beginning of the 20th century. The owner of Aseri and Koogu Manors, the district magistrate Hermann Otto Schilling, instigated the building of the cement factory. A joint-stock company with the name of "Asserien" was created, which also lent the name to the village. By 1905, the factory buildings, the workers' dwellings and a power plant had already been built and a water supply had been installed at Meriküla on the lands of Aseri Manor. The limestone quarry and clay quarry had been opened and a railway line branching off from Sonda station had been built. A small brick factory was also established there in the 1920s, which grew into a large joint-stock company "State Brick Factories" in 1935–1937. The Aseri factories quickly expanded and soon they entirely swallowed up the former fishermen's village, filling it with factory buildings and clay quarries. The production of bricks and roofing tiles continues to this day in Aseri.

The time-worn stone cross erected to Vasili Rosladen has lost one of its arms.

The restored Purtse Castle.

Young oaks in the Memorial Park to all Victims of Evil.

A museum introducing the history of the factories is located in the local sports hall (20, Kesk Street).

A three-storied **vassal castle** with a sleek tower can be seen near the Tallinn-Narva Road in **Purtse**. This is one of the largest fortified manor houses in Estonia. The castle was built by the von Taubes in the first quarter of the 16th century, when the new modern fashion for spacious palaces was starting to replace the old medieval castle layouts. Purtse Castle has several times been burnt to the ground; it suffered heavily in the Livonian War and the Northern War. After WW II it remained in ruins for several decades. No wonder people called it a "ghosts' castle". When its restoration began in 1987, many of its original features could only be guessed. Now, the restored castle houses a concert hall and exhibition rooms.

About 1 km towards the sea from Purtse, on a small ridge called Purtse Hiiemägi, grows the **Memorial Park to all Victims of Evil**, planted on the initiative of the Alutaguse "Memento" group. The first memorial oak was planted in the park on 14 June 1991, when 50 years had passed since the large-scale deportations of Estonians carried out by the Soviets in June 1941. The President of Estonia and the representatives of the Government, the counties and many organisations have already planted their trees there. The Estonian Map of Pain was created on the grass in the park in 1993. Each county on this map is marked by a sign giving the number of people who were deported from this county. A small belfry was erected in the park.

Lüganuse Church, standing on a bank of the Purtse River, was probably built in the 14th century. At the beginning of the 15th century, the building was turned into a 2-aisle church and a round

Lüganuse Church, heavily damaged in WW II, was restored at the end of the 1980s.

The splendid Lüganuse monument to the War of Independence was restored from photos.

tower, a vaulted choir and sacristy were added. The church lost its vaulting either in the Livonian War or in the following Russian-Swedish War, but it escaped destruction in the Northern War (1700–1721). It is said that somebody had put a Russian sign on the door of the church, saying: "True Christians will not damage this house, which is consecrated to Christ". The church was again damaged by the war in 1941, when its entire interior was destroyed. This was restored ten years later, but the spire was restored to its original appearance only in 1987.

The well-known man of letters and linguist Otto Wilhelm Masing was the Lüganuse pastor in 1788–1795 (see Viru-Nigula, Lääne-Virumaa). South of the church stands the monument to the War of Independence, which has been opened three times – in 1924, 1944 and 1989. The design of the present monument was made by the sculptor Tõnu Mellik from photos of the original monument, which had been made by his father, also a sculptor, Voldemar Mellik. The monument features a soldier, a woman and a child standing on a 6 m tall pedestal.

The Erra River flows underground for about 1 km between Lüganuse and Erra. This area is the **Uhaku Karst Field Nature Reserve**. The river surfaces again at Purtse Kõrgekalda, but water flows in the riverbed only during spring floods. The path of the underground river is marked by a chain of sink holes, the two largest of which are called Suurhaud and Pikkhaud. Some of the sink holes are so deep that they reach down to the water level of the underground river and some water can always be found at the bottom.

Maidla Manor is located about 5 km south of Lüganuse. It was created by a rich Estonian family, who acquired an elegant new surname after the name of their estate – Maydell. The manor changed hands many times and it

It is believed that the founders of Maidla Manor, von Maydells, were Estonian.

was destroyed in the Northern War. The von Wrangells built a new Baroque manor ensemble on the site in the 1760s. Its mansion with dark walls and contrasting white doors and window frames and other decorative details bears the coats of arms of the von Wrangells and the von Breverns. The dwellings of the estate manager and the gardener are the only other buildings of the ensemble still standing. Maidla Manor is among the most important historical monuments of Ida-Virumaa; its mansion has been beautifully restored. Since 1925, it has housed a school.

One of the most remarkable cup stones in Estonia, **Aravainu cup stone** with 202 hollows, is located in Vainu, north of Erra. It is not known why the ancient Estonians made hollows in some stones, it may have been related with fertility magic. About 2000 cup stones are known in Estonia.

The town of **Kiviõli** got its present name in 1928. By that time it had become clear how valuable the yellowish rock layer under the soil was. The first oil-shale quarry was opened there in 1922; the first gas and oil factory was built in 1931. Resulting from the decades-long quarrying, large man-made heaps of solid waste stand in the northern part of the town.

Driving through Kiviõli, we notice a black granite cross and a memorial plate to commemorate all war victims. This monument was erected on 14 June 1994 to replace a monument from the Soviet time to the people killed in a concentration camp during the German occupation. During WW II, the Kiviõli concentration camp was a transit camp for Jews and also a prison camp for political prisoners put there by different ruling powers. Flowers are brought to the monument to commemorate also the people who were deported from this area by the Soviet regime.

A commemorative stone to the narrow-gauge Sonda-Mustvee railway line stands at the engine depot in **Sonda**, west of Kiviõli. This railway line was opened in 1926 and it worked until 1972. The Sonda railway station served both the narrow-gauge and the broad-gauge lines; the present building is already the fourth at the same site. A slightly older building, the old wooden toilet of the Sonda station, was taken to the Estonian Railway Museum in Lavassaare in 2001.

Narrow-gauge railways are in the past now. Memorial stones like this one in Sonda have been erected in many places along the former railway lines.

AROUND KOHTLA-JÄRVE AND JÕHVI

The town of **Kohtla-Järve** was born thanks to oil shale and the oil-shale industry. Several legends tell us about the discovery of oil shale. One goes that some shepherds had made a ring of yellowish grey stones around their fire, and were much surprised when the stones caught fire too.

Another says that a farmer had built a sauna of these stones and got the dreadful shock when the sauna burned to the ground. Although oil shale was mined there even earlier, it attracted serious attention only at the beginning of the 20th century. A joint stock company "The State Oil-Shale Industry" was created in 1922 to mine and process this valuable raw material. Villages grew by the quarries and mines; Kohtla-Järve became a town in 1946.

This monument to miners was erected in Kohtla-Järve in the Soviet era.

A museum was established in the former Kohtla mine.

Kohtla-Järve **Oil Shale Museum** is located in the building of the Kohtla-Järve Town Government. It introduces the history of oil-shale mining and processing in Estonia.

The **Kohtla Mining-Park Museum** is also connected with oil-shale mining; it is located in Kohtla-Nõmme, about 2 km south of Kohtla-Järve. The museum was established in the former Kohtla mine that was closed in 2001. The museum opened in the autumn of the same year; in addition to viewing a display about the history of the mine, visitors can see underground mine tunnels, ride an underground railway and try out miner's drills. Appointments should be made beforehand to visit the underground museum. 122-m high solid waste heaps at Kohtla-Järve are the highest artificial relief forms in the Baltic countries.

The tallest **waterfall** in Estonia is located in **Valaste**, it falls over the Clint edge from a height of 26 m.

The beauty of Valaste waterfall can be admired from a sightseeing platform and spiral steps leading to it.

However, this is not a natural waterfall, it gets its water from a large irrigation drain. A viewing platform with spiral steps has been built at the waterfall and visitors can also admire the different layers of limestone in the klint wall.

Kukruse Manor, located between Jõhvi and Kohtla-Järve, about 1 km towards Jõhvi from Kukruse, was bought by the von Toll family in 1762. They built a wonderful manor ensemble in the 19th century. Now the manor is owned by the county government and it is in an acute need of repair.

South of the manor, across the Tallinn-Narva Road, an alley of oaks leads to Kabelimets, the family cemetery of the von Tolls.

A monument in the shape of a sailing ship was erected there to the explorer of Polar areas, a graduate of the University of Tartu **Eduard von Toll** (1858–1902). He was lost when searching for the mythical Sannikov Land in the New Siberia Archipelago. His ship got stuck between the sheets of ice and he attempted to reach the Siberian coast by sledges with his crew. A bay on the coast of Taimyr Peninsula, a river on Taimyr Peninsula and mountains on Bennett Island and Novaya Zemlya have been named after von Toll.

The sturdy **Jõhvi St Michael's Church** is the biggest one-aisle church in Estonia. The stronghold church was probably built in the mid-14th century. The slender western tower and a fortification system with a moat were added to it before the Livonian War. The present spire was restored in 1984 on the basis of the original 19th-century one. The Baroque pulpit was made by Johann Valentin Rabe in 1728.

A museum was opened in the vaulted cellars under the altar of the church in 2002, displaying rare archaeological finds from the Jõhvi region. The display includes the oldest iron objects found in Estonia, excavated from Jäbara burial site, and sacrificial offerings from Alulinn.

There is also the model of the medieval fortified church of Jõhvi. The second room of the museum is designed as a medieval crypt chapel, where the healing relic was kept. A curious niche to the left of the chapel altar could have

Kukruse Manor acquired its present appearance at the time when it belonged to the von Tolls.

Polar explorer Eduard von Toll perished when searching for the legendary Sannikov Land.

Oru Palace has been destroyed, but its beautiful park still reminds us of its former splendour.

been the place for the relic. The most valuable object in the church is a silver chalice made in the 17th century.

Toila, located north-east of Jõhvi, was called the air spa in the early years of the Estonian Republic that emerged in 1918. In addition to the beautiful beach, visitors could also enjoy the healing effect of the ozone-rich air of pine forests.

The development of Toila into a popular summer resort started in the second half of the 19th century and was further accelerated by the opening of the rail service between Tallinn and St Petersburg in 1870. Estonian intellectuals, writers, and artists spent their summers in Toila.

The beautiful nature of the place attracted also Russian visitors. The building of summer houses was soon under way. Poets Marie Under and Henrik Visnapuu wrote many of their well-known works there.

The St Petersburg merchant Grigori Yelissejev bought Pühajõe Manor near Toila in 1897, and had a luxurious villa built on the right bank of the River Pühajõgi. The palazzo-type **Oru Palace** with numerous balconies, terraces and a tower, built by the architect Gavril Baranovski, had 57 rooms. Grapes, peaches and palms were grown in a horseshoe-shaped winter garden; nearby was a kennel for 70 dogs and a dovecote.

A large and abundant park was planted at the mouth of the Pühajõgi River. After WW I, the palace was abandoned. Estonian industrialists bought it in 1935 and gave it as a present to the President of the Estonian Republic for his summer residence. Oru Palace was destroyed in WW II, but the restoration of the park began at the end of the 1950s. Now the park has almost recovered its former splendour.

The first theatre in the Estonian countryside was built by a Toila farmer and public figure Abram Siimon (1844–1929). Siimon, who had founded a fire fighting association, a choir and a brass orchestra and two schools in Toila, staged more than 60 plays in the new theatre. The wooden theatre burned to the ground in 1901, and Siimon constructed a

than 5000 men, Estonians and Germans, are buried there.

The 70 m long **Koltsina inn** building, standing by Jõhvi-Mustvee Road in Rajaküla village, is one of the longest of its kind in Estonia; only that of Voltveti (Pärnumaa) is longer – 85 m. The stone building is privately owned and is in good order.

Kiikla Manor, south of Kohtla-Järve towards Mäetaguse, was probably created in the 17th century; starting from the early 18th century, it belonged to the von Rosens. Friedrich von Rosen established a small home theatre there in 1780, where he held the premiere of the play "The Hermit", written by his friend, a young playwright August von Kotzebue. One of the most prominent writers in Estonia at the time of the Enlightenment, **Friedrich Gustav Arvelius** (1753–1806), was a tutor at Kiikla Manor at the same time. Here, Arvelius wrote his most important Estonian-language works – A Nice Book of Tales and Morals I–II (Üks Kaunis Jutto- ja Õppetuse-Ramat I–II) (1782–1787) and Ramma Josep's Book of Help (Ramma Josepi Hädda – ja Abbi-Ramat) (1790).

A memorial stone marks the site of the first country theatre in Estonia.

Russian poet Igor Severyanin chose to live on the beautiful northern Estonian coast.

new, stone building which still exists. Siimon is buried at Toila cemetery. The site of the country theatre is marked by a commemorative stone in the yard of the house at 62, Pikk Street.

Near Siimon's theatre, at 58, Pikk Street, was the house of the Russian poet **Igor Severyanin** (1887–1941). Severyanin, who translated Estonian poetry into Russian and promoted it abroad, first came to Toila in 1912 and after that spent the next summers there. In 1918, he settled permanently in Toila and lived there for 18 years. The place where he lived is marked with a memorial stone.

In the seaward end of Toila there is the cemetery of soldiers who were killed in WW II. More

A peculiar literary character, Ramma Joosep, meant to be an example for the peasants, was created at Kiikla Manor.

The first part of the book of tales and morals, which praised the peasants' life, to whom "nobody can do any wrong, because manor lords help and protect them", was not overly popular among the peasants.

The same goes for the second part, telling a tale of a model peasant Ramma Joosep, who saved his manor lord from the robbers, but was himself left a cripple. When his lord offered him freedom from serfdom for his deed, he refused this and preferred to continue his life of a serf. He only asked to be allowed to preach the Christian word on Sundays. No wonder that such an example did not impress the peasants who rather thought the character to be a fool.

Contrary to that, The Book of Help offered plenty of useful advice, for example, how to make sure a person is only unconscious, not dead, or how to help people who have been poisoned by carbon monoxide or suffered frostbite. The extremely large number of copies – 10,000 – were all distributed among the peasants free of charge.

Now, Kiikla Manor belongs to a non-profit organisation "An Open Gate", who will open a children's home there.

In 1736, the notorious Livonian Land Magistrate Otto Fabian von Rosen bought **Mäetaguse Manor**, located south of Jõhvi and 3 km west of the Jõhvi-Mustvee Road. In 1739, he signed the memorial compiled by the Livonian Land Magistrates, also called the Rosen Declaration, proclaiming that Estonian peasants were serfs from that moment on and they became the property of estate owners. Everything the peasants had also became the property of the estate owners, who could tax them any way they pleased.

Beating was an obvious means of punishment, but the killing of peasants was inadvisable. This document perpetuated serfdom in Estonia for less than 100 years. The peasants' laws, adopted in Estonia in 1816 and in Livonia in 1819, ended serfdom. The peasants still had to wait for almost another generation, until 1849 and 1856, respectively, for the permission to buy farms.

The Classicist mansion of Mäetaguse Manor, which was built at the end of the 18th century and later repeatedly rebuilt, is in a very good condition. Its ground floor houses the local community government; a concert hall is on the first floor. The painted ceilings, a wooden staircase and the oaken doors of the mansion are remarkably beautiful. To visit the mansion, an appointment has to be made with the Mäetaguse community government. In the manor park grows the tallest ash tree in Estonia, reaching a height of more than 30 m. A wooden chapel can be seen at the cemetery north-east of Mäetaguse. A monument to the Baltic Battalion – the unit of Baltic-Germans who participated in the War of Independence – was opened at the cemetery in 1936, and it miraculously stood there, unvandalised, for the whole Soviet time.

AROUND SILLAMÄE

Sillamäe, located on the seashore, was a favoured summer resort for the St Petersburg intellectuals already at the end of the 19th century. For example, the outstanding Russian physiologist Ivan Pavlov (1849–1936), the discoverer of conditioned reflexes and the winner of Nobel Prize in

1904, spent 25 summers there.

Oil-shale processing was started in Sillamäe at the beginning of the 20th century. After WWII the Soviets founded a uranium refinery, which was a part of the Soviet war industry. The workers were brought from Russia, the town was closed to outsiders and everything was kept in deep secret. In 1970, the plant started processing rare-earth metals; now it is working under the name of AS Silmet.

Sillamäe town museum-exhibition hall (17 a, Kajaka Street) gives an overview of the history of Vaivara parish and community and Sillamäe town, and exhibits a unique collection of rocks.

The area surrounding **Vaivara Sinimäed (Blue Hills)**, southeast of Sillamäe, has been the site of large battles over many centuries. Bloody battles were fought in these hills that blocked the road to Tallinn in the Northern War and in the War of Independence. The most serious wounds were dealt to the region in the battles of 1944.

Narva fell to the Red Army on 26 July 1944, and after that the main war activities moved over to Sinimäed, to the Tannenberg Line, built by the Germans in 1943. Despite furious attacks, the Russians managed to take these positions only on 18 September.

A memorial wall was erected to commemorate the Estonians and Norwegians who fought with the German troops, and an Estonian map was shaped by flowers at the old Sillamäe cemetery.

The hardest ever battles in Estonian history were fought in the three hills of Sinimäed. The defence line was held, together with Germans, also by Danes, Norwegians and Dutchmen and 15.000 Estonians, who bore the blue-black-and-white emblems on their uniforms. These units were vastly outnumbered by the manpower and arms of the Red Army. The men of the Estonian Rifle Corps were fighting there among the Soviet troops. Again, Estonians had to fight each other at the front line, brother against brother.

War historians call the Sinimäed battle a miracle. Both sides lost more than 10.000 men; many of them were never buried. Naturally, the Estonians hoped that by fighting at Sinimäed they would be able to keep their homeland free and independent; wishful tales were told that the English

The steps descending towards the sea, built when Stalin was still alive, are one of the sights in Sillamäe.

Tall memorial crosses were placed at the battlefield at Sinimäed.

would come to help them.

Unfortunately, everything was the other way round. The great powers had already decided upon the fate of Estonia behind the backs of the desperately fighting men. On 18 September, the German army command ordered the retreat, since the Red Army was rapidly advancing from the south and there was a danger of getting encircled. The whole area was full of artillery fire, all farms were destroyed and only broken tree trunks were standing in the woods. The Estonian Legion had to fight the Estonian Rifle Corps again in three days at Porkuni (see Porkuni battle ground, Lääne-Virumaa).

A hiking path runs along the old battle grounds, taking visitors over all three hills – Tornimägi (the western hill), Põrguhauamägi or Grenaderimägi (centre hill) and Pargimägi or Lastekodumägi (the eastern hill). A tall metal cross has been erected on Põrguhauamägi and an information board stands nearby. Traces of war – bomb craters and trenches – can even now be seen all over the area, which is a kind of an open-air museum. A tour guide can be engaged and detailed maps of the area can be acquired at the Vaivara museum at 2 Pargi Street, Sinimäe. In recent years, Vaivara community has also become famous for its new depository for dangerous waste.

A yearly war game, the **Utria** Landing, is enacted in Utria, north of Sinimäed. This event commemorates the successful landing of Estonian marines and Finnish volunteers on the Utria coast on 17 January 1919; these units were able to free Narva from the enemy in the War of Independence. A modest monument to this landing stands in Utria.

NARVA AND NARVA-JÕESUU

The summer resort of Narva-Jõesuu is located north-east of Narva. The golden beaches, pine forests and parks attracted rich visitors at the end of the 19th century, especially after the opening of the rail service. The old fishermen's village called Hungerburg developed into a much-loved

A curiosity from the Soviet era by the Narva River.

summer resort, the so-called Nordic Riviera, for the cream of St Petersburg and Moscow society. Beautiful villas, pensions and places of entertainment were built.

Most beautiful among them were the **Villa Capriccio** with its white columns and portico, built in 1874, and the wooden building of Kuursaal, decorated with sawn-out ornaments, constructed in 1882. A large part of Narva-Jõesuu, including the above-mentioned buildings, was destroyed in WWII. One wing of the Kuursaal was restored to house a club. The remaining old wooden villas now stand side by side with the large blocks of sanatoria, built in the Soviet time, many of which are already falling to pieces.

An exhibition about Narva-Jõesuu history can be seen in the Museum of Local Lore at 38, Nurme Street.

Besides the Narva-Jõesuu – Narva Road, about 4 km from Narva-Jõesuu, stands the only preserved **tank-monument** in Estonia, marking the Soviet offensive on the Narva front in 1944. In the Soviet era, such monuments were found everywhere all over the Soviet Union. In Estonia, some other tanks stood in Valga

The Town Hall is one of the few pre-war buildings in the formerly beautiful town of Narva.

and near Pärnu, on the bank of the Reiu River.

The town of **Narva** on the eastern border of Estonia emerged and developed as a fortified town. Over many centuries, Narva had to resist attacks from the east and often suffered much damage. In 1944, the whole historical centre of Narva was destroyed.

Narva finally lost its former appearance in the post-war years, when all damaged houses were torn down and Soviet-style dwelling blocks were erected in their place. Only the Town Hall (built at the end of the 17th cen-

Two castles stand face to face across the Narva River; for many people they are symbolising the two worlds – the West and the East.

tury) and a few dwelling houses in Koidula Street were restored. The present-day centre of the town is located west of the historical centre.

The Kreenholm Manufacture has been working in the town district with the same name, south of the railway, since 1857. Its buildings were damaged in the war and they were rebuilt by 1962. Eduard Vilde describes the hard life of the workers of the Kreenholm spinning factory in his grim novel The Iron Hands (Raudsed käed).

The Baltic and Estonian Power Stations and the Narva oil shale quarry are located in the southeastern part of the town, near the Narva Reservoir. The Narva Reservoir, created in 1956, is the third largest body of water in Estonia.

Hermann Castle was built on the western bank of the Narva River in the 13th century. In the mid-14th century, when the king of Denmark sold Northern Estonia to the Livonian Order, the old castle was rebuilt into a powerful convent, which was surrounded by fortifications. An additional belt of bastions was built around the castle in the 17th century, under the Swedish rule; the bastions have withstood the turmoil of history and they can still be seen.

A fierce battle was fought at Narva between Swedes and Russians in 1700. The Russians outnumbered the Swedes threefold, but the Swedish King Charles XII was a competent army commander and managed to defeat his enemy. This battle is commemorated by the so-called **Swedish lion**, standing on a tall pedestal in Narva. In 1704, the tables were turned and the Russians took Narva by storm.

Narva Castle was damaged in WWII, too; restoration of the castle started in the 1950s. In 1986, the Narva Museum moved into the restored western and southern wings of the castle. Three rooms with historical interiors are open to visitors, who can also climb the Pikk Hermann tower of the castle.

In 1991, a branch of the Narva Museum was opened in the former army storage in 21, Vestervalli Street. This is an art gallery exhibiting Western European and

A bronze lion reminds us of the heroic deeds of King Charles XII.

Narva's Alexander Church used to be the largest church in Estonia, built to accommodate all of the 5000 workers of the Kreenholm factory. Now the church is being restored and it is used as a concert hall.

Russian works of art from the 18th and 19th centuries and the works of Estonian and Narva artists. The main part of the art collection was bequeathed to the town by a philanthropic Narva merchant S. A. Lavretsov in 1902.

IISAKU, TUDULINNA AND AVINURME

Tärivere hill, standing northwest of Iisaku, is the highest hill in Alutaguse, reaching 94 m above sea level. The sightseeing tower on the hill offers views over the large bogs and deep forests of Alutaguse; in good weather, one can even see the large man-made semi-coke heaps on the horizon.

Robert Theodor Hansen (1849–1912), the local school teacher and founder of the Iisaku choir and an amateur composer, is buried at Iisaku cemetery. Round crosses can be seen on the graves of the Peep family. The best-known member of the family, the actor **Helend Peep** (1910), was born in Vaikla village, south-east of Iisaku. He is an opera singer and a film and drama actor.

A museum was opened in Iisaku (58, Tartu Road) in 1983. The history of Ida-Virumaa, old farm tools and handicraft, the school life of the early 20th century, the history of local fire fighters and Alutaguse nature are displayed in seven rooms. A special room has been furnished as an old-time teacher's living room.

The largest **barrow complex** in Estonia can be found in **Jõuga village**. Less than a half of the 260 mounds have been studied so far. The burial site was used by the Votians, a small Finno-Ugric tribe, who buried their dead there from the mid-12th century until the first half of the 16th century.

Bronze and silver jewellery have been found among the grave-goods, and even such ornaments that were unknown to Estonian women. A reconstruction of one barrow is displayed at the Iisaku museum.

The construction of the **Tudulinna power station** was started on the Rannapungerja River in 1947, almost at the same time with the restoration of the Leevaku power station in Põlvamaa. The Tudulinna power station was activated three years later, but it was stopped after the renovation done in 1959. The power station was again activated in 1999.

Two Lutheran churches have for many years stood side by side in **Tudulinna**, near the road from Tallinn. The older one, built in the 18th century, is in ruins, but the newer one, built in 1939 as a

A sightseeing tower stands on Tärivere hill, the highest hill in Alutaguse.

result of a quarrel among the congregation, is still used. The quarrel broke out in 1923, when a new Pastor, Voldemar Kuljus, came to serve the Tudulinna congregation. He was a well educated man and a talented speaker; his sermons touched upon wider spheres of life than merely the Scriptures; he told his congregation about literature and scientific achievements. Unfortunately, the more conservative members of the congregation did not like his sermons and the congregation split in 1929.

The conservative part of the congregation met in the prayer house of the local Moravian Church and called themselves the Peace Congregation. They wanted to use the church, which the other part of the congregation did not allow.

Thus a new church was built in 1939. A peculiar feature of the church is that its tower stands at the eastern wall of the building, against the tradition of placing it at the western wall. The two congregations did not manage to end their quarrel before the war. The valuable items in **Tudulinna Church** include glazed Dutch tiles from the 18th century, which are remarkable works of art. The

The Tudulinna power station is working again.

The new Tudulinna Church was built in 1939, when the local congregation had split up.

The old church was used as a kolkhoz grain dryer.

Unique forged crosses can be seen at Tudulinna cemetery.

dilapidating old church was made a grain dryer in the Soviet time.

The only "volcano" in Estonia is also located in Tudulinna. The hill-fort with a large hollow in the middle was drawn on the map, made in the 18th century by the famous cartographer Ludwig August Mellin (1754–1835) (born at Tuhala Manor), as an extinguished volcano. The mistake was corrected in the later maps. Mellin's main work is The Atlas of Livonia (Liivimaa atlas), completed in 1810, which contained 7100 place names.

Avinurme, located in the southwestern nook of Ida-Virumaa, in the Alutaguse forests, has for a long time been known for its woodwork. Since the suitable land for fields was scarce, but forests were large, the men of Avinurme earned money with woodwork. The skills were taught in the families and in the course of time it turned out that people in certain areas made certain kinds of wooden artefacts.

Examples of the local woodwork can be seen in the museum of local lore (6, Võidu Street), displaying a large range of tableware from the 19th century and other household objects.

Alexandr Pushkin's friend Wilhelm Küchelbecker spent his youth in Avinurme.

Avinurme Historicist Church was designed by the Riga architect Wilhelm von Stryk and built in 1909. The stone building is decorated with brick fringes around the windows and on the corners of the building.

The narrow-gauge railway passed through Avinurme in 1916–1972. A 100 m length of this railway was restored to commemorate the 75th anniversary of the line in 1991. A newly painted engine and two carriages are displayed on the rails.

The Russian writer and Decembrist revolutionary Wilhelm Küchelbecker (1797–1846) spent his youth in Avinurme Manor. He was one of the noblemen who organised an unsuccessful uprising in 1825 against Tsar Nicholas I.

The place where he lived is marked with a commemorative stone in the former manor park. Küchelbecker, who was a friend of the famous Russian poet Aleksandr Pushkin, wrote a story titled Ado, based on the ancient fighting for freedom of the Estonians, and set it near Avinurme.

One of the first journalists in the Baltic countries to voice an

100 m of the old railway was restored in Avinurme.

opinion against serfdom, **Johann Georg Eisen** (also Eisen von Schwarzenberg) (1717–1779) worked as a tutor at Avinurme Manor for 5 years. In addition to writing articles that condemned serfdom, Eisen, who also worked as the Pastor in Torma in 1745–1775, was interested in agriculture and experimented with the drying of vegetables in order to store them, and with the making of potato starch.

The writer and linguist **Otto Wilhelm Masing** (1763–1832) was born in Lohusuu village. It is not known in which house he was born, so a commemorative plaque has been placed on the wall of Lohusuu schoolhouse. A commemorative stone for this famous linguist is also standing in Äksi village, Jõgevamaa, where he was the Pastor during the last years of his life and a memorial plaque is on the wall of the parsonage in Viru-Nigula, Lääne-Virumaa.

Masing was a progressive man who sought more rights for the Estonian language and enriched it by applying a new letter – "õ". He wrote school textbooks and, for some time, edited the Estonian-language newspaper Country People's Weekly (Marahwa Näddalaleht) (see Viru-Nigula, Lääne-Virumaa).

AROUND KUREMÄE AND VASKNARVA

According to a legend, the grave of the mythical hero Kalevipoeg is located on **Kuremäe drumlin**, north-east of Iisaku. Another legend tells us that Kalevipoeg's legs, which were chopped off by the enemy when the hero was sleeping, were buried under the Kuremäe sacred oak. Running on his knees, Kalevipoeg had pursued his enemy up to Kivinõmme, where he had dropped down dead. He was buried at the same place. In this case, his death was not caused by his sword, which had been condemned and buried in the bottom of the Kääpa River.

Five onion cupolas adorn the roof of the Cathedral in Kuremäe Convent.

The lighting of candles is an inseparable part of Orthodox rituals.

Still another legend goes that a sacred grove of the ancient Estonians had been growing on Kuremäe hill. A large oak tree with the girth of 4.3 m, called Sacred Tree, is still standing on the hill. The tree is surrounded by a fence to prevent its visitors, craving for pieces of the 'sacred bark', from scratching it entirely off the tree. There is also a legend about the appearance of the Virgin Mary; when the site of the appearance was searched later, an icon, adorned with silver and pearls, was found on the hill.

The **Kuremäe Convent**, or rather, the Pühtitsa Dormition Convent, was founded by the Governor of Estonia, Prince Sergei Shakhovskoy, at the end of the 19th century. The general plan of the convent and the buildings in the tradition of early Russian church architecture were designed by the Professor of the St Petersburg Academy of Arts, Mikhail Preobrazhensky. The wooden dwelling of the nuns, a winter church and refectory and a hospital were built in 1892.

The convent is surrounded with a thick granite wall; a rectangular entrance gate – the Sacred Gate – has a belfry. The main Cathedral of the convent, that of the Dormition, was rebuilt from a Lutheran Church, the building of which had started in 1884, but was not completed because of the wave of Russification that swept over the country.

At the beginning of the 20th century, the cathedral was rebuilt and it acquired five cupolas; it has three altars and a rich iconostasis, carved of pine wood. The most sacred relic of the church is the icon "Dormition", depicting the Mother of God on her death bed, and Jesus, surrounded by angels and apostles, who is holding the soul of his mother in his hands.

The Convent acquired an official status in 1892 and it is subordinated to the Patriarch of Moscow and All Russia Alexy II. More than 170 nuns are living in the Convent now. Large numbers of the faithful arrive at the Convent each year on 15 August, when the holiest day for the Convent is celebrated, to participate in the walk led by the cross and drink the water from the holy spring.

Another legend connects these areas with Kalevipoeg. The name of Dobrina village, located a few kilometres off from Kivinõmme towards Vasknarva, has been related with a Russian mythical hero Dobrynya Nikitich. Kalevipoeg is said to have fought with him on the fields near the village. Local inhabitants of Russian origin have already for a long time called the wood around Kalevipoeg's grave the Dobrynya Wood.

Moving on along the Narva River away from the northern coast of Lake Peipsi, we reach **Gorodenka** village that got its name (gorodenka - a small town in Russian) from a glass factory that worked there in the 18th century. A small town-like village grew around the factory to house its workers.

A museum room has been organised in the Gorodenka Punamäe border guard station, exhibiting a collection of all kinds of WWII weapons and war machinery that have been found in the forests by the Narva River and restored to working order. Igor Sedunov has created this collection on his own initiative and without any outside help.

When walking in these forests on the bank of the Narva River, we can see abandoned military equipment everywhere. The river bank is edged with trenches and bunkers, rusting machinery and empty shells. The trees growing in these forests are full of shell splinters and they cannot be used in the wood industry.

Vasknarva village, located at the starting point of the Narva River on the northern coast of Lake Peipsi, is an important local fishing centre. A border guard station is located in Vasknarva as well.

The border castle, built here in 1349 by the Livonian Order, was meant to keep an eye on the important waterway of the Narva River. Unfortunately, the Russians destroyed the castle soon afterwards. It was rebuilt and fortified with a surrounding wall and powerful round towers with splits for artillery in the 15th century.

Vasknarva border castle guarded the Narva River until it was destroyed in the Livonian War.

Vasknarva Castle was destroyed again, probably in the Livonian War, and subsequently was not used or restored.

Vasknarva got its name from the one-time German name of the Castle – Neuschloss, meaning a new castle (vastne linnus) in Estonian. Russians called the place Syrenets. Leaving aside the Castle, no other building has remained in the village from the pre-war time.

JÕGEVAMAA

JÕGEVAMAA

Typical features of Jõgevamaa are the drumlins that stretch from north-west to south-east. Many lakes seem to do the same, and also some of the main roads. The drumlins were shaped by the departing glacier that left behind these gravel moraines at the end of the Ice Age.

The 13th century hill-forts of Jõgevamaa witnessed fierce battles with the invaders. The Teutonic Order built two powerful strongholds - Laiuse and Põltsamaa.

In the 16th century Põltsamaa became capital of the Livonian kingdom and headquarters of Duke Magnus, made king by the Russian Tsar Ivan the Terrible (1530–1584). The peculiar kingdom lasted no more than seven years and expired together with the Russians' plans to seize the Estonian territory. Jõgevamaa was ruled by the Poles and the Swedes, followed again by the Russians. A longer period of peace arrived only after the Great Northern War which ended in 1721.

Laiuse stronghold sheltered one of the most famous crowned heads in the Nordic countries - the militant Carl XII (1682–1718) who wintered there.

Another typical feature of Jõgevamaa is the coastal area of Lake Peipsi populated by the Old Believers, Russians who fled to Estonia because of religious persecution. The first Russian Old Believers appeared in Estonia on the coast of Lake Peipsi near Mustvee in the late 17th century. Today there are about 15,000 members in 11 congregations of Old Believers in Estonia.

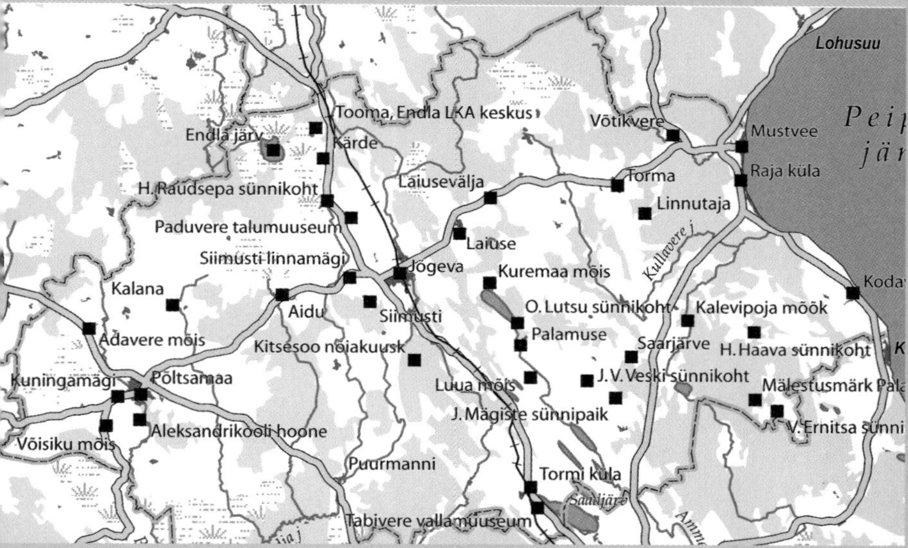
Lohusuu
Tooma, Endla LKA keskus
Võtikvere
Mustvee
Endla järv
Kärde
Raja küla
Torma
H. Raudsepa sünnikoht
Läiusevälja
Linnutaja
Paduvere talumuuseum
Laiuse
Kullavere j
Siimusti linnamägi
Jõgeva
Kuremaa mõis
Kalana
Aidu
Siimusti
O. Lutsu sünnikoht
Kalevipoja mõõk
Adavere mõis
Palamuse
Kitsesoo nõiakuusk
Saarjärve
H. Haava sünnikoht
Kuningamägi
Põltsamaa
Luua mõis
J. V. Veski sünnikoht
J. Mägiste sünnipaik
Aleksandrikooli hoone
Võisiku mõis
Puurmanni
Tormi küla
Saadjärv
Tabivere vallamuuseum

AROUND VÄGEVA AND VAIMASTVERE

About 5 km from Vägeva towards Jõgeva the signpost points to the centre of the **Endla Nature Reserve** at Tooma. The centre is located in the former schoolhouse that also has a small museum introducing the history of the Reserve. The Endla mire expanse has been researched since 1910 when a centre of paludological (bog science) research was established at Tooma.

The bog system and springs emanating from the edge of the Pandivere Upland are today under protection, although in the past local people were doing the opposite – trying to turn the bogs into arable land or plant forests.

The **wooden walkway** in the **Männikjärve bog** was the first of its kind. There are now dozens of walkways in Estonian bogs. A nature study path takes the visitor from Männikjärve Lake to Endla Lake. Despite its much reduced size due to drainage, Endla is nevertheless the biggest bog lake in stonia. It is famous for its bird population.

Männikjärve bog is the best known in Endla mire expanse.

Kärde Peace House was probably built by the local manor lord.

The former Kärde manor centre is primarily famous for its **Kärde Peace House** where on 1 July 1661, the Russians and the Swedes reputedly signed a peace treaty that ended the war (1656–1658) between them. The little house was probably built later by a local manor lord to mark the place where the treaty was signed – it is certainly difficult to imagine such an important event taking place in a hut.

On Kärde Hill at the other side of the Rakvere-Jõgeva Road stands a memorial stone known as **Preilikivi (Maiden's Stone)**. This marks the grave of Margarethe Victoria, daughter of the last owner of the manor, Viktor von Stackelberg. The maiden drowned herself in 1903 because of unrequited love. The stone bears the coat of arms of the Stackelbergs and an alley of silver firs.

In fine weather, Kärde Hill offers a splendid view of the surrounding area.

The playwright **Hugo Raudsepp** (1883–1952) was born in the family of a gardener of the manor. During the Estonian independence period in the 1920s and 1930s Raudsepp's plays achieved huge popularity. He also wrote short stories, novels and memoirs and

Preilikivi commemorates the unfortunate daughter of von Stackelberg.

The memorial stone in front of the new schoolhouse commemorates the popular playwright Hugo Raudsepp.

The house where Betti Alver was born.

was a prolific theatre critic. His life ended in a Siberian prison camp.

A monument commemorates Hugo Raudsepp in the manor park. The mansion burnt down and a schoolhouse was built in its place.

A private **Farm Museum** operates in **Paduvere**, a few km from Vaimastvere towards Jõgeva. The displays describe the life of rural people in the 18th and 19th centuries. In addition to the usual exhibits, the museum has a collection of oak sculptures of famous people of the area.

JÕGEVA AND THE SURROUNDING AREA

Jõgeva got its name from Pedja river ('jõgi' means 'river') when the first settlement was located by the river. It began developing faster after the Tapa-Tartu railway line was completed in 1876. The railway station was established a few km south from the former manor house, and plots of land were sold nearby.

One of Estonia's most prominent poets, Elisabet Lepik, better known as **Betti Alver** (1906–1989), was born in a house near the station. Her father worked on the railway. Alver studied Estonian language and literature at Tartu University and devoted her life to literary pursuits. She has written short stories as well and translated world classics, although she is loved in this country mostly for her poetry.

Betti Alver married Heiti Talvik (1904–1947), also an excellent poet who was declared an enemy of the state and deported to a Siberian prison camp after WW II where he died.

Alo Mattiisen (1961–1996), a well-known and popular composer, was also born in Jõgeva. He became famous during the perestroika period, or the time of the Singing Revolution in Estonia in 1988–1989. He wrote five patriotic songs that were much needed at the time and are still often sung today.

It is planned to establish a museum to both Betti Alver and Alo Mattiisen in Alver's birthplace. At present the house has a memorial plaque to the poet.

The Jõgeva Plant Breeding Institute is located in the former Jõgeva manor, a few km north of the town on the riverbank. It was founded in 1920 by **Mihkel Pill** (1884–1951) who acted as director until his death. He was fondly known as 'the father of Estonian white bread'. Pill was keenly interested in science and was one of the first to make use of the achievement in genetics. Over 80 years now, the main commitment of the Jõgeva plant breeders is the development of new varieties of winter rye, winter and spring wheat, barley, oats, field pea, potatoes, vegetables, forage grasses and legumes. Around 270 new varieties have been bred of which one fourth is constantly used.

Another great man in our plant breeding, **Julius Aamisepp** (1883–1950) also lived and worked in Jõgeva. He focused his efforts on potato, and was also involved in breeding new varieties of peas, black currents, mangelwurzel and turnip. He gathered the world's largest potato collection that contained 1500 varieties.

Near **Aidu**, by the Jõgeva-Põltsamaa Road northwards stands the memorial to battles fought in late 1918 and early 1919 in the **War of Independence**. Estonian

Plant breeding started in Jõgeva in 1920. The greatest achievements in this field belong to Mihkel Pill and Julius Aamisepp.

The Estonian defence line halted the onslaught of the Red troops at Aidu.

Ceramics have been produced at Siimusti over one hundred years.

Jaan Poska's house bears a commemorative plaque to the great statesman.

defence lines were attacked by the Red Army who was successfully thrown back.

The monument was destroyed by communists but restored in 1989.

The small town of **Siimusti** about 5 km south-west of Jõgeva is known as the centre of clay industry. For the past 120 years, people have been producing ceramics there. The local enterprising merchant **Joosep Tiiman** (1857–1934) was the first to start the pottery business in 1886 and became successful very quickly.

The need for his products continued through WW I and the independent Estonia of the 1920s and 1930s. During the Soviet era, the factory worked in three shifts in order to meet the demand. The business is still going well.

A museum of Estonian ceramics opened in Siimusti in 1997.

An ancient fort-hill is located north-west of Siimusti in Viruvere.

AROUND LAIUSE AND TORMA

In Laiusevälja by the Jõgeva-Mustvee Road is the birthplace of the prominent Estonian statesman

Jaan Poska (1866–1920).
Jaan Poska was born in the family of a clergyman and schoolteacher. He was initially educated at a theological seminary, but later he chose legal profession and studied at Tartu University. He worked in his chosen field in Tallinn and took an interest in politics.

During WW I he was mayor of Tallinn. After the war he was convinced that Estonia should make use of the turbulent times in Russia and strive for independence. Poska was briefly the foreign minister, then deputy prime minister. Largely thanks to his diplomatic skills the Tartu Peace Treaty was signed with Russia on 2 February 1920.

A commemorative plaque now marks the house where he was born.

Historians do not agree as for the age of the **Laiuse Order Castle** at Laiusevälja. Opinions suggest any time from the 13th to 15th century. The castle escaped the Livonian War with relatively little damage.

After the Teutonic Order, the castle belonged to the Russians, the Poles and then the Swedes. During the Northern War, Swedish

Carl XII spent a winter at Laiuse and planted a lime tree before he left in the spring.

The cellars of Laiuse castle are reputedly full of gold and silver.

King Carl XII spent the winter of 1700/1701 at Laiuse, taking a rest from warfare. Next year the castle was destroyed in battle.

Today it is possible to walk among the conserved ruins, admire the high walls and the foundation of a corner tower. Archaeological excavations have revealed arrowheads, stone and iron cannonballs, bullets, brooches, coins, clay pipes, stove tiles and other objects.

The so-called **Carl XII lime tree** grows in the Laiuse churchyard. Unlike many trees all around Estonia that were allegedly planted by Swedish crowned heads, this one probably was, as the age exactly corresponds to the time when he was there.

The 19th century **Kuremaa Manor** stands north-east from Laiuse in the northern tip of Kuremaa lake. In 1934 another storey was added to the mansion. Today it houses an agricultural school and a small museum. The manor was always run efficiently and turned a profit. Its products were sold in St Petersburg.
The park surrounding the main building is rich in various plants.

Kuremaa Manor was a progressive enterprise during the tsarist times.

Torma is located by the Jõgeva-Mustvee Road. A century and a half ago the important Riga-St Petersburg Road passed through here. Since 1844 until his death, **Adam Jakobson** (1817–1857) worked here as a schoolteacher and clergyman. He is mostly known for his enterprising sons Eduard Magnus, an artist and book illustrator, and Carl Robert, a radi-

Monument to Carl Robert Jakobson who was born here.

cal fighter against the privileges of the Baltic German aristocracy, a founding member of the Estonian Learned Society and editor of the newspaper Sakala (see also Pärnumaa).

The great Estonian linguist **Paul Ariste** (1905–1990) was born in Rääbise in Torma parish. Professor Ariste developed the research of Finno-Ugric languages at Tartu University.

Only the park and ruins remain of Rahuoru or **Friedenthal** estate by

G. J. Schulttz-Bertram was a censor and was interested in Estonian folk poetry.

the road from Torma towards Tartu. This place is connected with **Georg Julius Schultz-Bertram** (1808–1875), a prominent figure of the National Awakening period. Between 1862 and 1864 he ran an eye hospital at Friedenthal. From 1867, Schultz-Bertram had the important job of the censor of the Estonian-language literature. He was interested in folk poetry, collected it himself and supported the publication of Estonian national epic Kalevipoeg (Kalev's Son). He occasionally picked up the pen himself, writing poems and several books about the history of the surrounding areas. A large stone in the park commemorates the enterprising Baltic German.

AROUND MUSTVEE

The town of **Mustvee** lies at the estuary of Mustvee river and has, besides the Estonian name, also one in Russian – Chorny (Black). About half the population speaks Russian and has lived there for at least 5–6 generations.

In the mid-17th century Patriarch Nikon started reforming the Orthodox church in Russia, causing bitter friction between the innovators and the traditionalists. The first prevailed, and the latter, known as Old Believers, fled to the edges of the Empire. The first refugees arrived in Estonia in the early 18th century, settling mostly on the shores of Lake Peipsi, around Kallaste, Kolkja-Varnja, Piirissaare and Mustvee-Raja. They have abandoned all religious sacraments except baptism and confession and always elect the next priest from among the community. There are about 10,000 Old Believers living in Estonia at present.

Mustvee town stretches along the low banks of the lake, with most people engaged in fishing and vegetable growing. There are two Orthodox churches, one Lutheran church and two secondary schools. In the town centre the visitor can get an overview of the Old Believers in a small museum.

The street names in small Estonian towns often show little variety – Aia (garden), Jõe (river), Kivi (stone) and Pargi (park) crop up everywhere. A welcome change in this respect occurs in Mustvee. A nice small street is called Benito Agirre. He was a pilot in the Red Army who had a crash landing on the ice of Lake Peipsi in 1944.

He started towards the shore but was caught in the fire as local men had noticed him. Heavily wounded, he had finally put a bullet through his own head. Later it turned out that the unfortunate Benito was Basque whose correct name was Inazio Agirregoikoa Benito. It is most unlikely, however, that the people of Mustvee are going to correct the street name to which they are already used.

Travelling south from Mustvee we see rows of wooden houses by the road, each with a corner for the icon, that form the villages of the Old Believers. South of Mustvee in Raja village stands a church of the Old Believers with unique icons that can be viewed during the Sunday morning service. Their best known icon painter, **Pimen Sofronov** (1898–1973) comes from Tiheda village near Raja. He studied his craft locally, but later lived and worked in many parts of Europe. During WW II he stayed in the Vatican and left for the USA after the war.

The villages by Lake Peipsi consist of one street, lined with houses.

Mustvee Museum is located near the Orthodox Church

The Basque Benito Agirre was a pilot of the Red Army.

A large bench that would suit the hero of the national epic, Kalevipoeg.

A charming belfry adorns the church in Raja village.

Jürissaare Farm Museum is located in Võtikvere by the road towards Avinurme (off the Mustvee-Jõgeva Road). It is a converted old barn, displaying an old living rooms and household items.

AROUND SAARE AND PALA

Turning east from the Saareküla bus stop on the Tartu-Jõhvi Road we come to Kääpa river with a peculiar monument to the sword of Kalevipoeg, the hero of our national epic. Standing on the bridge, one can see a massive hilt of a concrete sword.

According to a legend, this was the place where our hero perished. Evil sorcerers stole his sword and Kalevipoeg uttered a curse, but unfortunately got his

The former Saare schoolhouse today accommodates a museum about Kalevipoeg and local history.

words slightly mixed up. He wanted to make the sword cut off the legs of whoever was carrying it at the time, but instead he told the sword to cut off the legs of who had it before. The sorcerers dropped the sword in Kääpa river where Kalevipoeg, in pursuit, stumbled upon it. The cursed weapon obeyed the order and cut

A plaque in the birthplace of poet Anna Haava shows the way of life 150 years ago.

off the hero's legs, thus inflicting him a mortal wound.

A museum dedicated to Kalevipoeg was opened in the former Saare schoolhouse. Seven rooms give a thorough overview of the national epic and its compiler, Friedrich Reinhold Kreutzwald. Another display tells about the local lore.

Between Saare and Pala is the village of Haavakivi, birthplace of one of the most significant lyrical poets **Anna Haava** (1864–1957). Her real name was Anna Rosalie Haavakivi. She was also a prolific translator, especially of Goethe, Schiller and Shakespeare.
A stone and a plaque in her memory now stand near the house where she was born.

The linguist and famous figure in Estonian temperance movement **Villem Ernits** (1891–1982) was born near Nõva south of Pala. With short intervals, he worked at the Tartu University for nearly 50 years.

Russians and Votians (a small nation who nowadays number only a few dozen) arrived in **Kodavere** area by Lake Peipsi in the 12th–13th centuries, and therefore the locally spoken language contains various peculiari-

Kodavere Church is remarkable for its blunt tower.

The memorial stone to the perished Pala children bears the writing: "Our unlived lives must exist somewhere."

ties. **Kodavere Church** is remarkable for its low blunt tower with a rooster perched on top. The early classicist church was completed in 1777. Its most valuable treasures include the altar painting and the 18-register organ of German origin.

The 4.41 m tall monument to those killed in the War of Independence (1918–1920) was set up in Kodavere cemetery on 31 August 1924. The black granite stone was transported here from the shore of Lake Peipsi 7 km away. The stone weighed 8 tonnes and it took 17 horses 4 days to get it to Kodavere.

By the Nõva-Sõõru Road at Vea village stands a monument to the tragic event in 1996 when eight Pala schoolchildren were killed when their bus collided with a lorry.

PALAMUSE
AND THE SURROUNDING AREA

Järvepera village on the south bank of Kuremaa lake was the birthplace of **Oskar Luts** (1887–1953), certainly one of the most popular Estonian writers of all time. A large boulder with a plaque marks his house. A museum (at Köstri allee 3) was opened in 1987 in the former parish school of Palamuse where Luts studied. This is the most famous schoolhouse in Estonia as every-

Memorial stone to Oskar Luts at the bank of Kuremaa lake.

body knows it by Luts's books, especially his Kevade (The Spring) that describes the life and many adventures of children at the fictional Paunvere (Palamuse) school.

Luts whose father was a cobbler, studied pharmaceutics at Tartu University, but later became a freelance writer. Kevade was followed by Suvi (Summer), Tootsi pulm (Toots's Wedding), Sügis (Autumn), Talv (Winter) and many others. He also wrote hugely popular plays. No less than five films have been made after his books and Kevade has seen 19 reprints.

Oskar's younger brother Theodor (1896–1980) was born at Palamuse. He later became a well-

A museum operates in the former Palamuse parish school.

The Luts family lived in a house at Palamuse that later worked as a pharmacy.

known filmmaker and cameraman who studied in Paris and Berlin and later produced several features and documentaries at home, including the first sound film in Estonia. After WW II he moved to Brazil where he worked as cameraman.

Besides Oskar Luts, the museum describes earlier centuries as well, as the first school for peasant children was opened there in 1687.

Palamuse Church was probably built in the first half of the 14th century. However, it is known that a priest was working here as early as in 1234.

The church at Palamuse stands in the middle of the village.

The school at **Luua Manor**, located a few kilometres south of Palamuse, has offered instruction to foresters for over half a century. Luua Forestry School operates in the mansion that has been largely rebuilt. Young people can study landscape planning, forest management and survey and other subjects. With its great variety of plants and trees – 800 altogether – the park is certainly among the most beautiful in the country. A pretty house with wooden lace carvings stands beside the mansion.

Luua Manor educates foresters.

AROUND PÕLTSAMAA

A signpost on the Tallinn-Tartu Road just before Põltsamaa says Mõhküla. This is a reminder of an ancient Estonian county called Mõhu. The stone castle of Mõhu that belonged to the Teutonic Order later developed into **Põltsamaa** settlement.

The shape of the **stronghold** built of boulders and limestone on the right bank of Põltsamaa river was square, with each side stretching to one hundred metres. Next a convent was built and the

A nice house with wooden lace stands next to the mansion.

walls made higher until they reached eleven metres. In the 16th century a cannon tower was added.

In the early years of the Livonian War (1558–1582) the castle was invincible, at least until the Livonian Order fled the castle and left it to the Russians. In 1569 Põltsamaa suddenly found itself as the capital of the newly born Livonian kingdom. The ambitious Duke of Holstein Magnus, brother of the Danish King Frederik II, arrived in time to claim a share of the new kingdom.

The territory of today's Latvia and Estonia were still without a proper master. Magnus managed to convince the Russian tsar Ivan the Terrible that he was the man to take charge and remain loyal to the great neighbour Russia. To prove his intentions, he married the tsar's niece. After settling in Põltsamaa, Magnus set out to conquer Tallinn. Thanks to the Swedes, however, the town resisted successfully until plague chased the Russians away in 1571.

Next year the tsar and his faithful duke fared much better. In 1577 Magnus was once again at the doors of Tallinn, but it still proved difficult. At the same time Duke Magnus sought new allies in Poland. In 1578 the Russian tsar, having lost his patience, stormed Põltsamaa castle and burnt it down. The new kingdom had collapsed and the king fled. Poland then attacked Russia from the north-west and Sweden did the same from the north. Ivan the Terrible had to withdraw.

The castle was rebuilt by the Swedes, but again destroyed by the Russians in 1703.

The 18th century brought a desired relief and flourishing to Põltsamaa. The most important figure was the manor lord, major **Woldemar Johann von Lauw** (1712–1786), who built a luxurious castle with marble halls and rococo boudoirs. The walls were adorned with silver incrustations and Venetian mirrors.

Von Lauw even had his own theatre troupe, musicians and a painter. He established a copperworks, starch factory and a tannery and started to produce glass as well. He was the one to open

The strong rectangular castle of Põltsamaa.

the first rural pharmacy in 1766. Soon he added the china and mirror factory. Again on von Lauw's initiative a hospital was opened nearby, inviting Peter Ernst Wilde who had studied medicine in Germany, to run it. Wilde later established the first private print shop in tsarist Russia.

After von Lauw's death in 1786 his property was sold piece by piece. Most workshops and factories closed.

The museum at Põltsamaa castle offers an overview of the colourful history of Põltsamaa and a display of the Põltsamaa blue-and-white china, much valued at the time of production and a rarity today.

An eminent figure of our National awakening period, **Karl August Hermann** (1851–1909) was born near Põltsamaa in Võhmanõmme. Despite his humble origin, he received a good education and even studied at Leipzig University for his doctorate in philosophy.

During the Russification period in the 1880s he became involved in the national movement, writing articles about the Estonian language and literature and establishing the first musical monthly. Hermann belonged to various cultural societies and wrote songs which became quite popular.

He acquired the paper Perno Postimees and turned it into Postimees where he encouraged people to maintain their national spirit. It was at the meetings of the

Karl August Hermann was a tireless promoter of music. His monument stands in the park of the castle.

The gate of the house where Hermann was born.

Estonians collected money to establish the Alexander schools for 16 years.

The owner of Võisiku Manor made an attempt to further democracy in Russia, and was thrown in prison.

Von Bock, made famous by Jaan Kross's novel The Tsar's Madman, lies in his family burial place in Kundrussaare.

Estonian Student Society, held at his home that the idea of a blue-black-and white flag first emerged. His wife Paula in fact sewed the first flag that has miraculously survived.

Hermann's house still stands and today bears a plaque to his memory.

Põltsamaa is also connected with a large-scale undertaking of the Awakening period – the **Alexander school**. In the early 1860s some progressively-minded men came together and decided to establish secondary schools in the Estonian language. In order to obtain permission from the authorities, they proposed to name it after tsar Alexander I under whose reign the peasants of Estonia and Livonia were freed from serfdom.

In 1869 the permission was granted, and an extensive money collecting started. In the course of 16 years, people donated 95, 218 roubles and 22 kopecks. A suitable house for the school was found near Põltsamaa and on 20 August 1888, the new school was consecrated. Alas, it bore little resemblance to the school that was originally intended. Classes had to be in Russian, the only exception being the Estonian language lessons.

The 6-year school received children who had graduated from a village school. Before its closure in 1906, 284 children were able to study there.

Today the building houses the Põltsamaa Agricultural School and a museum about the Alexander School that provoked so much enthusiasm, hope and disappointment.

Turning towards Kolga-Jaani from the Põltsamaa-Võhma Road, we come to the **Võisiku Manor** that belonged to the von Bock family in the early 19th century. It was here that the veteran of the Napoleonic Wars,**Timotheus Eberhardt von Bock** (1787–1836), compiled a new, democratic constitution, and sent it to Alexander I in 1818. As a result, he was thrown into prison from where he emerged as a broken man. He committed suicide and was buried in Kundrussaare cemetery about 1 km from the manor.

Von Bock's 'misunderstanding' with Russia is described by Jaan Kross in his novel The Tsar's Madman (translated into many languages.

Võisiku Manor has been restores and operates as a home for the elderly.

Adavere windmill is a well-known sign by the road.

A monument to the famous linguist Julius Mägiste in Kassema village.

Adavere Manor by the Tallinn-Tartu Road was a schoolhouse for most of the 20th century. Due to that the building has been properly maintained and is in good condition. The classicist mansion with a grand staircase was completed at the end of the 19th century. The park around the house is but a pale shadow of the old grand Adavere park.

A bit towards Tartu from Adavere, right by the road, stand striped posts that mark **the centre of mainland Estonia**. This, however, is not the one and only centre. If to consider our islands as well, the central point would be elsewhere.

By the road towards Tallinn from Adavere stands a **Dutch windmill**, known as a convenient place to stop and have something to eat between Tartu and Tallinn. It was restored in 1980.

About 9 km north-east from Põltsamaa, near **Kalana** (north of Kalana in Nurga village), is the Otisaare fort-hill and **limestone quarry** (south of Kalana in Mõisaküla), that used to provide high-quality dolomite or the so-called Kalana marble. The dolomite has been widely used in building. The quarry is still operating. Samples of various stones can be seen at Põltsamaa Museum.

AROUND MAARJA, TABIVERE AND PUURMANI

Kassema village by the Maarja-Kudina Road is the birthplace of the famous Estonian linguist **Julius Mägiste** (1900–1978). A memorial stone and a signpost stand by the road.

Before WW II Mägiste lectured at Tartu University and edited the magazine The Estonian Language. During the war he left the country and worked at Lund University in Sweden at the faculty of Finno-Ugric languages. He was especially interested in the etymology of words in various Finno-Ugric lan-

Veski introduced numerous new words into Estonian. The memorial stone in Vaidavere.

The keen cyclists of Vaidavere built a cycle track at Saadjärve a hundred years ago, but it has not survived.

guages. In the early 1960s he translated The Chronicle of Henry of Livonia (Henrici Chronicon Livoniae, probably written in 1224–1227) into Estonian.

Another eminent linguist, **Johannes Voldemar Veski** (1873–1968) was born in Vaidavere village south of Kudina. Veski lectured at Tartu University for 35 years and compiled various dictionaries. His contribution to the development of the Estonian language is overwhelming.

In Tormi village north of Tabivere stands a monument to the old 350-m long cycle track built by the Saadjärve Cycle Society one hundred years ago. It was the first rural sporting society in Estonia.

The name of **Puurmanni** derives from the mid-17th century when the local manor belonged to Christopher von Buhrmeister. After the Northern War (1700–1721) the **Puurmanni Manor** was the property of the

The Puurmanni Manor is adorned by a tall octagonal tower.

An ancient steam engine catches the eye in front of the local museum at Tabivere.

von Manteuffels who built the mansion seen today. The most striking elements of the mansion are certainly the 25-m high tower and a grand staircase. The house is in reasonably good condition as it has been accommodating a school from 1926.

During the War of Independence, lieutenant **Julius Kuperyanov** formed his partisan group in the last weeks of 1918 namely here at Puurmanni Manor (see also Valgamaa).

The military activities of Julius Kuperyanov's partisans started at Puurmanni.

A few hundred years ago Puurmanni was an important centre of lime burning that mostly provided the buildings in Tartu.

TARTUMAA

Ignatsi Jaak
1670 – 1741
Forseliuse andekas õpilane, koolmeister

TARTUMAA

Tartumaa lies on the banks of River Emajõgi between two lakes, flanked by Lake Peipsi on the right and Lake Võrtsjärv on the left. Here you can find higher plateaus, boggy flatlands and in some places, also rolling landscapes with small lakes here and there. In ancient times, this area was the heart of the powerful Ugandi County, governed by the well-fortified Tarbatu stronghold. Later, Tartu became the seat of the bishops, who ruled the whole surrounding area up to the present-day Setomaa.

The life of Tartumaa is undoubtedly determined by its being in the neighbourhood of the university town and large cultural centre – Tartu. We can find numerous old schools in Tartumaa, such as in Kambja, where a school for the peasants' children was founded already in the last decades of the 17th century. Since Tartu has through ages been a great attraction for different conquerors, Tartumaa has greatly suffered from pillaging, burning and deportations. The first known poet of Estonian origin, Käsu Hans, did not in vain list the misfortunes of Tartu in his Lamentation for the Destruction of Tartu in the beginning of the 18th century. Desperate battles were held in the vicinity of Tartu during WWII as well, when the brave unit of Estonians, who had already fought in the Finnish Winter War, gave their best to halt the onslaught of superior forces of the Red Army.

The poet Juhan Liiv was born on the northern border of the county, in Alatskivi; the home of the poet Gustav Suits was in Võnnu in the south. Both of these great masters occupy a place in the focal moments of our cultural history, and they make us to think about the meaning of being an Estonian. How much of the darkness of the old times of slavery can still be found in our souls, and how much of the knowledge that we are a part of Europe, which has always meant spiritual light?

Tartumaa and its university town have always been the source of spiritual light, where educated people found already long time ago that if their only wish was to become Germans, they would have no path into the future.

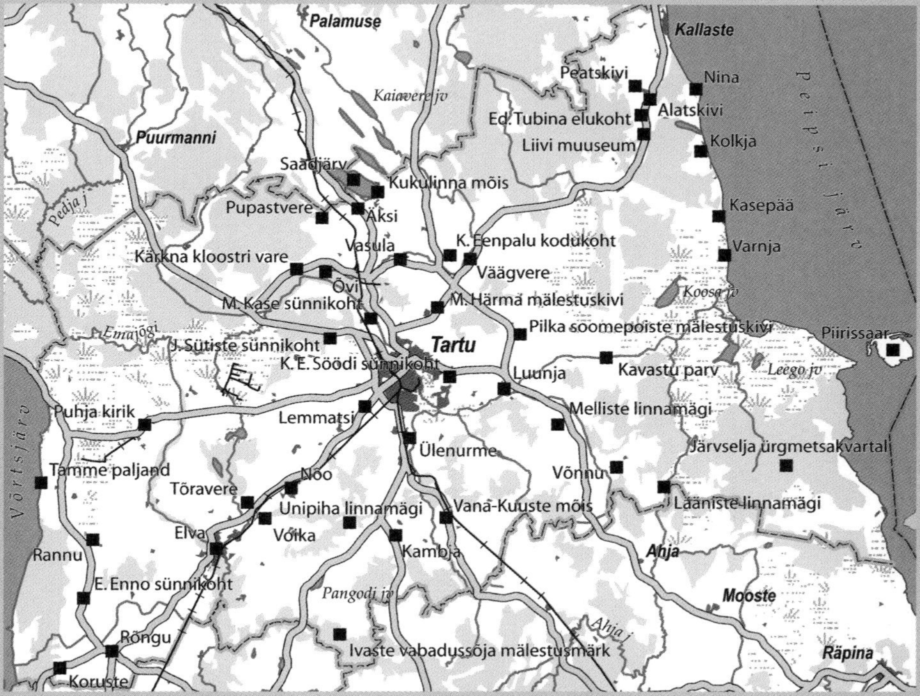

Palamuse
Kallaste
Peatskivi
Nina
Kaiavere jv
Alatskivi
Ed. Tubina elukoht
Kolkja
Puurmanni
Liivi muuseum
Saadjärv
Kukulinna mõis
Pedja j
Pupastvere
Äksi
Kasepää
Peipsi järv
Vasula
K. Eenpalu kodukoht
Varnja
Kärkna kloostri vare
Väägvere
Õvi
M. Kase sünnikoht
M. Härma mälestuskivi
Koosa jv
Emajõgi
Pilka soomepoiste mälestuskivi
Piirissaar
J. Sütiste sünnikoht
Tartu
K. E. Söödi sünnikoht
Luunja
Kavastu parv
Leego jv
Puhja kirik
Lemmatsi
Melliste linnamägi
Võrtsjärv
Ülenurme
Järvselja ürgmetsakvartal
Tamme paljand
Nõo
Võnnu
Tõravere
Unipiha linnamägi
Vana-Kuuste mõis
Lääniste linnamägi
Elva
Võika
Kambja
Ahja
Rannu
E. Enno sünnikoht
Pangodi jv
Mooste
Ahja j
Rõngu
Ivaste vabadussõja mälestusmärk
Räpina
Koruste

AROUND ALATSKIVI

The name of Alatskivi means 'the lower mill' in Estonian. In the neighbourhood there is also the village of Peatskivi, referring to the fact that once there had been another, "the upper mill". The neighbourhood of Alatskivi has beautiful landscapes, a splendid palace and a thick cultural layer.

The Neo-gothic mansion of **Alatskivi Manor** was designed by the estate owner, Baron Arved von Nolcken from Luunja. He was inspired by his travels in Scotland, where Balmoral, the royal summer residence, impressed him so much that he had a similar palace built for himself in 1885. The right part of the mansion has two storeys, the left part – only one; it is decorated by several towers and a turreted balcony on columns over the front entrance. The great hall of the palace with large fireplaces, a balcony and Corinthian columns extends through two storeys in a true English style. The Baron used this palace for summer residence, where he could walk with his lady in the beautiful park, adorned with pavilions and sculptures. None of these adornments are in its place now; one of the sculptures, a copy of Belvedere's Apollo, was taken to the Tallinn Art Museum in 1937. A splendid rose garden was once growing behind the palace; now it is marked only by lawn terraces.

Since the nationalisation in 1919, the palace has housed a school, a border guard staff, a casino and a state farm centre. Now, it is owned by the local community and it is open to visitors. The renovation is under way and visitors can already get the idea of the one-time splendour and design of the palace.

In 1858–1861, the poet **Juhan Weitzenberg** (1838–1877) worked as a parish and manor clerk in Alatskivi. He had studied in Tartu County School and had for some time been a tutor with C. R. Jakobson's family in Torma. Here he wrote his popular poems Tönnis Laks or the Estonian's Fatherland (Tönnis Laks ehk eestlase Isamaa, 1862) and An Old Steward's Lamentation (Vana hopmanni Nutu-laul, 1864).

The story about Laksi Tõnis is about the idea of emigration, which was popular at that time; Laksi Tõnis had hoped to find a better life in some other country, but his fate was sad. Laksi Tõnis (1808–1861) is buried at Alatskivi cemetery; his grave is marked by a tombstone featuring a chained hand with fingers pointing to the ground.

The first **Alatskivi Church** was probably built already in the time of the Livonian Order, but it has not survived. The stone church, built under the Swedish rule, has also been destroyed. The interesting church that is today standing on Kirikumägi hill was built by the estate owner von Stackelberg in 1777–1782; it has been altered later, and its spire was completed only in 1890. The church was dam-

Alatskivi mansion copies the English architectural style.

Old stone crosses in the Alatskivi churchyard indicate that several hundreds of years ago the place was a cemetery.

aged by vandals in the 1970s; in 1993, it was restored with the financial help of Aksel Kiiss, a one-time inhabitant of Alatskivi, who lived in the USA after the war. The church had probably been built in an old cemetery; two stone crosses, much older than the church, stand by its walls. One of them marks the grave of Äkkemäe Rein (see a passage below).

A nature path takes visitors from the shore of the lake behind the palace to **Alatskivi hill-fort**, which was presumably used in the 13th and 14th centuries. The nature path passes **Punane allikas (Red spring)** and **Truuduse tamm (Oak of Fidelity)**. Punane spring, flowing out of an outcrop of red sandstone, was known for its clear water that had been used to cure eye diseases. People came from far away to cure their eyes, and the local manor owner had his drinking water brought from the spring. The protected Truuduse oak, (circumference 4.2 m and height 25 m) got its name from the belief that the oath of faithfulness, given under the tree on St John's night, could not be broken. Young couples come even today to pledge fidelity to each other under the oak tree.

According to a legend, **Kalevipoeg's bed**, located north-west of Alatskivi, at Peatskivi near the Tartu-Kallaste Road, had been assembled by Kalevipoeg, who was tired and wanted to take a rest. Another legend goes that later, a Black King had lived on the hill; one of his sons had been a free peasant at Äkkemäe farm in Haapsipea. The Äkkemäe farm had been very rich, having a distillery already before the Northern War, and a strong fence with iron gates had surrounded its premises. Äkkemäe Rein, whose grave is marked by the stone cross bearing the date 1693 that stands by Alatskivi Church, had been living in that farm.

A memorial stone marks the birth place of the writer **Jakob Liiv** (1859–1938) at the location of Veski farm in **Kassiveski**. His father Benjamin Liiv had farmed it up to 1862, when the manor owner had had the farm demolished and houses for manor workers built at the place. The Liivs moved over to Riidma, where their son Juhan was born. In 1866, the

Juhan Liiv's older brother Jakob was born in Kassiveski near Alatskivi.

family moved to Oja farm in Rupsi village, which now is the location of the Juhan Liiv Museum (see below).

Jakob Liiv spent his best working years in Virumaa, being a teacher in Avispea, Pandivere and Uniküla and a bookseller in Väike-Maarja, where he wrote several collections of poems and a number of plays. From 1913, he lived in Rakvere, working as a bank clerk and also a mayor of the town. His bronze bust stands in a park behind Väike-Maarja Museum; his grave at Rakvere Cemetery is marked by a monument.

The birth place of **Juhan Liiv**, the youngest son of the Liiv family, in Riidma village, a couple of kilometres east of Alatskivi, is also marked by a memorial stone. Juhan Liiv (1864–1913) is among the best-known and most loved Estonian poets. His simple and beautiful poems about homeland and its nature are sad and very moving.

When talking about Juhan Liiv, people usually put together his poetry and his fate, both of which are intertwined with tragedy, loneliness and hopelessness. Liiv is always depicted as a pessimistic and introverted man, with eyes full of melancholy and unfulfilled yearning. The poet fell ill with

Juhan Liiv is buried at Alatskivi Cemetery.

Juhan Liiv, the poet with a tragic fate, was born in Riidma village near Alatskivi.

schizophrenia when he was 30 years old, and suffered from it for the rest of his life, of about 20 years. When he was well, he worked as a journalist with several newspapers (Virulane, Sakala, Olevik). His first collection of poems was published on the initiative of the literary group "Young Estonia" only in 1909. The second edition of this collection (1910), beautifully designed by the artist Kristjan Raud, is a classical work of Estonian book design.

Juhan Liiv, who was a poet par excellence, wrote and published also short impressionist stories and realistic stories. His best-known short story "A Shadow" ("Vari") is, to a certain extent, based on his own life. He started publishing his stories already in the 1890s.

During the years of his illness, Liiv lived with his relatives and friends in the neighbourhood of Alatskivi. He died of tuberculosis and was buried at Alatskivi Cemetery, where his grave is marked with a tall monument with his bas-relief portrait and a line from one of his best-known poems.

A couple of kilometres off Alatskivi towards Tartu is Rupsi village, where Oja farm, the former home of the Liiv family, houses the Juhan Liiv Museum that introduces the life and work of Juhan and Jakob Liiv. The stress is laid on the brothers Liiv, but a special exposition introduces the composer Eduard Tubin, who was also born in the neighbourhood.

The composer **Eduard Tubin** (1905–1982) spent his childhood in the Naelavere village school, located between Alatskivi and Rupsi. His older brother was a teacher and his parents kept the farm that had been given for the teacher's use by the local parish. The brothers Liiv also attended this school for some years.

Eduard Tubin is foremost known for his ballet "Kratt", but he also wrote two operas ("Barbara von Tisenhusen" and "The Reigi Pastor"), 10 symphonies and several concertos, orchestra pieces, sonatas, chamber music and choral songs. He was a prolific composer and the most recognised Estonian author of symphonies. He wrote the main part of his works in Sweden, where he escaped from Estonia in 1944.

The former Naelavere school house is now privately owned; a commemorative plaque to Tubin has been put on its wall. Tubin's birth place in the former Torila village, which has by now become a part of Kallaste town, is marked by a memorial stone in the yard of a private house in Oktoobri Street. Driving to the east or south-east from Kallaste, we reach the shore of Lake Peipsi with **fishing villages** inhabited by **Russian Old Believers**.

The first settlers of the villages of Nina, Kolkja, Kasepää, Varnja and others were the people who fled from Russia because of the

Juhan Liiv Museum is open at his former home in Oja farm.

Commemorative stone to Eduard Tubin stands in Kallaste.

The Kolkja house of worship of the Old Believers.

A room-museum in Kolkja shows an exhibition of the life and customs of the Old Believers.

persecution after a church reform in the late 17th century. They bought the fishing rights from the local manor owner and rented a piece of land and fishing equipment. They remained true to their faith and built their houses of worship and characteristic villages, where houses are situated close to each other along a kilometres-long village street. There is a sacred corner with an icon in every Old Believer's house; onions are grown in each garden. The growing of onions is a specific branch of agriculture here and in autumn, all villages are full of large heaps of drying onions.

The Old Believers still worship in the Church Slavonic language. To preserve the traditions, children are taught Church Slavonic at Varnja School and they have religious instruction. The celebration of traditional feasts (according to the old calendar), such as Christmas (6 January), Passover (the first Sunday after the spring equinox), Trinity Day (seven weeks after Passover), the Feast of Dormition of the Mother of God (29 August), St John's Day (7 July) and Maslenitsa (before Lent, at the end of winter), is very important for Old Believers.

The **Museum of Russian Old Believers** is located in the Kolkja Basic School, displaying a typical living room in the Old Believers' home with beds, a table, a chest of drawers and a mirror. The exposition includes clothing, Church Slavic books, neck crosses, etc.

AROUND LAKE SAADJÄRV

For some reason or other, Lake Saadjärv has been divided between two counties. Five sevenths of this largest lake of the Vooremaa region, or 5 sq km, belong to Tartumaa, the remaining 2 sq km belong to Jõgevamaa. The greatest depth of **Lake Saadjärv** stretches to 25 m.

Several large erratic boulders can be seen on the lake shores; legends tie them with Kalevipoeg and his brothers. Kalev's three sons had once had a stone-throwing competition – the winner, who would throw his stone farthest, would become the king of the land. The youngest of the brothers, Kalevipoeg, threw his stone farthest. The stone of the middle brother fell on the shoreline and the stone of the oldest brother fell into the lake.

Today, the large boulder standing on the shoreline in Põltsamaa village, on the southern shore of Lake Saadjärv, is known as the middle brother's stone and the stone standing on the eastern shore of the lake is called Kalevipoeg's sling-stone. On the northern shore of the lake, about 500 m from the water-line, across the road, stands still another large boulder – a cup-stone with about 70 hollows – which is also known as one of Kalevipoeg's slingstones.

East of Lake Saadjärv is a Kalevipoeg bed-type hill-fort from the beginning of the 2nd millennium.

The architecturally interesting mansion of **Kukulinna Manor** stands at the south-eastern end of Lake Saadjärv near Äksi village. The wooden Neo-gothic mansion is decorated with columns imitating castle towers, which are its most characteristic details. This charming building was completed in the second half of the 19th century, when the manor was owned by the Koskülls.

In the 1920s, the mansion was a summer house of the Tartu Art School Pallas; probably due to this fact there are many beautiful paintings of Saadjärv views around in Estonia. During the Soviet time, the mansion housed a young pioneer summer camp. Today it is, unfortunately, empty and in need of repair.

The first wooden church was built in **Äksi** village in the mid-15th century. This building and the next one on the site perished in fire. The new stone church was built in 1730; it got its present Neo-gothic appearance at the end of the 19th century.

The linguist and writer **August Wilhelm Hupel** (1737–1819) and the compiler of Estonian-language school textbooks and calendars **Otto Wilhelm Masing** (1763–1832) were both Pastors at Äksi Church. A memorial stone to Masing stands in front of the former parsonage (about Hupel, see Põltsamaa, Jõgevamaa; about Masing, see Viru-Nigula, Lääne-Virumaa).

A curious memorial stone has been erected by the Tartu-Jõgeva Road at Puhtaleiva, near Äksi, commemorating the so-called **Witch of Äksi**, Hermine Elisabeth Jürgens (1892–1976). A large stone on the roadside field marks the last home site of the famous healer, where she received her patients and other visitors. A large eye painted on the stone seems to say that a "witch" can see you everywhere. A survey, held in Estonia about a decade ago revealed that about a half of the

Kukulinna mansion is characterised by original wooden columns.

An all-seeing eye is featured on the memorial stone to the so-called Witch of Äksi, Hermine Jürgens.

population still believes in witchcraft in spite of 800 years long fight against paganism held by the clergy and the progress of science and technology.

A road leading to the north-west from Kärkna railway station takes visitors to **Pupastvere** village, the birth place of the sculptor **Jaan Koort** (1883–1935). The village lies on a drumlin, the road ends in the village, and a mire begins behind it. The home of the sculptor stands on the highest point of the drumlin.

Jaan Koort studied at Hugo Treffner's school in Tartu and at Baron A. Stieglitz School of Technical Design in St Petersburg, later also in Paris and Moscow. The adventurous artist travelled much and even visited Australia. Working in Moscow, he fell ill with pneumonia and died.

He was an innovative artist and created sensitive portraits, sculptures of women and figures of animals. His sculpture "Roe Deer", the copy of which has for a long time stood in a small green park between the high steep bank of Toompea Hill and Nunne Street in Tallinn, is one of his best-known works.

The house of the artist is marked with a marble plaque; his distant relatives are still living in the house.

A marble plaque marks the house of the innovative sculptor Jaan Koort.

A commemorative stone marks the location in Pupastvere village, where the **"Finnish Boys"** – Estonians, who fought in the Finnish Army in WWII – fought their **first battle** after having returned to Estonia in 1944.

At the beginning of 1944, the JR 200 (200th Infantry Regiment) was formed in Finland of Estonian volunteers. The Regiment consisted of Estonians, who had escaped to Finland in 1943, the so-called Finnish Boys, led by Captain Karl Talpak. The Regiment participated in battles against the Red Army on the Karelian Isthmus in 1944.

The situation on Estonian fronts had become critical by that time and many Finnish Boys wanted to return to fight for their homeland. After long negotiations between Finns and Germans, the men were given the permission to return on 12 August 1944. 1752 of them came back; their representatives met with the Prime Minister of the time, Jüri Uluots, who thanked them for their brave decision.

The ship carrying the Finnish Boys arrived in Paldiski, where a memorial stone marks the place of their landing. The Regiment became a part of the 20th Estonian Waffen-SS Division and was divided into two battalions. The 2nd Battalion, which had been incorporated into a reserve regiment, was dispersed in September 1944, after having fought at the Narva Front. The 1st Battalion was sent to the Tartu Front; already on 28 August 1944, they participated in a fierce battle at Pupastvere village, recapturing the village from the Red Army.

After three days of hard battles, they threw the enemy, who was supported by armoured vehicles and artillery attacks, back across the River Emajõgi. They halted the onslaught of the Red Army for three weeks. The Red Army started a great offensive on 17 September by forcing the Emajõgi River and the whole Estonian front collapsed after that. The battalion of Finnish Boys, who had fought the Red Army units at Pilka village, had to retreat as well. The Pilka battle field by the Tartu-Kallaste Road (north of Luunja) is marked by a commemorative stone.

A room-museum dedicated to the Finnish Boys has been opened in Äksi village, north-east of Pupastvere, by the Tartu-Jõgeva Road, displaying the map of the battles and introducing the history of the units.

Turning towards Vasula from the Tartu-Jõgeva Road, we reach **Vasula Manor**, which belonged to the assessor of the Tartu Court of Appeal Georg von Stiernhielm (1598–1672). Stiernhielm, who is also considered as the founder of Swedish poetry, came to Estonia with Johan Skytte, who became the first Chancellor of the University of Tartu. Skytte owned Haaslava Manor south-east of Tartu.

At the time when Stiernhielm lived there, Vasula Manor became the centre of free thought. Its library was the place where many heated discussions were held on various scientific subjects. Georg von Stiernhielm returned to Sweden after the Russians burnt his manor to ashes in 1656.

The Stiernhielm family owned the manor until the early 18th century, when it went to the famous Russian General Field Marshal Count Sheremetyev.

A home economics school was founded in the manor in 1924. Now, only the stairs that once led to the front door of the mansion have remained. A commemorative stone to the enlightener and poet Georg von Stiernhielm stands beside the stairs.

The home place of the politician and statesman **Kaarel Eenpalu** (1888–1942) is in Kobratu village by the Tartu-Jõhvi Road. In the 1920s and 1930s, Kaarel Eenpalu (until 1935, Karl August Einbund), fulfilled the positions of Riigivanem (President), Auditor General, Chairman of the Riigikogu (Parliament), Minister of Internal Affairs and Prime Minister. He was a close co-worker of Konstantin Päts, being in favour of authoritarian regime. He initiated the campaign of Estonianisation of family names, leading the way himself. He is also considered to be the founder of Estonian Police.

In addition to being a politician, Eenpalu was engaged in farming at his training and experimental farm in Aruküla village, Harjumaa. He was arrested in 1940 by the Soviet

The Finnish Boys managed to halt the enemy at Pupastvere.

The room-museum devoted to the Finnish Boys displays battle maps and war equipment.

authorities and sent to a prison camp, where he died. His former home place is marked with a commemorative stone.

North-west of Tartu, by the Tallinn-Tartu railway line, lies the village of Kärkna. 3 km west of the village stand **the ruins of Kärkna Monastery**. The largest Cistercian Monastery in Livonia was founded in the 13th century by Bishop Hermann of Tartu, who spent there the last years of his life. Kärkna Monastery was the first Cistercian monastery in Estonia; all in all, there were five of them, in Kärkna, Tartu, Lihula, Padise and Tallinn. The Cistercian Order was a religious order of military nature; its members followed to the precision the rules of common life concerning prayers, work, and education through reading, laid down by St Benedictus.

Kärkna Monastery was surrounded by a strong stone wall and a deep moat full of water. When firearms came to be used on battlefields in the 15th century, an artillery tower was built to improve the defence of the monastery. The large one-aisle church of the monastery had an exceptionally large crypt with side altars, where the monks were buried. Bishop Hermann was also buried there. The monastery existed in Kärkna up to the Livonian War, when it was destroyed. After the war, the Cistercians left Estonia.

A battlefield has been marked in Õvi village, by the Kärkna-Kärevere Road, where the Finnish Boys destroyed the Kärevere bridgehead of the Read Army in August 1944. At Õvi stone field nature reserve we can see boulders with the diameter of 1–1.5 m, which have been washed out of moraine. The forest growing at the protected area is full of smaller stones mostly with about half-a metre diameter.

A large boulder commemorates the battle of the Finnish Boys in Õvi village.

In Kärkna, only ruins have remained of the largest Cistercian Monastery in Livonia.

AROUND TARTU

The birthplace of the poet **Juhan Sütiste** (1899–1945) is about a couple of kilometres north of Rahinge village near Tartu, quite near to the Tartu-Tallinn Road. The house where the poet was born is marked with a commemorative plaque.

Juhan Sütiste (until 1936,

Johannes Schütz) was a realist poet who believed that true literature had to be just 'close to life'. He wrote more than ten collections of poetry and several long poems and plays. In 1940, he welcomed the Soviet coup d'etat with a poem "The World Turns to the East".

Sütiste is always remembered as a good athlete – in 1927, he won the first place in javelin throw at the Students' Olympics in Rome.

Vorbuse was the home place of the well-known radio broadcast doctor **Mihkel Kask** (1903–1968). A professor of the University of Tartu, Mihkel Kask was an enthusiastic promoter of public health; he taught courses in public health and wrote dozens of popular scientific articles on the subject. He is remembered by his contemporaries as a 'radio doctor' whose weekly broadcasts on health were extremely popular before and after WWII.

Mihkel Kask's home is marked with a memorial stone, standing among a grove of birches.

The birthplace of the composer **Miina Härma** (1864–1941; until 1935, Hermann) is in the former Kõrveküla school house beside the Tartu-Jõhvi Road. Miina Härma studied composition and organ at St Petersburg Conservatoire and gave piano concerts in Russia and in several European countries. Back home, she founded a mixed choir in Tartu, encouraged local society to engage in music and took an active part in the creating of the Tartu Higher Music School. She conducted joint choirs at song festivals.

Her choral songs are much loved; she wrote more than 200 songs, many of which have become standard repertoire. Her most popular song "Tuljak" (1902) has been performed at all song

The birth place of the composer Miina Härma in Kõrveküla and a commemorative stone.

festivals. A commemorative plaque marks her former home; a memorial stone stands in the old schoolyard. The Miina Härma Gymnasium in Tartu is among the best Estonian schools; a sculpture of the composer is standing in the yard. An exhibition of her life and work can be seen at Kõrveküla School.

Village of **Väägvere**, lying beside the Tartu-Kallaste Road, is well-known for its brass band, founded already in 1839. At first, the members of the band studied music on their own; in 1846, **David Wirkhaus** came to teach at the local school, and started to supervise the band as well. In 1851–1912, his son David Otto Wirkhaus (1837–1912) led the band that won the first prize at a brass band competition held during the first song festival in 1869. The Väägvere brass band is still active today.

David Otto Wirkhaus, who was born in Lohkva village near Tartu, inherited the love for music

People of Väägvere appreciate their famous compatriots

from his father. Like his father, he worked for a long time as a teacher at Väägvere School, first as his father's assistant, later as the head of school.

On his initiative and encouragement, more than 100 brass bands were created all over Estonia. Wirkhaus helped them to improve their playing skills, ordered sheet music and organised joint concerts. He was the general conductor of brass bands at several consecutive song festivals.

The poet **Karl Eduard Sööt** (1862–1950) was born in a former mill farm in Lohkva village by the Tartu-Räpina Road, near Tartu. When he was six years old, the family moved to Ilmatsalu village, where he spent his childhood and youth. He started writing poetry already at school. After finishing school, he returned to his home parish and worked for some time as the parish clerk. Later, he worked as a journalist; he became a publisher and had a printer's shop and a bookshop.

Sööt was an affectionate and lyrical poet; he wrote for adults and also for children. The Luunja Community is now issuing the Karl Eduard Sööt prize for children's poetry.

Sööt's birthplace in Lohkva and his former home in Ilmatsalu are both marked with commemorative stones. David Otto Wirkhaus, a composer and a long-time conductor of Väägvere brass band, was born in Lohkva village (see Väägvere).

An antitank ditch was dug near Tartu in Lemmatsi village, by the Tartu-Valga Road, in 1941. Many prisoners were killed there during the German occupation. About 12,000 people found their grave there. **A dolomite memorial wall**, featuring a sculpture group of nine figures on its highest part, was erected at the site in 1964.

EAST OF TARTU

The centre of **Luunja Manor** lies by the Tartu-Räpina Road. At first, Luunja Manor was located in Vanamõisa; it was moved to its present location during the Polish rule in the 16th or 17th century. The manor has had many different owners; some of them have been quite famous.

After the Northern War, the manor together with several other neighbouring manors belonged to the famous Russian general Boris Sheremetyev (1652–1719). Later it was owned by General Field Marshal Count Burkhard Christoph von Münnich, who led the Russian troops in the Russian-Turkish War (1735–1739) and supervised the construction of the Paldiski military port and the fortifications of Riga.

The leader of conservative noblemen and an active member of the Livonian nobility, Baron Georg von Nolcken (1789–1853), is the best-known member of the family of the next owners, the von Nolckens. Georg von Nolcken fought actively against the agrarian reform of the 1840s, arguing against the selling of land to the peasants and against the legalisation of monetary rent for peasants.

Since 1920 up to WWII, the manor was used by the Estonian

Seed Grain Society, who started growing the seeds of grain, grass, and vegetables and created a nursery and an orchard. After WWII, the Luunja state farm grew seed grain and also bred horses. In the 1980s, the growing of flowers was added to the list of activities. The state farm worked in Luunja up to the early 1990s, when it was reorganised into a joint stock enterprise, which has by now ceased to operate.

The mansion of Luunja Manor was destroyed in WWII; the cattle sheds of the manor have been preserved and now they are used to keep horses. In 1990, on the 70th anniversary of the state farm, a large bronze sculpture of a horse, made by the sculptor Endel Taniloo, was erected in the manor park.

When driving from Tartu towards **Pilka** and passing through Luunja, we see a roadsign pointing right, to a **WWII battlefield**, where among others, the 1st Battalion of the Finnish Boys fought the Red Army units on 17 September 1944. A memorial stone marks the battlefield.

Another memorial stone, standing in Veskimäe village between

The spacious Võnnu Church consists of the nave and the transept.

Mäksa and Kavastu, marks the battles held on the Kastre-Võnnu line. The stone had first been erected in the manor park, but it was moved and now it is standing in the yard of a local inhabitant who had also participated in these battles.

A ferry takes people across the Emajõgi River in **Kavastu**; the ferry has been operating there already since 1899.

A large heap of stones called **Lingutusmägi** stands on a hill-fort near Melliste. A legend goes that already in the ancient times people had hurled stones from this heap at the enemies, giving the hill its name (Sling Hill). People have started bringing new stones to the heap, which has been given a poetic name "Cover the Evil with Stones".

Võnnu Church is one of the largest rural churches in Estonia. It was built in the 13th century and has been repeatedly restored and rebuilt since that time. Baron von Nolcken erected a black marble grave monument inside the church to the memory of his son who was killed at the Borodino Battle in 1812.

A large bronze sculpture of a horse was erected in Luunja Manor Park in 1990.

The old **Võnnu Cemetery** lies a kilometre to the south from the church. At the cemetery stands an obelisk-shaped chapel of the owner of Kurista Manor, General A. G. de Villebois (ca 1717–1781), erected in 1781. Due to his family ties (his mother was a step-sister of the Empress Catherine I) and his successful military career, de Villebois had an excellent standing at the Russian Imperial Court and he was assigned the task of supervising the construction of fortifications in the towns of the Baltic provinces of Russia. At home in Kurista, he was known as a strict master to his peasants.

The red brick rocket-like chapel is overgrown with young birches and offers a surprising sight to visitors.

Near Võnnu, by the road to Lääniste, stands a ring of specially planted trees and a commemorative stone marks the birthplace the poet **Gustav Suits** (1883–1956). A memorial plaque has also been set on the wall of the former Võnnu schoolhouse, where the father of the poet worked as a teacher for some time and where Suits started his schooling. He graduated from the Tartu grammar school with a gold prize and entered the University of Helsinki, studying literature of European countries. He married his fellow student Aino Thauvon and worked for some time as a teacher.

Suits returned to Estonia in 1917, and plunged into political life and joined the Socialist-Revolutionary Party. He was one of the first to voice the idea of independent Estonian statehood and he promoted the idea of an Estonian-Finnish federation. Since the adapting of the University of Tartu into national university in 1919, Suits was the professor of literature there. He taught the history of Estonian literature and the literature of Western Europe and Russia.

He was also one of the best-known Estonian poets. Having moved most of his life in academic circles, Suits was one of the initiators of the "Young Estonia" movement, and its leader. At the beginning of the 20th century, he was one of the most important promoters of the idea of entering the European cultural space. Every-

The rocket-shaped chapel of General de Villebois is covered by young trees.

The poet and scholar Gustav Suits started his schooling in the former Võnnu schoolhouse.

body knows the slogan voiced by Suits in 1905, "More of culture! More of European culture! Let us remain Estonians, but let us also become Europeans!"

Suits left Estonia during WWII in 1944, and continued his literary work in exile in Sweden.

Lääniste hill-fort of Kalevipoeg bed-type is located east of Võnnu, on the western bank of the Ahja River. The hill-fort was used as a stronghold at the end of the I millennium. In the 19th century, it was a local orthodox cemetery.

The oldest Estonian forest reserve, established in 1924, is located at **Järvselja**. The owners of Kastre Manor, the von Essens, paid much attention to the forests of the area already in the 19th century. They appointed a forester, organised the melioration of the area and regenerated the forest. During the first years of the Estonian Republic, the reserve belonged to the Training and Experimental Forest District of the University of Tartu; now, it is maintained by the Järvselja Training and Experimental Forest District Foundation. Several rare introduced tree species grow in the Järvselja virgin forests. The tallest spruce (43.8 m), the tallest pine (42.7 m) and the tallest birch in Estonia (36.5 m) grow here.

The island of **Piirissaar** guards the entrance from the large Lake Peipsi into the smaller Lake Lämmijärv. This extremely low island covers about 8 sq km and forms a separate community with the permanent population of about 100 people.

The natives of the island are Russians, the descendants of the

People of the island of Piirissaar earn their living by fishing in the lake and growing onions in their vegetable gardens.

The commemorative stone to Gustav Suits features some lines of his poetry.

Lääniste hill-fort has also been an Orthodox cemetery.

The inhabitants of Piirissaar are the descendants of the Old Believers.

Old Believers, who had long ago settled on the island. They are mainly engaged in fishing and onion-growing. The red-finned burbot can be seen on the coat of arms of the community. The house of worship of the Old Believers and the Russian Orthodox Church have both been preserved on the island.

AROUND ELVA AND KAMBJA

The Estonian Agricultural Museum is located in **Ülenurme** village, in the former Ülenurme Manor by the Tartu-Võru Road. The museum exhibits historical farming equipment and machinery and historical apicultural equipment. The exposition introduces the history of cattle and poultry farming in Estonia. An old windmill has been brought from the island of Saaremaa and set up at the museum. Historical farm machinery can be seen on the exhibition field.

Vana-Kuuste Manor, located south of Ülenurme, was a state manor in the Swedish time. After the Northern War, it was returned to the von Ungern-Sternbergs, who extracted the lands of the new Vastse-Kuuste Manor from it at the end of the 18th century. The notorious Ungru Count Otto Reinhold Ludwig von Ungern-Sternberg (1744–1811) was born at Vana-Kuuste Manor (see Suuremõisa and Kõrgessaare, Hiiumaa).

At the beginning of the 19th century the manor was owned by the Livonian Field Marshal Karl Gotthard von Liphart, who rented the manor together with its surrounding lands to the Agricultural Institute of the University of Tartu in 1833. The Institute worked at the manor in 1834–1839, using the best agricultural machinery in Russia.

The art historian Karl Eduard von Liphart (1808–1891), the son of K. G. v. Liphart, was born at Vana-Kuuste Manor. He complemented the art collection created by his father, which was the largest in the Baltic provinces in the 19th century. A part of his remarkable library of more than 30,000 volumes is held at Tartu University Library. Today, the mansion houses the Kuuste basic school.

Kambja, located 17 km off Tartu by the Tartu-Võru Road, has played an important role in the history of Estonian-language education. A first school for peasants' children was founded there more than 300 years ago. A beautiful **memorial complex with a fire altar** commemorates this important landmark. A part of the complex is a large stone book, made by the sculptor Endel Taniloo.

The beginning of the Kambja school is connected with a man called **Ignati** (also Ignatsi) **Jaak** (ca 1670–1741), who, as a very young boy, went to study at Bengt Gottfried Forselius' (*ca* 1660–1688) Teachers' Seminar.

The story of Ignati Jaak's and

his schoolmate Pakri Hansu Jüri's visit to Stockholm has become almost a legend. Forselius had wanted to demonstrate to the Bishop of Estonia and the King of Sweden, Charles XI that Estonian village boys had been able to learn so much at his school. The boys had read and sung so well that the King had given a gold ducat to each of them. The Bishop was satisfied as well and in spite of the opposition of local estate owners, it was allowed to establish peasants' schools in Livonia and Estonia.

Having graduated from the seminar, Ignati Jaak started to work as a schoolteacher. Before he became the sexton and teacher at Kambja, he taught in Otepää, Rõngu and Kavandu. He worked in Kambja for about 40 years, and with the help of local Pastor Albrecht Sutor, managed to escape the status of the serf.

At Kambja Cemetery, we can see memorial stones to Ignati Jaak, Albrecht Sutor, Bengt G. Forselius, and Pastor Andreas Virginius (Verginius), who probably had supported Ignati Jaak in getting to the teachers' seminar and who was one of the translators of the New Testament into Estonian. The birthplace of Ignati Jaak in Kavandu village near Pangodi has been marked with a commemorative stone.

Ignati Jaak studied at Bengt Gottfried Forselius' Teachers' Seminar and taught at Kambja for 40 years.

The hero of the War of Independence, **Julius Kuperjanov** (1894–1919), and the wrestler, **Johannes Kotkas** (1915–1998), were born near Kambja. Julius Kuperjanov studied to be a military officer and participated in WWI. When the War of Independence broke out, he gathered an about 1200 men-strong unit of partisans and fought in South Estonia. He died of a mortal wound received at the Paju Battle (see Paju Battle, Valgamaa).

Johannes Kotkas won the first place in classical wrestling (heavyweight) at the Helsinki Olympics in 1952 and belonged to the world elite of wrestlers in classical and free style in the 1950s. During WWII he also managed to set the record of the Soviet Union in hammer throw with the result of 53.88.

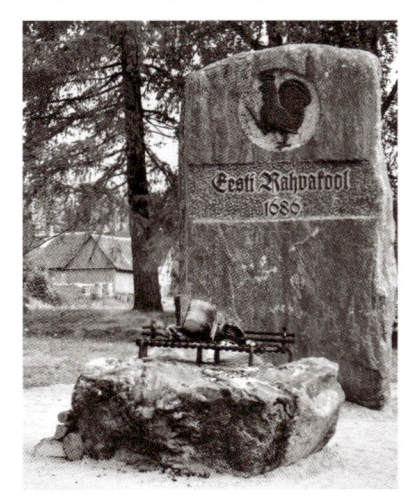

The memorial complex dedicated to Estonian rural schools.

Kambja Church, which was probably built in the 15th century, was destroyed several times. It was seriously damaged in WWII and restored only in the newly independent Estonia. The mansion of the former Kambja Manor now houses the community government.

Unipiha hill-fort is located about 2 km south-east of Unipiha, by the Kambja-Nõo Road. The hill-fort was probably used in the 8th–9th centuries; it was surrounded by a settlement.

Kambja Church was restored in the newly independent Estonia.

Nõo Church is one of the oldest churches in South Estonia and, in spite of many wars, it has almost preserved its original appearance. The church that belonged to Tartu Cathedral Chapter was built in the 13th century. It became a parish church in the 15th century and soon it also became a favourite destination for pilgrims. The church was also used for defence purposes; it has defence galleries and tall windows.

The organ of the church dates back to 1890, the largest of the church bells was cast at the beginning of the 19th century in Gatchina, Russia. The altar was carved by the sculptor Jaan Koort. Adrian Virginius was the Pastor in Nõo in the early 17th century.

Turning towards Lutike from the Otepää-Tartu Road at Nõuni, and driving north-east through **Lutike village**, we reach Ivaste village. A **monument** has been erected in the village to the **members of the League of Veterans of the Estonian War of Independence** (see birthplace of Aleksander Larka, Järvamaa).

Jaagupi tarand-grave is located in Voika village, south of Tõravere railway stop. The burial place was used in the 3rd–5th centuries. This is one of the largest tarand-graves in Estonia, being 55 m long and 19 m wide. The burial site is formed by 9–10 rectangular areas, fenced in by rows of large boulders – tarands. Numerous finds have been excavated from the graves, including plenty of jewellery – brooches, rings and bracelets. Six tarands have been left open for viewing.

At **Tartu Observatory**, located in Tõravere, 21 km south of Tartu, research is carried out in astronomy and astrophysics. The observatory was founded in 1964; it was given the name of the former director of Tartu Observatory and world-famous astronomer Friedrich **Georg Wilhelm Struve** (1793–1864) (about Struve, see Simuna, Lääne-Virumaa).

In 1997, an exhibition and lecture room "Stellarium" was opened at the observatory, where the visitors can study the model of the solar system and learn about the alternation of day and night and the seasons on the Earth and about the appearance of solar and lunar eclipses; they can watch videos about astronomy and handle a

Gardener's house at Luke Manor.

Gothic lanes, fashionable 150 years ago, and a romantic gardener's house can be admired at Luke Manor Park.

270-kg piece of an iron meteorite. The birth and development of the town of **Elva**, like that of many other Estonian towns and villages, is related to the railway or, to the building of the Tartu-Valga railway line in 1886–1889.

A settlement started growing around the railway station and many well-off inhabitants of Tartu acquired summerhouses there. During the first years of the Estonian Republic, Elva attracted more and more holiday-makers, mostly from Tartu and the rest of Estonia, but also from abroad.

A regular rail service was started between Tartu and Elva in 1927. Two years later, a wonderful beach and swimming pool were built at Lake Verevi. In 1934, Elva became a summer resort and its inhabitants were mostly engaged in servicing holiday makers. There were a restaurant and a guest house, several boarding houses, a swimming pool, a café in the railway station and a summer casino in Elva.

Elva is a summer resort even today; the pretty beach of Lake Verevi, a reservoir and peaceful atmosphere of the town attract

Tartu Observatory was named after Georg Friedrich Struve.

A bas-relief on the observatory wall commemorates one of its founders, Academician Aksel Kipper.

summer visitors.

The Tartumaa Museum is located in Elva (2, Pikk St.), displaying seasonal exhibitions. The collections of the museum contain a unique object – the first Estonian-language globe, made by Hurt-Mayer. The Estonian-language geographical maps reached Livonian rural schools in the last quarter of the 19th century. The only globe that has been preserved belonged to the family of von Middendorffs. Of Estonian place names, only Tallinn and Tartu are marked on the globe. A room-museum of the actor Leopold Hansen (1879–1964) has been opened at his former home (10, Vaikne St.).

Fierce battles were held at Rõngu Castle in the Livonian War.

AROUND LAKE VÕRTSJÄRV

Rõngu Church acquired its present appearance in 1901. Lossimäe Park and the ruins of a vassal castle, built probably in the 14th century are located near Rõngu village. The rectangular courtyard of the castle was surrounded by the main building and its wings, housing the knight and his men-at-arms. During the Livonian War, several battles were held at the castle between Russians and the troops of the Livonian Order. Russians, who had managed to capture the castle, were driven out by the Master of the Order Godert (Gotthard) Kettler, who later destroyed the castle. Some parts of the castle walls were used in building the mansion of Suure-Rõngu Manor. This manor has also been destroyed.

The Pikasilla-Rõngu Road passes through Koruste village (about 6 km before Rõngu). About 1 km after Koruste (when approaching it from the direction of Rõngu), there are commemorative stones to mark the homes of the painter **Elmar Kits** (1913–1972), the composer **Aleksander Läte** (1860–1948) and the writer and publisher **August Toomingas** (1892–1973).

The birth place of Elmar Kits, an outstanding representative of the Pallas Art School, was located on the shore of Lake Linajärv. Aleksander Läte spent the last years of his life nearby.

Of all of them, August Toomingas, or Kusta Toom, lived for the longest period near Koruste, in Salulaane forest east of Juka farm. He was the son of the Rõngu church sexton, Aleksander Toomingas. He was very ill when a child, as a result of which he was half

Aleksander Läte founded the first Estonian symphony orchestra; he lived for some time near Koruste village.

deaf and could not attend school. He taught himself to read and write in Estonian and in several foreign languages. At the same time, he was convinced of his vocation of becoming a writer.

Unfortunately, nobody else shared his belief. Being poor and without family, he went to live in a forest, built himself a shack in Salulaane forest near Koruste and sent numerous letters to different publishers. Finally, he established his own printing shop and started publishing magazine Tõrvik. The magazine was closed by the censors on some minor reason and he soon founded a new one, titled Hääl, which he printed himself in 150 copies. It was issued twice a month for seven years (1934–1941).

Toom got no profit from his enterprise. His shack was repeatedly broken into and his belongings were stolen. He had to stop publishing in the Soviet time, and then he devoted himself to music; his contemporaries have said that he had a good musical talent. But he could not enter a music school, since he had got no formal education. He lived the last years of his life at a home in Jämejala. He was buried at Rõngu Cemetery.

The birthplace of the poet **Ernst Enno** (1875–1934) is located in Valguta village, north of Rõngu, at the Teedla crossroad. He was born in Köödsa inn and spent his childhood in Soosaare farm.

Ernst Enno is wellknown for his lyrical nature poems and ballads. His children's poems have been much loved by several generations. A memorial stone marks his birthplace. The empty and derelict buildings of the former Valguta Manor are located near the site.

Rannu vassal castle, located on the southern edge of the former Rannu Manor park, was probably built in the 13th century. In the 15th century it went to the family of von Tiesenhausens, who owned it until it was destroyed in the Livonian War in 1558. Later, Rannu became a rich manor. Its owner von Claven had the ruins of the old castle torn down at the end of the 18th century and used the stones to construct the manor buildings and the surrounding wall. Today, only the old park of the manor and some outbuildings have survived.

An old legend about the tragic love story of young Barbara von Tiesenhausen is well known people. According to the legend, cruel brothers drowned their younger sister in an ice hole on Porkuni Lake; another legend says that it was done in Rannu.

The young lady had fallen in love with the manor clerk Franz Bonnius. Bonnius was a commoner, and the laws of the time prohibited noblemen's marriages to commoners. The young couple decided to escape to Riga, get married there and live abroad. They were caught and at the family trial it was decided to kill the girl because she had overstepped the law.

The sentence was carried out by the girl's brother, Jürgen. This cruel deed seems to have brought a curse upon the family, since all the

Kusta Toom believed until the end of his life that he was a genius. He lived in the forest near Koruste village.

members of the family were killed one by one and their castle was destroyed in the Livonian War.

The **Tamme outcrop and caves** are located on the eastern bank of Lake Võrtsjärv, near Neemisküla and Kaarlijärve villages. The outcrop of red sandstone extends to several kilometres up to the mouth of the outflow canal of the Tamme polder. The Dutch-type Tamme windmill, built in the 19th century, is still standing nearby.

Fossils of primordial fish have been found in the Tamme cliffs, which are under state protection. Lake water and the springs that flow out from under the cliffs have shaped the cliffs into natural sculptures.

An outstanding writer and the translator of the Bible Adrian Virginius was the Pastor at Puhja Church.

Puhja Church was built in 1499, but it was partly destroyed at the beginning of the 17th century. Only the choir with its star-shaped vaulting has preserved its original appearance. Several outstanding pastors have served at Puhja Church. In 1686–1694, Adrian Virginius (1663–1706) was the pastor; he translated the Bible into the Northern Estonian dialect there. His assistant was a writer and linguist **Johann Hornung** (1660–1715); together they published the New Testament and a self-help and song book in Northern Estonian dialect.

Adrian Virginius was the son of the Kambja pastor Andreas Virginius, who continued his father's work in publishing Estonian-language religious literature. Together with his father, he translated the Catechism, the psalms and the New Testament into Southern Estonian dialect. He also translated clerical books into Northern Estonian dialect. He was killed by Russians in the Northern War, being accused of spying for the Swedes. Johann Hornung was also arrested

Käsu Hans, the first Estonian poet, was a schoolteacher at Puhja.

in the Northern War and he died in a Russian prison.

In 1700–1730, **Käsu Hans** (Hans Kes) worked as a teacher and sexton in Puhja. He is considered to be the first writer of Estonian origin, based on his letter written in 1706 and a long Estonian-language poem Lamentation for the Destruction of Tartu, written in 1708. A commemorative stone to Käsu Hans and Adrian Virginius has been erected in front of Puhja Church.

PÕLVAMAA

PÕLVAMAA

At first, Põlvamaa was a part of the ancient Ugandi County; later, it belonged to the Teutonic Knights, the Tartu Bishop, Russia, Poland, Sweden and again, Russia. Põlvamaa was the "border state" between Russia and Livonia (part os southern Estonia and northern Latvia).

The natural character of Põlvamaa is shaped by numerous primeval valleys, the largest of which are, undoubtedly, those of the Ahja, Võhandu and Piusa Rivers. The beautiful sandstone outcrops or "walls" at the Ahja and Võhandu Rivers are known and admired by all Estonians. Many people visit them, and fortunately, less and less people scratch their names onto the high sandstone walls.

A marvellous natural environment encompasses the heart of Põlvamaa, where even some roads are known as historical landmarks – old winding roads have been beautifully fitted into the landscape. The truly impressive man-made Piusa Caves are again open to public. A walk in these cool sandstone cathedrals takes one deep into a totally different, mystical reality.

The shores of Lake Peipsi and Lämmijärv Lake are of an entirely different appearance. This is the ancient country of the Orthodox Setu people, where fields often grow onions instead of potatoes and rows of drying fish are hung like garlands under the eaves of the roofs. Setus inhabit areas near Lake Peipsi and some in today's Russia. The most famous Setu woman folk singer, Anne Vabarna, who knew more than 100,000 songs by heart, came from near Värska. In her time, she even visited Finland to sing her songs there.

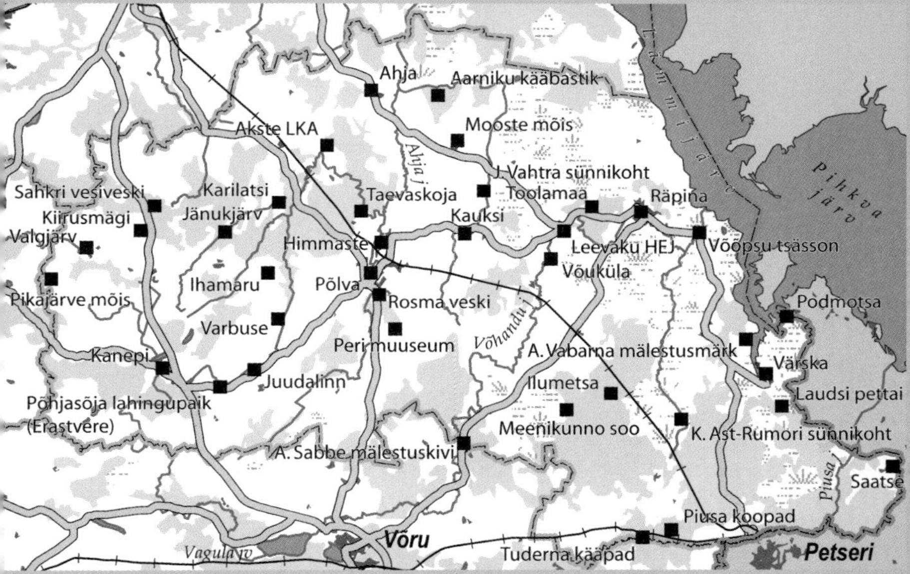
Ahja
Aarniku kääbastik
Mooste mõis
Akste LKA
Ahja j.
J. Vahtra sünnikoht
Sahkri vesiveski
Karilatsi
Taevaskoja
Toolamaa
Räpina
Kiirusmägi
Jänukjärv
Kauksi
Valgjärv
Himmaste
Leevaku HEJ
Võõpsu tsässon
Võuküla
Ihamaru
Põlva
Pikajärve mõis
Rosma veski
Podmotsa
Varbuse
Peri muuseum
Võhandu j.
A. Vabarna mälestusmärk
Kanepi
Värska
Juudalinn
Ilumetsa
Laudsi pettai
Põhjasõja lahingupaik
(Erastvere)
Meenikunno soo
K. Ast-Rumori sünnikoht
A. Sabbe mälestuskivi
Saatse
Piusa j.
Piusa koopad
Vagula jv
Võru
Tuderna kääpad
Petseri
Lämmijärv
Pihkva järv

AROUND SAVERNA

Pikajärve Manor lies on the road from Saverna to Otepää. A proud *Art Nouveau* style mansion, built in 1908, on a solid granite foundation, stands on a high lake shore. Earlier, in Soviet period, the mansion housed a nursing home, now it is privately owned and offers travellers food and shelter. A beautiful park and several stone outbuildings are situated near the mansion. Driving from Pikajärve towards Lake Valgjärv, you can admire the most beautiful rolling landscape of this region.

Picturesque Lake Valgjärv has attracted many painters.

The mansion of the Pikajärve Manor is characterised by its high granite foundations.

A memorial stone has been erected at Pikajärve Manor for **Valdo Pant** (1928-1976), one of the most renowned journalists of the Soviet time, who was born nearby. Pant brought back to Estonian broadcasting the concept of free conversation which had largely disappeared under the Soviet regime.

Journalist Valdo Pant was an innovator of radio and TV broadcasting.

One of his most important achievements was a 300-part TV series on WWII, „Today 25 Years Ago..."

Lake Valgjärv, located by the Saverna–Otepää Road, attracted the attention of several Estonian artists, the most famous of them being, undoubtedly, Konrad Mägi. His large painting "Valgjärv" (also known as "A Võrumaa Landscape"), created in 1916, was among his first works bought by the Estonian Art Museum in Tallinn. The Elva River starts its flow from this picturesque lake with three islets.

A long-time editor of the Estonian daily *Päevaleht*, **Georg Eduard Luiga** (1866–1936), was born in Valgjärve village. Besides his journalistic career, Luiga wrote short stories and poems. The modern reader is unlikely to be familiar with his collections of stories, but everybody knows a popular song about a field of rye swaying in the wind, the lyrics of which were written by G. E. Luiga.

A famous architect and interior designer **Johan Kuusik** (1888–1974) was also born in Valgjärve. He was among the founders of the Estonian Architects' Society, and for several decades taught at the Estonian State Art Institute. He designed the Tallinn Art Hall by the central square called Freedom Square, and the former building of the Central Assembly of Estonian Officers in Sakala Street, Tallinn, (now housing the Ministry of Defence).

The name of **Friedebert Tuglas** (1886–1971), one of the most significant Estonian short-story writers, literary critics and translators, is also connected with Lake Valgjärv. Having worked as a carpenter and granary keeper at the Ahja Manor, Jüri Mihkelson (1852–1926), the father of the future writer, moved on and rented the Tamme inn near Lake Valgjärv. The family lived there for two years and Tuglas started his school at the Maaritsa parish school. Later, Tuglas wrote that the Valgjärve landscape had much influenced his development. He depicted life at the parish school in his book *Memoirs of My Youth*.

In the early 20th century, a velodrome was located at the Sulaoja village by the Võru-Tartu Road, where all-Estonian competitions were held. The highest hill of the locality was named **Kiirusmägi** (Speed Hill) after the track.

Near Sulaoja, on the shore of a choked millpond on the Sulaoja stream, the Sahkri water mill still stands. The building is a typical example of numerous water mills that once worked on Southern Estonian rivers and streams, but which have now mostly fallen into ruins. The mill is privately owned.

Lake Jänukjärv is located north of Krootuse village by the Saverna-Põlva Road. North-west of the lake, in the Tiksi pine forest, lie the ancient burial mounds dating from the second half of the first millennium.

A legend about Lake Jänukjärv goes that Kalevipoeg, hero of the Estonian national epic had once come to the lake, very thirsty, and drunk almost all the water.

AROUND KANEPI

The first Estonian sculptor **August Ludwig Weizenberg** (1837–1921) was born near the small town of Kanepi, on the Tartu-Võru Road. He first trained as a cabinetmaker, and later studied at art academies in Germany and St Petersburg. He lived and worked in Rome, St Petersburg and finally, in Tallinn. He preferred to work with white marble, and created a number of busts of Estonian cultural figures from the time of the National Awakening in the second half of the 19th century, such as F. R. Kreutzwald, L. Koidula, A. Haava, and J. Hurt. He also depicted heroes of Estonian folk tales, such as 'Vanemuine', 'Linda' (in Tallinn, on Lindamägi, named after the sculpture), 'Dawn' and

A monument to the famous sculptor A. L. Weizenberg in front of the Kanepi village centre.

A memorial stone by the road, marking sculptor A. L. Weizenberg's birthplace at the Ritsiko inn.

'Dusk'. Weizenberg had many talents; he also wrote stories and plays and composed music.

Weizenberg's bas-relief portrait, set on a granite pedestal, was opened in front of the Kanepi village centre in 1937 to celebrate the 100th anniversary of his birth. Near the village, by the Kanepi-Otepää Road, on the bank of the Võhandu River, stands a memorial stone marking the artist's birthplace in the former Ritsiko inn.

The graves of Weizenberg's relatives in the Kanepi Mäe cemetery are adorned by his own sculpture named 'Hope' – a beautiful bronze figure of a woman raising her hand with a wreath. The sculpture was made in 1897.

Kanepi holds an important place in the history of Estonian culture and education. The first boys' parish school in Estonia worked there in 1804–1818, and a girls' school was opened soon afterwards. The history of the Kanepi School is closely connected with a Baltic-German Pastor **Johann Philipp von Roth** (1754–1818), who got on very well with the local peasants. He defended his parishioners against the local manor owners' arbitrary behaviour, and started to give the peasants family names already before the abolition of serfdom.

Together with his brother Carl August, his son Georg Philipp August and the Põlva Pastor Gustav Adolph Oldekop, he published the first Estonian-language (Tartu dialect) weekly newspaper *Tarto maa rahwa Näddali-Leht* (*The Weekly of Tarto Country Folk*) from March to December 1806. The newspaper had four pages, it appeared on Wednesdays, and all together 41 issues were published. It contained didactic and moralistic stories, useful pieces of advice, foreign and local news. The newspaper was closed and the published issues were collected together and destroyed, as Alexander I feared possible peasants' uprisings. For a long time, the histories of Estonian journalism claimed that no single

Kanepi Church is the only church in Estonia with a morning star at the top of its spire.

issue had been preserved. Only in 1995, were ten issues found in the Russian State History Archive in St Petersburg.

The Kanepi Song and Drama Society has had its role in Estonian cultural history. The society's choir participated in the first Song Festival in 1869 in Tartu. They managed to build a house for the society already in 1887, which is now one of the oldest of its kind in Estonia.

By the Kanepi-Põlva Road, quite near to Kanepi, north of the road at the village of Magari, stands a large stone commemorating a former Great Northern War battlefield. The war was fought against Swedish supremacy. On 9 January 1702 a battle was held near Erastvere, fought by 10,000 men of the Russian corps led by Count Boris Sheremetjev and 3,700 men of the Swedish field army led by General Major Wolmar Anton von Schlippenbach. The Swedes were outnumbered and beaten by the enemy and lost 1,400 men, while the Russians lost only 1,000. The Erastvere battle was the first major victory of the Russian army in the Northern War. Maybe already then the Swedish commander started to doubt his side in this war – it is said that 900 Swedes defected to the enemy. W. A. von Schlippenbach defected to Russians after the Poltava battle and served the Russian Tsar as a general in his army.

A couple of kilometres away from the battlefield towards Kanepi, in the former park of the **Erastvere Manor**, grows the tallest lime tree in Estonia, reaching a height of 35.5 m. The mansion has been destroyed; the famous Baltic German family, von Ungern-Sternbergs, who were the last owners of the manor, restored a small commemorative chapel to the family in the park by the road in 1990.

By the Kanepi-Põlva Road near Põlgaste there are the **Juudalinna burial mounds and cairns**, dating from the 3rd to the 5th centuries, where the ashes of the dead were buried. Bronze beads, rings and a rare brooch have been found in the mounds.

AROUND PÕLVA

The settlement of Põlva emerged sometime in the 15th century, when a church was built at the crossing of trade routes. The **Põlva Church** is one of the oldest in south-eastern Estonia and a legend is told about its construction, resembling the stories of the building of the Helme castle and Väike-Maarja church. The builders had not been able to raise the church walls, because all that was built during the day collapsed during the night – Old Devil came to destroy their work at nights. The builders had to follow a sage's advice and to wall in a kneeling virgin. The girl was tricked into her task just as it had been done in Helme. The builders asked the girls whether some of them wanted to become the keeper of church keys and one

A memorial stone to the Erastvere Battle in the Northern War stands near Magari village. The Swedish troops were outnumbered and beaten by the Russian army there.

girl, called Maarja, agreed. Later, when the church had been completed, it was named after her.

But time has shown that this wizardry did not help the church for long. It has been destroyed and rebuilt many times, which has been a regular fate of Estonian country churches, no matter whether somebody had been walled in or not.

The facade of the tower of the Põlva Church has some interesting architectural features. Inside the church there are a memorial tablet to Jakob Hurt, the altar painting created by Friedrich Ludwig von Maydell, and an organ made at the end of the 19th century.

According to a legend, a virgin called Maarja was walled in when the Põlva church was built.

Gustav Adolph Oldekop (1755–1838), the first journalist to write in the Estonian language, is buried in the Põlva **churchyard** near a small chapel. He was the Põlva pastor in 1781–1819 and had to give up his post because of his marriage that was unsuitable for his rank. He was a prolific writer – he compiled the *Eesti Ma-Rahwa Kalender* (*Calendar of the Estonian Country Folk*) that started to appear in 1796; together with the von Roths, he issued the *Tarto maa rahwa Näddali-leht*; he translated the peasants law of 1819 into the South Estonian dialect, and wrote many other pieces. He wrote a collection of poetry in the South Estonian dialect. The Estonian language of two centuries ago differs quite noticeably from the modern written language.

A crude stone cross bearing a memorial tablet stands on Oldekop's grave. The author of a one-time extremely popular textbook of one of the major dialects in Estonia, the Võru dialect, **Johann Georg Schwartz** (1793–1874), and artist **Jaan Vahtra** (1882–1947) are also buried in the Põlva cemetery.

An inscription on the gravestone says that Gustav Adolph Oldekop was the first journalist to write in the Estonian language.

The **Intsikurmu Song Festival field** and the nearby forest park form a kind of a trademark for Põlva. The first parish song festival was held at Intsikurmu in 1906. A new stage was erected in 1967, spacious enough for 500 singers. It was burnt down in a fire in 2002, but was restored very soon and the place again hosts all kinds of popular celebrations.

The inhabitants of Põlva have a long tradition of singing – the first local song festivals were held in Põlva in 1855 and 1857.

South-east of Põlva, in the near vicinity, at **Rosma**, stands a well-preserved water mill, now privately owned. In Rosma, closely packed houses line the old Värska Road that runs through the village, thus resembling the villages of Old Believers on the shore of Lake Peipsi. Old Believers are Christians who split from the Russian Orthodox Church in opposition to the Russian Church Reform introduced in 1653–1666 by Patriarch Nikon. The reform mostly applied to liturgical practices therefore the Old Believers differ from the official Russian Orthodox Church in their practices. In 1667 they were separated from the Russian Orthodox Church as they refused to accept some reforms, and were forced to flee the country.

The Society for Preserving National Heritage aims at maintaining such a style of housing. A famous educator **Johannes Käis** (1885–1950) lived in the old building of the Johannes School (located in the yard of the new building) by the Värska Road. Johannes Käis is primarily known as a teacher-trainer and as the innovator of pedagogy. He believed that directing pupils towards independent thinking was an important part of instruction. Käis's grave is at the Põlva cemetery, behind the chapel. A black granite obelisk, bearing words "The highest reward for an educator is when his ideas have been adopted by the open and grateful minds of his students", stands on his grave.

The Rosma hill-fort lies in the southern end of the village, by the Põlva-Võru Road, on a hillside by the deep valley of the Ora River. The fort was defended by a circular wall of soil; there could also have been a moat, filled with water from the dammed Ora River. The courtyard of the fort was about 100 m long and 80 m wide; it was used in the second half of the first millennium.

In **Mammaste**, north of Põlva, stands a memorial stone to a school for peasants, established in 1688. The stone stands on the location of the first primary school in Mammaste; it was opened on the 300th anniversary of the school in 1988. In 1687–1688, already 38 schools with about 900 pupils were working in Livonia. The opening of schools was inspired by the activities of the teachers' training seminar that took place in 1686–1687 near Tartu under the leadership of Bengt G. Forselius.

Writer **Richard Roht** (1891–1950) was born in the village of **Ihamaru** and attended the local Karaski village school. Roht had an adventurous life – he fought in WW I and the Estonian War of Independence (1918–1920), published a journal in Berlin, ran a farm and to top it all, he even went to jail for forgery. Roht was a prolific writer, publishing a number of realistic novels, a captivating series of memoirs and affectionate stories about nature for children, which remain in the treasury of Estonian children's literature.

The Põlva Peasantry Museum is located in the village of Karilatsi, about 2 km west of Koorvere on the Põlva-Tartu Road. It is interesting to note that there are two villages

PÕLVAMAA

A windmill of Dutch design at the Karilatsi Museum.

The Põlva Peasantry Museum in Karilatsi exhibits old farm buildings with authentic furnishings. Across the river on the picture below is the workhouse.

under the same name there; the museum is in the southern Karilatsi.

The **Karilatsi museum** is actually the central museum of the Põlva County, officially called the Põlva Peasantry Museum. This is a unique open-air museum with an area of 5 hectares. The buildings of the former Karilatsi (Kähri) parish centre, mostly built in the 19th century, are well preserved. They include a storehouse, the older building of the parish centre and the courthouse, which later became a workhouse; the new parish house together with outbuildings and a newer dwelling house for the schoolteacher. A classroom and a room where the teacher lived have been furnished in the former schoolhouse. The visitors to the museum can also view the granaries and an old smoke sauna, an old barn-dwelling house, a smith's farm, a windmill and the farm machinery and vehicles of the bygone times. Still another item of interest is an open-air model of Põlva County, exhibited on a couple of thousand square metres. There is a park by the museum, where numerous cultural and public figures have planted trees that are now known by their names.

The sandstone cliffs and walls (Taevaskoda) of the Ahja River are the symbols of Estonian primeval nature, just like the limestone klint running along the North Estonian coast. Many high sandstone cliffs can be found at the Ahja River. Two of them are the most beautiful and tens of thousands of people visit them each year. Suur-Taevaskoda and Väike Taevaskoda stand on the middle reaches of the Ahja River, downriver from the Saesaare Reservoir. Road signs point out the way to the cliffs from the Tartu-Põlva Road.

The 150 m long cliff wall of

Suur-Taevaskoda rises to the height of 24 m (the river valley is up to 38 m deep there); the ca 200 m long cliff of **Väike-Taevaskoda** is about 13 m high.

Neitsikoobas (Virgin's Cave) opens out from the Väike-Taevaskoda cliff; nearby, the ample spring of Emaläte (Mother Spring) flows out from under a cliff arch. According to local legends, Neitsikoobas hides virgins who have drowned in the river and the healing water of Emaläte cures eyesight. In front of the high wall of Suur-Taevaskoda stands the Salakuulaja (Spy) boulder A legend goes that once, a council of elders was held at Taevaskoda, and a guard noticed a spy in the river. The spy was killed by an arrow, and turned into a boulder.

A legend tells us that these places were called Taevaskoda (Sky Hall) because they were holy places, where people brought offerings and held councils. The 'council hall' had a high cliff wall, and the sky was its roof. The present-day Ahja Primeval Valley Nature Park covers the most beautiful, about 18-km long, run of the Ahja River from the Koorvere road bridge to the Valgesoo water mill.

The vicinity of Lake Kiidjärv, lying downstream of the Taevaskoda cliffs, with the **Otten water mill** is

The cliff wall of Suur-Taevaskoda rises to the height of 24 m.

The cave of Neitsikoobas at Väike-Taevaskoda.

A horse fell into the river form the Otten bridge in the cult film "The Last Relic".

The unfortunate young squire von Risbiter was thrown out of the coach at this road bend.

worth visiting as well. Some episodes of the Estonian cult film *Viimane reliikvia* (Last Relic), produced by 'Tallinnfilm', was shot here a few decades ago.

Himmaste village, north of Põlva, is the birthplace of one of the key figures of Estonian National Awakening, **Jakob Hurt** (1839–1907).

He was the son of the local schoolteacher and received a very good education for his time, studying theology at the University of Tartu. Development of the young man was advanced during the years spent as a private tutor with the family of Alexander Theodor von Middendorff in Hellenurme. Hurt became a leading figure of the national movement in 1869, when he gave a speech at the first Song Festival, declaring that the most important goal of the Estonians was the preservation of the Estonian language and Estonian nation. In the 1870s, he chaired both the Society of Estonian Men of Letters and the main committee of the Alexander School. He leant more towards the politics of C. R. Jakobson than that of J. V. Jannsen, who had become more and more obedient to the will of Baltic-Germans, removing him from the post of the editor of *Eesti Postimehe Lisaleht*. In 1872, Hurt became the minister at Otepää Church, but at first, he still applauded the start of C. R. Jakobson's newspaper *Sakala*, which was known for its anti-clerical position. Later, the disagreement between Hurt and Jakobson grew, as well as his antagonism with his German colleagues. Hurt remained between the two warring parties – those who believed in the kind Russian tsar, and those who preferred to do business with the Baltic German landlords. However, as history showed only too clearly later, nothing good came from either Russians or Germans. Those who relied only on their own enterprise, came out best.

Having tired of his post, Hurt finally decided to leave Estonia and he became the minister of the Jaani (St John's) parish of St Petersburg. The departure of Hurt in 1880 and

A memorial stone to Jakob Hurt lies under a large oak.

Jakobson's death in 1882 caused an ebb in the wave of the National Awakening movement, internal conflicts deepened and political fighting between different parties escalated. Hurt lost his important position in his homeland and turned more and more towards his long-time favourite occupation – collecting of folklore. His appeals launched the unprecedented activities of collecting folklore all over the country. With the help of about a thousand and a half collaborators he accumulated more than 100,000 pages of folkloristic material. He wrote numerous scientific articles on the Estonian language and popular culture and published the materials of his collections.

The house where Hurt was born has not been preserved, only a barn and a shed are still standing. A memorial stone marks his birthplace. Monuments to Hurt have been erected in Põlva and Tartu.

Leerimägi, a hill-fort dating from the early Iron Age – the 10th and 11th centuries – stands on the bank of the Lutsu River, east of the road near the village of Kauksi by the Põlva-Räpna Road. The cultural layer of the hill-fort is shallow, indicating only temporary use.

In past times, seven water mills have worked on the Lutsu River – the right-hand tributary of the Ahja River. An ancient Kauksi mill farm shows the life of a Põlva County water mill a century ago. The turbine and a pair of millstones have been preserved in the mill; some farm buildings are also intact.

A museum of local lore, containing historical objects, can be found at the centre of **Peri** village (a former **collective farm**), a few kilometres south of Põlva, east of the Võru Road.

Turning off from the Põlva-Kanepi Road towards Krootuse, we reach

Road Museum, open since summer 2005, at the former Varbuse horse post station.

the Tilleorg Nature Park. At the edge of the park, by the old Tartu-Võru Road, stands the **Varbuse Post Station**, built in 1861–1863. The post station was closed in 1931, and the building housed the Varbuse road repair inspecting centre. When it was later moved to Kanepi, the previous post station was found to be a suitable place for the **Road Museum**, which was created in 2001.

The museum, opened in June 2005, offers a visitor an interesting display. Different road construction machines and an exhibition of decorative sculptures that were erected by roadsides in the Stalinist era are exhibited in the machinery hall.

The Varbuse Post Station complex has been almost entirely preserved, being unique in Estonia. All the buildings of the former post station– the main building, the stables, the coach house, the smithy and the dwelling house of the stable hands – are intact. The buildings are positioned around a rectangular courtyard, formed of walls.

Besides the historical post station, a narrow and winding road starting at the village of Vooreküla, located 25 km north of Varbuse (on the Põlva-Tartu Road), to the village of

Puskaru, has been preserved as a historical landmark. The Põlva Peasantry Museum is located on this road. In the Middle Ages, the connecting route from Tartu via Vastseliina to Pskov followed this road. The post road, opened in the 1860s, connected two county centres – Tartu and Võru – and facilitated regular transportation of mail and passengers. Two hill-forts – **Kantsimägi** and **Rõõmumägi** – are situated on the high brink of the valley on the spot where the old post road crosses the valley. A 4-km hiking path takes people across the beautiful landscape of Tilleorg valley. Following the path, you can admire one of the many oak-trees, planted by Karl XII, King of Sweden, and watch the beaver dam and a copious Meriooni spring that flows out from a cave in the Devonian sandstone cliff.

AHJA, MOOSTE AND THEIR SURROUNDINGS

The mansion of the Ahja Manor is a Baroque building completed in the 18th century. For a long time a school was working in the mansion, but after the school moved over into a new building, it has stood empty in recent years. The ponds in front of the mansion and the park are well kept. The ruins of the burial chapel of the last manor owners, the von Braschs, are in the park about 500 m away from the mansion. Our literary classic **Friedebert Tuglas** (1886–1971) described the burial of a young squire as seen through the child's eyes in his book *Little Illimar (Väike Illimar)*.

On 2 March 1886, son Friedebert was born to the estate carpenter and later granary keeper in an old barn at the Ahja Manor. He became one of the most influential figures in Estonian literature and literary life of the 20th century. In the whirl of the revolutionary unrest in 1905, he was an enthusiastic left-winger, who spent a short time in jail and lived abroad for ten years. Before that, he was one of the creators and the ideologist of a literary group "Young Estonia". "More of European culture!" was the slogan of "Young Estonia", and this slogan was Tuglas's motto all through his life. From 1917 he lived in Tartu; together with Marie Under, August Gailit, Henrik Visnapuu and others, he formed a literary group "Siuru", launched a literary magazine *Looming* and was its first editor; on several occasions, he was the chairman of the Estonian Writers' Union; he was a member of the boards of numerous societies and naturally, he was a writer. He wrote a large number of Neo-romanticist short stories, and volumes of literary criticism and essays, and translated mostly Russian and Finnish literary works. When he was fifty, he wrote a book that made famous his home at the Ahja Manor. *Väike Illimar* is, undoubtedly, a masterpiece of Estonian memoirs.

In Soviet times, Tuglas lived in Tallinn. At first, he was given an honorary title of People's Writer,

The childhood home of writer Friedebert Tuglas is located in the neighbourhood of the Ahja Manor.

and he was elected a corresponding member of the Academy of Sciences of Soviet Estonia, later he fell into disfavour and lived for years in constant fear of getting arrested; his books were not published at that time. His name was rehabilitated by the Soviet authorities in 1955, after Stalin's death when the cultural climate became somewhat more relaxed.

The house where he was born has not been preserved; the site has been marked with a **memorial stone** that lies near the crossroads in the centre of the village, some ten metres towards Rasina. A small museum has been created at the Ahja Secondary School, giving an overview of Tuglas's childhood, life and works.

Akste Nature Reserve lies near the Ahja—Vastse-Kuuste Road. This unique nature reserve was created to protect wood ants. Approximately 1,500 nests of Scottish wood ants can be found on the two hundred hectares of the reserve; the largest of the nests are 2 m high. The total number of ants at Akste could, it is estimated, reach three milliards of individuals, or twice the number of humans on the Earth.

South of the road from Ahja to Rasina, up to 1.5 km into a pine wood, there are several groups of moss-covered sand mounds – the **Aarniku (Arniko)** burial mounds. Among others, there lies also the longest burial mound in Estonia, 95 m long, 9 m wide and 0.8 m high. This ancient burial ground dates back to the Middle Iron Age, or to the 5th–8th centuries.

The first group of mounds is located 300 m south-west from the game keeper's farm, the second – 1.3 km south-east of it, the third – 800 m south-south-east and the fourth – 800 south of the farm.

Fortune hunters destroyed a part of the mounds in 1799 and found an earthenware pot, filled with bones and charcoal. It was probably an ancient burial urn. Archaeological study of the mounds was led by Harry Moora in 1925. Emergency excavations were held in 1973, since part of the mounds had been disturbed by logging. The finds included jewellery and earthenware moulds for making jewellery. Some mounds contained only burnt pieces of bones. Mainly, there had been cremation burials, but some bodies had also been buried. Among the finds was even a coffin, hollowed out of a tree trunk. Each mound usually contained a number of burials. Bigger mounds had been formed of many smaller mounds, which had grown with new burials and finally joined each other.

Mooste is located near the crossing of the Tartu-Räpina and Põlva-Rasina Roads. The settlement grew around the magnificent mansion and the centre of the Mooste (Moisekatsi) Manor. The mansion is in good condition and has for de-

The mansion complex of the Mooste Manor is surrounded by a high granite wall with wonderful gates.

cades housed the local school. The roof of the mansion, made of black slates, gives the building an especially dignified atmosphere. Many of the outbuildings of the manor have also been preserved, but are in a bad condition. The ensemble of outbuildings is surrounded by a stone wall with wonderful gates and a unique belfry. The last owners of the manor before the land reform in 1919 were the von Nolckens who left for Germany via Sweden in 1918.

The birthplace of artist and writer **Jaan Vahtra** (1882–1947) is located south of Mooste, in a village of Kaaru (Kaaro) near the road to Kauksi.

Jaan Vahtra was primarily a painter and a book illustrator. Clear Cubist and Futurist influences can be found in his paintings and he is considered to be one of the innovators of Estonian book design. The last decades of his life were devoted to writing; he also published a volume of memoirs, talking about life in Põlvamaa during his youth.

The farm, where Vahtra was born, is still there and in use. A sign by the Mooste-Räpina Road points to the memorial stone, standing by the road.

AROUND RÄPINA

8 km west of Räpina, by the Tartu Road and the Võhandu River, stands the **Leevaku Hydropower Station**. A watermill worked at this place already in the early 19th century; later, there were also a wool mill and a sawmill and eventually, an electricity turbine. The hydro station was destroyed in WW II by the Germans; it was restored by the Young Communist League shock brigades in 1947 and worked up to 1968. Since 1993, the Leevaku hydro station is again producing electricity in an amount sufficient to meet the everyday needs of private consumers of a medium-size village.

Juhan Smuul (1922–1971) wrote an epic poem about the restoration of the Leevaku hydro station. In the late 1940s, Smuul produced many poems dedicated to reconstruction work and the great leader, Stalin. His readers, however, appreciate much more his popular humorous works.

When hiking upstream from Leevaku on the shores of the Võhandu Reservoir, we reach the smallest hill-fort in Estonia, **Võuküla Kindralimägi**. The former fort was located on the high

A hydro station is still working at Leevaku on the Võhandu River.

The derelict Toolamaa Mansion is an ancient wooden building.

The Räpina mansion is known as the Sillapää castle.

The Räpina paper mill was already operating 275 years ago.

bank of a river bend; it was only 40 m long and 20 m wide. The place is also called a General's grave but nobody seems to remember his name any more.

The former **Toolamaa Manor centre** is located near Räpina, on the Tartu-Räpina Road near the Toolamaa crossroads. The archaic wooden mansion with the stone base is noteworthy for its age. Its wooden part dates back to the 18th century, the stone parts may be even older. Now it is used as a dwelling, but it is in dismal condition.

The **Räpina settlement** on the Võhandu River emerged near the church, the manor and the paper mill already in the 18th century, but it became a town only in 1993. The mansion of the former Räpina Manor, or the Sillapää castle, was built on a peninsula jutting into the river reservoir. The mansion is surrounded by a park, rich in different tree species, now under the care of the local gardening school. The beautiful Classicist mansion, built by the owners of that time, the von Sievers family, was completed in 1858. Today, the mansion is used by the Räpina Free Education Society and the local lore and gardening museum.

Räpina is famous for its paper industry, started by the manor owners already in 1730 and thus being one of the oldest industrial enterprises in Estonia. Water power was used to run the machinery; mostly rags were used for raw material, which resulted in the making of superior-quality products. The Räpina factory has even produced paper for bank notes. In older times, special agents were travelling around in South Estonia, exchanging rags for earthenware pottery and collecting rags for the Räpina factory. Paper production continues in Räpina even now; mostly, the factory makes drawing paper and cardboard.

The museum located in the Sillapää Manor offers a good historical overview of the work of the paper factory, the gardening school and the Räpina Parish. It also displays examples of the local paper with different watermarks and bank notes printed on the paper made at the Räpina factory.

The year of 1784 is an important date in the history of Räpina, when the so-called **War of the Wooden Fence** took place. The local peasants had gone to Riga to complain about the local manor owner von Löwenwolde for forcing them to work too much, and because they lacked any rights. When the manor

The dynamic monument to the Wooden Fence War is locally known as the Iron Man.

owner learned about it, he called all his serfs, the total of about 500 men, to the mansion yard and promised to tell them about the "laws" received from Riga. Instead of the laws, there were 60 soldiers, whom he had invited to come to help him. He demanded his serfs tell him the names of the complainers, but nobody obeyed, and the soldiers were told to shoot the peasants. A real battle broke out with the peasants pulling pieces out of the wooden fence and attacking the soldiers. Five peasants were killed and eight were wounded; four soldiers were wounded as well.

A monument has been erected on the bank of the Võhandu River near the paper factory to commemorate this conflict. The monument features a powerful bronze figure, called an Iron Man by the locals.

South of Räpina, on the border of the town, near Sillapää, is the 10,000 years old **Tsõõrikmäe meteorite crater**. A low circular wall surrounds the crater which has a diameter of 40 m, which has by now been buried in peat; the floor of the crater is hidden under an 8-metre layer of peat.

BETWEEN THE VÕHANDU PRIMEVAL VALLEY AND THE PIUSA RIVER

By the Võru-Räpina Road, 1 km towards Räpina from Paidra, stands the **commemorative stone for the last Estonian Forest Brother** (Forest Brothers were Estonian guerrillas who took to the woods after WW II) **August Sabbe**, who was killed in an armed conflict with KGB agents on 28 September 1978. To escape arrest, he jumped into the Võhandu River and drowned himself. He managed to hide from the Soviet authorities for more than 30 years. If he had been able to survive for ten more years and welcomed the new Republic of Estonia, he could have come out of the forest an honest man.

The Meenikunno (Meenikunnu) **bog** is the largest in South Estonia; a 2.4 km board-walk has been built there for hikers. The Meenikunno Nature Reserve can be reached when driving from Veriora towards

The memorial stone to the last Estonian Forest Brother, August Sabbe, was erected on the bank of the Võhandu River.

Võru, and turning to the south-west towards Nohipalo at Viluste, ca 2 km from Veriora. Two lakes are almost side by side on the edge of the bog, but they differ from each other like night and day. The water of Nohipalo Mustjärv (Black Lake) is dark brown, being one of the darkest lakes in Estonia; Valgjärv (White Lake) is among the lakes with the clearest water. One of the few competitors to the latter is the sapphire-blue water of Äntu Sinijärv (Blue Lake) on the Pandivere Upland in the Lääne-Virumaa County.

If we turn to the south towards Rebasmäe from the Põlva-Värska Road at the Ilumetsa railway station, we will reach the **Ilumetsa meteorite craters**. There are five rounded hollows in the ground there, two of which are, without doubt, of meteoritic origin. The easiest to visit is **Põrguhaud** (Hell's Grave) with the diameter of 80 m and depth of 12.5 m. A good path runs to it and views have been opened to the crater, making it easily accessible, like its famous counterpart on the island of Saaremaa – the Kaali main crater. A small log hut stands at the beginning of the path to Põrguhaud, where a small exhibition offers information about the meteorites.

The second Ilumetsa crater, **Sügavhaud** (Deep Grave), has been preserved in its natural state;

Old people related the Ilumetsa craters with devils.

Põrguhaud is the largest of the Ilumetsa meteorite craters.

no trees have been felled to make it more easily observable. Sügavhaud is about 50 m wide and 5 m deep.

The third larger hollow, the 25 m deep **Kuradihaud** (Devil's Grave), has sometimes also been considered as a meteorite crater, but no scientific proof has been found about it.

A stone of about 10 m-diameter fell from the sky near Ilumetsa about 6000 years ago and broke into pieces just before hitting the earth. The meteoritic origin of the craters was proved by geologist **Ago Aaloe** (1927–1980) only in the 1960s. But the locals had known already for centuries that these hollows were by no means ordinary ones, and that is why they were related with devils and Hell. A legend about Põrguhaud goes that once there had been a church at this site, and it had fallen into the earth when three brothers had entered it together. After that, Põrguhaud had been the nest of devils, where they had made fires at night. People also tell that it is not advisable to say the Estonians' favourite curse *kurat!* (Devil) near these hollows. Those who do it will then become the serfs of the Devil.

The Piusa caves are not of natural origin. The mining of valuable sand for making glass was started there in 1924, and about 10 km of caves were hollowed into the earth. An open sandpit was made at the same time. The area of caves stretches underground for about 6 hectares.

When the mining was stopped, it was found that the caves that had become a tourist attraction could easily fall down on the visitors. Some entrances to the caves were dynamited, and signs prohibiting entry were placed at others.

Since 2001, some of the caves are open again and thousands of people visit them. Dim colonnades, 5–6 m high, are chilly even on the warmest summer days. The area of the Piusa caves is actually a nature reserve that was created to protect bats. In winter, more than 3,000 bats of different species gather to hibernate in the caves. The Piusa bat colony is the largest in the Baltic countries and bats fly there even from a distance of 100 km.

Near the old Pskov-Võru Road, between the village of Tamme and the Piusa railway station, lie the **Tuderna burial mounds** (also, Piusa burial mounds) on both sides of the road. Stretching over 6 km, there are about 230 rounded mounds; the diameter of most of them is 6–8 m, and they are only about knee-high. But the largest rounded burial mound in Estonia was found there, too; it is 1.4 m high and its diameter is 22 m. Burials were held there probably in the second half of the first millennium and even later.

Before WW II, the highest railway bridge in Estonia was located on the Tuderna stream; it was constructed in the 1880s by Polish builders. During different wars, the bridge was blown up and rebuilt again several times.

The largest rounded burial mound in Estonia was found among the Tuderna burial mounds.

The Räpina-Vastseliina Post Road passed through Tuderna in the 16th–17th centuries. Naturally, a number of inns had been built by the road, such as the Liiva, Piiri and Tuderna inns.

When we drive about 3 km south of the Orava railway station towards the village of Niitsiku (Niidsiku), and turn to the south-east at Kahkva village, we arrive in the **village of Päävakese**, the birthplace of writer and politician **Karl Ast-Rumor** (1886–1971). The buildings of his home are intact and bear a memorial tablet, but they are empty and derelict. In 1905, Karl Ast (Rumor was his literary alias), took an active part in political struggle where people demanded their social and political rights from the tsarist regime and the local Baltic Germans. Ast was even jailed for a period. Later, he was a member of the Constituent Assembly and the Estonian Parliament, and was twice appointed a minister. In the 1930s he travelled much and represented Estonia in Paris and Stockholm. After the occupation of Estonia by the Soviets, he lived in

Brazil, Canada and the USA. He published short stories and later, in exile, his memoirs.

BETWEEN VÄRSKA AND SAATSE

North of Värska, by the border with Russia at **Podmotsa**, stands a beautiful **Setu** 'tsässon' (a small chapel), which was built in the 1760s and is the oldest of its kind in the **Setu** region. In the cemetery near the chapel there are several stone crosses made at the time of the Russian-Livonian War (1558-1582).

In the Setu region, each village used to have its own chapel, called 'tsässon'. About 80 of them have been preserved up to now, including those located across the Russian border. Usually, they are small wooden prayer houses; their interiors are decorated with many icons, votive scarves, candles and flowers. The chapel roof is adorned with a modest Orthodox cross. Each village built its own chapel, which was maintained by all inhabitants of the village. Each chapel, like each church, had its own patron saint.

The name of the chapel originates from a Russian word for hour, because hour-long services were held in them. In the olden times, chapels and churches were open for everybody, and travellers were also able to sit and meditate in them. Now the village elder or the nearest neighbour holds the key to its door. The name day of the patron saint is celebrated with a large party for the whole village. In some cases, the party is held even twice a year, like in Võõpsu, where the chapel is dedicated to St. Nicholas – there are two St. Nicolas's days in the calendar. Burial services are also held at these chapels.

On the shore of Värska Bay, in Võpolsova (Võporsova), where the Karisilla stream flows into the bay, stands a granite memorial stone marking the birthplace of the **folksinger Anne Vabarna** (1877–1964). She is without doubt the most famous Setu folk singer; more than 100.000 verses of her songs (6000 pages on paper) have been recorded. She was the creator of the Setu epic *Peko*. This illiterate woman, who had a phenomenal memory, performed her songs in Helsinki and in Moscow. She was a skilled improviser and creator of songs; she knew numerous riddles and sayings. Her grave in the Värska churchyard is marked by a stone with her bas-relief.

Looking at the newly renovated 'tsässon', it is difficult to believe that it was built in 1760.

Anne Vabarna was the most famous Setu folk singer.

The Laudsi pine tree was believed to have power over the dead in the other world.

Exhibition in the barn of the Setu Museum.

South of Värska, between Värska and Verhulitsa, grows an ancient pine tree, which mediated between our world and the other world. The straw from the dead person's bed was burnt under the Laudsi (deathbed) pine tree and her or his earthenware crockery were broken there, closing for ever her or his way back to the living world.

The Värska Orthodox Church was completed in 1904. It is a beautiful church built of red bricks and granite with an arched gate bearing the words "Come back, children of Men!" Folksinger Anne Vabarna was buried in the churchyard; the church is adorned with many wonderful and maybe even miracle-working icons.

Since the summer of 1998, the Setu Farm Museum has been offering its visitors a unique opportunity to get acquainted with the Setu farm architecture, old tools and the rich handicraft of the late 19th and early 20th century. Authentic farm buildings from North-Setu region, including a dwelling house, a granary, a workshop, a pottery shed, a smoke sauna, a cattle shed, a smithy and a barn, have been re-erected at the museum. The museum constantly arranges exhibitions devoted to some specific subject; in summer, local folk musicians, such as the folk groups Leiki and Kuldatsäuk, give concerts there.

A 'tsäimaja' (teahouse), opened at the museum in 2004, serving authentic Setu food.

Another **Setu Museum** is located in **Saatse**. The museum opened in 1974 and it holds more than 20,000 objects collected from the Setu region. It also exhibits art works of Renaldo Veeber, the son of the founder of the museum. The museum is located just on the border with Russia and is now a branch of the Värska Setu Farm Museum.

An inscription on the gate of the Värska churchyard calls back the children of Men.

VÕRUMAA

VÕRUMAA

No wonder that on some maps, issued in Estonia, Võrumaa is coloured almost dark brown - it is the roof of Estonia. Võrumaa does, indeed, have more hilly landscapes than other Estonian regions. Wooded hillocks with small lakes in between are the symbols of Võrumaa. Suur Munamägi and Vällämägi are the highest hills of the Haanja Upland.

Another important characteristic of Võrumaa is the local dialect, which the people living in the area have started to protect and develop. For a number of years now, Võro children can learn to read from a primer in their own dialect. Estonia is a large country indeed, it even has several languages!

Bordering with Latvia in the south, with Russia in the east, and having the Seto people somewhere in between, Võrumaa, too, is a "border state". Life can be quite uncomfortable when the enemy starts raiding. The ancient fight for freedom started in Võrumaa, which once was at the margin of the old Ugandi County. Germans, who became the new masters, also did not feel safe and started to build castles as they settled there. They erected the powerful stone castles of Kirumpää and Vastseliina.

A stone sculpture of the Seto 'mother of songs' – 'lauluimä' – stands on a high reservoir shore in Obinitsa. The building of the wooden Obinitsa Church coincided with the death of Stalin. And Obinitsa is a strange place in itself, since all mortals, the living men and those who have already passed on, meet at the local churchyard each summer.

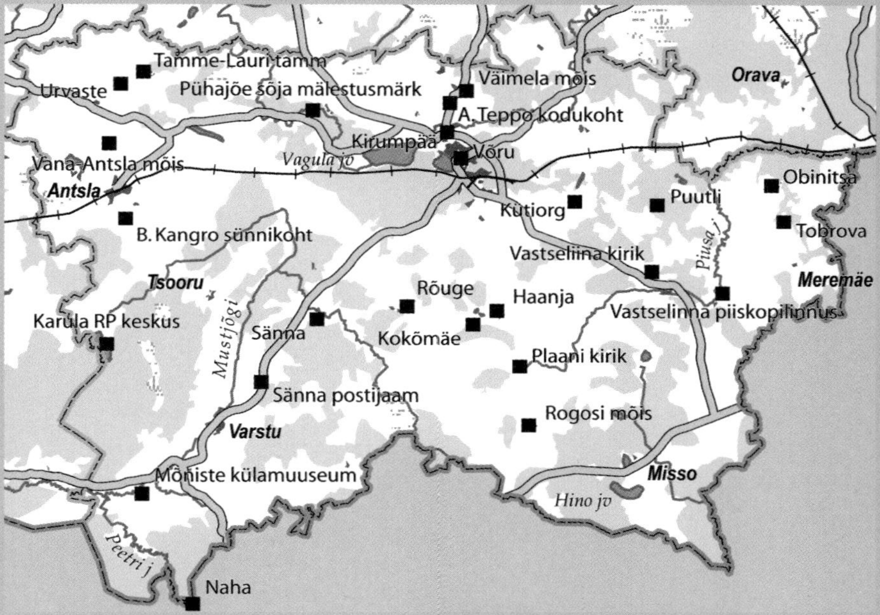

Tamme-Lauri tamm
Urvaste
Pühajõe sõja mälestusmärk
Väimela mõis
Orava
A. Teppo kodukoht
Kirumpää
Võru
Vagula jv
Vana-Antsla mõis
Antsla
Obinitsa
Kütiorg
Puutli
B. Kangro sünnikoht
Tobrova
Piusa j
Vastseliina kirik
Tsooru
Meremäe
Rõuge
Haanja
Vastselinna piiskopilinnus
Karula RP keskus
Mustjõgi
Sänna
Kokõmäe
Plaani kirik
Sänna postijaam
Rogosi mõis
Varstu
Misso
Mõniste külamuuseum
Hino jv
Peetri j
Naha

URVASTE, SÄNNA AND TSOORU

Urvaste is located in the northwestern corner of Võrumaa; its beautiful landscapes are made even more expressive by a primeval valley that cuts deep into the earth, and by two deep, long lakes – Lakes Uhtjärv and Lõõdla.

Urvaste Church is the only basilica-type country church still standing in Estonia; it was first built in the late 13th century, but due to later pillaging and fires, it has been rebuilt many times. The ground plan of the church has remained the same. It is believed that the altarpiece of the church was made by sculptor August Weizenberg.

Johan Gutsleff was the Pastor at Urvaste from 1642 to 1656. He compiled a Latin-language grammar of the South-Estonian dialect and a German-Latin-Estonian dictionary containing 1,800 entries. Probably, he also translated the Old Testament into the South-Estonian dialect. Being a devoted man of God, he tried to convert heathens to Christianity and even wrote a book to explain why the Võhandu River is not a holy river. Linguists have said that Gutsleff's knowledge of Estonian was better than that of the author of the first Estonian grammar, Heinrich Stahl (See Järvamaa County, Järva-Madise).

A memorial stone to the founder of an elementary school (sexton school) in Urvaste, Pastor Matthias Uthander (1868–1906) stands in front of the church. An inscription on the other side of the stone commemorates the 300th anniversary of the founding of the first school in Urvaste.

In the 18th century, Urvaste was an important centre of the Herrnhuter or Moravian Church in Estonia. The local Pastor Johann Christian Quandt (1704–1750) had joined the movement and he founded a congregation in Urvaste in 1741. He also published a few books of moralist tales and songs in the Estonian language.

The Moravian Church was founded in Herrnhuth, Germany. This was a movement of religious awakening that preached the liberating of the world through religion. At its peak in the 19th century, the Moravian Church had about 50,000 members and more than 150 prayer houses in Estonia. An interesting fact is that Herrnhuters are active even today, as members of the Estonian Evangelical Lutheran Church.

A memorial stone to the poet **Marie Heiberg** (1890–1942) stands in the park behind Urvaste Church. Her verses attracted attention when she was only 16 years old, when she published her first collection of poetry Songs of a Child of Sorrow. She also wrote short stories, mostly about life in Võrumaa. Unfortunately, at the age

Urvaste church is the only basilica-type country church in Estonia.

Poet Marie Heiberg published her first collection of poems when she was only 16 years old.

The Tamme-Lauri oak tree in Urvaste is the thickest tree in Estonia.

of 29 years, she became mentally ill, as happened to Juhan Liiv.

Urvaste can boast the most powerful tree in Estonia. An oak tree with the girth of 8.25 m that grows on the land of the Tamme-Lauri farm, north of the village, is the thickest tree in Estonia. The tree used to be hollow, and 7 people are said to have fitted into the hollow. In 1960, the hollow was filled with concrete to prevent the tree from breaking apart. The oak is some 20 m tall and it is protected by a lightning rod. The Tamme-Lauri oak is 680 years old, which is more than ten times the average lifespan of Estonian men.

The Urvaste Lauri-Tamme oak is depicted on the back of the Estonian ten-kroon note.

There are three settlements called Antsla in Estonia - Antsla, Vana-Antsla and Uue-Antsla (Vahtsõ-Antsla). The latter two are former manor centres, which came into being when Antsla Manor was divided into two parts. Antsla village grew around an inn and a horse post station, its life was boosted by the opening of a railway station in 1889. Earlier, the village had first been called Siksälä and was later called Hauka; the name Antsla came into use when the railway station was named after the manor.

The **Vana-Antsla Manor** has a majestic park with many ancient oaks. The mansion, which now houses a vocational school, is in great need of repair. A 200-year-old door of the mansion can be noticed from afar. Terraces descend from the mansion towards a horseshoe-shaped pond. Among the outbuildings there is a curious rounded tower with a pointed roof that resembles a picture in a fairy-tale book. The tower is a former

The Vana-Antsla gardener's house is also called a bottle house.

VÕRUMAA

gardener's house and it has also been called an apple store.

An ancient avenue of broad-leaved trees leads from Vana-Antsla Manor to the centre of Uue-Antsla Manor. Uue-Antsla mansion has been destroyed.

When talking about Vana-Antsla Manor, the occasion should be mentioned when a prince was born there. The Duke of Södermanland, the later King Charles IX, stopped over at a castle there in 1601, during the Swedish-Polish war, and his wife gave birth to a son called Charles Philip. The later King is said to have been so happy with his son that he planted two oak trees in the park of the castle, which have now grown into real giants.

Oese village, a few kilometres south of Antsla, is the birthplace of the writer **Bernard Kangro** (1910–1994). Kangro lived for a long time in Lund, Sweden, where he published a literary journal Tulimuld for 43 years, and led the Estonian Writers' Co-operative Publishing House for almost as long a time. Being a prolific writer, he published more than ten collections of poetry, a number of novels and several volumes of memoirs. He also published long essays about Estonian literature, such as two volumes on the group of poets Arbujad (Soothsayers). A memorial stone marks the writer's birthplace.

Karula National Park was created to protect the local hilly national heritage landscape full of sparsely positioned farms. The area of the park is about 11,000 hectares, two-thirds of which are covered with woods. Lake Ähijärv is the largest among the 40 lakes in the park; the information centre of the park is located on the shore of this lake. An exhibition gives information about local nature.

A charming old wooden church in Kaika village, located in the park, is still standing, but unfortunately, it is in a bad state of repair and may fall down very soon.

The southernmost point of Estonia is located in Mõniste parish, in Karisöödi village near Naha forest keeper's farm. A sign in Naha village says that the southernmost corner of Estonia is nearby, but inaccessible as no roads go there. A unique open-air museum, thought to be the oldest in Estonia, is located 4 km south of Mõniste village, in Kuutsi. The Estonian Open Air Museum in Rocca al Mare was founded in 1957 and its buildings were opened in 1964.
Mõniste Open Air Museum was begun by the local enthusiast Alfred Lepp already in 1948. Its visitors can see farms complete with outbuildings and all kinds of household objects and tools from the Tsarist time and the time of the Estonian Republic.

Two writers are associated with Sänna, whose works have sprung from Võrumaa and Võro dialect. The poet **Artur Adson** (1889–1977) spent his childhood at Kaugu. The boy was brought from Tartu to be raised by his aunt when he was only three months old. His

A memorial stone to publisher and writer Bernard Kangro is located in the garden of a private house.

Poet Artur Adson grew up in the Kaugu school house in Sänna.

childhood among people speaking the Võro dialect left a strong impression on the soul of the future writer; most of his poems are written in this dialect and Võrumaa is frequently mentioned in them.

Adson and his wife Marie Under, also a poet, left Estonia in 1944. For many years he worked at the archive of the Royal Library in Sweden. In exile he mostly wrote memoirs, but also published some poems.

A memorial plaque to Adson has been put on the wall of the former Kaugu schoolhouse.

Another memorial plaque to another writer from Sänna, **Juhan Jaik** (1899–1948), is also on the wall of the same schoolhouse. Jaik was born in Sänna Manor centre and went to Kaugu School a few years after Adson. As a young man, he participated in a secret separatist movement and was banished to Russia near the Volga River. Later he was a volunteer in the Estonian War of Independence and worked for some time as a journalist. In 1944, he escaped to Sweden, just like Adson. He is best known for his adventure stories for young people; in some of them, the characters include numerous weird beings familiar from Estonian folklore. His best short stories have been published under the title Stories from Võrumaa (Võrumaa jutud); another collection, Kaarnakivi, collects his best children's stories. In ancient times, a strange stone, called Kaarnakivi (raven's stone), could be found in a raven's nest. The stone had miraculous power; if you rubbed the stone and said a wish, the stone would fulfil your wish.

A monument to Juhan Jaik (sculptor Tiiu Kirsipuu) stands in Rõuge Park, featuring Kaarnakivi (belemnite, thunderstone, a small black stone supposedly having magical powers). A bird's nest with Kaarnakivi is on the top of a tall column. A memorial stone marks the writer's birthplace some 50 m off the dilapidated wooden mansion of Sänna Manor.

Juhan Jaik was a master of ghost stories.

Sänna landscapes have been shaped by the Pärlijõgi River that sends its clear waters down the Haanja Upland. A few centuries ago, large numbers of freshwater pearl mussels were caught in the river. Precious pearls found in them were sold even in St Petersburg. Today, freshwater pearl mussels are among the rarest and most endangered species in Estonia and they have disappeared from South Estonia. The last of them are hidden in a small stream in Lahemaa.

In Kangsti village by the Võru-Valga Road stands **Sänna Post Station**, which was used from the early 18th century up to the War of Independence. The post station was built at least 200 years ago and it is one of the oldest post stations in Võrumaa, which has also preserved its original outbuilding. According to legend, Empress Catherine II stopped overnight there. The building is in good repair.

AROUND VÕRU

The upper reaches of the Võhandu River have from times immemorial been known as the Pühajõgi River (Holy River) and the home of water spirits. For many centuries after the arrival of Christianity people brought offerings to sacred groves on riverbanks. Pastors barked from their pulpits on their still-heathen congregations, but nothing helped. One of the most enthusiastic fighters against such heresy was the Urvaste Pastor Johan Gutsleff (see above, Urvaste).

The Pühajõgi flowed lazily in its bed until Sõmerpalu Manor owner built a mill there, which the local peasants hated. Rains did not stop in 1642 and all crops failed. Everybody knew that the river revenged such "desecration" and a warring group of 60 peasants went and demolished the mill. Only the soldiers, summoned by the manor owner, were finally able to pacify the angry peasants. Today, this event, known as the "Pühajõgi War" is commemorated by a stone erected in Osula near the Võru-Viljandi Road.

Väimela Manor centre stands north of Võru, beside the Põlva Road; a farming school has been working there since 1920. Today it bears the name of Võrumaa Vocational Training Centre.

In the Pühajõgi War the peasants fought to defend the spirit of the river.

Terraced steps lead from the Väimela mansion to the lakes in the park.

The mansion of the Manor was built and rebuilt in the 19th century; about a dozen outbuildings are also intact, including a distillery, a granary and a dairy. A large park with two beautiful lakes – Lakes Alajärv and Mäejärv – belongs to the Manor. The ruins of the manor owners' burial chapel are near Alajärv Lake. There is a legend about a clever valet of the manor, who had won back the manor that its owner had lost in a card game. The grateful manor owner gave him free keep and a place in his own burial chapel.

The ruins of **Kirumpää Bishop's Castle** stand north-east of Võru, beside the Võru-Põlva Road – a few wall fragments on a high hill from where the visitor can see the Võru Church tower and some buildings of the town. The Tartu Bishop built Kirumpää Castle to defend the land against Russians from Pskov. The castle was already standing there in 1322, when, according to chroniclers, Lithuanian Prince Gediminas besieged and conquered Kirumpää.

The Bishop and the Livonian Order started their raids on the eastern areas from this castle. The Russians, naturally, did not like it and several times they attacked and burnt this enemy's nest. By the beginning of the Livonian War, the castle was surrounded by a large settlement of merchants and craftsmen, which was swept from the earth during the invasion by a Russian army in 1558. Kirumpää Castle was completely destroyed during the Swedish-Russian War in the mid-17th century. Later, people used the stones from the ruins to build houses in Võru town.

The birthplace of the accordion-maker **August Teppo** (1875–1959) stands north of Võru, in Loosu. A memorial stone has been erected in the corner of the garden of the famous master's home. The wife of his grandson is now living in this farm.

The famous accordion-maker and player August Teppo made his first instrument when he was 15 years old. Four years earlier, he had mended his brother Aleksander's accordion. He taught himself the craft and made all his tools. He made his last accordion when he was 84 years old; he died in the same year. During his life, Teppo made about 150 instruments, which are now highly valued. The oldest among them has been used for music-making for already 107 years.

The town of Võru can be glimpsed from the high site of Kirumpää castle.

On festive occasions people play the accordion beside the memorial stone to August Teppo.

Teppo's accordions are remarkable for their clear and pleasant timbre and exceptionally good tuning. When still young, Teppo was a much sought-after musician at parties; he also wrote music for his instruments.

Võru, the capital of Võrumaa lies almost in the centre of its county on the edge of the large and wide Võru Vale, on the shore of Tamula Lake. The town was named after the Veeru Stream, which first gave the name to the local manor. Today, it is called the Koreli Stream.

A 4,000 years old site of an ancient settlement has been found on the shore of Tamula Lake. Arrow points, stone axes, amber beads and a large amount of bone scraps of the game, including those of big-horned aurochs, caught by ancient hunters, were found when the site was excavated.

The Mediaeval predecessor of Võru was the stone castle of Kirumpää (see above, Kirumpää), from where the townspeople harvested building stones for their houses. The seed for the town was sown on 27 August 1784, when Empress Catherine II decreed that a new county was created, covering most of the present Võrumaa; Võru Manor, standing beside the Tartu-Pskov post road, was bought to become the centre of the new county. At first, it was planned to locate the county centre at Vana-Koiola, but the present location proved to be much more suitable. The newly appointed county officials moved from Vana-Koiola to Võru Manor just on this date.

The brand-new county centre developed at a snail's pace, its population was small and its enterprises were still smaller. By the mid-19th century, Võru had gathered fame as an educational centre – there were several schools of different types there and the local Germans readily sent their children to attend them. The most famous school of the time was H. Krümmer's boarding school for boys.

The older cultural history of Võru is very closely connected with the physician and man of letters, **Friedrich Reinhold Kreutzwald** (1803–1882), who was born in Virumaa, but moved to Võru after having graduated from Tartu University in 1833. He lived in Võru for the next 44 years and worked as a town physician.

After moving to Võru, Kreutzwald married Marie Elisabeth Saedler, the daughter of a Tartu tinsmith of German descent, and had three children with her. His wife arranged her household in such a meticulous petty bourgeois order that to escape from it, he often found refuge in the attic. In that very attic, he wrote most of his voluminous literary work. In the 1840s, he was a prolific contributor to a German newspaper

The monument to Friedrich Reinhold Kreutzwald has become the symbol of Võru.

Inland, published in Tartu, and offered its readers quite truthful descriptions of peasants' lives, earning the wrath of the nobility and endless persecution by the authorities.

Kreutzwald was constantly haunted by a lack of money, since he had borrowed to buy his house and publishing his works was often very costly. Once he even had to sell his horse and carriage to make both ends meet. He jokingly wrote about it, "then we had to eat horse meat".

Being known, foremost, as the author of Kalevipoeg, he actually wrote in almost all genres – he published poems, and didactic stories to educate the public, and translated stories and poems from German. He wrote a play The Plague of Vodka (Wina-katk) promoting temperance, memoirs titled A Couple of Steps in the Road of Travels (Paar sammokest rändamise-teed), a satirical story about simpletons who did everything in their own way, a popular scientific The World and What Can Be found in It (Ma-ilm ja mõnda, mis seal sees leida on) and a health handbook Home Doctor (Kodutohter). This list is far from being exhaustive and Kreutzwald is rightly taken as the founder of Estonian national literature.

His correspondence with Baltic-German Estophiles, German, Finnish and Russian scientists and young Estonian intellectuals is of immense cultural and historical value. Corresponding with friends and fellow scientists with similar intellectual interests enabled him to withdraw from the dull everyday routine of a provincial town.

Kreutzwald is called the "Father of Songs" and the "Viru Singer"; there are more monuments to him than to any other person in Estonia. The monuments stand in Võru, Tartu, Rakvere and Tallinn and memorial stones in Jõepere, Virumaa, and Kaarli, near Rakvere. The most impressive monument stands in Võru, on the shore of Lake Tamula. This bronze sculpture and several bas-reliefs, made by sculptor Amandus Adamson, were cast in Italy and erected in Võru in 1926. The sculpture was paid for by public donations.

The Memorial Museum to F. R. Kreutzwald, located in the house where the writer once lived (31, F. R. Kreutzwaldi Street) gives an excellent overview of his life and

Empress Catherine II donated money for the building of Võru Church. The all-seeing eye decorates the facade of the church.

work. The wooden building from the year of 1793 has by now been carefully restored and the museum is open to visitors.

Võrumaa Museum (11, Katariina Street) gives an overview of Võrumaa history from the ancient times up to the present day, although it focuses on the battles of the War of Independence.

The **Võru Lutheran Church** was built in the final years of the 18th century. Empress Catherine II again played her role here, donating 28,000 silver roubles, a remarkable sum of money for that time, for the building of the church in the county centre. Naturally, the church was dedicated to St. Catherine. The Classicist church building can boast a handsome spire.

In the park next to the church stands a **monument** to the Võrumaa people who perished on the ferry Estonia in 1994. The ferry sunk in the stormy Baltic Sea, and over 700 people died a horrible

The Võro Institute is engaged in the preservation of the unique Võru dialect.

death. The author of this deeply emotional sculpture is Mati Karmin.

When in Võru, the visitor should certainly find time to walk along the shores of Lake Tamula and cross the suspension bridge leading to Roosisaar. This is the longest suspension footbridge in Estonia; its length is almost a cable – 180 m.

RÕUGE

The neighbourhood of Rõuge is not as hilly as Haanjamaa, but it offers breathtaking views from the high verge of the primeval valley. The area is slashed by a 10 km long and 45 m deep primeval valley and its numerous side gullies. A number of lakes lie on the valley floor; among them is the deepest inland body of water in Estonia. Lake Rõuge Suurjärv is 38 m deep. A legend tells us about a magnificent church with silver bells, which was drowned in the lake. Now, after each St. Michael's day, a bridge is said to appear over the lake, a black monk steps on the bridge and cries that the time will soon come when the church would surface again.

The best-known side gully has been given the romantic name of Ööbikuorg (Valley of Nightingales); this steep-sloped gully is a couple of hundreds of metres long and full

The bronze hands, reaching out from the granite pedestal commemorate people from Võrumaa who perished with the ferry Estonia.

The neighbourhood of Rõuge offers breathtaking views over lakes and hillocks.

The water-ram pumps water without any external energy supply.

of the song of nightingales in spring. A wonderful view opens on the high edge of a neighbouring gully, Tindiorg, towards Lake Liinjärv in the bottom of the gully. A low sightseeing tower, which is also a swing, has been built on the edge of the gully.

An ancient Rõuge hill-fort stands between Ööbikuorg and Lake Liinjärv. The fort was permanently settled up to the 8th–11th centuries.

Remains of different buildings have been found in the fort. There were 5–6 simple dwelling houses with hearths and clay floors and a smithy. The fort was surrounded by a log wall; it has been burnt down six times. The fires refer to battles. Animal bones indicate that the inhabitants of the fort hunted elk, beaver, wild boar and bear, and ate beef, pork, lamb, goat and horsemeat. All this was revealed by thorough excavations which took place in 1950. The whole cultural layer of the fort, extending to a half metre, was excavated then.

Traces of an ancient settlement were found near the fort, where people lived in the 5th –11th centuries.

A nature path, starting at the sightseeing tower, follows the bottom of Tindiorg, taking the visitors past a rare bubbling piece of machinery with the funny name of 'water-ram'. Water-ram is an extremely environment-friendly hydraulic pump, able to lift water to the height of 24 metres. It is activated by hydraulic energy produced by a clever system of valves. Forcefully opening and closing valves take water uphill and one water-ram can meet the daily water needs of a farm. The first water-ram in Rõuge was built by a local farmer Friedrich Johanson.

Rõuge Church, built in the early 18th century, is exquisite in its simple and laconic way. The organ of the church was made by local masters, the brothers Kriisa, and it was fitted into the church in 1930. Across the road, opposite the church, a bronze soldier holding a sword stands on a tall pedestal – a monument to the War of Independence.

In 1945, the Soviets destroyed the monument and buried the bronze soldier in the ground. A local man Aksel Ollmann happened to see this; he dug the sculpture out and hid it somewhere else. Restoration of the monument was discussed in 1988, and then Ollmann's widow revealed the hiding place of the solder. It rose from the ground, where it had lain for 40 years and is now again standing on its pedestal.

HAANJAMAA

Turning off from the Võru-Luhamaa Road at Verijärve towards Noodasküla, we arrive in the northern corner of **Kütiorg valley**. The Küti Mäeveski mill has been working there since 1868. The mill is in working order. 5 km long and up to 70 m deep Kütiorg is the deepest valley in Estonia. Such deep slopes have attracted skiers, who have made the once wild natural area a winter resort.

Before the arrival of the skiers, the painter **Valdur Ohakas** (1925–1998) lived there during the warmer half of the year, as long as the weather permitted, and painted numerous wonderful pictures of the valley. This bohemian artist also kept a donkey at Kütiorg. The Open Studio is working at Kütiorg now, initiated by the photographer Peeter Laurits and his wife Leelo.

The birthplace of **organ makers, the Kriisas**, is west of Haanja, at Kokõmäe. A large memorial stone, dedicated to three generations of

Rõuge Church stands on the shore of the lake where, according to the legend, there should be another church.

The bronze soldier from the Rõuge monument to the War of Independence had to wait for 40 years in the ground until he could rise again onto his pedestal.

Memorial stone at the home of the brothers Kriisa, the organ-builders. They made organs for more than 20 Estonian churches.

organ makers, stands at the roadside.

The organ-making was started by three brothers – Juhan (1858–1942), Jakob (1861–1949) and Tannil (1866–1940) Kriisa – in the 19th century. Tannil was the designer and he did the finest work, Jakob made the pipes and Juhan worked on the bellows and bodies of the organs.

The first organ was made in 1886; it was installed at Misso church. Later, the brothers Kriisa provided organs for many churches all over Estonia including on Saaremaa Island. The enterprise of the three brothers made altogether 20 organs.

Tannil's son Eduard (1902–1968) represents the second generation of organ-makers; he studied the craft with his father and continued the work after his death. He made only two organs, but repaired many of them.

Today, the work is continued by Eduard's son Hardo (b. 1940).

Haanja is the roof of Estonia. Our highest peak, the hill of **Suur Munamägi**, reaching 317 m above the sea level, stands there; at the same time, the height of the hill from its foot to its top is only 62 m. The absolute height of a neighbouring two-peaked Vällamägi hill is 304 m, but its relative height is 88 m, making it the record-holder among natural relief forms in Estonia. The hill of the highest relative height has been amassed by man: the Kiviõli semi-coke heap rises up to the height of 115 m. As the mean relative height of Estonia above the sea level is about 50 m, Haanjamaa is about 4–5 times higher than the mean level.

Haanjamaa has been put together by hillocks, valleys, lakes and bogs and by rivers and streams coursing between them. There are 170 lakes and thousands of smaller swampy hollows. The Haanja Nature Park with its area of 17,000 hectares and headquarters in Haanja village protects local landscapes.

One of the best-known buildings in Estonia – the **sightseeing tower** on Suur Munamägi – is located at Haanja. The beautiful Functionalist construction was built on the site of an earlier and lower wooden tower in 1939. At first, the height of the new tower was 26 m, but in 1969, another storey was added and now the visitor, who has climbed the tower, stands at a height of 29 m. With good weather, the view from the tower extends to about 50 km.

At the foot of the hill stands a stone to commemorate the brave fighting of the 1st Cavalry Regiment in the War of Independence. The architecturally outstanding mansion of Rogosi Manor stands about 10 km south of Haanja, in Ruusmäe village. The mansion was

The sightseeing tower, with its functionalist design, was erected on Suur Munamägi on the site of the former wooden tower.

The mansion of Rogosi Manor with its closed courtyard resembles a castle.

built on the site of a mediaeval castle and with its closed courtyard, it also resembles a castle. The name of the manor comes from its first owner, a Pole Stanislaus Rogosinsky. The mansion acquired its present shape in the 19th century, but the original layout of the building has been little changed. A small lake and a park with a band-shell lie behind the mansion, which is now housing an elementary school and a small museum.

After the nationalisation of land in 1919 the **Rogosi manor** owner's son, Guido von Glasenapp, was given a farm in the centre of the manor, called Uus-Rogosinsky, for his participation in the War of Independence. He built a new house for himself and lived there, and the mansion remained empty and fell to the prey of vandals. Fortunately, the local parish decided to open a school in the mansion and it was repaired. Later, it has been maintained and restored. Otto von Glasenapp, the son of the former owner, visited Rogosi in 1990 and was delighted to see the home of his fathers in such a good order. He was especially happy to see that the former mansion was being used as a schoolhouse. A relative of his, Patrick von Glasenapp, initiated a campaign in Germany to help to restore the Stone Bridge in Tartu.

The **Plaani Orthodox Church** was built beside the Haanja-Ruusmäe Road in 1873 to acquaint more Estonians with the official faith of the Russian tsars. The church, built of red bricks and stones, has been snugly fitted into the beautiful Haanjamaa landscape. The roof of a relatively small church accommodates even five onion domes, which have recently been covered with new tin roofs. The church was used for storage during the Soviet time and its renovation was time and effort-consuming. In the long term, the Orthodox Church plans to establish a monastery at Plaani Church.

THE SETO REGION IN VÕRUMAA

The **ruins of an ancient Bishop's** Castle, located 6 km off Vastseliina, at Vana-Vastseliina, are the symbol of the area. In the Middle Ages, there was only one settle-

Plaani Orthodox Church is a stone building wellfitted into the landscape.

ment called Vastseliina, which stood near the stone castle and was destroyed together with it.

The initial castle was built by the Livonian Order and by the Tartu Bishop in the mid-14th century. The original powerful defence tower was rebuilt into a strong stone castle, and more towers were added. Massive artillery towers were built at the corners of the castle in the 16th century. Unique ornamentation, resembling that of the Tartu Dome, can still be seen on the walls of the eastern tower. In the Middle Ages, the chapel of the Vastseliina Castle was the pilgrims' destination wellknown all over Europe. A holy cross that had been kept in the chapel gave a 40-day pardon from sins, confirmed by Pope Innocentius VI in 1354.

Vastseliina Castle was situated on the border between the East and the West, on the trade and military road between the former Old-Livonia and Pskov. This is the reason why the castle has changed hands on so many occasions. It has been ruled by Germans, Russians, Poles, and Swedes. Under the rule of the King of Poland in the late 16th and early 17th centuries, it was even an administrative centre and was called Novogrodek.

Russian Tsar Peter I visited Vastseliina in 1697 and found that the local Swedish garrison did not show enough respect towards him. The revenge taken in the Northern War that followed was severe. The castle was erased from the earth together with the settlement that had grown around it.

The settlement of Vastseliina was rebuilt several kilometres away from its former site. The castle proved to be a useful mine for building stones. Today, only some tall wall fragments and thick lower parts of two artillery towers are still standing.

Vastseliina Castle is remarkable for still another aspect. The white stork, which today is a very common bird species in Estonia, is actually quite a recent arrival. It has been recorded that the first pair of white storks, who had arrived in Estonia, built their nest in the Vastseliina Castle ruins in 1841.

The Piiri Inn, which has been open at one and the same place ever since 1695, stands in the neighbourhood of the castle next to the road and is another reminder of the border between the East and the West. The heyday of the inn was in the 19th century, when it started to sell the production of the distillery of the local manor.

After the destruction of the castle and its chapel, the local population was left without a church. The new church was built about 10 km west of the castle ruins, in Külaoru village, but for some reason, no village grew around the church, as it would have been customary. Vastseliina emerged a couple of kilometres away from the church. The local manor owner, Gotthard Lionel von Liphart, was much respected and very friendly and

The lower parts of the massive artillery towers have been preserved at Vastseliina Castle.

Vastseliina Church stands on a hill a few kilometres from the town.

understanding towards his peasants. He lies at rest at the cemetery near the church.

Almost the same story as in Rõuge happened to the monument to the War of Independence in Vastseliina. As usual, the Soviets dynamited the monument and cast the bronze sculpture of a soldier into the bushes. The local farmers picked it up and buried it. It was dug out in 1988, and now it again stands in the middle of Vastseliina.

A monument to the local Forest Brothers was erected in the wood near **Puutli village**, east of the Vastseliina-Loosi Road, in 1989. Five men and two women, who had managed to hide from the Soviet authorities, were killed in an armed conflict there in 1965. The stone monument bears the names of five people, but the names of the other two are still unknown.

The charming wooden Orthodox Church in Puutli village is worth a visit. It was built by nine families who had settled here from Russia in 1935.

Although **Obinitsa** is located in Võrumaa, it is actually an important centre of Setomaa. Since 1983 a powerful sculpture of the **Seto Lauluema** (Mother of Songs) – one of the symbols of Setomaa – has stood on the high shore of the reservoir on the Tuhkvitsa stream. Memorial stones to other much-loved folk singers have been placed around the sculpture.

The song (leelo) has been an inseparable part of the Seto way of life; the mother of songs was the most important singer. The singing choir consists of 5–6 singers, the most skilful of whom are the lead singers. The lead singer first says the verses and the choir repeats them with two voices. One high voice gives additional colouring to the song.

The experienced lead singers were called the mothers of song; some of them knew more than 30,000 verses by heart. Songs accompanied almost all activities of life in Setomaa, but best-known among them are the wedding and work songs and laments. Laments were sung when the bride left her father's house and naturally, at the funerals.

Singing and remembering songs was more woman's business in Setomaa. Mothers taught their daughters, and sung for the collectors of folklore. This does not mean that the Seto men were mute; they have many songs, but their repertoire is more humorous and suitable for singing when walking in a village street in high spirits.

The most celebrated Mother of Song of the Obinitsa region was **Hilane Taarka** (1856–1933). When the Setos were given family names by the Estonian State in

1921, her name was Darja Pisumaa. She came from Hilane village and could not marry, because the parents of her groom did not allow him to wed so poor a girl. Hilane Taarka's fame grew also as a result of her visit to Finland, where she sang to the President. Later, the state of Finland presented her with a nice farmhouse with a chimney, as she had formerly lived in a house without one, and the state of Estonia paid a small pension to her. Hilane Taarka is buried at the Obinitsa cemetery. Another famous singer, **Miko Ode** (1864–1924), knew 20,000 verses by heart and could sing them all whenever there was a patient listener.

The Seto dialect resembles the Võro dialect, but there are differences in pronunciation and vocabulary. The Seto dialect is thought to be more ancient and it has many Russian loans, which is no surprise, Russia being the large neighbour of this small border region.

The Seto Museum Hut exhibits the old Seto way of life.

The **Seto Museum Hut** was opened in Obinitsa in 1995. One room of the museum is furnished with antiquarian Seto objects. Among other things, the visitors can see two life-sized mannequins clothed in traditional Seto folk costume. The museum offers a good selection of literature on Setomaa and Võrumaa. The road turning into the yard of the house in front of the museum passes through a beautifully carved log gate.

Obinitsa Church also has a story of its own. At the beginning of the last century, a quite unique school and church was built, complete with a tower, as a church should be. Children studied on the ground floor, and on the first floor, services were held. When the Soviets came, the tower was dismantled and the house was turned into a school. The local people did not like it; the local priest Vileomon Talomees was the least content among them.

In 1950, the congregation acquired a piece of land and, led by the priest, the construction was started. Despite all difficulties, the two-towered Orthodox Church of the Transfiguration of the Lord was completed in two years. The most populous festive event in Setomaa – the celebration of Passover on 19 August is held at Obinitsa church. A

The Seto Mother of Songs commemorates all famous folksingers from the area.

festive service is held and a procession led by a cross walks around the church, watched by about 3,000–5,000 people. After the service, people go to the cemetery and eat and drink on the graves of their relatives. Food and drink are left there for the deceased as well; the Setos are well aware of the contacts between generations. Our ancestors have given us the gift of life and it would be a great sin to forget them. Meeksi Church, southeast of Vastseliina, was built by the local population during the Stalinist time. 7 July is the holy day at Meeksi Church.

Several ancient burial mounds have been found in the vicinity of Obinitsa Church. The 600–700 hundred years old burial places, walled with stones, are right in the cemetery.

Across the Obinitsa reservoir, on its farther shore, towers a sandstone cliff with a large cave. The cave is called **Juudatarõ** (Devil's house) and a legend goes that some sort of devils live in the cave. People had once wanted to build a church on the stream bank near Obinitsa, but the devils had come at night and destroyed everything that had been built during the day. The church builders had plucked up their courage and went to see, what was there in the cave. They found a table covered with a red cloth and dishes, but not a soul could be seen. Later, the church was built farther off from the stream.

Each Setomaa village has a small wooden chapel or **tsässon** – a simple building with a cross on its roof, built by the local people. The name tsässon originates from Russian, meaning an hour, since one-hour-long services were held there. 11 such chapels have been preserved in Meremäe parish, where Obinitsa belongs. These small chapels are adorned with icons, candles and holy scarves that are used to cover the icons. The old Obinitsa chapel was destroyed in 1950. One of the best-known chapels of the area is the Tobrova stone chapel, located on the 6th kilometre from Tobrova on the Obinitsa-Meremäe Road (see also Põlvamaa, Setomaa).

Obinitsa Church was built by all the inhabitants of Obinitsa, including the priest.

Serga tsässon is a simple building in the village street.

VALGAMAA

VALGAMAA

The triangular-shaped Valgamaa stretches along the Estonian border, which is, again, losing its original meaning. At many different times, Estonia and Latvia have been ruled by the same central power. On these occasions, the Konnaoja stream, which the Pope's legate, Wilhelm of Modena (1184–1251) – an important peace mediator from Europe – nominated as the border between them, is again simply the Konnaoja (Frog) Stream, which everyone can cross at will. Estonian Valga and Latvian Valka are separated by a river and have more than once in history been called sister towns.

In ancient times, most of Valgamaa belonged to Ugandi County, the southern part of which was ruled by the strong Otepää hill-fort. Estonians, Russians, Germans and Latvians fought each other at this hill-fort.

Valgamaa stands out for its many-towered manor houses. Those of Taagepera, Holdre and Sangaste Manors are gems in their own right among the buildings that have been preserved until the present day. A special sight is the austere and beautiful mausoleum of Prince Barclay de Tolly with a rather worn-out avenue of larches. The motto of the Prince, who had loyally served his Tsar fighting against Napoleon, was 'Loyalty and patience'. We do not know the motto of young Lieutenant Julius Kuperjanov, who was mortally wounded in the Paju battle against Russians in the War of Independence. In this battle, the enemy lost his last hold in Estonia; a tall pyramid monument has been erected to commemorate the battle by the Valga-Tartu Road.

Count Friedrich von Berg of Sangaste Manor was one of the most renowned manor owners and innovators in the late 19th century and early 20th century in Estonia, who created a unique monument for himself. When crops are ripening, his modest grave under the ancient trees at the Sangaste cemetery is adorned with the long slender stalks of Sangaste rye, which he had bred.

One of the Estonian writers with the best romantic imagination, August Gailit (1890-1960), was born near Sangaste, in Kuiksilla village. His writing-desk was recently brought to his birthplace from Sweden. Although the desk has never before stood in that house, it seems to be the most natural place for it.

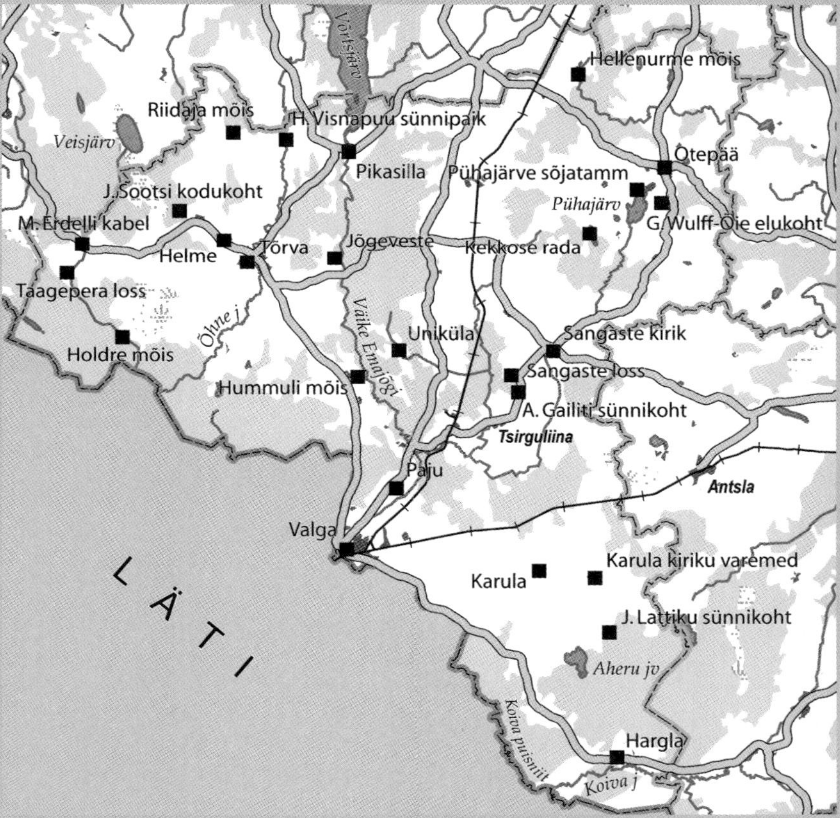
Võrtsjärv
Hellenurme mõis
Riidaja mõis
H. Visnapuu sünnipaik
Veisjärv
Otepää
Pikasilla
Pühajärve sõjatamm
J. Sootsi kodukoht
Pühajärv
M. Erdelli kabel
G. Wulff-Õie elukoht
Tõrva
Jõgeveste
Helme
Kekkose rada
Taagepera loss
Õhne j
Väike Emajõgi
Uniküla
Sangaste kirik
Holdre mõis
Sangaste loss
Hummuli mõis
A. Gailiti sünnikoht
Tsirguliina
Paju
Antsla
Valga
Karula kiriku varemed
Karula
LÄTI
J. Lattiku sünnikoht
Aheru jv
Koiva puisniit
Hargla
Koiva j

AROUND PIKASILLA AND RIIDAJA

The composer **Aleksander Läte** (1860–1948) was born in the former inn of Aakre Manor, in **Pikasilla** village, at the southernmost end of Lake Võrtsjärv. Läte, who at first was a schoolteacher in Puhja village and later a sexton and organist in Nõo village, went to Germany in the 1890s and graduated from the Dresden Conservatoire. He was the chief conductor at the Fourth Song Festival in 1891; in 1900 he founded the first symphony orchestra in Estonia. In the 1930s he had a piano repair shop in Tartu; he made some improvements to the construction of such a complicated instrument as the piano. He wrote symphonic music, but he is still better known as the author of many lyrical choral songs.

The house in Pikasilla village, where he was born, burnt down in WW II; a new house was built on the foundation of the old one. The connection of the place with Läte has not been marked. A memorial stone to Läte has been erected in Koruste village, about twelve kilometres towards Tartu from Pikasilla, where he lived after WW II. Nearby are the memorial stones to the artist Elmar Kits and the writer August Tooming (Kusta Toom), who both lived in Koruste village.

A few kilometres west of Pikasilla, in Purtsi village, **Elmar Maasik** has organised a private museum. He exhibits a barnful of artefacts from the time of the war until the end of the Soviet period, and he can tell exciting stories about each of them.

The birthplace of the poet **Henrik Visnapuu** (1890–1951) is located near the county border with Viljandimaa, in the beautiful landscape north of **Leebiku** village. A road sign in Leebiku village shows the way to the place.

Visnapuu became a primary school teacher when he was 17 years old; soon he started writing for newspapers. At the time when the Estonian Republic was born in 1918, he created a literary group 'Siuru' together with Marie Under, Friedebert Tuglas, August Gailit and Artur Adson. Having initially been a rebellious and defiant poet, he later wrote elegiac nature poetry and during WW I, a number of gloomy ballads.

In 1944, Visnapuu went to Germany and later to the USA, where he lived until his death. His memoirs under the title The Sun and the River (Päike ja jõgi) were published in Sweden, and were reissued in Estonia in 1995.

Driving west from Leebiku towards Kärstna, we arrive in **Riidaja** village, the centre of Põdrala parish. **The mansion of Riidaja Manor** is one of the few preserved wooden Baroque buildings in Estonia. The manor was constructed in the mid-18th century; for a long time it served as a schoolhouse, and in Soviet times as a collective farm. Today it houses a library and the local handicraft circle. 0.7 km from the mansion (indicated by a sign)

Poet Henrik Visnapuu, a well-known author of ballads, was born in Leebiku village.

stands a beautiful red brick chapel, which was restored in 2001. The family members of the former manor owners, the von Stryks, are buried next to the chapel. The grave markings have been destroyed, just as has happened in hundreds of country cemeteries all over Estonia. Those who want to see the interior of the chapel have to get the key from the farm standing on the left-hand side of the road opposite the chapel.

Andres Dido (1855–1921), a prominent figure of the Estonian National Awakening Movement in the second half of the 19th century, was born in Riidaja village. He was an active collaborator of C. R. Jakobson and published articles in his newspaper Sakala; later he was given a prison sentence for his links to Russian exile democrats. After being released from prison, he was not allowed to live in the Baltic region and he went to Paris, where he published a few issues of an Estonian-language legal journal Õigus and translated our folklore into French.

General **Jaan Soots**'s (1880–1942) home lies south of Riidaja, about 1.5 km west of Linna village. It is marked with a memorial stone. Soots, the son of the owner of the Küti farm, studied at Helme parish school and as a boy, participated in Jakob Hurt's folklore-gathering campaign. In 1900 he volunteered for the Russian Army, graduated from the Vilnius Military School and the St Petersburg Military Academy. He fought in WWI, but returned to his homeland in November 1917. On 6 December the same year, he was appointed the Chief of Staff of the newly formed First Estonian Infantry Division, and until Johan Laidoner assumed the post, he also acted as the temporary com-

The wooden Baroque mansion of Riidaja Manor is nice and homely.

The owners of Riidaja Manor, the von Stryks, built a beautiful red brick burial chapel.

The birthplace of General-major Jaan Soots is marked by a memorial stone.

mander of the Division. For the greater part of the War of Independence, Soots was Chief Commander Laidoner's main assistant; after the end of the war he was promoted to major-general and decorated by Estonia, Finland, Latvia and Poland. Estonia also awarded him a sum of money and the Karula manor near Viljandi. In 1920, Soots left active service and became a politician. He participated in the Tartu Peace Conference, was the Minister of War, a member of Parliament and the Mayor of Tallinn. In September 1940 he was arrested in his home in Tallinn and taken to Russia. Major-general Jaan Soots was shot in the Ussolje prison camp in Perm District, Russia, on 6 February 1942.

AROUND TÕRVA

Ala village is located by the Pärnu-Valga Road, 16 km from Tõrva. The owners of the Taagepera Manor, the von Stackelbergs, had a small stone church with a wooden tower built in Ala village in the 18th century. The family burial place of Mats Erdell, an Estonian farmer, is worth noting in Ala graveyard.

Mats Erdell (1792–1847) was the owner of Sõnni farm in Taagepera. One of his descendants, Hans Erdell, bought the Roobe Manor in 1868. It was one of the earliest purchases of the kind in the history of Livonia, since the Riga Landtag had, only two years earlier, given common people the right to purchase manors.

The Finnish writer of Estonian descent, **Hella Wuolijoki** (1886–1954), was born in the former Ala inn, her maiden name was Ella Marie Murrik; her mother Kadri Murrik was the inn-keeper at that time.

Wuolijoki started writing in Estonian, but later continued her literary work in Finnish. She moved to Finland in 1904. Her series of plays, depicting the life in the large Niskamäe farm, brought her international renown. She participated in political life and was elected to the Finnish Parliament. Her five books of memoirs are full of interesting cultural historical information and have been translated into Estonian.

About 2 km south of Ala stands the art nouveau mansion of **Taagepera Manor** with national romantic elements. The manor had already been established by the first half of the 16th century; its name was derived from the name of the von Stackelbergs (local peasantry found the name Stackelberg too difficult to pronounce and thus it gradually turned into Takelberg, Taagelberg, Taagepera), who owned it in 1674–1796. In the 19th century, the manor belonged to the von Stryks. Hugo von Stryk built the wonderful palace that has been preserved up to our days on the site of the old mansion, which was burnt down in 1904. The mansion, built after the designs of the Riga architect Otto Wildau, was completed in 1912. We can notice the weather wane featuring a half-moon and stars at the top of the tower. The weather wane was

Mats Erdell, one of the first Estonian huge farm owners, built a funeral chapel for his family.

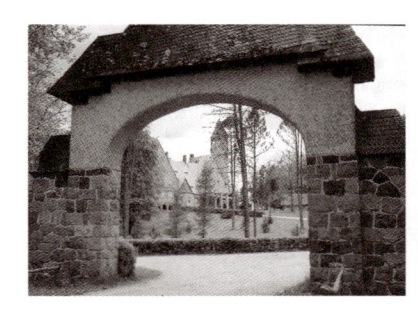

The mansion of Holdre manor resembles that of Taagepera, but it is much smaller.

The mansion of Taagepera Manor with its 40-m tower and national romantic style resembles several castles built in Finland in the early 20th century.

inspired by the lady of the manor, who was a Turk by nationality.

The mansion is surrounded by a park rich in different tree species; the park is surrounded by a granite wall. During the first years of the Estonian Republic, the mansion housed the first sanatorium for sufferers of tuberculosis; now the mansion is privately owned and it is operating as a hotel and a conference centre. A neighbouring Functionalist building once belonged to the sanatorium; now it houses a home for the elderly.

Holdre Manor lies about 7 km south-east of Taagepera. The first reports about the manor date back to the 16th century. The manor has had many different owners, the last of them, Woldemar Dimitri von Ditmar, built the mansion in 1910 that has been preserved up to now. The art nouveau building resembles the Taagepera mansion, as it was built by the same architect, Otto Wildau but it is much smaller. During the Soviet time, a Young Pioneer summer camp worked in the mansion; now, the sadly rather dilapidated building is privately owned.

Helme is located by the Pärnu-Valga Road, 3 km before Tõrva. The best-known local sight are the ruins of an ancient **Order Castle**. The crumbling fragments of castle walls stand like stone teeth on a high hill that is difficult to climb - a natural place for a castle. The castle was large, about the size of a football field, built of granite stones probably at the beginning of the 14th century. An interesting aspect of the castle is that all of its buildings had been erected along the inner side of its wall. Another exceptional feature was that the fortified gate was located on the other side of the moat, which was crossed by a stone bridge.

A legend goes that a virgin was

walled into the Helme Castle when it was built. This was not a punishment to the girl, as it was with the prototype of the White Lady of the Haapsalu Castle Church. A simple farm girl was asked whether she wanted to be the keeper of castle keys. The girl had thought that the idea was attractive and had agreed, not guessing that she would have to do it inside a wall. The same legend also tells us that the castle was invincible until the enemy found out the name of the girl who had been walled in. Eventually, an enemy soldier had persuaded an old washerwoman to tell him the girl's name – Anne – and the castle fell into the hands of the attackers. Lehte Hainsalu has used the legend in her ballad Ohver (A Victim), written in 1974.

Helme Castle was ruled by Germans, Russians, Lithuanians and finally, Swedes, who destroyed it in 1658. A settlement of craftsmen emerged in the vicinity of the castle in the Middle Ages. The castle was destroyed, but the settlement remained.

The **Helme caves**, located north of the castle ruins, have suffered from serious collapses. Once the cave system contained seven larger rooms connected with tunnels, which were several hundred metres long. The caves were located in the park of the nearby manor, the owner of which had them widened. The caves are of natural origin, hollowed into soft sandstone by spring waters. The largest of them, called Vanakuradi vats (the Old Devils belly), was 3 m high. According to the legends, one could go from Helme to the local church and even further, to Viljandi, along the underground tunnels. One of the tunnels was said to go straight to the Old Devil – to Hell. None of the brave men who entered the tunnel to Hell ever returned. Three cave mouths can be explored today, but it is not advisable to go further underground.

Two springs near the castle ruins: **Ohvriallikas** (Sacrificial spring) at the foot of the castle hill and **Arstiallikas** (Healing spring) on the bank of the Õhne River. Young girls are said to have offered beads to the springs to help them to preserve their beauty.

The Helme Manor ensemble, which is among the most representative manors of its time in South Estonia, was raised near the Order Castle at the end of the 18th century. The Baroque mansion with an attic was built by Jakob Gustav von Rennekampff in 1760–1770. He created an English-style park with numerous pavilions; bridges crossing the moat connected the park with the castle floor. The park has not been fully preserved, but the remaining parts are kept in good order. Some reports mention that the earliest monument to the famous German writer Friedrich von Schiller (1759–1805) was erected in Helme manor park already in 1805, but it has not survived.

The Helme Agricultural School started to work at the manor in

Helme Order castle changed hands many times in wars; it was used for 350 years.

1924; now it is still working under the name of the Valgamaa Vocational Schooling Centre. One of the rooms in the building is used as a classroom.

Helme Church is located 3 km south of the town in Kirikuküla village. The church was probably built in the 14th century and it was seriously damaged in the wars of the 17th century (its vaulting was destroyed), as well as in the Northern War, but it was rebuilt again and again. Now, the church has been in ruins since 1944. The Helme Corpus Christi Chapel, which was probably built in the 15th century, is in ruins too.

The former Helme parsonage houses a museum of local lore.

The former parsonage now houses the Helme Local Lore Museum, displaying various objects and documents describing the local history and everyday life in the past.

About 50 m north of Helme cemetery, on the bank of the beautiful primeval valley of the Keisripalu stream, stands a stone with two large hollows called **Orjakivi** (Slave's stone). According to a legend, an orphan was running from pursuers and climbed the stone to rest for a while. He very pitiably asked the stone for a soft resting-place. When the pursuers reached him, he was lying dead on the stone. The place where he had sat can still be seen on the stone.

Helme Church has stood in ruins since WW II.

Traces on the stone where an orphan rested for a while.

Only 150 years ago, an ancient coniferous forest was whispering in the winds on the site of the present-day **Tõrva**, and the only building standing there was an inn with stone walls. The settlement that emerged there later was named after a tar-maker called Tõnis, whose tar pits had all the time been belching smoke behind the inn (tar – tõrv in Estonian).

The settlement started to grow after the local manor owner von Stryk started to sell construction plots there. A tailor came to settle; a mill, a post station and a fire station were built. Around the turn of the 19th century, a school was founded and a house was built as the parish centre.

The former inn is the oldest building in Tõrva.

Tõrva can be proud of its beautiful nature – the town lies on the high slopes of the Õhne River primeval valley. Lake Vanamõisa and an ancient hill-fort, known as Tantsumägi (Dance Hill), also belong to the town. An open-air stage and a festival field are located on **Tantsumägi**. The fact that Tantsumägi is, actually, a site of a hill-fort was discovered only in 1930.

One of the most characteristic features of Tõrva is its concert hall, fitted into an old stone church building, situated by the Valga

Tõrva Tantsumägi is the local festival site.

Road that passes through the town.

Driving south-east of Tõrva, turning to the left at Roobe crossroads, we reach Jõgeveste village. There stands the **mausoleum** of the Russian army commander Prince **Michel Andreas Barclay de Tolly** (Mikhail Bogdanovich) (1761–1818). M. A. Barclay de Tolly was born in what is today Northern Lithuania , but his family originates from Scotland. He served in the cavalry and his gallantry was noted in the Russian-Turkish War (1787–1791) and in the Russian-Swedish War (1788–1790). In 1810–1812, he was the Russian Minister of War and at the beginning of the Russian-French War, the Commander-in-chief of the 1st Western Army. In the famous Battle of Borodino, he was the commander of the right wing and the centre of the Russian army. He was awarded the title of Count when Russia won the Battle of Nations at Leipzig. When Napoleon was finally defeated and the Russians and their allies reached Paris, Barclay de Tolly led the attack on Paris. For this battle, the Tsar promoted him General Field Marshal and made him Prince.

Hard campaigns had ruined his health; he retired from active service and lived for some time at the Jõgeveste Manor, which he had inherited. He died when he was on his way to a spa in Bohemia. His body was embalmed and buried in the beautiful mausoleum in his manor. The Classicist mausoleum was built in 1823 on the order of Princess Barclay de Tolly (architect Apollon Schtschedrin). The 4 m tall monument inside the mausoleum was made by the renowned Russian sculptor Vasili Demut-Malinovski. The sarcophagi of the Prince and Princess are inside the mausoleum; their son Ernst Magnus, together with his wife, is buried at the cemetery next to it. A 100 m long avenue of Siberian larches leads to the mausoleum. The centre of the former estate is a couple of kilometres off from the mausoleum; the house has been destroyed.

Prince M. A. Barclay de Tolly led the seizure of Paris in the Napoleonic Wars.

AROUND VALGA

Hummuli is located by the Valga-Pärnu Road. Here, a visitor should see the red brick mansion with a tall corner tower of **Hummuli Manor** that resembles a castle. It was built in the 19th century. The exterior of the building has already been restored, the work is continuing on the inside. Since 1930, the manor has housed a school. The park with its several ponds is in good order.

The mansion of Hummuli Manor with its corner tower houses a school.

A monument in front of the school commemorates the fierce Battle of Hummuli, fought here in July 1702 during the Northern War. In this battle, the Swedish field army, led by Woldemar von Sclippenbach, was three times outnumbered and defeated by the Russian corps, led by Boris Scheremetjev. The Russians lost 1,500 men in the battle, the Swedes 3,500.

The birthplace of the poet **Friedrich Kuhlbars** (1841–1924) is in **Uniküla**, north-east of Hummuli, across the Väike-Emajõgi River. Kuhlbars has written lyrics to several well-known and much loved popular songs. A grey stone marks the site of the former schoolhouse, where the poet was born.

Paju Manor is located by the Valga-Elva Road some 5 km northeast of Valga. The bloodiest battle of the War of Independence was fought here on 31 January 1919. Paju Manor, the last defensive position of the Red Army in Estonia, was defended by 1,200 Latvian Red Rifles and an armoured train. The Estonian unit of 683 men consisted of Lieutenant Julius Kuperjanov's Partisans and Finnish volunteers. After a day-long battle, Estonian troops managed to take the manor in a fierce combat in the arriving dusk. On the Estonian side, 156 men were dead or wounded; the Russians lost twice as much.

Lieutenant **Kuperjanov**, who later was hailed as the greatest hero of the War of Independence, was mortally wounded in this battle. He died three days later in Tartu and was buried at the Raadi Cemetery. During the Soviet time, students, defying the KGB, brought flowers and candles to his grave on 24 February, Estonian National Day. One of the best units of the current Estonian Defence Forces – Kuperjanov Single Infantry Battalion – proudly carries his name. A monument has been erected by the Tartu-Valga Road to commemorate the battle, and an information board stands near the monument. A memorial stone to the unit of Finnish Volunteers – Põhja Pojad (Sons of the North) – was set up in the manor park.

The border town of **Valga** is the southernmost Estonian town, separated from the town of Valka – the northernmost town of Latvia, only by the narrow Konnaoja Stream. When talking about Valga and the Konnaoja, we should recall the Pope's Legate, Modena Bishop Wilhelm, who was sent here to sort out the quarrels between the Order of the Brothers of the Sword and the local land owners of the neighbourhood in 1226. In the South, the dispute over the border was held with the Tartu Bishop, and the Pope's legate drew the border on the bed of Konnaoja. The border remained there during the Livonian War, and also after the War of Independence, when Estonia and Latvia had a serious disagreement about the border at Valga. To settle the dispute, the British Colonel Stephen George Tallents was asked to act as an arbitrator between them. On 1 July 1920 he fixed the border between Valga and Valka.

St John's Church and an early Classicist chapel in the centre of Valga were both built after the designs of the architect Christoph Haberlandt who was also active in Riga at the end of the 18th century. Valga Church is remarkable as the only oval-shaped church in Estonia. Its mansard hip-roof is also rare in Estonia.

The late-Classicist wooden town

The seizing of Paju Manor marked the end of the War of Independence.

The pyramid-shaped memorial to the Paju battle.

The tower of Valga St John's Church gets graduall thinner.

The border divides the town into Estonian Valga and Latvian Valka.

The wooden building of the Valga Town Hall has been carefully renovated.

hall, built in 1866, is a sight worth seeing. The former Säde club hall in Vabaduse Street was built in 1911. This building has been burnt to the ground and then rebuilt several times; it was renovated to house a museum in 1999. The permanent exhibition of the museum shows the history of Valga and Valgamaa from ancient times up to now, displaying artefacts found at archaeological excavations, introducing the course of the famous Paju Battle, presenting prominent people from Valgamaa, showing the building of railway, etc. One of the wax figures shown at the museum represents Johan Märtson, the first mayor of Estonian origin in Valga and in the whole Estonia. The life-size model of the railway carriages in which Estonians were taken to Siberia is very moving.

In 1999, a monument was erected in Jaama Avenue to celebrate the 100th anniversary of the Estonian-Pskov railway connection. The monument depicts a green locomotive that forms a symbolic background for the present-day rails.

The Church of St Issidor the Priest Martyr, built in the Classicist style at the end of the 19th century, is located near the locomotive monument, in the corner of Ernst Enno and Pargi Streets.

The first Estonian winner at the Olympic Games, **Alfred Neuland** (1895–1966), was born in Valga. He won a Gold Medal in weight lifting at the Antwerp Olympics in 1920. Four years later, at the Paris Olympics, he won the Silver medal. He managed to set 12 world

The weightlifter Alfred Neuland was the first Estonian Olympic winner.

records during his sports career. In 1995, his bronze bust was unveiled in the corner of Vabaduse and Kuperjanovi Streets. A memorial stone to the victims of Soviet repressions at Valgamaa was opened in the Säde Park in 1990.

About 20 km west of Valga, near the road to Lüllemäe village, stands the **village of Karula**. Of the former manor ensemble, only an interesting stone house resembling a castle, where the estate manager lived, and another house about 50 m north-west of the former, where the manor hands lived, have been preserved. The large and beautiful Karula Manor was destroyed in a fire in 1919. The stone outbuildings of the manor (now privately owned) are all standing and they are being restored. A shady avenue of broad-leaved trees leads about 500 m to the west from the manor, to the cemetery of the manor owners, the von Grotes, where a brick chapel is standing on the Krootimägi hill.

Karula village is known already from history books, because of the peasants' rebellion in 1784 and the subsequent events. The manor lord had decided to punish the peasants, who had rebelled against the establishment of a new tax and summoned a group of soldiers. All local peasants had to watch the trial of the leaders. They did not watch quietly when their brothers were flogged, but attacked the soldiers with everything they could lay their hands on. For some time it even seemed that they could win, but a new and larger group of soldiers arrived and all whom the manor lord named, were punished. Some of the rebels were deported to the Siberia, from where they were not allowed to return.

During WW II and after, the forests around Karula offered good hiding places for the Forest Brothers; several sites of their bunkers have been identified. Best-known among them are the brothers Mõtus, who hid in the Karula

The house of the manager of Karula estate resembles a castle.

The new church next to the ruins of the old one.

Johann Hornung, who translated the Bible, was the Karula Pastor for a long time.

forests for 23 years. Their bodies were recently reburied in Lüllemäe cemetery.

In the village of **Lüllemäe**, the former centre of Karula parish, stand the ruins of Karula St Mary's Church. The church was built probably in the 14th century; it was bombed in 1944 and was never restored. Beside the ruins of the old church stands the new church, built in 1997.

In the Northern War, a battle between the Swedes and the Russians took place near Karula church on 2 January 1708, where the Swedes were defeated. The water of a nearby stream is said to have been red with Swedish blood, giving it the name of Verioja (Blood Stream). Several streams in Estonia have been given the name of Verioja for the same reason. One of them, although it has dried up by now, is near the ruins of the St. Mary's Chapel in the neighbourhood of Viru-Nigula, in Lääne-Virumaa. There is another legend, telling us that the two large oaks, growing on the hillside, were originally two oaken sticks, stuck into the ground by Peter I. The king of Sweden is said to have hidden under the bridge called Kuningasild (King's bridge).

The writer and politician **Jaan Lattik** (1878–1967) was born in Mäkiste village by the Lüllemäe-Hargla Road. A large monument has been erected by the road; an avenue of oaks leads to the house, where the future politician was born. In 1920–1930, Lattik was the leader of the Christian People's Party; he was a member of Parliament and a minister in the government, and a representative of Estonia in Lithuania. After 1944, he lived in exile in Sweden, working mostly as a pastor. Lattik has published numerous short stories and books of memoirs in his homeland and abroad.

The present-day **Hargla Church** was built in 1821 on the site of a former wooden church. A church had been in Hargla already in the 17th century, but it was destroyed in the Northern War. The church was rebuilt in the Historicist style in 1873. The western tower and choir were added, the latter is separated from the body of the church by a wide triumphal arch. The gem of the otherwise simply furnished church is a painting "Deposition" by the German artist E. Jacobs, which dates from 1859.

The pine forests that lie right on the Estonian-Latvian border offer unforgettable sights for city people. The whole area was covered with

Monument to Jaan Lattik stands by the road in Mäkiste.

such woods when our ancestors started to make their homes here many hundreds of years ago. The Koiva Pine Forests Reserve was created in 1975 to protect the forest on the right bank of the Koiva River. The age of the oldest trees in the forest is about 120 years.

AROUND SANGASTE AND OTEPÄÄ

Driving from Paju village through Tsirguliina and Laatre to the northwest, a kilometre before Lossiküla village, we reach **Kuiksilla** village, the birth place of the writer **August Gailit** (1891–1960). A memorial plaque is on the wall of the building where he was born (a long white house by the road); one room of the house has been furnished as a memorial room to the writer, displaying his works and his writing desk, which was donated by his daughter. The desk was brought here from Sweden a few years ago.

Gailit is one of the most singularly talented Estonian writers. His imaginative novels Toomas Nipernaadi, Ekke Moor and Do You remember, Dearest? (Kas mäetad, mu arm?), written in exile, are full of interesting characters, romance and unique, sometimes sad humour. When talking about Estonian literature, Gailit and Tammsaare are positioned on opposite ends of the scale. Both are unsurpassable masters of their genres – Gailit in his playfulness, Tammsaare in his monumentality.

Two of Gailit's books, Toomas Nipernaadi and The Cool Sea (Karge meri) have been made into films; Toomas Nipernaadi is, undoubtedly, one of the best Estonian films.

The **Sangaste Manor** is located in Lossiküla village. During the Middle Ages, a manor belonging to the

August Gailit's home in Kuiksilla and his writing-desk in a room at the house.

Tartu Bishop stood on the same site. In the 17th century, it went into private hands and in 1808, the von Bergs became its owners. The new luxurious mansion was built by **Count Friedrich von Berg**, probably, on the example of palaces he had seen in England. It was designed by the architect Otto Pius Hippius; in 1879–1883, the building was erected at a site 100 m away from the previous 18th-century mansion. It has been said that Berg built such a magnificent palace to avenge an insult he had had to swallow in England, when an English nobleman had not given him his daughter in marriage, calling him a savage from Russia.

The building is the best example of Estonian Historicist architecture, it has towers and attics and spacious rooms. Originally, there was 99 rooms (only the Tsar was allowed more than 100 rooms in his palaces), but later rebuilding has much reduced the number. Among the more interesting outbuildings there are a water tower and the stables, built in the same style as the palace. A rich park surrounds the manor.

The Sangaste Count was known as an innovator of agriculture in Russia. He studied in France and was later an inspired breeder of crops. If Mihkel Pill, who worked at Jõgeva, is called "the father of Estonian white bread", then Friedrich von Berg can well be called "the father of Estonian black bread", since he bred a yielding variety of rye, "Sangaste", which grew well in Estonian climate. Breed stallion Hetman, who played an essential role in breeding the Tori horse, also came from Sangaste (see Pärnumaa, Tori). We should also say that Sangaste Manor with its extremely modern mechanical farm equipment was named the best agricultural enterprise of Tsarist Russia in 1912. Today, the manor with its hotel and seminar centre is under the care of the local community. The Ballroom, Spanish Room and Hunting Room and the former Library are open to visitors, who can also see a small exhibition of old photos about the life of Count Berg.

Sangaste village, located 4 km north-east of Lossiküla (Palace village), was built at the crossing of larger local roads as a typical church village and for a long time, it was called Kirikuküla (Church village). One side of the road from Lossiküla to Sangaste is bordered by a row of large oaks.

In 1742, **Sangaste Church** was built on the site of an old church, which was destroyed in the Northern War. The church has a unique organ, built in 1924 by the brothers Kriisa who have produced a number of organs for our churches. The most renowned lord of Sangaste Manor, Count Friedrich von Berg (1845–1938), is buried at the cemetery one kilometre off from the church. (A sign is pointing to the cemetery.) His grave is marked with a modest tombstone; rye is sown on his grave every year.

The predecessor of the town of Otepää was a village called **Nuustaku**, which was renamed Otepää on the initiative of Matthias Johann Eisen in the early 1920s. The name derives from the name of an ancient stronghold, called Otipea (Bear Head; Odenpe after Henry of Livonia). The bear can be seen on the flag and the coat of arms of Otepää, but it looks much milder that the bear on the coat of arms of Vändra, the other "bear town" of Estonia.

Originally, there were 99 rooms in the mansion of Sangaste Manor.

The stables of Sangaste Manor.

A permanently settled **stronghold** of ancient Ugandi County was already established by the 7th–8th century at Otepää Linnamägi. After Tartu, this was one of the most important strongholds of the region, known also to the Pskov Russians, who came to raid the area. During the ancient fight for freedom, Otepää stronghold repeatedly changed hands. Brothers of the Order of the Sword conquered it in 1208. In 1217, the Ugandians together with the Russians attacked the Germans, who had fortified themselves there, and won the stronghold back. The Teutonic Knights finally conquered Otepää in 1224 and started to build a stone castle there. This was one of the first stone castles in South Estonia and also the oldest brick construction in Estonia. The building was begun by the Bishop of Estonia (Lihula), Hermann I von Buxhoeveden, who 10 years later became Bishop of Tartu.

The Bishop's castle was destroyed in the late 14th century by the troops of the Livonian Order, who repeatedly raided the Tartu Bishopric. The stronghold was finally abandoned after wars with Moscow in 1480–1481. Archaeologists have found a very rare object under the ruins of the castle – a bronze gun, which is one of the oldest preserved guns in the world. This muzzle-loading gun without a lock had been broken into pieces; it is now kept at the Institute of Estonian History. Some parts of the old castle walls have been excavated and they can be seen on Linnamägi.

Mediaeval Otepää had three

The organ of Sangaste Church was built by the brothers Kriisa.

Every year, rye is sown on the grave of the Sangaste Count von Berg.

The stone castle built on Otepää Linnamägi in the 13th century is the oldest brick construction in Estonia.

The first blue-black-white flag was consecrated at Otepää Church in 1884.

The Otepää monument to the War of Independence.

churches – one inside the stronghold and two outside its walls for the peasants' use. A large stone cross on a hill behind Linnamägi marks the site of the first peasants' church.

The present-day **Church of St Mary** is located on the border of the town, beside Kanepi Road. The old church was rebuilt in the Neo-gothic style at the end of the 19th century. An altarpiece by the artist Albert Sprenael is worth mentioning in the interior of the church. Two bas-relief commemorative plaques devoted to the Estonian flag, made by Voldemar Mellik, are on the facade of the building. Services are held in this church only in summer and during the more important winter holidays (Christmas, Easter).

In winter, Sunday services are held in a much warmer and more comfortable so-called Winter Church, remodelled from an outbuilding of the old parsonage, the actual name of which is the Chapel of Orphans and Widows. At the traditional Otepää winter music festival, some concerts are held in the Winter Church.

A monument to fighters in the War of Independence has been erected on a hill in front of Otepää Church.

In 1996, the **Estonian Flag Museum** was opened at the former Otepää parsonage, displaying a permanent exhibition on the history of the Estonian flag. The blue-black-and-white flag of the Estonian Students' Society, sewn by Karl August Hermann's wife Paula, was inaugurated at Otepää Church in 1884. Hardly anybody could then guess that in 34 years, this flag would be the official flag of the Estonian Republic.

As fitting for the winter capital of Estonia, the **Skiing Museum** was established in Otepää in 2001, located under the same roof as the Estonian Flag Museum. The museum introduces the history of skiing in Estonia, stressing the role of famous Estonian skiers.

A monument to **Jakob Hurt** (1839–1907), who was the Nuustaku Pastor in 1872–1880, is standing near Otepää parsonage. In those years, he was most active in the National Awakening Movement and paid much attention to the opening of schools and equipping of them with study aids. Residing in Otepää, Hurt chaired the Learned Estonian Society and the Main Committee of the Estonian Alexander School (see Põlva-

The Otepää Skiing Museum and the Estonian Flag Museum are under the same roof.

maa, Himmaste). School life in Otepää was outstanding; the Estonian-language Pro-gymnasium, opened in 1907, was the first of its kind in Estonia. Two men from Kambja village have stood at the beginnings of education in Otepää – Adrian Virginius (1663–1706) and Ignati Jaak (1670–1744). Adrian Virginius established the first school in Otepää and invited a recent graduate of B. G. Forselius's teachers' seminar, an Estonian Ignati Jaak, to teach there (see Tartumaa, Kambja).

When talking of Otepää, people often mention the so-called energy

The energy column is simply a tree trunk.

column, erected in 1992, which is supposed to catch positive cosmic energy. The site of the column – a thick tree trunk with a large cupola – in Mäe Street (the last street of the town, when we drive towards Pühajärv Lake) was chosen by people claiming to be extra sensitive. Bear figures, wrought of iron on the Smiths' Day in 1993, adorn the column. The energy column has even been mentioned in The Estonian Encyclopedia, which is expected to be a rather emotionless publication. But faith is powerful and a tree trunk could hardly catch any energy without the strong faith of those who erected it. Sceptics are, however, wondering how the energy can be drawn out from the tree trunk. In recent years, energy columns have been erected in other places, too – why should all good things happen only in Otepää.

The poet **Gustav Wulff-Õis** (1865–1946) spent his old age in the Lõhmuse farm by Lake Nüpli, south-east of Otepää. Every Eston-

Jakob Hurt was the Otepää Pastor when the National Awakening Movement was at its height.

ian knows his lyrics to the song "Tender Nightingale" ("Õrn ööbik") and the song has become a kind of a anthem for Otepää. A small museum introducing his life and work is has been established at the Lõhmuse farm, the birthplace of Wulff-Õis's wife, the owner of which is Wulff-Õis's grandchild Mari-Ann Karupää.

Near the Otepää-Sangaste Road, 500 m off the Pühajärve Spa, stands a powerful well-branched oak – **Pühajärve Sõjatamm** (Pühajärve War Oak) which is about 380 years old. Its girth is about 7 m and its height about 22 m. Its name, War Oak, originates from the events of the winter of 1841, when angry peasants held war councils under the branches of the tree. The war began in the autumn of the same year.

Rumours started to spread in Livonia at the beginning of 1841 that emigrants would be given land free of charge in South Russia. In summer, numerous envoys from the peasants came to Riga to ask the provincial government for permission to emigrate, hoping to get free land in the "warm country". Governor General Pahlen, meeting the demands of the nobility, ordered that the envoys should be severely beaten and sent back home like criminals, with their heads shaved. This news spread

Pühajärve Sõjatamm is also a monument to peasant unrest in the 19th century.

over the whole province and general dissatisfaction grew still more.

Peasants from the vicinity of Pühajärve drew up lists of emigrants, and the local manor owner summoned soldiers to help him to cope with them. To counteract, angry peasants, armed with wooden clubs, attacked the manor on 20 September, but were thrown back by the soldiers. In December, the rebellious peasants were severely punished near the manor – each of them was whipped 500 times with twigs and 30 had to run the gauntlet – an old military punishment in that country was to send the victim, stripped to the waist, through a double line of men, each armed with a stick with which to hit him as he passed.

The movement to change faith, which ebbed only by 1848, when about a tenth of all peasants of Võrumaa, Tartumaa and Viljandimaa and about a third of those of Saaremaa had changed to the Orthodox faith, was also connected with emigration. People became Orthodox in the hope of getting free land when they adopted the faith of the Tsar.

A wooden sculpture in the park on the shore of Lake Pühajärv (Holy Lake) commemorates the

The poet Gustav Wulff-Õis lived for some time in Lõhmuse farm near Otepää.

historical visit of His Holiness the 14th Dalai Lama to Lake Pühajärv and his blessing of the lake in 1991.

Driving to the south of Lake Pühajärv and turning to the south-west at Sihva, the visitor reaches the popular **ski centre** of **Kääriku**. A monument to a sports teacher of international renown, **Fred Kudu** (1917–1988), who initiated the building of this recreation and sports centre, has been erected in Kääriku.

A 15 km long hiking and ski trail, known as the Kekkonen Trail starts from the Kääriku ski stadium. The President of Finland at that time, Urho Kaleva Kekkonen, skied the trail in 1964, partly to escape his KGB minders. Since that time, a traditional Kekkonen Ski Event is held there annually on the first Sunday of March.

Harimägi, one of the highest hills of the Otepää Upland with a sightseeing tower, stands 3 km south-west of Kääriku. Friedrich Georg Wilhelm Struve (1793–1864), an astronomer and geodesist of international fame, conducted geodetic surveying on Harimägi in 1816–1819. He built a triangulation tower, the stone base of which can still be seen there.

Hellenurme Manor Ensemble is located north-west of Otepää; from 1850, it belonged to the von Middendorfs. The Baroque mansion was built in the second half of the 18th century; a number of outbuildings are also intact. Young Jakob Hurt worked as a tutor with the von Middendorffs. Now the mansion, surrounded by a rich and beautiful park, houses a kindergarten and a home for the elderly.

About a kilometre west of the mansion, in a small park around a chapel, is the family cemetery of the von Middendorfs, where lie the graves of an outstanding scholar, Alexander Theodor von Middendorff and his son, Ernst von Middendorff.

A member of the St Petersburg Academy of Sciences, A. T. von Middendorff (1815–1894) was one of the best-known scientists of Baltic-German origin of the 19th century. He was an explorer, who studied the distribution of animal species. Together with K. E. Von Baer he visited Lapland and the Kola Peninsula and in 1842–1845, he led an expedition to North Siberia and the Far East. During his travels to Novaya Zemlya and the coasts of Iceland, he conducted meteorological and hydrological measurements, which are now of great value. A. T. von Middendorff is considered to be the founder of ecological zoogeography; birds and their migration was his special interest. In addition to nature studies, he was also engaged in agriculture, participating in the breeding of Estonian red cattle and the Tori horse. Several plant and animal species have been named after him, also a bay on the Taimyr Peninsula and a cape on Novaya Zemlya. His elder son Ernst (1851–1916), who was one of the best-known ornithologists of his time, inherited from his father his interest and love for nature.

Fred Kudu initiated the foundation of a sports resort in Kääriku.

VILJANDIMAA

SIIN MURSI TALUS SÜNDIS
10.(22) DETSEMBRIL 1868. A
EESTI SILMAPAISTEV KULTUURI-
JA POLIITIKATEGELANE, PROFESSOR
JAAN TÕNISSON

VILJANDIMAA

Viljandimaa connects the ancient Sakala to Mulgimaa, where the more self-confident and wealthier farmers and intellectuals played a special role in our national awakening in the 19th century. Although Carl Robert Jakobson worked his farm on the border of Pärnumaa, separated from Viljandi by the woods and bogs, his activities were, nevertheless, focused on Viljandimaa.

The Lõhavere stronghold and the site of the old hillfort of Viljandi Kaevumägi remind us of the might and power of Sakala. The spirit of our ancient hero Lembitu has not been lost.

Henrik Adamson's poems in the Mulgi dialect and August Kitzberg's humorous plays show us something of the essence of Mulgimaa. People living in these parts have their own language and frame of mind. And the memorial stone to the local breed of apple tree, standing in the centre of Suislepa Manor, shows something very characteristic of Viljandimaa. Sweet apples, and what a beautiful name, Suislepp!

The town of Suure-Jaani is a birthplace of many famous musicians. The families of the composers Kapp and Mart Saar were close neighbours.

The cultural layers of Viljandi are so thick that a true monograph should be written about them. During the period of National Awakening in the second half of the 19th century, C. R. Jakobson and his newspaper Sakala were a powerful lighthouse for the whole of Estonia. Viljandi was the hometown of a much loved writer August Kitzberg; this is also the place, where Friedrich Kuhlbars wrote his famous song "When People of Kungla" (Kui Kungla rahvas), which is now sung everywhere as a folk song. Juhan Liiv, the sad poet from Alatskivi, was once a journalist in the heart of Sakala.

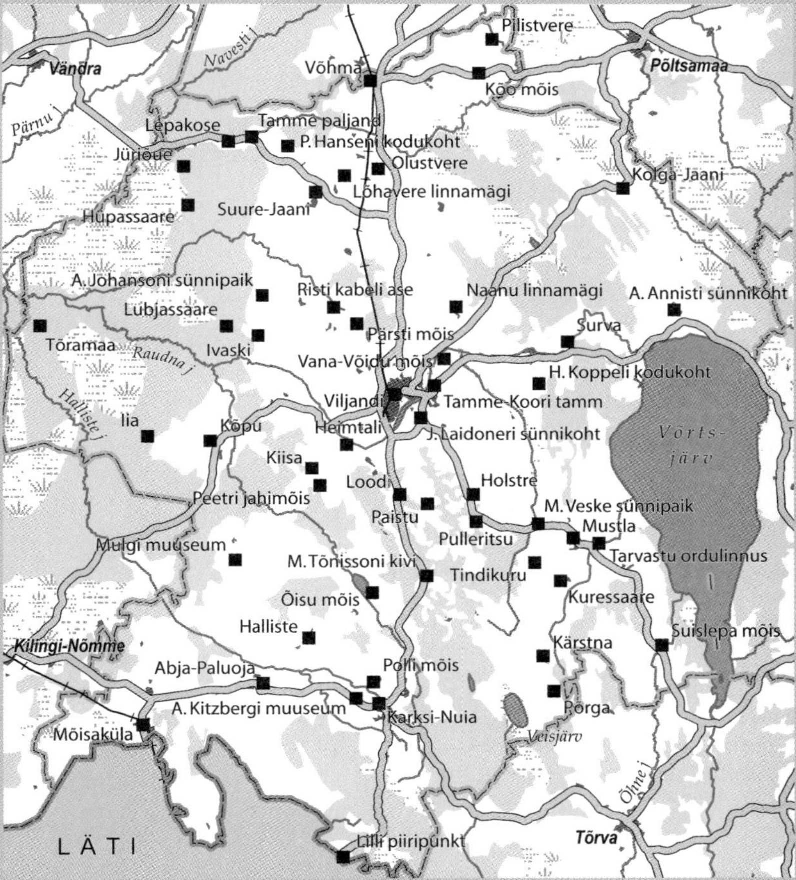

Pilistvere
Vändra
Navesti j
Võhma
Põltsamaa
Kõo mõis
Pärnu j
Lepakose
Tamme paljand
Jüriõue
P. Hanseni kodukoht
Olustvere
Kolga-Jaani
Lõhavere linnamägi
Hüpassaare
Suure-Jaani
A. Johansoni sünnipaik
Risti kabeli ase
Naanu linnamägi
A. Annisti sünnikoht
Lubjassaare
Pärsti mõis
Surva
Tõramaa
Raudna j
Ivaski
Vana-Võidu mõis
H. Koppeli kodukoht
Viljandi
Tamme-Koori tamm
Halliste j
Iia
Kõpu
Heimtali
J. Laidoneri sünnikoht
Võrts-järv
Kiisa
Lood
Holstre
Peetri jahimõis
M. Veske sünnipaik
Paistu
Mustla
Pulleritsu
Mulgi muuseum
Tarvastu ordulinnus
M. Tõnissoni kivi
Tindikuru
Kuressaare
Õisu mõis
Halliste
Suislepa mõis
Kilingi-Nõmme
Kärstna
Abja-Paluoja
Polli mõis
A. Kitzbergi muuseum
Põrga
Karksi-Nuia
Mõisaküla
Veisjärv
Õhne j
LÄTI
Lilli piiripunkt
Tõrva

VILJANDIMAA

AROUND VÕHMA AND PILISTVERE

The ancient village of Võhma, located in a loop of the northern boundary of Viljandimaa, started developing after the building of a narrow-gauge railway in 1900. In the 1930s, the area was famous for its rapid economic development and it was called the Chicago of Estonia. A modern slaughterhouse was built and meat was exported to places as far away as England. In the Soviet period, the Võhma factory almost monopolised the meat production in the country. After the restoration of independence, and after the closing of the large market to the former Soviet Union, the enterprise went bankrupt in the mid-1990s. The once flourishing meat industry is now remembered only by a yellow bull and crossed butcher's cleavers on the coat of arms of the town.

Pilistvere St. Andrew's Church can boast the tallest tower of any Estonian country church. The sleek spire, renovated in 1990, is 70 m tall and offers a good landmark to visitors of Pilistvere.

Pilistvere stone church was built in the second half of the 13th century. As elsewhere in Estonia, the church was heavily damaged during the wars of the 17th century and in the Northern War; it was completely restored only in 1762. The most valuable items in its interior are the Baroque pulpit, made by the Tartu master Thomas Öhrmann, probably in 1686, and the fragments of figural ornamentation on the impost of the southern portal.

The monument to a former politician, **Jüri Vilms** (1889–1918), and a cross to commemorate the War of Independence, unveiled in 1932, are both standing in the churchyard. The cross is one of the few original monuments to the War of Independence that escaped destruction by the Soviets. A member of the national awakening movement, **Jaan Jung** (1835–1900), is buried at Pilistvere cemetery. Jung was born in Tammeküla village, Imavere parish, the former Pilistvere church parish. Being a serious enthusiast of history and archaeology, he translated the Chronicle of Henry of Livonia into Estonian (published in 1881–1883) and published a collection of writings on Estonian archaeology. For these, he gathered material at archaeological excavations in the neighbourhood, where he also discovered the hill-forts of Sinialliku and Naanu. He was the first scholar to voice the opinion that the stronghold of an ancient Estonian leader, Lembitu, mentioned by Henry of Livonia, could have been located on Lõhavere hill.

Pilistvere stone mound is growing each year.

A monument to all Estonian victims of Communism stands near Pilistvere cemetery. A large mound of stones, the building of which was started on the initiative of the local Pastor Vello Salum in 1988, has by now grown into a large hill. A new, steel cross has replaced the wooden cross, around which the stones were brought at the beginning. 15 large stones of about a man's height, each bearing the name of a former Estonian county, have been arranged in the park to surround the stone mound, commemorating all people who perished in the hands of alien powers. The fate and the graves of many of them are still unknown. The territory of the memorial park is about 1,000 hectares. The planting of a memorial grove of trees has been started, too, and the relatives of the victims or other people who want to remember them have already planted more than a thousand trees.

Estonian Alexander Agricultural School operated for some time at Kõo Manor.

The owner of Põltsamaa castle, Woldemar Wrangell, established **Kõo Manor**, located near Pilistvere, in 1670. The manor was soon made a state manor and at the end of the 18th century, it was given to the Ambassador of Russian Empress Catherine II, diplomat and general Heinrich von Weymarn, for helping the lover of the Empress, Stanislaw August Poniatowski, to the Polish throne. Diplomacy was not Von Weymarn's only skill. He was a good writer and helped August Wilhelm Hupel (1737–1819) in his studies of local lore and journalistic activities (see also Jõgevamaa and Põltsamaa).

Having become a manor owner, von Weymarn started a large-scale construction, completing the late Baroque mansion in 1774 and a number of outbuildings in the following decade. The Estonian Alexander Agricultural School started working at the manor in 1914. In 1920, the school was moved over to Olustvere Manor (see Viljandimaa, Olustvere).

Today, the privately owned Kõo mansion is empty. The outbuildings house the local community office, library, outpatient surgery and kindergarten.

AROUND KOLGA-JAANI AND TÄNASSILMA

The Kolga-Jaani **St John's Church** was built probably in the early 14th century; its vaults were built at the end of the same century. A rare item in the church is an altar crucifix from the 14th century and the oldest Baroque chandelier in Estonia dating from 1750. The stained-glass windows, made at Emil Tode's workshop in 1903, are also worth mentioning.

A monument to **Villem Reiman** (1861–1917), a long-time Pastor of Kolga-Jaani Church, featuring

Villem Reiman was the Pastor of Kolga-Jaani for 27 years.

Kolga-Jaani Church can boast of a 600 year old crucifix.

A naivist sculpture of an elk stretching its neck in the middle of Kolga-Jaani.

his bronze bust on a granite pedestal, has been erected near the church.

Villem Reiman was one of the more important figures of the National Awakening. Being a moderate, he was against the excessive favouring of both Germans and Russians and published numerous articles on culture and history. He was among the first scholars to study these fields in Estonia and he published a collection of articles titled Estonian Culture (Eesti Kultura). He also took time to chair temperance societies and the Estonian Students' Society. He was one of the founders of the Estonian Literary Society and the Estonian National Museum, and he assisted Jaan Tõnisson in publishing the newspaper Postimees. He studied Estonian history and his century-old research work is still highly valued, since when gathering information, he always turned to original sources. A memorial room to Reiman has been established at the Kolga-Jaani parsonage.

A cup stone with 31 hollows can be seen at the edge of Kolga-Jaani cemetery.

A memorial plaque marks the home of folklorist **August Annist** (1899–1972), who was born near **Leie** village. August Annist, a PhD in philology and a long-time professor at the University of Tartu, published numerous papers on Estonian folklore of the 19th century. Over many years, he revised new editions of the Estonian national epic Kalevipoeg; he translated the Finnish epic Kalevala and Homer's Iliad and Odyssey into Estonian. In 1945–1951, he was in prison on fabricated political charges. After that, he was for many years a senior researcher at the Institute of Language and Literature of the Estonian Academy of Sciences.

Jaan Tõnisson (1868– ?; it is not known when exactly he was murdered by the Russians), a well-known Estonian politician and member of the National Awakening movement, was born in Surva village near Tänassilma.

Tõnisson was born on a large farm; he received a good education at school and graduated from the University of Tartu as a lawyer. He went into politics in the 1890s as a member of the learned Estonian Society; later his work at the newspaper Postimees demanded political participation. For a time, he worked as a lawyer in Orel, Russia. Back in Estonia, he bought Postimees together with Oskar Kallas and Karl Koppel and became seriously involved in the National Awakening Movement.

He promoted co-operative movement, organised the work of the Tartu Estonian Agricultural Society, supervised courses and organised popular exhibitions of agricultural produce. In the whirlwind of the revolution in 1905, he founded the National Progress Party (Eesti Rahvameelne Eduerakond) and in 1906, participated in the work of the first Russian Duma in St Petersburg as a representative of the Estonian people.

Tõnisson was given the mandate to travel abroad and seek foreign support for Estonia; he also participated in the Paris Peace Conference in 1919. The Tartu Peace Treaty was signed between Estonia and Russia on 2 February 1920; at that time, Tõnisson was the Prime Minister of Estonia. Later, he was a member of five successive Estonian Parliaments – Riigikogu, the state elder (Riigivanem), the Speaker of the Riigikogu, the Minister of Foreign Affairs, and the leader of the Estonian delegation at the League of Nations. During all his political life he was also an active member of the Estonian Students' Society and was its Chairman from 1905 to 1917.

In the early 1930s, Konstantin Päts eased Tõnisson out of politics. The latter was not in favour of the increased role of the president. The death of his son, Ilmar Tõnisson, a promising politician and social scientist, who was murdered by his wife in 1939, affected him very much.

Tõnisson was arrested in December 1940 and killed in the prison of the KGB probably sometime in 1941. A memorial plaque marks his birthplace.

The birthplace of the renowned medical scientist and educator **Henrik Koppel** is located about 3 km south of **Tõnuküla village** in Viljandi-Tartu Road.

Koppel was a physician and a social scientist; he was among the developers of Estonian-language

The farm, where Jaan Tõnisson was born, has been preserved in Surva village.

higher education. On his initiative, the Estonian language became the official language at the University of Tartu in 1928. He was the Rector of the University in 1920–1928 and also the head of the clinic for internal diseases. He paid much attention to the development of public hygiene and founded the journal Tervis (Health) in 1903. He was an eager naturalist and worked towards the creating of nature reserves.

AROUND SUURE-JAANI AND VASTSEMÕISA

In Vihi village by the Vändra-Suure-Jaani Road, a smaller road turns to the south-west and runs between forests and bogs. After 12 km, the visitor reaches Hüpassaare, on the edge of Leetva mire – the birthplace of the composer Mart Saar. **Hüpassaare** is a very remote place between large forests and wetlands, bordering on the large Leetva mire; probably no other Estonian composer has shown such deep affection to his home as Mart Saar. His ancestors had settled in Hüpassaare by the early 19th century; to escape serfdom they became foresters.

Mart Saar Museum is based at the composer's home in Hüpassaare.

Mart Saar (1882–1963) studied the organ at the St Petersburg Conservatoire and composition with Nikolai Rimski-Korsakov. Saar is well known primarily for his choral songs, the roots of which were often in archaic folk songs. Among his widely sung choral songs is Põhjavaim (Northern Spirit), inspired by the country around Hüpassaare.

The Mart Saar House Museum was established at Hüpassaare after Saar's death in 1964, but then its activities ceased for a while. It was opened again after renovation in 1982, when the 100th anniversary of Mart Saar's birth was celebrated. The museum gives an overview of his life and work; among the exhibits is a home organ, which had been given to him in his childhood. One of his relatives made organs and almost all members of the family could play it. An open-air stage was erected at Hüpassaare in 1997 and several choral concerts have been given there. A path of wooden boards begins near the museum, taking visitors to Kureso mire in Soomaa National Park – to the landscapes that inspired the composer.

Mart Saar moved to Hüpassaare in 1932, after his wife had gone to the USA with their daughter. She had hoped that her husband would follow them in search of a better life abroad, but the composer could not leave Estonia and remained true to his home and country. In the Soviet era, he taught composition at the Tallinn Conservatoire. He was buried at Suure-Jaani cemetery. His grave is marked by a modest tombstone, nearby are the graves of the Kapp family members, described below.

The specialist for Mart Saar's work, Johannes Jürisson, writes that the families of Saar and the Hansens, and even the Hansens

The birthplace of A. H. Tammsaare's mother, Anne Backhoff, is marked with a memorial stone.

Painter Johann Köler was buried at Suure-Jaani cemetery.

and the Jannsens (Koidula) are tied together in Hüpassaare, since brides were usually brought home from the neighbouring villages. About 4 km north of Hüpassaare are the lands of the former Jüriõue farm. **Anne Backhoff**, the mother of the writer Anton Hansen Tammsaare, was born there. Her family was relatively well off, as they were able to provide a good education to both of her brothers, who trained to be schoolteachers.

The **Lepakose** ancient settlement site, used in the 6th–4th centuries BC, lies near the Vändra – Suure-Jaani Road. When driving from Lepakose towards Suure-Jaani, a road soon turns to the left towards the Tamme outcrop. This is a unique outcrop, where layers of sandstones are lying on limestone. An old water mill is waiting for restoration on the nearby Navesti River.

In the small town of **Suure-Jaani**, we can find Lembitu Avenue and Köleri Street. Both of these famous men are also there, cast in bronze.

The Suure-Jaani monument to the War of Independence ties together the ancient fight for freedom and the 20th century.

Wounded Lembitu is holding his sword high on a monument to the War of Independence; the painter reaches his brush towards an invisible palette at the cemetery. The local cultural life has for more than a century been connected with the large family of musicians, the Kapps.

Suure-Jaani emerged and started to grow in the neighbourhood of a church about 150 years ago. In 1920, it became a rural town and in 1938, it was given the town rights. Its development was somewhat hindered by the fact that the local manor owner did not allow the railway line to cross his lands, and the railway station was built in Olustvere.

Schoolteacher **Joosep Kapp** (1833–1894), who worked at the local school in 1853, stood at the cradle of cultural life in Suure-Jaani. He was a real educator in the best sense of the word and he was much loved and respected by his pupils and their parents. He clearly favoured Estonian national ideas and Estonian-language teaching. It was he who said that an Estonian foot does not fit into a German boot. Being a music lover, he founded several choirs, a wind and violin orchestra and a song and drama society Ilmatar in Suure-Jaani.

His elder son **Hans Kapp** (1870–1938) continued his work as a teacher and furthered musical life.

His second son **Artur Kapp** (1878–1953) became a famous professional musician in the 1930s. Among his students were Gustav Ernesaks (1908–1993) and Roman Toi (1916). Artur Kapp was a wonderful composer, organ virtuoso and conductor, he was known for his impulsive and colourful personality. He studied music at the St Petersburg Conservatoire, where his teacher of composition was Nikolai Rimski-Korsakov. At the beginning of the 20th century, he worked for more than a decade as a director of a music school in Astrakhan, Russia. Back in Estonia, he taught at the Tallinn Conservatoire. He has written a number of symphonies and choral songs.

Monument to Artur Kapp.

The Kapp House Museum in Suure-Jaani.

Artur Kapp's son Eugen (1908–1996), born in Astrakhan, continued his father's work as a teacher at the Tallinn Conservatoire and was its director for more than ten years. He taught many Estonian composers. He was awarded several honorary titles, including that of the People's Artist of the Soviet Union.

Eugen Kapp was a prolific author of operas and ballets; he wrote such operas as Tasuleegid, Tabamatu and Rembrandt and ballets, such as Kalevipoeg" and Kullaketrajad.

The third composer in the Kapp dynasty was Hans Kapp's son

Villem (1913–1964), who also taught at the Tallinn Conservatoire. His best known work is a choral poem Põhjarannik (Northern Coast); he also wrote symphonies and more than 70 choral songs. The Kapp's House Museum is located near the town government building; earlier, the house belonged to the Kapp family. The display gives a good overview of the work and lives of these musicians, it includes Eugen Kapp's piano; from time to time, concerts are held at the museum.

An organ built by the brothers Kriisa is a treasure of Suure-Jaani Church.

Suure-Jaani Church was first built in the 14th century, but during the wars that followed, it was repeatedly destroyed and rebuilt. The church acquired its present look in the second half of the 18th century. An interesting detail of its interior is a stone cross, dating from 1598, which has been fixed on the wall. This is supposedly the second oldest stone cross to mark a grave of an Estonian in the whole country. It used to stand on the grave of **Anne Ratisepp**, who had, according to a legend, selflessly cared for the victims of the plague during the Livonian War and earned a worthy place for her grave next to the church.

An urn-shaped tombstone to the Olustvere manor owner, Count **Hans Axel Fersen** (1755–1810), general in the Tsarist army, also stands in the church. The legend goes that his carriage driver from Olustvere accompanied him in the battles and brought, according to his wish, his heart home from the war. The heart was placed into an urn full of spirits, and the sexton was supposed to add spirits to the urn when necessary. Unfortunately, he fancied the spirits and the general's heart eventually dried up.

Suure-Jaani Church can boast of two excellent musical instruments. One of them is an organ made by the brothers Kriisa, the other is a concert grand, received as a gift a few years ago. It was donated by an American businessman of Estonian origin, Paul Weserstein, who wanted to pay homage to the home country of the composers Kapp and Mart Saar.

Lõhavere stronghold, which probably was the stronghold (castrum Leole) of the Sakala leader Lembitu, mentioned by Henry of Livonia in his Chronicle, is beside the Olustvere – Suure-Jaani Road.

A hill-fort was built at Lõhavere already as early as in the 11th century. At the beginning of the 13th century, with the coming of difficult times, it was fortified with an up to 3.5 m high and 5–6 m thick earthen wall and reinforced by a log wall. The top of the earthen wall was paved with logs and probably there were 3–4 towers as well.

The Teutonic Knights reached Lõhavere only in spring 1215 (Viljandi had already been besieged in 1211), when the troops from Riga, together with the Teutonic Knights, Livonians and Latvians forced their way into Northern Sakala and attacked Lõhavere (Leola) stronghold. According to Henry of Livonia, the stronghold surrendered and peace was negotiated with the Germans; Lembitu and his people were baptised. The same year, units from Sakala and Ugandi took part in revenge attacks on Germans in what is now Latvia, but they were still not able to conquer Riga, as they had hoped. Frequent raids by Latvians followed this event and the people of both Ugandi and Sakala sent letters to Riga announcing that they were willing to be baptised. A large-scale baptism campaign soon followed, but later, people washed off the holy water again.

In September 1217, an elite troop of 3,000 men, consisting of Germans, Livonians and Latvians, again marched to Sakala. The Master of the Order Folkvin himself is said to have been the commander-in-chief of this campaign. On St Matthew's Day, 21 September 1217, the invaders clashed with the Estonian troops on a site of about 11 km north-north-west of Viljandi in a battle that appeared to be the largest one in the ancient fight for freedom. Although Estonians outnumbered their enemy, they were defeated, Lembitu was killed, and Estonians were forced to continue living under the peace terms settled in 1215.

On 29 January 1223, Estonians, who had been living in Viljandi Castle together with the Germans, killed almost all Germans there. The same happened in Leole. In Järvamaa, the Sakala men caught the local bailiff, Hebbe, who was a Dane, and cooked his heart over the fire and they ate it all together "to grow strong to defeat the Christians". Messages were sent from Viljandi to Otepää and Tartu, where Germans were killed, too. In a short time, a third of the Teutonic Knights were killed in Estonia, among them all their leaders in South Estonia, and almost all Estonian territory was free of alien powers, except for Tallinn. Estonians pressed on to Toreida in Latvia and fought a battle there, which was the last battle the ancient Estonians were fighting as free men outside the borders of Estonia.

The war machine of the Order was unstoppable and in August, the Teutonic Knights, crusaders, Latvians and Livonians were again besieging Viljandi Castle. Estonians were forced to accept Christianity again and promised large retribution to the conquerors. The peace that was then made meant the arrival of slavery.

In 1224, the Teutonic Knights, led by Bishop Albert, started to prepare for the last and decisive attack against the Estonians. Tartu fell in August, and Estonian lands were divided among the conquerors. The division did not pass without quarrels – everybody wanted to get their share, including the King of Denmark. Sakala became the share of the Teutonic Knights. Wilhelm of Modena, the Pope's Legate, who visited Viljandi next year, preached that Estonians and Germans should live together in a friendly manner.

History has, however, shown that no great friendship was ever born among the former enemies. A large granite monument was erected on Lõhavere Linnamägi in

The stronghold of the Estonian leader Lembitu was located at Lõhavere.

1969 to commemorate the ancient fight for freedom and the defenders of the old Sakala.

Olustvere Manor had already been established at the end of the time when the Order governed the land, but it was located at Papioru, slightly north of the present site. Valentin von Schilling moved the manor over to its present site in the early 17th century. In the 18th century, the manor went to the von Fersens as the dowry of a bride.

The present mansion was built by the von Fersens in 1903; it is an asymmetric two-storey stone building in English style with a two-storey high central hall. Many stone and brick outbuildings were erected together with the mansion and a rich English-style park was created.

Today, one wing of Olustvere mansion houses a kindergarten; a museum introducing the history of the mansion and several renovated halls are open to the visitors in the other wing. Since 2002, the display at the museum includes wooden figures carved by the local inhabitant Voldemar Luha, featuring horses and people engaged in different farm activities. Luha is said to have made his first horse of linen cloth and sawdust when only five years old; after retirement, he started woodworking in earnest. He has altogether made about 500 wooden horses, about 50 of them are on display.

Alexander Agricultural School, founded at Kõo Manor in 1914, was moved over to Olustvere Manor in 1920. Today the school is called the Olustvere School of Service and Rural Economics. A new building for the school was erected next to the mansion in the old orchard; now it is used also by the local primary school. A museum of local lore has been opened in the schoolhouse, introducing the history of Olustvere, as well as that of the local schools.

A bronze bust of **Jaan Adamson** (1824–1879), a schoolteacher and member of the 19th century National Awakening Movement who was born in Kurnuvere, near Olustvere, is standing near the schoolhouse.

Adamson, who was the schoolteacher at Pulleritsu school, in Holstre parish, was a man with an alert mind; he was a founding member of the Estonian Society of Literati, as well as one of the initiators of the idea of the Alexander School and a member of its main Committee. He worked enthusiastically to further cultural activities,

Olustvere Manor is surrounded by a beautiful park with a pond, well-kept outbuildings and a unique well.

founded song and drama societies in Paistu parish and created a private loan library. His attitude towards the national movement was quite radical and he clearly supported Carl Robert Jakobson. In 1866 and 1871 he participated in political activities, being a representative of Holstre parish among a group of envoys who took a petition to the Tsar, asking for better living conditions for peasants.

Jaan Adamson's birthplace in **Kurnuvere** village has been marked with a memorial stone; he was buried at Paistu cemetery.

The founder of Estonian painting, **Johann Köler** (1826–1899), was the seventh child of the leaseholder at Lubjassaare Farm, in Ivaski village, on the edge of the large bogs and mires of Soomaa. Although the family was poor, he managed to go to school and his talent was soon noticed. He made his first step towards an artist's career thanks to the manager of Vastsemõisa Manor, who recommended him as a journeyman to his brother, who was a painter in the Latvian town of Cesis.

The strong-willed young man made every effort and arrived in St Petersburg in 1846 with only 75 kopecks in his pocket. He worked to earn his living, and studied at the same time. After a hard struggle, he graduated from the St Petersburg Academy of Art with the small golden prize and went to further his skills in abroad.

He travelled in Germany, France and Italy, where he painted his first famous works. Having returned to St. Petersburg, he became the drawing teacher of the daughter of Emperor Alexander II. He was much honoured, but also extremely well paid for the exciting task of painting the first portrait of the new Emperor, Alexander III.

When talking about Johann

Johann Köler's home stood at the edge of the Soomaa mires, at Ivaski.

Köler, we cannot neglect his political activities, which was the second most important aspect of his life after his painting. He was an active and important figure in the Estonian national movement. Since he lived in St. Petersburg, he was politically inclined towards the sympathisers of Russia, and he was an obvious supporter of the idea that the unnaturally harsh conditions of the Estonian peasants under the Baltic-German estate owners can only be relieved by the kind help of Russian officials. He offered encouragement to Carl Robert Jakobson and gave him financial support as well. Jakobson could hardly have gained the permission to publish his newspaper Sakala without the help of Professor Köler and his friend Philipp Karell, the personal physician of the Emperor.

Köler was compromised as a public figure by his utopian plan, formulated in 1882, to buy some land in the Crimea and build a "flourishing Estonian settlement" there. Jakob Hurt as the Chairman of the Main Committee of the Alexander School tried to prevent such enterprise as much as he could, but he was forced to resign from the post and Köler, who became the next Chairman, continued to work on his project of land purchase. The project came to its bitter end when Köler went bankrupt and the Main Committee was dissolved after Hurt's complaints. The Alexander School, which should have been an Estonian-language school, started to work in the Russian language (see also Jõgevamaa and Põltsamaa).

In 1890, Köler was elected the President of the Society of Estonian Literati, but he did not have much support and the Society closed down a few years later.

The renowned artist and fighter for Estonians' rights was buried at Suure-Jaani cemetery. A huge crowd of people attended his burial. In 1913, a monument commissioned by Estonians living in St Petersburg, featuring his bronze bust made by sculptor Amandus Adamson, was placed on his grave.

A memorial stone stands at Köler's home at Lubjassaare. **Johann Köler Homestead Museum** is open at Lubjassaare, introducing the farm life of the time and Köler's life and work. Hiking paths starting at the farm offer the visitors the opportunity to walk along the paths of the artist's youth.

The ruins of Risti Chapel, built in the 15th century, stand east of Vastsemõisa by the road to Pärsti village. A small wooden sign points the way to the chapel at Rattama crossroads. Nobody seems to know exactly why the chapel was once built, although many legends are told about it. There is a story about a blind prince who suddenly got his eyesight back when he had sat down to rest on this hill, and later he had the chapel built on the site.

Another legend tells us that the chapel was erected to commemorate the victory over the Estonians in the St Matthew's Day battle (1217). Although, according to Henry of Livonia, the battle was fought somewhere in the vicinity of

Not much has been preserved of the Risti Chapel.

Vanamõisa village, no historical sources link the building of the chapel with this event. It is still believed that the toponym of Risti (Cross) symbolises the victory over the pagans.

Archaeological excavations testify that Risti Chapel was several times burnt to the ground over the centuries. The walls that had survived the fires were torn down in 1777 on the orders of the local clergy. The reason was, probably, the fact that people from the neighbouring villages used to hold yearly pagan rites in the chapel on 2 May. But according to still another legend, the chapel had been named after the spring holiday of the cross on 2 May.

Only the foundation of the chapel has been preserved. A rough limestone sculpture of Lembitu stands near the chapel ruins.

Tammemägi, supposed to be a site of an ancient shrine, is located on a wet pasture of the former Rattama farm. According to a legend, the Estonian elders used to hold councils on this hill and to mark the meetings, lit a fire on one of the two stones standing on the hill.

People have also believed Tammemägi to be the grave of the Sakala leader Lembitu. Although archaeological excavations have

The figure of Lembitu, made of limestone, near the ruins of Risti Chapel.

not confirmed that the place had been a burial site and no fires had been lighted on the stones in ancient times, the legends still live on. A large stone has been erected on Tammemägi with a text Lembitu 1217.

Madi burial mound, which has also been connected with the Battle of St Matthew's Day, can be found a few kilometres north-east of Risti Chapel. According to a legend, the Estonian fighters of Lembitu's troops, who had been killed in the battle, were buried in this mound.

The mound is, actually, situated on a burial ground of an ancient village and some men from the neighbourhood of Pärsti village, who had fought in the battle, could well have been buried there. About 2,000 finds have been unearthed at Madi; mostly they were pot shreds, but knives, fragments of bronze jewellery, pieces of scythes and sickles, and spearheads and war axes have also been found.

Pärsti Manor, located north-west of Viljandi, existed already before the Livonian War; it has changed both its owners and its location in the course of history. The old mansion stood near Lake Kuuni, where now only of group of large old trees and some outbuildings hint to its former location. The centre of the manor was moved to its present location only in the 18th century.

The mansion is already the second one on the site; it was built in 1872 after the old mansion had been destroyed. At the time when Peter Georg von Colongues was the owner of Pärsti manor, he had a telephone line brought in from his town house in Viljandi and the first telephone in the countryside was installed in his mansion. Pärsti Manor was closed down during the land reform in 1919, its lands were distributed among the veterans of the War of Independence and among the manor hands and some of the buildings were dismantled and taken away.

In **Lemmakõnnu** village, a memorial stone has been erected at the birthplace of the first Estonian agronomist who received special education, **Ado Johanson** (1874–1932).

Johanson studied agriculture in

The mansion of Pärsti Manor is decorated with wooden lattice-work

Finland, Sweden, Denmark and Germany. He was an agricultural adviser, but in addition to that, for many years he helped to edit the agricultural magazines Põllumees, Talu and Kaja and published research articles on the improvement and reclamation of new land. Twice, he was a member of the Riigikogu.

AROUND KÕPU

In our minds, **Soomaa National Park** is mostly connected with spring floods, called the fifth season, on the flood plain grasslands on the banks of the Halliste River, and with huge mires and raised bogs. This is a real wilderness, a hiding place for numerous animals and birds and a home for rare plants.

Soomaa is also connected with the culture of dugout boats. Such boats are still made there and the craft is taught to everybody who is interested in it.

The visitors' centre of Soomaa National Park in Kõrtsi-Tõramaa offers information about the park, its sights and nature paths.

Suure-Kõpu Manor ensemble, located in Kõpu village, contains the late-Classicist mansion (built in 1837–1847; since 1921, a schoolhouse), the estate manager's house and the park. The mansion, one of the grandest in South Estonia, is among the last Classicist mansions in Estonia.

The former Suure-Kõpu parish centre is the birthplace of the folklorist Oskar Loorits (1900–1961). A memorial stone has been placed in the yard of the house.

Oskar Loorits studied the religion of Estonians and related Finno-Ugric peoples. He compiled several collections of folkloristic materials, modernised the Estonian

A memorial stone to the folklorist Oskar Loorits stands in the yard of the Vana-Kõpu parish office. The text on the stone is in Estonian and Livonian.

language, and published epigrams, feuilletons and articles on current affairs in newspapers. He studied the spiritual world of Estonians, the sources of Estonian patriotism and the features of the psychology of Estonians. From 1944, he lived in exile in Sweden, where he continued his research.

Väike-Männiku Farm Museum is located at Iia, west of Kõpu, by the road to Tipu. The museum exhibits old farm tools, stuffed animals and an old wooden contraption for drying cones.

At Napsi, a smaller road turns to the south, towards Abja-Paluoja, from the Kilingi-Nõmme – Viljandi Road. **Mulgi Museum** is located in Koskila village. The museum occupies two buildings. An old-time kitchen, a living room and a classroom have been furnished on the first storey of the local schoolhouse; a display shows the history of the local school. An old granary has been brought to the school-

The old granary, exhibited at Mulgi Museum, has been brought there from elsewhere.

yard and old farm tools are exhibited there. This lovely and simple museum was born on the initiative of local enthusiasts; although no signs point it out, it can easily be found just across the road at Kosksilla bus stop.

AROUND HALLISTE, ABJA-PALUOJA AND MÕISAKÜLA

Õisu Manor ensemble is considered as a real gem in Viljandimaa. It consists of the Classicist mansion, built in 1760–1770, large outbuildings and a beautiful English-style park. Until quite recently, the visitors were greeted by two marble figures of the goddess of justice, Justitia, and the symbol of wisdom, Prudentia, standing on the large granite outer steps of the mansion. Now, these two figures that are the most valuable late Baroque park sculptures in Estonia have been relocated into the hall. The sculptures were probably made by an Italian artist Giovanni Antonio Cybei. From 1744 until the land reform in 1920, the manor belonged to the von Sivers'. Today, it houses the Õisu College of Food Industry and the local library.

Õisu has its own Hell, too. About a kilometre off the road, in the valley of the Vidva River,

Exhibits of Mulgi Museum fill several rooms.

stands an 8 m tall Devonian sandstone cliff with a large cave, which could as well be the mouth of a tunnel leading to the dwelling of the Old Devil.

The Mansion of Õisu Manor is more than 200 years old.

Halliste St Anna Church is among the first churches built in the newly independent Estonia. The church has burnt to the ground four times during its history; it was finally restored on the initiative of the local Pastor Kalev Raave in 1991. The large altarpiece of the church, "Christ", was painted by Jüri Arrak. A sculpture of a mother, made by sculptor Aime Kuulbusch, is standing in the church.

During the previous four centuries, an earlier church had four times been reduced to ruins. First, it was destroyed in the Livonian War and it was rebuilt in the 17th century. The church with wooden roof was again burnt to the ground in the Northern War, but by 1721, it had been raised again and 60 years later, a new tower was added to it. The church was hit by lightning in 1863 and again, only smoking ruins were left. The new church building was constructed under the supervision of Swiss architect Ruedi Häusermann to stand larger and more magnificent than ever before and it was consecrated in 1867. Unfortunately, there was a fire again in 1959. This time, only the sacristy was saved from the flames.

Writer **August Kitzberg** (1855–1927) started his working career in Halliste, at the former Pornuse parish office in 1872. In the vicinity there are numerous places connected with Kitzberg's work, such as the Lopa cliff and the 25 m long cave called Lopa Hell. The main character of his play The God of the Purse (Kauka jumal), Mogri Märt, is said to have lived in Lopa farm. The so-called Maimu's cave or another Hell is located in Mägiste, on the Halliste River, related to Kitzberg's short story Maimu.

Kitzberg's main works are the tragedy Werewolf (Libahunt), the drama The God of the Purse and the comedy A Damned Farm (Neetud talu). But in addition to these, he has written many village comedies and dramas that are much loved by the audiences.

Kitzberg was a fluent narrator and found interesting characters for his plays, such as the tailor

Halliste Church has burnt down several times.

Õhk. He also wrote children's stories and an interesting book of memoirs Youth Memories of an Old Good-for-Nothing (Ühe vana "tuuletallaja"noorpõlve mälestused).

When reading Kitzberg's pleasant and charming stories, it is difficult to believe that for most of his life, he worked as a parish clerk, a bookkeeper and even as a bank clerk. Monuments to Kitzberg have been erected at Tartu Raadi Cemetery (sculptor Jaan Koort) and in Karksi-Nuia, near the Viljandi Road. A memorial stone marks his birthplace in Puldre. The writer's room-museum was opened in Pöögle village near Karksi-Nuia.

South of Halliste, in **Kaubi** stock-farming manor, is a memorial stone to the diplomat and politician **Friedrich Karl Akel** (1871–1941), who was born there.

Akel, who was born in the family of Kaubi manor owners, studied medicine at the University of Tartu and worked for a period as an ophthalmologist. He also participated in the work of different societies and political parties. He started his more serious political activities in Jaan Tõnisson's National Progress Party, and left it in 1921 for another party, The Christian People's Party. Akel was one of the best-known centrist politicians in Estonia. Since 1922, he was the Estonian Ambassador in Finland, and later, the Estonian Ambassador in Sweden, Denmark, Norway, Germany and the Netherlands. In 1924, he was the Riigivanem (state elder) and several times fulfilled the post of the Minister of Foreign Affairs. He was also the Chairman of the Estonian Olympic Committee, and, for a period, a member of the International Olympic Committee.

Akel was arrested by the Soviets in September 1940 and was killed in 1941.

About 200 years ago, the neighbourhood of **Abja-Paluoja** became an important flax growing centre. The first co-operative flax processing factory in Estonia was founded there in 1914; later, flax mills started to work there as well. The flax processing factory worked there in the Soviet time, too, but the raw material was mostly imported then. Flax processing has now stopped in Abja-Paluoja.

The Abja autumn fair, held at the Paluoja Inn, was the largest cattle market in Estonia 100 years ago. The most remarkable construction in this town is the building of the former bank, built after the project of the professor of architecture Edgar Johan Kuusik (1888–1974), which now houses the post office.

Karl August Hindrey (1875–1947), a man of many talents, was born in Abja Manor, 2 km east of Abja-Paluoja. He was known as a sharp caricaturist as well as an author of psychological

F. K. Akel, who was born in Kaubi stock-farming Manor, was an active politician.

The most stylish building in Abja-Paluoja was designed by Professor Edgar Johan Kuusik.

The history of Mõisaküla and its railways is on display at the local museum.

short stories and funny and moralist children's books. The mansion of Abja Manor is located on the high bank of the primeval valley of the Halliste River; the park of the manor stretched down to the river. The mansion and some of the outbuildings, including a large granary with columns in front, have been preserved. Today, a border guard unit is located in the manor.

Since the end of the 18th century, Abja Manor belonged to the von Stackelbergs, who started selling farms to peasants already in 1843. Many farmers of the area grew flax and became rich, and started to buy up farms in the neighbourhood. The arrogant new rich were soon called mulk, derived from the Latvian word mulkis, meaning stupid. At the turn of the 20th century, well-off people in the area owned about a dozen local manors.

The narrow-gauge railway, running through **Mõisaküla**, has played an important role in the history of this town. The building of the Pärnu-Valga narrow-gauge railway was started in 1895 (completed in 1896). In 1897, a rail service was started between Mõisaküla and Viljandi. The railway accelerated the development of Mõisaküla and the whole of Mulgimaa for the next 75 years, furthering the local economy and giving the locals a valuable means of transportation. The neighbouring villages grew and Mõisaküla became a town in 1938.

Mõisaküla was an important centre for machine building and flax processing up until the 1970s, when it was decided in Moscow that the narrow-gauge railway should be closed. Since the plan, which had been prepared by faraway officials, had no economical basis, unfair methods were used to force it. The railway timetables were made uncomfortable for the passengers and the goods transported by rail were taken to places, where it was not possible to load and unload them. The narrow-gauge railway was closed on 3 June 1973. The last narrow-gauge train in Estonia went from Ikla to Mõisaküla and then to Valmiera, in Latvia, on 30 September 1975, gathering and pulling away the carriages from all the stations en route. Another railway linked Mõisaküla and Tallinn.

The closing of the railway was such a serious blow to Mõisaküla that the economy of this small town has still not recovered 30 years later.

Mõisaküla Museum, located at 4, J. Sihveri Street, gives an overview of the history of Mõisaküla and its railways.

The **Mõisaküla Lutheran Church** was built in 1934 and it

was among the most outstanding examples of Estonian church architecture of the 20th century. The church was designed by architect Alar Kotli. The church burnt to the ground in 1983 and is now being restored.

KARKSI-NUIA

The **Karksi Order Castle** was built on the site of Karksi hill-fort in the first half of the 13th century. The building of a stone castle to replace the former wooden one was probably started at the end of the same century, after raids by Lithuanians. The castle walls were reinforced and built higher during the following century. The castle was damaged in the Livonian War and the Polish-Swedish wars; it could not withstand the Northern War and it was destroyed in 1708. Today, only ruins remind us of the old castle.

Karksi St Peter's Church with its slanting tower was built partly on the foundation of the castle in 1773–1778, on the spot of the earlier castle chapel. The church is of an extremely simple design: a tower with its Baroque spire stands next to choir; a sacristy has been built against the eastern wall of the church. As an exception, the church was orientated from north to south (Estonian churches are mostly orientated from west to the east, with the tower at the western wall).

The tower of Karksi Church has leaned to the west for more than 2 metres.

Noteworthy objects in the church are the late Baroque altar with Rococo motifs from 1770, and the organ decorated with paintings. The former castle wall that had been used as an outer wall of the church proved to be unstable and the tower soon started to slant. Today, the tower has leaned more than 2 metres towards the west.

The mansion of the former **Karksi Manor** has been destroyed. The granary and the manager's house have been preserved; the houses have been restored and are now used by the parish centre. Carl Gottlieb Reinthal, who made the first translation of Kalevipoeg into German, was born at Karksi Manor.

A monument to the writer **August Kitzberg** (1855–1927) stands on the high bank of the primeval valley of the Halliste River, by the Viljandi Road. The sculpture, made

Karksi Order Castle is in ruins.

The sculpture of August Kitzberg is sitting on the brink of the Halliste primeval valley and gazes over familiar landscapes.

by Jaak Soans, was erected in 1991 (about Kitzberg, see also Viljandimaa, Halliste).

Old Devil has lived and played his tricks around **Karksi** for a long time. Traces of his activities can be found at many places. In ancient times, the devils and their families lived in four caves (Hells) near Karksi. One of them lived near the castle, the second in the Koodiorg valley, the third in Mägiste (Allaste village) and the fourth came out from a large stone called Iivakivi (Sudiste village). They had good relations with the local people and sometimes even helped them.

It is surprising that in Karksi old tales, the devils are depicted as good and industrious beings. A rich devil called Lasna lived in the castle ruins. His good friend was another devil called Lisna, who lived in Koodiorg at Vana Kariste village. Lasna baked bread twice a week and each time threw a couple of loaves to his friend Lisna with a crust. The devil in Koodiorg threw the crust back with his own loaves. The devil who lived in Mägiste cave was poor; the other two did not communicate with him.

At the time of Christianisation, the Mägiste devil left his cave, putting a curse on the bulls of local farmers, and on the local girls too.

People believed that a door to Hell opened in the Iivakivi stone that stands in the forest at Sudiste village through which the devil came and went.

The devil that lived in the castle took the form of a black cat and is even now guarding the barrels of gold and silver in the castle cellar. Unfortunately, nobody knows the way to the cellar.

Polli Manor, 2 km north of Karksi-Nuia, was probably formed as the stock-farming manor of the Karksi castle at the end of the time when the Order ruled the area. Polli was made an independent manor in 1744. An unconventional mansion with a one-storey central part and two-storied wings was built at the end of the same century. Many of the outbuildings of the manor have been preserved, but mostly they are empty and derelict now.

The mansion is waiting for a new owner, but the Polli Horticultural Institute is working in the rest

Fruit trees and berries are grown at Polli Manor.

of the ensemble, dealing with the introduction of new varieties of fruit trees and berries. An important aspect of the Institute's work is the preservation of the genome bank of all Estonian varieties of fruit and berries.

Pöögle village is 3 km from Karksi-Nuia towards Pärnu; the writer August Kitzberg lived and worked there for a period of time. The writer's Room-museum is open in the village, introducing the local farm life and Kitzberg's life and work. The caretaker of the museum, Asta Jaaksoo, conducts (driving) tours to the 'literary places' of the neighbourhood, connected with Kitzberg, K. A. Hindrey and Hella Wuolijoki. (About K. A. Hindrey, see Abja Manor, Viljandimaa; about Wuolijoki, see Ala inn, Valgamaa.)

At the **Lilli border point**, 14 km south of Karksi-Nuia, a memorial stone was opened in 1999, on the 10th anniversary of the Baltic Chain, to commemorate the chain of people that reached from Estonia to Lithuania, demanding their freedom. This memorial stone is one among the many of its kind (see also Särevere, Järvamaa).

A memorial stone to Mats Tõnisson, a compiler of calendars, is located by the Viljandi – Karksi-Nuia Road, just before the Tuhalaane crossroads (see Vändra, Pärnumaa).

The birthplace of a scholar of medicine and the Rector of the University of Tartu, **Henrik Koppel** (1863–1944), is beside the Viljandi-Tartu Road, south of the Tõnuküla crossroads. The house is marked by a memorial plaque.

VILJANDI AND ITS NEIGHBOURHOOD

An ancient Estonian stronghold was located at **Kaevumägi**, on **Viljandi Castle Hill**. It was the main defence centre in the ancient fight for freedom. When the lands were divided among the conquerors, the stronghold was given to the Order of the Brothers of the Sword, who started to build a stone castle there.

In its time, Viljandi Castle was the most powerful among the castles of Old Livonia, and the Viljandi Order commanders resided there. The settlement that grew at the northern wall of the castle was soon given the town rights and in the 14th century, it became a member of the powerful Hanseatic League as an important stopping place on the trade route to Russia.

In the Livonian War, the castle changed hands many times and by the 17th century, it had lost its military importance. The town of Viljandi and the castle were seriously damaged in the Northern War, and the castle has since then stood in ruins. Today, the castle hills are a favoured recreation area for the townspeople.

Viljandi Town Hall was built between 1768 and 1774; at that time, it belonged to Johann Nicolaus Otto, who was the chief official of the town. In 1783, it was rented to house the new magistrate of the town. This hip-roofed house, like other stone town houses of the time, had been built in Baroque style. The Town Hall was radically rebuilt in 1931, when only the walls of the ground floor remained. An electric clock bought from the firm of Siemens in Germany was installed in the tower of the building. The clock first struck on St John's Night in 1932.

Viljandi Order Castle lost its importance 400 years ago.

Viljandi Town Hall is adorned by a sleek clock tower.

The Soviets turned the Viljandi St John's Church into a furniture warehouse.

The Viljandi Museum dates back to 1878. On the initiative of the teacher of history at the Viljandi Rural Secondary School, Theodor Schiemann, owner of Uue-Vändra Manor, archaeological excavations were started at Viljandi castle ruins with the financial support of Friedrich von Ditmar. The collection containing the finds of the excavations was called the Ditmar Museum up to 1936. In 1940, the museum that had already been named the Viljandi Museum, moved over to the building of the former chemists at 10, Laidoneri Plats.

The display in the museum introduces Estonian nature and the development of Viljandi and Viljandi County starting from the earliest times. A detailed model of Lembitu's stronghold and of the Viljandi Order castle are on display. Among the other exhibits, we should mention the original copies of August W. Hupel's works, the issues of the first Estonian-language magazine A Short Instruction... (Lühhike öpetus...), published in 1766 by Hupel and the local physician, Peter E. Wilde, and a copy of the first Estonian-language Bible, published in 1739.

The history of **Viljandi's St John's Church** dates back to the building of the Franciscan monastery in 1466–1472. The monastery that had been burnt to the ground in the Livonian War was later rebuilt as a town church, dedicated to St John. The church was working up to 1950, when it was closed and made into a furniture warehouse. It was restored in the last years of the Soviet era and the first service was held there at Christmas of 1991.

The other church in town, **St Paul's Church**, was built after the design of architect Matthias von Holst in 1863–1866, using the characteristic Viljandi building materials – granite and red brick. Viljandi Manor owner Baron von Ungern-Sternberg gave a piece of his land for the building of the church. The writer, clergyman and politician Jaan Lattik was the Pastor of the church in 1910–1939 (see also Mägiste, Valgamaa). In 1866, K. C. Andreas's altarpiece Crucifixion and an organ made by G. Knauf were installed in the church.

A memorial stone to Captain Anton Irv stands next to the church. Captain Irv was a legendary commander of an armoured train in the War of Independence, who was killed in North Latvia just before the end of the war.

Viljandi Trepimägi (Stairs hill) was built at the end of the 19th and beginning of the 20th centuries to improve traffic between the town and the lake. The largest obstacle in the way, the ancient moat, was filled with the rubble from the fire of 1894. The five-stage staircase has 158 steps; the young trees that were planted by the stairs were brought from the park of the secondary school. Trepimägi was reconstructed in 1991.

The bronze Johann Köler is still painting in Viljandi.

The beautiful monument to **Johann Köler** was erected at the Town Square in 1976, when the 150th anniversary of the birth of the creator of Estonian painting was celebrated. The sculpture is by Edgar Viies, the architect of the monument was Rein Luup (about Köler, see Ivaski village, Viljandimaa).

The cultural history of Viljandi is awesomely rich. At the corner of Jakobsoni and Liivi Streets stands the house where one of the editors of the newspaper Sakala, Juhan Liiv, lived and worked in 1888–1889. The building that housed the editorial office of the newspaper in 1878–1879, located between Tartu, Lossi and Tallinn Streets, is also marked. The monument to Carl Robert Jacobson stands at the corner of Lossi and Tartu Streets.

An original monument stands near the lake, in a small park at the corner of Ranna Avenue and Supeluse Street. It was erected to mark an important sports event –

Vana-Võidu mansion houses a vocational school.

Selles majas asus C. R. Jakobsoni ajalehe *Sakala* toimetus aastail 1878–1879

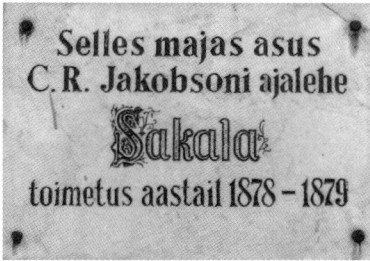

Cultural history in Viljandi is closely connected with Carl Robert Jakobson.

Races around the lake have been held in Viljandi for more than 75 years.

the annual race around Lake Viljandi. The names of all winners, starting with the year 1928, have been engraved onto the monument, but the list is still incomplete.

To the left of the Viljandi-Tartu Road, about 7 km of Viljandi, stands the ensemble of **Vana-Võidu Manor**, built at the beginning of the 19th century. The late Classicist mansion is surprisingly similar to Kuremaa Manor house in Jõgevamaa, and both of them are probably designed by one and the same architect. Similarly to Kuremaa, the heart of Vana-Võidu Manor houses a vocational school – the Viljandi Joint Vocational Secondary School.

One of the most famous Estonian trees, **Tamme-Koori oak**, stands by the Tartu Road just a short distance before a smaller road branches off towards the manor. The oak has been made famous by the artist Eduard Viiralt in his print Viljandi landscape (about Viiralt, see more in Varangu, Lääne-Virumaa and Koeru, Järvamaa).

The birthplace of **Johan Laidoner** (1884–1953), a general and emi-

Picturesque Viiralt's oak stands near the Viljandi-Tartu Road.

The sculpture of Johan Laidoner in Viljandi was the first equestrian monument in Estonia.

nent politician, is located at Vardja-Viiratsi, south of Viljandi. Here Laidoner lived until the age of seven, when his family moved to Viljandi town. A monument was erected at the site of the former Raba farm and an avenue of trees was planted. The monument was restored in 1990.

Young Laidoner chose a military career to escape economic hardship. The army clothed and fed its own. He studied at the Vilno Military School, served in the Yerevan grenadier regiment in Caucasia, which was an elite troop of the time, and entered through hard competition the Nicholas War Academy, which trained general-staff officers. In WWI, he was a reconnaissance officer and became a lieutenant colonel.

In 1917, he accepted the task of creating the Estonian Army. Starting with nothing, he created an army that halted the enemy offensive and drove them back well beyond what are now the borders of Estonia. When Estonia became independent, Laidoner went into politics, but there he was not half as successful as he had been in military service. During the crisis of the 1930s, he should have run for president, but instead he collaborated with Konstantin Päts. It is believed that without his help, Päts would not have been able to organise the coup d'etat on 12 March 1934.

During the following years Laidoner, who had been appointed the commander-in-chief of the army, kept a low profile. Recently heated discussions have broken out in Estonia about whether Laidoner had been right in concluding a treaty on military bases with the Soviet Union in 1939. The army, which he himself had created, was ready to fight. Laidoner was among the very first to be repressed. Together with his wife of Polish origin, Marie Kruszewka, he was arrested as early as the second day after the Soviet invasion of Estonia and sent to prison in Russia. He died in prison eight days after the death of Stalin.

The Laidoner Museum was opened in Viimsi, near Tallinn, in 1994; in June 2004, an equestrian monument was unveiled in the centre of Viljandi, which is the first of its kind in Estonia.

Naanu hill-fort, also known as Tantsimägi, is located north-east of Viljandi, at the northern edge of Saarepeedi village. The triangular-shaped promontory hill-fort is said to have been made of the remains of a ship.

The hill-fort was used for a very short time in the 11th and 12th centuries. By the time the Teutonic Knights invaded, in the early 13th century, it had probably already been abandoned. This is confirmed also by archaeological excavations – no traces of fighting and no arms were found in the cultural layer of the hill-fort. The clearest evidence about battles with the Germans – the crossbow arrowheads – were entirely missing there.

West of Viljandi at **Lõmsi**, near Pinska village, was the centre of the Viljandi model state farm. This institution was subordinated to the Estonian Institute of Cattle Breeding and Veterinary Science and worked as a testing facility for scientific research, its activities included the breeding of small agricultural animals, research in artificial insemination, etc. Many workers of the state farm were given state awards, for example, everybody in Estonia knew a Hero of Socialist Work, farm milker Leida Peips.

We can reach the former state farm centre when turning to the right from the Viljandi-Pärnu Road, to a row of large trees. Today, the office building is a dwelling house; furniture is made in one of the outbuildings.

An interesting **handicraft museum** is located in **Heimtali** village, displaying beautiful handicraft objects, old tools and toys. The owner of the museum is a textile artist, professor Anu Raud, daughter of writer Mart Raud (1903–1980), who was born at Vanausse, near Heimtali.

Heimtali Manor ensemble is located 6 km of Viljandi, on the brink of the primeval valley of the Raudna River. First reports about a manor called Linseni and later, Kurwitza date back to the early 16th century. Since 1793, the manor is called Heimtali. Peter Reinhold von Sivers, who inherited Kurwitza manor from his father, who was also the owner of Õisu Manor, renamed the place in memory of his bride Luise Heimthal, who had died young.

Von Sivers was an enterprising man, who increased the productivity of his manor by inventing the best ways of improving his lands. At the progressive Heimtali Manor, the peasants started paying rent

Heimtali Manor was an innovative agricultural enterprise during the early 19th century.

The exotic dairy of Heimtali Manor has sometimes been mistaken for a distillery.

instead of working for the manor already in 1810.

The Classicist mansion was built at the beginning of the 19th century; today, the manor houses the Raudna Basic School. The outbuildings of the manor are spectacular. The most interesting among them is the dairy, built in 1857–1858, (which has sometimes been mistakenly taken as distillery). This building with its high tile roof, strong stone walls and four corner towers looks like a medieval castle. The cheese, made there under the supervision of a Swiss master at the turn of the 20th century, sold well also in the neighbouring countries. Today, the house is privately owned and in good order.

The riding court and circular stables, cattle shed, pigsty and the stable hand's room, are an interesting sight. The construction has been neglected, but the local community plans to build a sports complex for the Raudna school there.

A peculiar building stands on the rim of the valley, which housed a granary, grain dryer and cellar. The manor owner developed a unique grain dryer in 1860, which became known as the Heimtali dryer all over the Baltic area and even farther off. The same dryer was working in this building, too.

Heimtali Manor is surrounded by a beautiful and well-kept park, which was created at the beginning of the 19th century and is now a protected area as a part of the Loodi Nature Park. The Heimtali park with many dissecting valleys is among the most beautiful manor parks in Estonia, featuring ponds, springs and numerous rare deciduous trees.

The **Loodi Nature Park** with an area of 3,500 hectares (established in 1992) is full of interesting sights. One of the many Hells – Loodi or Paistu Põrguorg – is located in Paistu primeval valley. Devonian sandstones outcrop in this narrow but about 20 m deep valley.

Three springs flow out of the valley; the largest of them opens up just in front of the large Põrguorg cave. An old story goes that during great wars and other upheavals, local people hid in the cave. It is also said that a long time ago, treasure and a dead body in a silver coffin were buried there.

The largest grove of larches in Estonia, planted in 1820, stands in Loodi park, at Püstmägi. An ancient grove of sacred oaks is growing at Tõllamägi; the largest oak in the grove is 21 m tall and with a girth of slightly less than 6 m. In the past, different religious and social rites were practiced at this six-branched oak. A memorial stone to folk singer Epp Vasara (1828–1895) stands in the park.

Local people are said to have hidden from the enemy in Paistu Põrguorg.

One of the several Estonian blue-water springs, called **Siniallikas** (Blue Spring), is located in the Loodi Nature Park, near Ramsi, south of Viljandi. It is called Suur Siniallik (Large Blue Spring). The peculiar bluish tinge of its water is caused by blue clay at the bottom and also by bluish algae.

The spring has been believed to cure sickness and people have thrown offerings, mostly silver coins, into the water. Old people tell many tales about the spring. Some of them are about a blue-eyed slave girl, seduced by the manor lord, who had drowned herself in the spring; others are about pots of money that have been dropped into the spring.

The spring has lent its name to the neighbouring Sinialliku Lake, as well as to a hill-fort of the so-called Kalevipoeg bed-type.

The hill-fort was discovered by an outstanding Estonian archaeologist and historian Jaan Jung. Later excavations have shown that the hill-fort was probably used from the first half of the 11th century to the mid-12th century. It was damaged when the Viljandi-Mõisaküla railway line was built; to make room for the railway it was necessary to flatten the eastern side of the hill. Later, people have mined gravel there and searched for limestone suitable for making lime.

About 3.5 km south-west of Heimtali, by the road to Abja-Paluoja, stands **Kiisa village** – the birth place of the poet and politician Johannes Vares Barbarus (1890–1946). The house where he was born is marked with a memorial plaque. The house is in such a bad need of repair that local people say that the plaque will soon weigh it down altogether.

Johannes Vares (Barbarus was his pseudonym) was a physician with leftist views, living in Pärnu. During the time of the pre-war Estonian Republic, Vares Barbarus was an innovative and rebellious poet. Due to his worldview, he attracted the attention of the occupational authorities in the 1940s. He was first made the Prime Minister of the first red government and soon after, he was appointed the Chairman of the Supreme Soviet of the ESSR – the post which was

The largest grove of larch trees in Estonia stands in Loodi park.

The birthplace of Johannes Vares-Barbarus in Kiisa village.

equal to that of the head of the state. But during the Soviet time, the most important person in the state was the Chairman of the Central Committee of the Communist Party. Vares Barbarus died in Kadriorg Palace in 1946 under mysterious circumstances. He was either murdered, or decided to commit suicide because he was disappointed with political life at that time.

Still further down to the south by the same road, about 4 km west of Heimtali, stands **Peetri Hunting Manor**, established at the beginning of the 20th century. The beautiful mansion of the manor is now privately owned.

1.5 km west of Loodi is the former Loodi narrow-gauge railway station. The station building was constructed in 1898, together with its outbuildings, the station complex has been preserved in its original state. Today, the complex is privately owned and in good repair. Nothing has been left of the railway, but its bed is still there and local people use it as a walking and cycling path.

PAISTU AND HOLSTRE

In the 1860s and 1870s, Paistu parish occupied a special place in Estonian political and cultural life – this was the heart of the national movement and the centre of the fight against the Baltic-German nobility. Here was born the idea of creating the Alexander School, and the campaign of petitions was run from here in 1864.

People sent petitions to the Tsar and sincerely believed that he would help them. The common belief was that the Tsar, the Father to his people, simply did not know how unfairly the manor lords were treating the peasants. He should only be informed of the true state of affairs, and he would right all injustice. So far, the good Tsar had not helped them only because the local manor lords had misinformed him all the time.

The petition campaign of the first half of the 1860s differed from earlier similar actions for its better organisation and because this time, intellectuals were also involved in it. The campaign was led by Jaan Adamson, Adam and Peeter Peterson, Johann Köler and others. The peasants demanded acceptable land prices and rent tariffs, abolition of serfdom and corporal punishment, wider use for the Estonian language, and, to make it more palatable for the Tsar, they also suggested that the Russian language should be taught at basic schools. The petitions were presented to Alexander II in November 1864 with the help of the so-called St Petersburg patriots (Köler and others).

The only visible result of the campaign was that the Livonian officials arrested the authors of the petitions and more enthusiastic collectors of signatures. In spite of this, petitions were sent to the Tsar even later, for example, in the early 1880s, when a revision of social and educational conditions in the provinces of Livonia and Kurland was held, supervised by Senator Manassein.

The poet, linguist and leader of the national movement **Mihkel Veske** (1843–1890), the playwright, poet, educator and member of the national movement **Juhan Kunder** (1852–1888), **Mart Raud** (1903–1980), who later became left-wing writer, and an altogether red writer and revolutionary Hans Pöögelmann (1875–1938), the journalist Jaan Tomp (1882–1943) and many others went to the former Paistu parish school. In 1880–1911, the composer Friedrich August Saebelmann (1851–1911) worked as a Paistu parish school teacher, and composed many of his famous and much-loved songs there. The schoolhouse was destroyed in ire in 1941.

Paistu Church was probably built in the last quarter of the 13th century. Only walls have been preserved of the original nave that survived war damage in the 17th and 18th centuries and the great fire in 1817, caused by lightning. The present-day Neo-gothic interior of the church, as well as its western tower, made after the project of the architect Matthias von Holst, were completed in the mid-19th century.

Paistu Church with its tall tower, located on a high hill, has lent its name to the whole parish (the name means "can be seen from afar"). Old people have said that the spire had even been seen as far as at the Baltic Sea and it had been a landmark for sailors. The church stands on a hill and it really can be seen from afar, especially when the trees are bare, but it could never have been a beacon, not even for Lake Võrtsjärv.

The communist poet, journalist and politician **Hans Pöögelmann** was born a few kilometres south of Paistu, in the Puiste farm of the former **Aidu Manor** in 1875. He studied at the Alexander School and also in Leipzig, Germany, where he got acquainted with Karl Marx's theories. After that, he became a revolutionary. He participated enthusiastically in the dethroning of the Russian Tsar and during the War of Independence, he attempted to get Estonia back under the Russian rule. He lived in Russia for a long time.
Another centre of the National

Paistu Church stands on a high hill.

Awakening was Pulleritsu village, south of Holstre. **Jaan Adamson** (1824–1879), one of the leaders of the National Awakening, worked there as a schoolteacher. He was one of the initiators of the Alexander School, a founding member of the Society of Estonian Literati and a leader of the petition campaign. As a schoolteacher, he taught Mihkel Veske and Juhan Kunder. The school building is now privately owned, but a memorial plaque

A memorial stone to the enthusiastic patriot Jaan Adamson stands in Holstre Manor park.

has been placed on its wall. A memorial stone to Jaan Adamson has been erected in the former Holstre manor park, which is now a school park.

Holstre Kindralimägi is located on the shore of Lake Mustjärv. More than 100 years old oaks stand over the ruins of an old chapel, where the last owner of Holstre Manor, General von Berg, was buried in 1784.

The poet **Juhan Kunder** (1852–1888) was born in Holstre village. A memorial stone for him and his half brother Hain Henno, a member of the national movement, has been placed in the yard of Kovali farm where they lived.

Kunder was a writer and schoolteacher; in addition to that he participated in the National Awakening movement, favouring its more radical wing. He fought for the establishment of the Alexander School and, for a period, was the vice president of the Society of Estonian Literati.

Kunder wrote in newspapers and often published criticism on his fellow writers, therefore he is considered to be one of the founders of Estonian literary criticism. He studied natural sciences at Kazan University, wrote a number of textbooks on natural history, revising Estonian terminology of the field, and published a few popular scientific works.

As a playwright, he wrote a number of village comedies which are still staged and much loved by the public.

A monument to Kunder stands in Rakvere, where he lived and worked for a long time (see also Rakvere, Lääne-Virumaa).

MUSTLA, KÄRSTNA, SUISLEPA

The birthplace of the linguist and member of the National Awakening movement, **Mihkel Veske** (1843–1890), is located at Viliimeeste by Viljandi-Mustla Road. His patriotic poems have been made into popular songs; one of them was the closing song of the Song Festival in 2004.

Mihkel Veske, Jakob Hurt and Karl August Hermann were awarded doctoral degrees in linguistics long before the Finno-Ugric languages were included into the curricula of the University of Tartu. Veske studied in Leipzig, and while Hurt started to study and collect folklore, Veske was a true linguist. He was the first lecturer of the Estonian language at the University of Tartu, who was also of Estonian descent. In 1879 he published a book on Estonian phonetics, where he suggested that the Estonian literary language should be based on the North Estonian central dialect and that the phonetic system of spelling should be adopted. Field trips to collect examples of different dialects took him to visit other Finno-Ugric peoples – the Maris and Mordvinians. During the last years of his life, Veske was the professor of Finno-Ugric languages at Kazan University.

Mihkel Veske, who was born at Viliimeeste, taught Finno-Ugric languages at Kazan University during the last years of his life.

A poet who wrote in Tarvastu dialect, **Andres Rennit** (1860–1936), was born in **Kuressaare** village, south of Mustla.

Rennit had a printing shop in Viljandi, where he also sold books. He wrote poems, plays and some short stories.

Driving to the west from Mustla, we pass through Koidu village and reach **Tinnikuru**, the home place of famous plant breeder, Mihkel Pill (1884–1951).

Mihkel Pill studied natural science at the University of Tartu and in abroad; he created the plant breeding station in Jõgeva and was its director for a long time. He founded several societies to improve Estonian plant breeds. He was justifiably called "the father of Estonian white bread", since resulting from his research and popularisation work, wheat production in Estonia increased several times. Pill bred 19 breeds of cereals and was one of the first scientists in the world to apply the modern theory of genetics. He was awarded a doctoral degree for his achievements without having had to write a thesis (see also Jõgeva Plant Breeding Institute, Jõgevamaa).

Mustla is the centre of Tarvastu parish. Mustla has a secondary school and one of the oldest libraries in Estonia, founded in 1860. Mustla started developing near the former Mustla inn as a village of poor manor hands. Local manor owners attempted to settle their cheap labour in the village. The Mustla monument to the War of Independence resembles the monument in Tudulinna. Among locals, it is known as Vabaduse Jaan (Freedom Jaan).

Ruins of an **Order Castle** stand in **Tarvastu park**. They are quite

A house with a tower is a landmark in Mustla.

Mustla people call the monument to the soldiers of the War of Independence Freedom Jaan.

hard to find. One has to drive to the south, past Tarvastu Church, and look for a sign saying 'Tarvastu metsapark'. A road bordered with trees runs through the centre of the estate and after about 1.5 km, we can see a sign with the name of a farm by the road. Driving along the road towards the farm, we arrive at a no through-road sign and a small parking area. To reach the castle ruins, we have to pass through the yard of the farm mill and cross the Tarvastu River by a footbridge. Across the river, near the footbridge, a flight of steps takes us up the castle hill.

Tarvastu Castle was built probably in the 14th century on the site of an ancient Estonian stronghold. After 1410, the Order commanders became frequent visitors there and the castle was further fortified. In 1481, the castle was attacked by the troops of Ivan III; in the Livonian War, the castle was first overthrown by Russians, then by Poles and in 1577, by Swedes. The castle was destroyed by an explosion of gunpowder storage.

The **Tarvastu manor** owners, the von Mesenkampffs, built a burial chapel with a pyramid roof and porches with double columns on the castle hill in 1825. The chapel has recently been renovated and gives a mystical air to the overgrown castle hill.

A monument to the former owner of Kärstna Manor, with a bronze lion lying on a huge boulder, has been erected near Kärstna village on Kabelimaägi (Chapel Hill). General lieutenant Reinhold von Anrep was killed in a battle with the French in East-Prussia in

The newly renovated burial chapel of the von Mesenkampffs at Tarvastu castle hill.

A beautiful view over the neighbouring landscape from Tarvastu castle hill.

A lying bronze lion commemorates the General Lieutenant von Anrep who was killed in Prussia.

1807. The stone is about 1 km off the manor centre. The von Anrep family cemetery is in the forest behind the stone; the chapel built in the 19th century is in ruins.

Kärstna Primary School is now working in the mansion of Kärstna Manor. A monument to the longtime teacher of the school, poet Hendrik Adamson (1891–1946) stands in front of the school. Adamson's home place in Metsakuru village near Lake Veisjärv has been marked with a memorial stone. Adamson wrote poems in the Mulgi dialect, as well as in the Estonian language, and short stories and witty philosophical novellas. He took an interest in the Esperanto language and wrote stories and poems in it. These works have been translated into Estonian. Today, Tarvastu parish issues the Henrik Adamson Prize for poetry written in dialect.

The text on a memorial stone to the poet Henrik Adamson in front of the former Kärstna mansion is in Livonian.

South of Kärstna, at **Põrgamõisa**, stands a monument to the **brothers Pinka**, who commanded a scouts regiment at the War of Independence. The younger brother, Friedrich Karl Pinka (1895–1942), was a colonel, the older brother, Herbert Pinka (1890–1919), was a lieutenant at the time he was killed. The Soviets arrested F. K. Pinka in 1941 and killed him in a prison camp.

Driving south off Tarvastu via Viljandi-Valga Road, we reach **Suislepa Manor**. A breed of sweet summer apples of the same name originates from the orchard of the manor.

Today, Suislepa mansion houses a local school. A giant lime tree stands in front of the school on a well-kept lawn. A commemorative stone to the famous Suislepa apple breed stands in the orchard next to

A memorial stone to the brothers Pinka at Põrgamõisa.

A stone has been erected to the sweet Suislepa breed of apples in the orchard of Suislepa mansion.

Hunger caves were made by peasants in the years of great famine.

the school. A tree of the breed has been planted by the stone.

Behind the mansion, on the bank of the Õhne River, there are the caves where, according to the legend, the local peasants had scraped sand during a great famine in 1695–1697 and exchanged it for grain in the manor. A stone stands next to the so-called Näljakoopad (Famine caves) to commemorate those hard times.

JÄRVAMAA

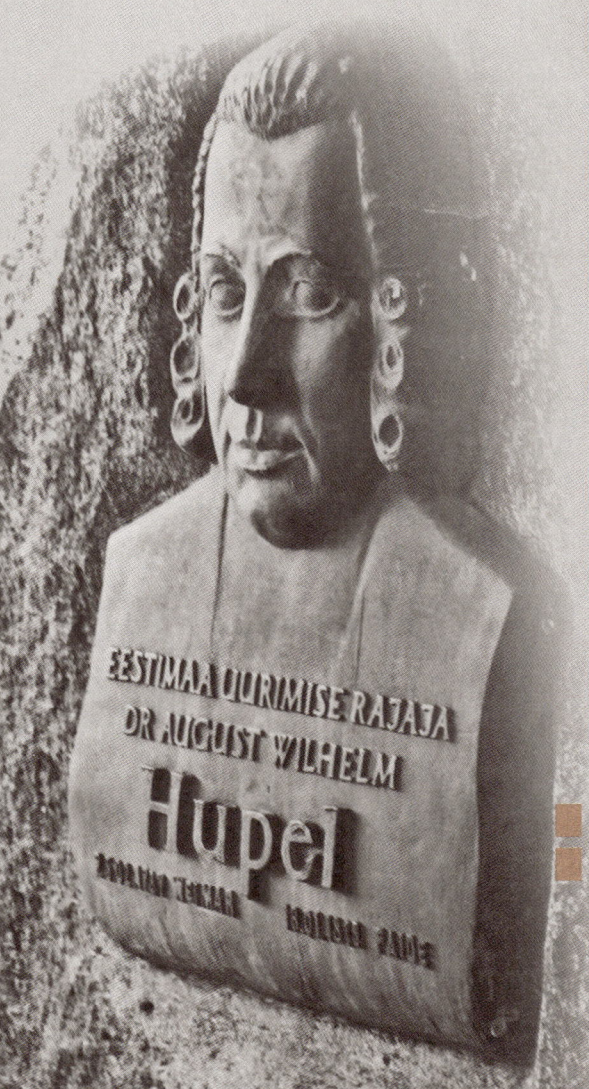

JÄRVAMAA

Järvamaa is the heartland of Estonia and the most fertile fields of our country are also in this region. Järvamaa is the concluding chapter of this book, of our brief excursion in our homeland, Estonia.

A memorial stone to August Wilhelm Hupel stands at Reopalu cemetery, in Paide. This gentleman with mild eyes and baroque curls, who lived in the town of Põltsamaa, translated into the Estonian language the stories that were helpful to peasants. Together with a physician of German origin, Peter Ernst Wilde, he was the publisher of the first Estonian-language magazine.

The tower of Paide Castle has been erected and destroyed and built up again with unwavering persistency. A modest memorial stone to four Estonian leaders, or kings, who were killed in a provoked struggle in Paide Castle 660 years ago, stands on the lawn near the tower. This was one of the reasons that quenched the fires of St George's Night Uprising for a very long time. On the strength of the legends, this fire was symbolically lighted again by the social democrats of the early 20th century. The land of the castle lords was divided among the people of the land, and the successors of those kings of the old times regained the land with the strength of their weapons.

Järvamaa is the birthplace of one of our greatest writers and thinkers, Anton Hansen Tammsaare. His deep understanding of people and society is revealed in his journalism, as well as in his novels.

Near Türi, a monument with a cross, although slightly neglected, commemorates the Baltic Chain – the longest known chain in history consisting of human beings holding hands. In August 1989 people of the three Baltic republics expressed their will for freedom. We hope that Estonia will never again be threatened by an enemy, so that this record will not be broken. North of Paide, another unique remnant of the lost times – the Viraksaare wooden walkway in a bog – encourages lively imagination. Standing before it, we could ask ourselves how it would feel to flee along it with all our belongings to escape the approaching enemy.

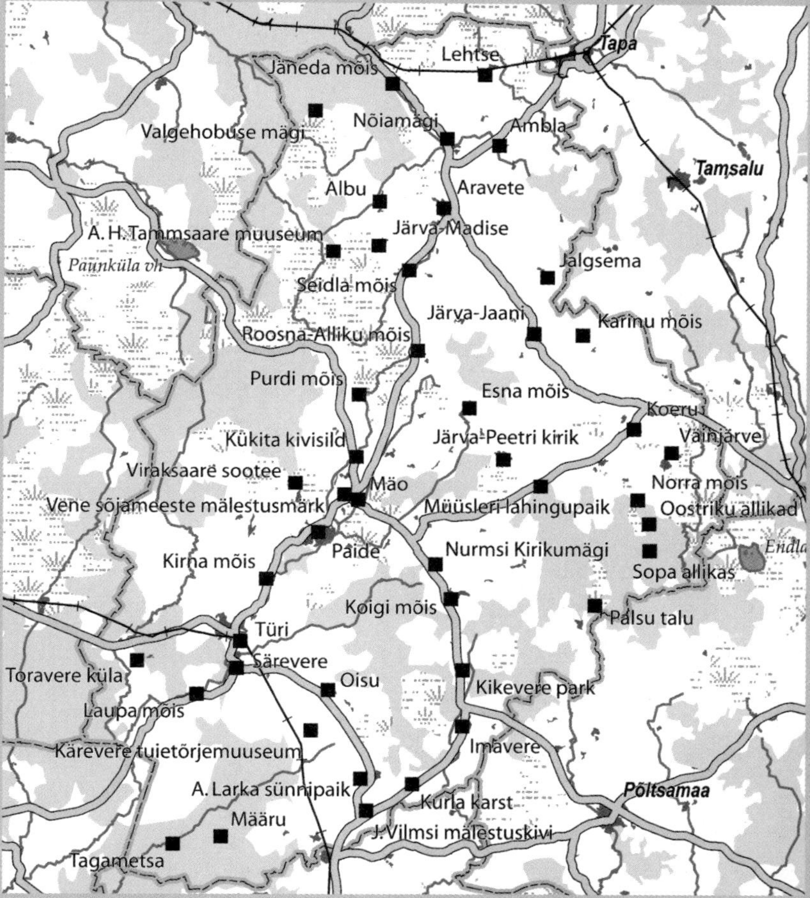

Tapa
Lehtse
Jäneda mõis
Nõiamägi
Ambla
Valgehobuse mägi
Tamsalu
Albu
Aravete
Järva-Madise
A. H. Tammsaare muuseum
Paunküla vh
Jalgsema
Seidla mõis
Järva-Jaani
Karinu mõis
Roosna-Alliku mõis
Purdi mõis
Esna mõis
Koeru
Kükita kivisild
Järva-Peetri kirik
Väinjärve
Viraksaare sootee
Mäo
Norra mõis
Vene sõjameeste mälestusmärk
Müüsleri lahingupaik
Oostriku allikad
Paide
Nurmsi Kirikumägi
Endla
Kirna mõis
Sopa allikas
Koigi mõis
Palsu talu
Türi
Särevere
Toravere küla
Oisu
Kikevere park
Laupa mõis
Imavere
Kärevere tuietõrjemuuseum
A. Larka sünnipaik
Põltsamaa
Kurla karst
Määru
J. Vilmsi mälestuskivi
Tagametsa

AROUND JÄNEDA AND LEHTSE

Driving from Aegviidu to the south towards Lehtmetsa, we arrive at the highest hill of Järvamaa, **Valgehobusemägi** (Hill of the White Horse). The top of this hill is 107 m above sea level; a sightseeing tower stands on the hill, making it still higher. In a good weather, one is supposed to be able to see as far as the Tallinn TV Tower. An old tale goes that Valgehobusemägi is the body of Kalevipoeg's white horse that was killed by wolves. The hero had again slept so hard that he had not heard when the wolves were killing his horse.

Valgehobusemägi is a part of the Mägede small drumlin field, containing many hills and ridges and interesting deep-sloped and flat-topped drumlins. At the beginning of the 20th century, the Albu manor owner established a brickyard in Mägede village, where bricks and drainpipes were made. The brickyard operated for several decades.

Composer Urmas Sisask's studio is in the tower of Jäneda mansion.

The Mägede small drumlin field is a recreation area of growing popularity, where people go skiing in winter and hiking in summer.

The central building in **Jäneda**, located 7 km off Aegviidu by Piibe Road, is the romantic red-brick Neo-Gothic manor house with towers, built about 100 years ago. Numerous outbuildings, including a distillery with a tall chimney and a granary with an arcade, have been preserved. The centre of the manor ensemble lies west of the road, but a beautiful stone building of a dairy, which has more or less kept its original form, stands east of the road. Today, the building houses a shop.

About half a kilometre southwest of the **mansion**, behind a drumlin in the wood on the shore of Lake Kalijärv, stands a wooden hunting lodge with a mantel chimney.

A modern white wing was added to the historical mansion in 1968–1977. The park of Jäneda

A bright red viewing tower stands on Valgehobusemägi hill.

Manor with its ponds and a spring lake is breathtakingly beautiful. For many years, whooper swans nested in the park and local people fed them in harsh winters. Rein Maran made a nature film about the swans and the sad death of the male swan.

For already five years, the Jäneda Days of Gardens and Flowers are held in the manor park. The competition of making wooden sculptures is a popular part of the events. The winning works of the previous competitions are displayed in the park.

Starting from 1921, an agricultural school, training also distillers among others, operated at the manor. In the Soviet era, the school was called the Jäneda State Farm and Technical School, teaching agronomy and landscape architecture. The school is closed now, and a Teaching and Advisory Centre, training and advising entrepreneurs and farmers functions there. The well-known Estonian writer Juhan Smuul and the current President of the Republic, Arnold Rüütel, have studied at Jäneda. Both of these men have been members of the Central Committee of the Communist Party of the ESSR, as well as the Supreme Council of the USSR. The one time spiritual leader of the Estonian non-Christian faith of Taaraism, Marta Utuste, writers Ernst Peterson-Särgava and Veera Saar, the biologist Johannes Piiper and the linguist Andrus Saareste have been among the teachers of the school. A monument, featuring an iron plough on a large boulder, was erected in front of the mansion at the 80th anniversary of the school in 1998 to commemorate the oldest **agricultural school** in Estonia. Actually, that agricultural school had been founded in Tallinn in 1918 and moved to Jäneda 3 years later.

Before the 1919 land reform of the Estonian Republic, Jäneda had belonged to the von Benckendorffs for more than 90 years. The last manor lord, Hans von Benkendorff, was murdered under suspicious circumstances on a road in the wood near his mansion in 1919. **A hunting lodge near Lake Kalijärv** was left to his family. His widow, Maria Zakrevskaja-Benckendorff-Budberg, a Russian lady with excellent education and great charm, was an extremely colourful and scandalous person. In her youth, she had been the private secretary of the Russian writer Maxim Gorky (1868–1936) in Italy. Later, she had very close relations with the English writer Herbert George Wells (1866–1946), who visited her in 1934 and spent some time at Lake Kalijärv. Gorky visited

The hunting lodge of Jäneda Manor has lost its original appearance.

A memorial stone with a plough marks the site of the old agricultural school.

Estonia too, and spent some time in Tartu, but 35 years earlier than Wells. The **Jäneda Museum** introduces both the history of Jäneda and the interesting life of the Baroness. The composer Urmas Sisask established a unique combination of an astronomical observatory and music studio in the tower of Jäneda mansion, where he installed a telescope and a small **planetarium**; he also gives concerts there. With a prior agreement, Sisask shows the tower to the visitors, tells them about the stars and performs his music that has been inspired by the movement of the stars.

The existence of an ancient hill-fort at Jäneda was discovered only in the 1930s. It is located on a narrow steeply sloping ridge between Lake Kalijärv and the River Jänijõgi. The courtyard of the hill-fort was about 100 m long. The fort was used in the 10th to 12th centuries.

Lehtse, located by the Jäneda-Tapa Road, emerged after the building of the St Petersburg-Paldiski railway in the 1870s. The Lehtse railway station, built about twenty years later, is a good example of the railway architecture of the time; the nice red brick building is decorated with wooden ornaments.

Lehtse **museum of local lore** is situated in a stylish two-storied house built at the beginning of the 20th century. The building has housed a bank, a cinema, and a local cultural centre. Among the more curious exhibits of the museum we should mention a walking stick-seat, which had belonged to the last Baron of Lehtse manor.

Lehtse Museum is located in the former cinema and cultural centre.

Lehtse railway station is an example of the official railway architecture of the time.

The former of Lehtse Manor can now only be guessed by its ruins.

Only the ruins of the tower of the once splendid **Lehtse Manor** are now standing at its site. The manor can still boast of a unique record in Estonian history. The series of phenological observations, made by **Baron Friedrich Alexaner Georg von Hoyningen** during 50 years, are the longest of their kind that have been recorded at one and the same place. The Baron, who was keen on ornithology and phenology, is buried at Ambla cemetery.

The renowned geographer **Jakob Kents** (1883–1947) was born in Lehtse. He wrote numerous school textbooks and he was the first to specify the geographical area of Kõrvemaa and to describe its nature.

AROUND ALBU, ARAVETE AND AMBLA

Albu is located by the Lehtmetsa-Kaalepi Road, 4 km north of Järva-Madise. In the centre of the village stands the beautiful well-kept **Albu Manor**, which has housed the local school for the last 80 years. The mansion was restored in 1995, and wonderful paintings were discovered on the walls and ceilings of the building.

Albu children can study in a schoolhouse with beautifully painted walls and ceilings, where once an academy for young noblemen worked.

The restored stone bridge is in harmony with the renovated park of Albu Manor.

The house is open for visitors in summer.

The manor park, stretching towards the Ambla River on two terraces, is also in good order. A **stone bridge**, built in the last quarter of the 19th century, crosses the river.

When talking about Albu Manor, we should mention the higher school for orphans from the ranks of the German nobility, or a **'knighthood academy'**, established on the model of similar schools in Western Europe, which worked in the manor in the first half of the 18th century. Young noblemen were taught everything necessary, such as languages, geometry, ethics, history, philosophy, military skills, fencing, riding and dancing. The graduates of the academy became military officers. The academy worked for a couple of decades; some Estonian and Russian young men have also been among its students.

A memorial stone to commemorate the so-called **Albu massacre** stands in front of Albu community centre. On 1 November 1861, the soldiers, summoned by the manor lord, fiercely beat the local peasants. The manor lord had thought that his peasants were too keen on the idea of emigrating and the beating was meant to put some sense into them. It was the time when Juhan Leinberg, better known as Prophet Maltsvet, was very popular in Harjumaa and Järvamaa. He encouraged rural people to emigrate to the Crimea, where they were to find an easy life. In May and June 1861, his most convinced adherents were waiting for a "white ship" on the high sea shore at Lasnamäe, near Tallinn, which should have come to take them to the promised land. The ship did not come, and the faith of even the most enthusiastic followers of the prophet dissipated.

A memorial plaque to Albu peasants who suffered severe punishment for their hopes for better life.

The **village of Järva-Madise**, located by the Lehtmetsa-Kaalepi Road, plays an important role in Estonian cultural history. The great master of Estonian literature, **Anton Hansen Tammsaare** (1878–1940), was born near here, in Vetepere village. The local inhabitants honoured him already in his lifetime, erecting a monument for him in front the community centre in 1936. The sides of the monument are covered with bronze bas-reliefs depicting scenes from Tammsaare's main work Truth and Justice (Tõde ja õigus).

Järva-Madise Church is very old and relatively small. It was built at the end of the 13th century and resembles the churches found in Läänemaa and Saaremaa. No other church in Central Estonia has a stone baptismal bowl. Tammsaare's father and mother, as well as several prototypes of the characters of his novels, among them Oru Pearu alias Jakob Sikenberg, are buried in the church yard.

Heinrich Stahl (1600–1657) was the Pastor at Järva-Madise Church in 1623–1633. Later he became the Provost of Järvamaa and then, the Dean of the Tallinn

Jakob Sikenberg, the prototype of Oru Pearu (far above) and A. H. Tammsaare's father (centre) and mother (above) are buried at Järva-Madise cemetery.

The monument to A. H. Tammsaare, standing in front of Albu community centre, is famous for its bas-reliefs depicting scenes from Truth and Justice.

Cathedral. Stahl wrote and published the first textbook and dictionary of the Estonian language in 1637. He also wrote a four-volume German-language church book and a collection of sermons. He was the first to mention the Estonian mythical hero, Kalevipoeg, in a written work (see also Kadrina, Lääne-Virumaa).

A road to Tammsaare's home starts from Järva-Madise, turning first to the west and then to the south-west. **A. H. Tammsaare** Museum is located about 7 km off Järva-Madise, at Vetepere. The road that passes it gradually vanishes among large mires. The farm buildings are standing among the fields, and people call the place Vargamäe after the home place of the characters of the book Truth and Justice (Tõde ja Õigus).

The museum was opened in 1958. The only original building from that time, the granary, was built by the writer's father, Peeter Hansen. Other buildings, including the dwelling house, have been restored. The nearby cottager's home with a chimneyless dwelling, a cow shed and a granary have also been restored. The museum, telling the visitors about Tammsaare's life and work, is located in the new dwelling house, built in the 1930s. The house actually belonged to Tammsaare's brother August. Walking paths start from the museum yard, taking the visitors through beautiful landscapes of the heart of Kõrvemaa and the literary places known as Vargamäe. Here is the drain on the border between two farms that

The farm buildings that now house the museum are located on high fields.

Of the farmhouses built by Tammsaare's father, only the granary is still standing.

caused many quarrels among the neighbours; one of them, Oru Pearu, built dams on the drain and the other, Mäe Andres, pulled them down.

About 200 m of the museum stands the Järvamaa Culture Grove, planted around a hill called **Kiigemägi** (Swing hill). The first trees were planted there in 1992; traditionally, the winners of the Järvamaa Cultural Award plant trees there. Nearby stands the huge **Vetepere oak** that could have lent the place its name – Tammsaare (Oak Island). We should add that Vargamäe is the most often visited literary site in Estonia.

The great Vetepere oak grows near Järvamaa Culture Grove.

Seidla Manor is located by the Paide-Rakvere Road, between Aravete and Roosna-Alliku; its mansion is among the most stylish early Classicist manor houses in Järvamaa. The granary with a beautiful colonnade has already been renovated and the mansion is being restored. The manor is privately owned. A yearly fair of antiquities is held at Seidla in July.

Driving from Aravete towards Roosna-Alliku and turning to the east at Seidla, we reach **Seidla suurkivi** (Seidla Large Boulder) or **Ausammaste kivi** (the Boulder of Monuments). Pieces from this boulder were used to build the monument to the War of Independence and the Tammsaare monument in Järva-Madise and the Monument to the Mother Tongue in Kadrina.

Aravete is located by the Tapa-Paide Road, 23 km of Tapa, about 1 km west of the road. **Kurisu manor house**, standing in the village, houses a local museum, displaying rooms devoted to different subjects – the manor room, women's room, school room, teacher's room, threshing room, machinery room, fire fighting room, and the political stagnation room – the Red Corner. History of Kurisoo Manor is also on display, among other objects we can see a wickerwork perambulator, which belonged to the lady of the manor. It is interesting to note that the manor, as well as several neighbouring farms, has been named after a huge swallow hole (Est. kurisu) north of Aravete by the new road. Karst crevices can be seen in the bottom of the swallow hole with the diameter of about 20 m.

Kangrumägi song field, the open-air concert site surrounded

Kurisoo Manor got its name after a large karst hollow.

by park wood, is located in the southern end of the village. A unique feature of Kangrumägi is that 18 different species of ants live there. The largest ant hills reach to the chest of a grown man. The habitat of ants is under protection.

By the Piibe Road, 1.5 km before Käravete, near the Lehtse crossroads, there is a hill covered with young pines in the middle of a field. This is an ancient place of sacrifice, **Nõiamägi** (Witch hill), which was probably used at the beginning of the 2nd millennium. Old legends talk about a treasure that is hidden under the hill, but it cannot be retrieved without some special spells.

Ambla is located by a smaller road connecting Tapa with the Piibe Road. Here stands the oldest church in Järvamaa, built in about 1250 and consecrated to St Mary; it has also been called **Suur-Maarja Church** (Lat. Ampla Maria – ampla meaning great, all-embracing) to differentiate it from Väike-Maarja Church in Virumaa. Differing form churches in Saaremaa and Läänemaa, where towers were added to the churches later, **Ambla Church** was originally built complete with a tower, being the first church in Estonia built with a tower. Archaic stone carvings, as well as the general outlook of the church resembles that of the churches of Gotland therefore, it is believed that the master builders came from Gotland. The church has a Renaissance altar from the beginning of the 17th century and the late-Renaissance pulpit.

The burial chapel of the von Maydells stands in the church yard; behind it we can see an interesting grave marking, a sculpture A Boy with Poppies,

Nõiamägi is covered with a grove of young pines.

made by Amandus Adamson. There is also a monument to those killed in the War of Independence and WW I, made by Anton Starkopf, featuring a peace angel with a wreath.

The Ambla cultural centre, built in 1893, standing by Tamsalu-Ambla Road, is a good example of rural architecture of the time.

Ancient cult stones, now under state protection, can be found near the stadium of Ambla school.

AROUND JÄRVA-JAANI

The small town of Järva-Jaani grew around a church. The large one-aisled church was built in the last quarter of the 13th century and it was probably a fortified church. The church has a beautiful polychrome pulpit, made in the mid-17th century, and a splendid retable. An interesting item – a pillory stone – stands next to the pulpit. The sinners had to stand next to that stone during the Sunday service. Unwed girls with children had to stand by the stone for three Sundays in a row.

A Classicist grave monument to major-general Carl von Schilling has been placed to the southern outside wall of the church.

Christian Kelch (1657–1710) was the Pastor at Järva-Jaani Church in 1682–1697. He was the author of the valuable historical sourcebook Chronicle of Livonia, or A Short Description of Memorable Tales of War and Peace from Estonia, Livonia and Latvia (Liivimaa kroonika ehk Eesti-, Liivi- ja Lätimaa mälestusväärsete sõja- ja rahulugude lühike kirjeldus). Pastor Kelch sympathised with peasants and, being inspired by B. G. Forselius, he opened a peasants' school in Järva-Jaani in 1685, which was among the first such schools in North Estonia. Later, he moved to Virumaa and then to Tallinn, where he died of plague in 1710.

Eduard Karl Franz von Gebhardt (1838–1925) was a son of a Pastor of Järva-Jaani; later he worked for a long time as a professor at Düsseldorf Art Academy, Germany. He had warm feelings for his homeland and he taught young Estonian students of art, such as Ants Laikmaa (Laipmann), and Kristjan and Paul Raud. He spent summers in Estonia and painted the portraits of local peasants. E. Von Gebhardt was a member of Dresden, Berlin, München and Vienna Art Academies and an honorary doctor of several universities.

The Järva-Jaani parsonage, where Kelch wrote his famous Chronicle and where the von Gebhardts lived, is located in front of the church by the Piibe Road. The limestone building has been restored and it is one of the most beautiful buildings in Järva-Jaani. The Järva-Jaani Association of Voluntary Firemen opened a museum in 1999, on the 100th anniversary of the association. The museum is located in the old fire engine house in 24, Pikk Street, which can be seen from afar, since it has been painted bright red. The museum shows old fire engines, and all kinds of fire fighting equipment. A sauna on wheels is a unique invention; Järva-Jaani firefighters tour Estonian country fairs with it. There is also an exhibition of about 20 old fire engines, mostly from the Soviet time. Appointments should be made to visit the museum, phone numbers can be found at the door of the museum.

Orina Manor is located in the northern end of the town. This is a one-storey gabled stone building; a portico was added to it in the 19th century. A local museum has been opened in the mansion; its most interesting exhibit is the equipment of the classroom where the students of the former vocational school were taught tractors. Another room displays the history of the school that worked in the mansion.

Orina Manor is the childhood home of the famous geographer and explorer **Admiral Nikolai von Schilling** (1828–1910). In 1873, von Schilling participated in the expedition to the Arctic

An old pillory stone stands next to the pulpit in Järva-Jaani Church.

The mansion of Orina Manor houses a museum.

A serious battle was held between peasants and soldiers at Karinu Manor in 1805.

Ocean, when Franz Josef Land was discovered. He had predicted the existence of these islands already beforehand, when studying the patterns of ocean currents. He also developed the theory of the origin of ocean currents.

On 28 February 1918, a fierce battle was held near Orina Manor between the local Red Guards and the oncoming German troops, where the Red Guards were defeated. A memorial stone was erected at the site of the battle, about 20 m north-east of the crossing of Tamsalu and Piibe Roads, in 1959.

The derelict centre of **Karinu Manor** is in an old park in Karinu village, by the Järva-Jaani – Väike-Maarja Road, 6 km east of Järva-Jaani. A glass workshop, which can be visited, is working in the former dairy of the manor. If we turn towards Väike-Maarja at Karinu, we can see a cup-stone with many small holes in it, called **Orjakivi** (Slave stone). According to legends, slaves had come and complained of their hard life and cried at the stone. Their tears had hollowed the cups into the stone.

In the autumn of 1805, a real battle was fought on a field of the manor between 120 soldiers and the peasants of the local manors. One peasant was killed and several were wounded; several soldiers were wounded too. After the battle, the leaders of the peasants were severely beaten and sent to Siberia. Karinu rebellion is one of the largest peasants' rebellions in Estonia in the 19th century.

Admiral **Johan Pitka** (1872–1944) and **Peäro August Pitka** (Ansomardi) (1866–1915) were born in Jalgsema village, north of Järva-Jaani. Both brothers were officers, the older brother served in the army, the younger one – in the navy. Peäro studied at the St Petersburg cadets' school, participated in the Russian-Japanese War and in WW I. He was at the Polish front, where he was promoted to a lieutenant colonel; he was killed in this war. He is also the author of lovely children's stories and stories depicting soldiers' life.

Johan Pitka studied to be a master mariner, was the commander of Estonian Navy in the War of Independence, and among the founders of the Estonian National Defence League. He was

The memorial stone at the home place of the brothers Pitka.

a member of the Estonian Constituent Assembly. Before WW II he went to Finland to find support and help in liberating Estonia of the Soviet occupation. In 1944 he returned to Estonia and attempted to restore the Estonian Republic at the time when Tallinn was defended against the Soviet troops. He was killed when he was hiding from the NKVD (see J. Pitka Museum, Harjumaa). A memorial stone stands by the Pitkas' home. A road sign points from Piibe Road towards Jalgsema.

AROUND KOERU

At Müüsleri, south of the Koeru-Mäeküla Road, stands the monument to the **Müüsleri battle ground** of the War of Independence. The beautiful monument, designed by the sculptor August Roosileht and featuring a granite pyramid standing on a disc-shaped platform, is reached by a flight of steps and surrounded by a grove of trees. It was opened by Konstantin Päts in 1934, destroyed later by the Soviets, and opened again in 1988.

At Müüsleri Battle (5-9 January 1919), the Reds were stopped and eventually thrown back. The enemy never reached Paide.

Järva-Peetri Church, located in Peetri village, is the youngest but the largest among medieval churches of Järvamaa. This three-aisled church was probably built in the first half of the 14th century. The 67.5 metre tower, added to the St. Peter's Church in the 19th century, is among the tallest church towers in Estonia.

Karl Espenberg (1761-1822), the first physician of Estonian origin to circumnavigate the globe, is buried at Peetri cemetery by the church. His friend Adam J. von

Until the completing of the new tower of Pilistvere Church, Järva-Peetri Church was the tallest country church in Estonia.

Krusenstern offered him a position of the ship's physician during the planned circumnavigation and Espenberg accepted. The expedition was on its way in 1803–1806; Espenberg had a chance to study changes in the health of the crew under hard oceanic conditions. Otto von Kotzebue, who also participated in the expedition, later named a cape in Alaska the Cape Espenberg. School director and founder of churches, Gustav Heinrich Beermann, and his son, Provost Christoph Wilhelm Beermann, are also buried at the same cemetery.

At Palsu farm by a gravel road leading towards Vao village north of Päinurme, stands a monument to commemorate the so-called Vaali Republic, created to protect landless peasants in 1905. Palsu farm was the birthplace of the later minister of the Estonian Republic, August Jürima (1887–1942). The master of Palsu farm Mart Jürmann, Voldemar Jürmann, Madis Resev and an enthusiastic collector of folklore, tailor Hans Anton Schultz proclaimed the Estonian **Vaali Republic**, assembled militia and wrote a constitution. A group of marines was summoned from Kronstadt by the local authorities; the rebels were arrested and shot in Koeru on 24 December. Another monument to these brave men has been erected in Koeru.

Koeru Church is one of the oldest churches in Järvamaa, built at the end of the 13th century. The church has medieval wall paintings, an old retable and altar, a late Renaissance pulpit and a large carved crucifix.

In 1844, the author of the Finnish national epic Kalevala, Elias Lönnrot, who was on a walking tour in Estonia, visited the Pastor of Koeru, Dietrich Georg von Mickwitz.

A number of relatives of the world-famous naturalist, Karl Ernst von Baer (mother Juliana Louise, brother Ludwig, sister Helene and his sons Alexander and Hermann) are buried at the cemetery by the church. The founders of the Vaali republic, executed in 1905, are buried at the old Koeru cemetery, about 1 km towards Rakke from the church. A **monument**, designed by Juhan Raudsepp, was erected to them in Koeru in 1935; it stands in front of the community centre by Paide Road.

In Koeru, we can again see the usual positioning of the inn and the church just opposite each other. Across the square in front of the church stands an imposing inn with 13 columns in front, built in 1833. Later it functioned as a post station in Tallinn-Tartu Road. The inn had separate rooms for German visitors and peasants and

Järva-Peetri monument to the War of Independence.

A memorial stone in the centre of Koeru offers thanks to our ancestors who rebuilt the parish after the Livonian War.

The parents of natural scientist Karl Ernst von Baer are buried at Koeru cemetery.

Koeru inn is located just in front of the church.

The monument to the founders of the Vaali Republic.

separate stables for their horses. During the Soviet time, **Koeru inn** was a restaurant; now it houses a shop.

The beautiful Classicist mansion of **Aruküla Manor** is located in Koeru. The last owners of the manor before the land reform of 1919 were the von Tolls. Carl Friedrich von Toll (1777–1842) served in the Russian army under the generals Barclay de Tolly and Kutuzov; he also participated in the Russian-Turkish War in the cavalry led by Johann Michelson, who came from the nearby Väinjärve Manor.

The mansion was once surrounded by a long fence of wrought iron, which has by now fallen to the prey of vandals. **The von Tolls' Neo-gothic burial chapel**, which was recently

The Classicist mansion of Aruküla Manor.

The wrought iron fence around Aruküla mansion has suffered under the attacks of several generations of vandals.

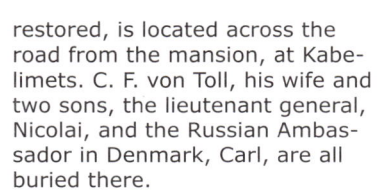

The burial chapel of the von Tolls stands across the road of the manor house.

restored, is located across the road from the mansion, at Kabelimets. C. F. von Toll, his wife and two sons, the lieutenant general, Nicolai, and the Russian Ambassador in Denmark, Carl, are all buried there.

At the edge of Koeru, at 20, Järva-Jaani Road stands the building of the former German private school; our most renowned graphic artist, Eduard Viiralt (1898–1954), studied at this school in 1911–1913. The house is marked by a memorial plaque. In 1909, the Viiralts moved over to Varangu Manor, where his father was the estate manger. Eduard attended the Koeru school, first the Estonian-language primary school, later – another school, where all subjects were taught in German, except history and geography, which were taught in Russian. He is said to have lived in the neighbouring house during his school years. The contemporaries recall Eduard as a modest and quiet boy, who was interested in drawing and sport.

The well-known poet **Kalju Lepik** (1920–1999) was born in Koeru, near the road leading from the church towards Lake Väinjärv. He lived most of his life in exile in Sweden. The house has not been preserved, but the site is marked with a commemorative stone that was erected there already during the poet's lifetime. A well-known Estonian graphic artist **Aino Bach** (1901–1980) was born in Koeru, too.

The largest lake in Järvamaa, Lake **Väinjärv**, lies near Koeru. The mansion of Väinjärve Manor with a tall eight-sided tower is located near the lake; the terraced park of the manor stretches toward the lake. Johann Michelson, a boy of peasant origin, served as a valet with the lord of Väinjärve Manor. He managed to educate himself to such extent that he could join the army when he ran away from the manor.

He made a brilliant career and eventually became a general. He led the Russian Army in the Russian-Swedish War in 1788–1790 and the Russian-Turkish War in 1806–1807. He helped to stifle the Pugachev Rebellion at the time of Empress Catherine II and Count Potjomkin, sending numerous captured rebels to build the town of Paldiski (see Paldiski, Harjumaa).

The story of a valet who became a general is the subject of Jaan Kross' famous book The Matriculation of Michelson (Michelsoni immatrikuleerimine). Michelson invited his father and mother – Estonian peasants – to the ceremony of his matriculation into nobility, causing a large scandal.

Norra Manor lies south of Koeru. A gravel road turns to the south from the Koeru-Paide Road a short distance after Aruküla Manor. The manor was named after the von Knorrings who had owned it for more than 300 years. Norra mansion was once famous for its magnificent wall paintings, but they were destroyed when the building stood empty and in ruins for several decades. Today, the mansion is privately owned and the new owner has started the restoration work.

Norra Park with its spring lake, lying between the mansion and the road, is worth seeing. The Oostriku River flows through the lake. Once, there were many ponds in the park, connected by canals. Nearby was a water mill, where the famous Prophet Maltsvet, alias Juhan Leinberg, was a miller for some time.

Moving to the south from Norra, we pass the **Oostriku** springs and reach a road that takes us to Sopa spring, hidden in the forest. The rounded funnel-shaped bottom of this spring, one of the deepest in Estonia, lies 5 m deep under the water. The spring yields 5 buckets of water a second; this is the beginning of the Sopa stream, flowing into the Oostriku River.

AROUND ROOSNA-ALLIKU

Roosna-Alliku Manor is located in Roosna-Alliku village by the Rakvere-Paide Road. The building is in good order and houses a school; a white brick wing, added in the 1960s, spoils the outlook of beautiful mansion.

The mansion, designed by the government architect Johann Schultz, was built at the end of the 18th century. (Schultz has also designed the Toompea Palace in Tallinn.) For 200 years before the land reform in 1919, the manor belonged to the von Stack-

Väinjärve Manor was the home of Johann Michelson, an Estonian general of the Tsarist army.

elbergs. The earlier owners had been the von Rosens, who had lent the place their name. Baron Otto Friedrich von Stackelberg was a man of modern views – in 1791, he decreed much milder rules for his peasants than those that had been fixed in the historical "von Rosen Declaration" (see Vohnja Manor, Lääne-Virumaa).

Roosna-Alliku is known as the birthplace of the Pärnu River. A group of protected springs at the edge of the Pandivere Upland yield more than 900 l/s of water. Numerous waterfowl spend winter at the ice-free Roosna-Alliku spring lake.

The mansion of Purdi Manor.

Roosna-Alliku Manor houses a school.

An alley, turning to the east from Tallinn-Tartu Road near Anna Church, leads to **Purdi Manor**, which belonged to the von Ungern-Sternbergs before the land reform of 1919. The Baltic-German writer, Baron Alexander Peter von Ungern-Sternberg was born in the manor in 1806. He has written a number of novels and published 6 volumes of memoirs of cultural historical interest. His works have not been translated into Estonian.

The late-Baroque mansion of Purdi Manor is now privately owned. The burial chapel of the von Ungern-Sternbergs is at some distance off the manor ensemble towards the Tallinn-Tartu Road.

Esna Manor and **Kareda village** both stand by Roosna-Alliku – Peetri Road. Fields around Esna are the best and most fertile ones in North and Central Estonia. That is why the region was densely settled already in the ancient times. Henry of Livonia mentions Kareda village several times in his Chronicle and praises it as a large, populous and beautiful village. All this attracted the Brothers of the Order. Kareda was raided in 1212 and 1217 and bloody battles were fought there. Wilhelm of Modena, the Pope's legate, visited Kareda when he came to Estonia to settle quarrels among the Danes and the Order of the Brothers of the Sword.

The mansion of Esna Manor, a simple wooden one-storey building, and numerous outbuildings are now privately owned. In the wood 1 km north-west of the manor centre there is the burial chapel and cemetery of the von Grünewalds, the one-time owners of the manor. More than 80 members of the family are buried there. The Neo-gothic chapel, although in ruins, is even now still imposing. The von Grünewalds have recently started the renovation of the family cemetery.

AROUND PAIDE

Driving from Tallinn to Tartu, we reach Mäo, which is considered the mid-point in the trip. Kükita stone bridge crosses the Pärnu River about 20 metres upstream from the Tallinn-Tartu Road. The limestone bridge was built in 1914; it has been renovated and can be seen across the road from the **Kükita Grill**.

Mäo Manor is one of the first manors that were taken under protection in 1933, but it is still in an immediate need of repair. The Classicist mansion was built in the first half of the 19th century and is surrounded by a park of tall lime trees. The manor centre can be seen from the Tallinn-Tartu Road at the Mäo crossroads.

Mäo Manor is connected with the famous Russian composer Nicolai Rimski-Korsakov (1844–1908), who came to visit his sister-in-law, who was living there. Rimski-Korsakov was a professor at St Petersburg Conservatoire and taught Estonian composers Artur Kapp, Mart Saar and Rudolf Tobias.

Coming from Tallinn and turning towards Paide just before Mäo, we can see a tall **dolomite obelisk** standing north of the road. It was erected by Mäo manor owner,

Kükita stone bridge stands near the Tallinn-Tartu Road.

Mäo Manor, now in urgent need of repair, belonged to the von Stackelbergs.

Baron Olaf von Stackelberg in the memory of Russian soldiers killed in the Livonian War, when they besieged Paide Castle in 1573. Among the dead was Maljuta Skuratov, the favourite of Ivan the Terrible. No wonder that the local peasants fled to the Viraksaare mire to hide from the bloodthirsty Russian troops.

The obelisk is quite hard to find; there is a sign that gives only a general direction, but the obelisk stands in a grove of trees in the middle of a field.

The **memorial** to all **policemen**, who have been killed in service stands at the Mäo crossroads.
On 15 December 1994, the smugglers of illicit alcohol attacked the policemen who had stopped their van to check its load. The smugglers opened machine-gun fire and killed two policemen and seriously wounded the third one.

A log path, made in the second half of the 16th century, was found in Prääma bog, north of Paide, in 1985. This secret path was made of about 2 m-long birch and pine logs, placed into the mire; the path probably led from Viraksaare to **Palivere bog** island. The logs that were buried in peat are relatively well-preserved, even the traces of axe cuts can still be seen. The logs sank into peat and only those who knew the path could walk it. Now, the path is under 70 cm-layer of peat. A couple of dozens of metres long fragment has been opened for viewing. The Viraksaare Road running to the north from Paide takes the visitors straight to Prääma bog. The secret path is about 5 km off the town of Paide.

The Viraksaare secret path into the mire was made of pine logs.

The memorial to all policemen killed in service stands at the Mäo crossroads.

The symbol of **Paide** is an eight-sided castle tower that, after having been rebuilt, again stands on Vallimägi hill. The building of the castle started in 1265, when Järvamaa became the property of the Livonian Order. Earlier, the King of Denmark had also had some designs for the area. At that time, **Vallimägi** was only a slightly higher hill rising from relatively flat and wet land. The 30 m-tall tower of six stories was built of white limestone, giving the town its German name – Weissenstein (white stone).

We do not know what the castle looked like in 1343, when the leaders of Estonians went there to negotiate with the Brothers of the Order. The convent had, probably, already been built. Later, the castle was surrounded with a strong wall; four bastions were built before the Livonian War.

The castle changed hands during the Livonian War, it was conquered by the Russians and Swedes, then by the Poles and again, by the Swedes. In 1636, the castle that had been destroyed in wars was simply abandoned.

Vallitorn, the highest tower also known as Pikk Hermann, was restored at the end of the 19th century, but the retreating Soviet Army blew it up in 1941. At the beginning of the 1990s, the symbol of the town was rebuilt again.

The castle tower that now belongs to the **Järvamaa Museum** is open to visitors. Its exposition introduces the older history of Paide and Järvamaa starting from Stone Age up to the Livonian War. The most remarkable exhibit is the treasure of different coins hidden during the Livonian War, found at Kihme.

The main exposition of the Järvamaa Museum is located at 5, Lembitu Street, in Lembitu Park. The museum gives an overview of Järvamaa nature and landscapes and of its history from the Livonian War up to WWII. Several thematic rooms have been furnished in the museum, such as a drugstore and a manor room. The Museum and the tower are opened at the same days and times.

A memorial stone to St George's Night Uprising stands on Paide Vallimägi hill, commemorating the four Estonian leaders, also called kings, and their three men-at-arms, who were killed in the castle on 4 May 1343. The St George's Night Uprising broke out in Harjumaa on St George's Day of the same year, when 10,000 peasants took up arms against German and Danish vassals.

The Estonian leaders were tricked into coming to negotiate with Germans by the Order Master Burchard von Dreileben. A quarrel was provoked and the kings of Estonians were killed. The Estonians were finally outnumbered and defeated by the Order troops on the Estonian mainland at the end of 1343 and on Saaremaa, in 1345. After this uprising, The Danish King gave up his possessions in Estonia and sold them to the Teutonic Order who, in its turn, sold them to the Livonian Order.

Paide Church has been repeat-

Paide castle tower has been rebuilt several times.

A memorial stone to Estonian leaders who were treacherously killed.

edly destroyed and rebuilt like many other Estonian churches. As result, we can today see quite a singular building, the tower of which seems to be detached from the body of the church. Contrary to the tradition, the tower does not stand at the western end of the church, but in the middle. The church obtained its present appearance in the mid-19th century.

The most important cemetery in Paide, **Reopalu cemetery**, is located at the western margin of the town. August Wilhelm Hupel (1737–1819), a renowned linguist and historian of local lore, is buried there.

For a long time, Hupel was the Pastor at Põltsamaa Church; he moved over to Paide in 1804. He gathered a rich collection of materials on the everyday life, history and geography of the Baltic countries and published it in many books, the most important of which is the three-volume Topographische nachrichten von Lief- und Ehstland. He helped Peter Ernst Wilde in the publishing of his first Estonian-language magazine A Short Instruction... (Lühhike öppetus...) by translating his articles. Hupel also compiled a grammar of the Estonian language and the most thorough German-Estonian dictionary of its time (see also Jõgevamaa and Põltsamaa). A large field stone marks Hupel's grave.

The world-famous modern Estonian composer Arvo Pärt (1935) was born in Paide. In 1999, a sculpture "Limestone Symphony", made by the sculptor Riho Kulla, was placed near the composer's birthplace at the corner of Väike-Aia and Kitsas Streets.

The tower of Paide Church seems to be detached from the body of the church.

A. W. Hupel was the editor of the first Estonian-language magazine together with Ernst Wilde.

The Manifesto of Estonian Independence was read to people here by the town commander Jaan Maide.

AROUND TÜRI

Turning to the south from the Türi-Rapla Road at Kolu Manor, and then turning to the east when the gravel road starts, we reach Toravere village, where there is a memorial stone to Pastor **Harald Meri** (1917–1990) and his domestic help **Valve Klein**.

In 1990, there were still quite serious conflicts between the adherents of independence and those who favoured Moscow and were against independence. The killing of the Pastor and his help and the burning of Türi parsonage in April 1990 were connected with political reasons, since Harald Meri was actively working to promote the idea of the restoration of the Estonian Republic.

This crime, which shocked the whole Estonia, has remained unsolved.

The memorial stone stands in a grove of trees behind a gravel quarry, where the bodies were found. No sign points out the stone and it is quite hard to find.

The mansion of **Kirna Manor**, located between Türi and Paide, has a beautiful portico. At the beginning of the 19th century, the manor belonged to Carl Magnus von Osten-Sacken, who was, among other activities, also the tutor of Russian Tsar Paul I and Grand Duke Constantin. The present-day owner of the manor claims that it is situated in a location with healing powers and he earns his living by offering cures to the people who believe in this questionable power.

The garden town of **Türi** is known as the spring capital of Estonia and as a location of large gardening and flower fairs. Türi became a town at the beginning of the 1920s. A large role in its developing into a beautiful garden town was played by the gardening school that was founded near the town, in Särevere, in 1924. Türi is characterised by hedges and immaculate gardens, even the coat of arms of the town features a branch of an apple tree.

Looking around in the present-day Türi it is hard to believe that the town was seriously damaged at the beginning of WW II. More than 100 houses were destroyed and the Soviet Army blew up many buildings of essential importance to the town, such as the radio station, the bridges, and the buildings of the Paper and Cardboard Factory that had worked there since the beginning of the 20th century. Despite the fact, monuments to the Red Army were erected there which are still standing to remind the people of the horrors of war.

The oldest construction in Türi, **St Martin's Church**, was built at the end of the 13th century using different materials – bricks, limestone and granite. Brick churches can mainly be found in South Estonia, limestone churches in North Estonia. The church has two entrances; one is in the western wall under the tower, the other – in the southern wall. The valuable pulpit and retable date back to the 17th century. No other church in Estonia has a polychrome rooster on the tip of its tower.

Besides a branch of an apple tree, the Türi coat of arms shows radio waves, reminding us of a construction that used to be important for the whole Estonia. In 1937, a modern radio transmitting station was built in Türi, complete with a 196.6 m tall steel mast that weighed 70 tons. At that time, this was the tallest freestanding radio mast in Europe. The station and the mast were destroyed in the battles in 1941.

In 2001, on the 75th anniversary of national broadcasting, the **Estonian Broadcasting Museum** was opened in Türi. Among the exhibits we can see a model of Türi radio transmitting station, and a wax statue of the most famous Estonian 'radio voice', Felix Moor (1903–1955). The museum offers a thorough overview of the development of Estonian broadcasting before and after WW II and exhibits all models of radio receivers made at the Tallinn Radio Factory RET.

The Estonian Broadcasting Museum is located in 11, Vabriku Avenue, near the railway crossing.

Türi Museum works in the same building with the Broadcasting Museum, introducing the history of Türi town and parish and exhibits works made by local artists.

On the territory of Türi railway station, we can see two old steam locomotives. The narrow-gauge

The only polychrome church rooster in Estonia stands on the spire of Türi church.

The Museum of Estonian Broadcasting Museum is located in the centre of Türi.

An old locomotive in Türi.

The beautiful wooden mansion of Särevere Manor.

Särevere Manor was for a long time owned by the von Schillings.

locomotive stands in front of the railway station, the broad-gauge locomotive stands near a railway crossing in the centre of the town.

Särevere is 3 km off Türi towards Pärnu; the centre of Särevere Manor is located in a well-kept park. The wooden mansion houses the Museum of Türi Rural Municipality and Türi Technical and Rural Economy School, which gives a good overview of the history of Türi parish, the manor and its owners the von Schillings, and the gardening school. The Türi Co-educational Gardening Economy College was opened in Särevere in 1924; later it became the Türi Gardening High School.

The commemorative stone to the Baltic Chain stands south of the road at the beginning of a smaller road leading from Särevere to Kabala. The human chain stretching from Tallinn to Vilnius was formed on 23 August 1989 to remember and condemn the 50th anniversary of the Molotov-Ribbentrop Pact – the secret deal between Hitler's Nazi Germany and Stalin's Soviet Union, dividing Eastern Europe into different spheres of influence. Estonia and the other Baltic countries fell under the Soviet rule for the following 50 years.

The Baltic Chain was organised

The oak trees planted at the monument to the Baltic Chain.

Oisu Museum is located in the cellar of Oisu manor house.

An interesting monument to fighters for freedom stands in Oisu manor park.

by the Popular Fronts of the three Baltic countries; its length was about 300 km and approximately 2 million people stood in the chain, holding hands.

The art nouveau mansion of **Laupa Manor,** standing 6 km towards Pärnu from Särevere, is located on a shore of a pond in a small park. Numerous outbuildings are still standing, including the Baroque house of the estate manager. The mansion, which houses a school, has recently been restored, its facade is in good order and several classrooms have been renovated. A small exhibition in the school gives information about the former owners of the manor, the von Taubes, who were the greatest entrepreneurs in Türi. They participated in the building of the Tallinn-Viljandi railway and built the Türi Paper and Cardboard Factory. The manor owners had the first cars and the first telephone in Järvamaa.

A fire fighting museum is located in Kärevere village, exhibiting a number of fire engines the oldest of which come from the days of WWII. The selection of fire engines differs from that at the Järva-Jaani fire fighting museum.

Kärevere is located on the railway south-east of Türi. To reach the village by car, one has to turn to the south-west from the Türi-Viljandi Road at Oisu.

A museum of local lore can be found in Oisu village. The exhibition introduces the history of the neighbouring villages and exhibits old farm equipment.

KABALA AND SOUTH-WESTERN JÄRVAMAA

Kabala is located south-west of Särevere. Near Kabala, by the road leading to the west, stands a memorial stone marking the birthplace of major general **Andres Larka** (1879–1943). The farmhouses have not been preserved.

Andres Larka was major general already at the beginning of the War of Independence. He had graduated from the St. Petersburg General Staff Academy in 1912. During the War of Independence, he was for a short period the Chief of the General Staff, and later, the Minister of War (at those times, the Minister of Defence was called the Minister of War).

Since 1930, he was the leader

of the extreme right-wing League of Veterans of the Estonian War of Independence and was their presidential candidate. After the bill of constitution, drafted by the League, won the national referendum, Päts and Laidoner decided to prevent the League members coming to power and they organised a military coup d'etat on 12 March 1934. The attempted counter-coup d'etat of the Leaguers in 1935 was not successful and about 500 activists of the movement were arrested. Major general Larka was arrested twice in Estonia, but he died in a Soviet prison camp.

A memorial stone to **Jüri Vilms** (1889–1918), a young politician who played an important role in the creating of the Estonian Republic, stands by the Imavere-Viljandi Road, at Arkma, just before the Kabala crossroads. Vilms, who had trained as a lawyer, got into politics and founded the Estonian Radical Socialist Party in 1917; later the party was named the Estonian Labour Party. He was elected a member of the Committee for National Salvation. He was the Minister of Justice and the deputy Prime Minister at the first Provisional Government of Estonia. At the time the German occupation, he attempted to go to Finland across the Gulf of Finland on his way to Europe to find support to the Estonian Republic. Unfortunately, he was captured by Germans and executed in Helsinki. Vilms's death has given food to numerous speculations. It has been suggested that he could have been killed by Finns, not Germans, and maybe he altogether drowned. In this case, it is not certain that it is he who is buried at Pilistvere cemetery, in Viljandimaa.

Driving from Imavere towards Viljandi, we can see the **Kurla (Määru) karst field** west of the road, just before the Kabala crossroads. The largest sink hole is 80

The monument to army commander Andres Larka.

The legendary politician Jüri Vilms died under suspicious circumstances.

m long, 30 m wide and 2 m deep. A legend tells us that here is the gate to Hell, through which Kalevipoeg entered when he went to see the underworld.

The 13th Song of Kalevipoeg tells us about a cave through which the hero entered the Hell. When Kalevipoeg had returned to Estonia from the land behind Lake Peipsi he passed Lake Endla. He saw smoke rising from behind a hill and went to explore. Some verses from the first version, written in 1853, describe the place more thoroughly, but these verses were left out from the final version. According to folklore, this cave was located at Kabala, 6–7 km north-west from Pilistvere.

The road leading to the north from Võhma turns to the west after 2 km, and goes towards **Tõrvaaugu**. The permanent camp of scouts and guides is located at **Tagametsa**, which can be reached by the road turning to the north-west at Tõrvaaugu and proceeding towards Rassi. At Rassi, we must turn left. A monument to all Forest Brethren stands at Tagametsa. The monument is a 2 m tall heap of field stones; stones have been brought here from many places in Estonia and from the USA and Canada as well. A bunker of the Forest Brethren has been restored at Tagametsa; the renovation of the former hunting manor is under way.

Turning to the north-east at Tõrvaaugu, we arrive at Määru stone or the **Stone of Head Foresters**. The names of all Kabala Head Foresters have been carved into this 2.5 m tall stone. There are 20 names, the first of which was the Head Forester called Reigh, who started his work in 1850. The stone is pointed out by a sign.

A monument and the restored bunker of the Forest Brethren at Tagametsa.

The names of more than 20 chief foresters have been carved into the Määrdu Foresters' stone.

AROUND KOIGI AND IMAVERE

East of the Tallinn-Tartu Road, about 10 km after the Mäo crossroads, there is a low hill covered with stones in a field by the road – **Nurmsi Kirikumägi** (Church hill).

This is one of the largest tarand-graves in Estonia, which has been thoroughly excavated and studied. Burials in these graves date back to the 2nd–6th centuries and again to the 12th century and even later. The fenced-in graves, consisting of 12 tarands, extended about 50 m from the east to the west. Both cremation burials and body burials have been found in the graves.

According to legends, people had once wanted to build a church at Nurmsi, but the devil had torn everything down at night and the church was never completed.

Koigi Manor stands by the Tallinn-Tartu Road, between Mäo and Imavere. The one-storey early-Classicist mansion was built in 1771. The manor owners, the von Grünewaldts, favoured education and treated their peasants relatively well. Starting from the 1840s, they were the first to pay wages to their workers. In 1837–1854, they financed a seminar for village school teachers at Ataste. They bred horses and ameliorated their lands. There was a private school at Koigi Manor; among its students was the future sculptor Alexander Friedrich Bock (1829–1895), who later was a professor at St Petersburg Art Academy and taught Estonian sculptors August Weizenberg (1837–1921) and Amandus Adamson (1855–1929).

A monument to the villages that were ravaged by the Soviet destroyer battalions at the beginning of WWII stands in Kikevere park, east of the Tallinn-Tartu Road, after Käsukonna.

In July 1941, the retreating destroyer battalion burnt several villages and Risti Church; the neighbouring Orthodox Church was burnt to the ground by a local communist. The sites of both churches are marked by monuments. Dalai Lama visited the site of Kikevere Church in 1991 and planted an oak tree there.

The **Estonian Dairy Museum** is located in the building of the former dairy in Imavere village, at the beginning of the Paia-Viljandi Road. The museum was founded already in the Soviet time. This location was chosen for the museum because the first cooperative dairy that was owned by the farmers was founded in Imavere in 1908. The museum introduces Estonian dairy history since its very beginning. The first estate dairies were founded in Vaida and Kunda only in 1850. The exposition contains dairy equipment, older wooden items and later iron separators and other dairy machinery. In the first half of the 20th century, Estonia exported butter to several countries.

The gem of the exposition is the fully equipped cooperative dairy in several rooms, including the steam boiler that powered the machinery.

The Estonian Dairy Museum gives an overview of the history of Estonian dairy production.

INDEX OF PLACENAMES

Aakre 262
Aaspere 125, 134
Abja 134, 300, 301
Abja-Paluoja 298, 300, 301, 311
Adavere 190
Aegna 108
Aegviidu 120, 322
Ahja 230, 231
Ahja River 226, 227, 229
Aidu 178, 313
Akste 51
Ala 264
Alajärv 247
Alatskivi 194, 196-200, 282
Albu 322, 325, 326
Allaste 303
Alu 91
Alutaguse 122, 140, 152, 155, 167, 169
Ambla 325, 329
Ambla River 325
Andja 130
Angerja 80
Angla 43, 44
Anna 337
Antsla 243, 244
Ao 122, 149
Aravete 325, 328, 329
Ardu 96, 117, 119, 120
Arensburg, see Kuressaare,
Arkma 346
Aruküla (Harjumaa) 203
Aruküla (Järvamaa) 334, 336
Aseri 154
Aseriaru 154
Asva 32
Ataste 348
Audru 52
Avanduse 140, 141
Avaste 54
Avinurme 167, 169
Avispea 198

Baltic Sea 28, 132, 250, 313
Baltiiskii Port, see Paldiski,
Birkas 74

Cesis, see Võnnu
Cozzo, see Karuse

Dageida, see Hiiumaa,
Dobrina 171

Ebavere Hill 122, 148
Ellamaa 101
Elva 210, 213, 214
Elva River 220
Emajõgi River 194, 202, 203, 207
Emmaste 20, 22, 24
Emumägi 150
Endla Lake 176, 347

Erastvere 223
Ereda 154
Ermistu Lake 53
Erra 156, 157
Erra River 156
Esna 337

Finland, Gulf of 17, 108, 346
Friedenthal (Rahumägi) 181

Gorodenka 171
Gutanäs 64

Haanja 240, 250, 252-254
Haapsalu 10, 15, 62, 66, 68-72, 101, 266
Haapsalu bay 68, 71
Haapsipea 197
Haaslava 203
Haavakannu 116
Haavakivi 184
Hagudi 90
Haimre 87
Haljala 134, 135
Halliste 298-300
Halliste River 46, 297, 299-302
Hanila 74, 75
Hargla 273
Hari kurk 10
Harimägi 280
Harjumaa 82, 95-120, 203, 326, 332
Harju-Madise 96, 99, 100
Harju-Risti 96, 98
Harku 109
Hatu 98
Hausma 15
Heimtali 309, 310
Heinaste 50
Hellenurme 228, 280
Helme 223, 263, 265-267
Heltermaa 10
Hiiumaa 7-24, 28, 65, 70, 109, 210
Hilane 257
Hill of Oath 49
Himmaste 228
Holdre 260, 265
Holstre 293, 294, 312-314
Hullo 66
Hummuli 269
Hungerburg, see Narva-Jõesuu,
Häädemeeste 48-50

Ida-Virumaa 105, 151-172
Ihamaru 225
Iia 297
Iisaku 152, 167, 170
Ikla 49, 301
Illiku islet 31
Ilmatsalu 206
Ilumetsa 235
Ilumäe 125, 126
Imavere 346, 348

INDEX OF PLACENAMES

Ingliste 93
Iru 111, 112
Ivaski 294
Ivaste 212

Jalase 88, 89, 93
Jalgsema 331
Juuru 78, 81, 82
Jõelähtme 112-114
Jõepere 114, 249
Jõgeva 176-179, 293, 315
Jõgevamaa 170, 173-192, 200, 201, 285, 307
Jõgeveste 268, 269
Jõhvi 157, 159, 162
Jõuga 167
Jõõri 34
Jäbara 159
Jädivere 87
Jägala River 96, 113
Jägala-Joa 114
Jämaja 39
Jämejala 215
Jäneda 120, 322-324
Jänijõgi 324
Jänukjärv 221
Järise 43
Järva-Jaani 329, 330, 345
Järvakandi 93, 94
Järvamaa 242, 292, 319-348
Järva-Madise 325-327
Järvepera 185
Järvselja 209
Jüri 109, 110

Kaali 33, 34, 235
Kaarli (Lääne-Virumaa) 136
Kaarli (Võrumaa) 189
Kaarlijärve 216
Kaarma 34, 35
Kaaru (Kaaro) 232
Kabala (Järvamaa) 345-347
Kabala (Raplamaa) 89
Kaberneeme 114
Kabli 50
Kadarpiku 66
Kadrina 143-145, 328
Kahala Lake 116
Kahkva 236
Kaika 244
Kaisma 58
Kaiu 93
Kalana (Hiiumaa) 21
Kalana (Jõgevamaa) 190
Kalevi-Liiva 114
Kalijärv 322-324
Kallaste 181, 199
Kalvi 154
Kambja 210-212, 278
Kanavere 117, 118
Kanepi 221-223, 229
Kangsti 245
Kapa-Kohila 80

Kaplimägi 20
Karala 40
Karaski 225
Kareda 337
Karepa 129
Karilatsi 225, 226
Karinu 331
Karisilla 237
Karisöödi 244
Karja 44
Karjaküla 102, 103
Karksi 302, 303
Karksi-Nuia 300, 302-304
Karujärv 41
Karula 244, 264, 272, 273
Karuse 74, 76
Kasari 73
Kasari River 73
Kaseküla 75, 76
Kasepää 199
Kassari 22, 23
Kassema 190
Kassiveski 197
Kastre 209
Kaubi 300
Kaugu 245
Kauksi 229, 232
Kautla 120
Kavandu 211
Kavastu (Lääne-Virumaa) 134, 135
Kavastu (Tartumaa) 207
Keava 78, 93
Keedika 66
Kehtna 93
Keila 66, 102, 103, 106
Keila River 80, 102
Keila-Joa 96, 106, 107
Keisripalu stream 267
Keo 93
Kerema 12
Kernu 102
Kihelkonna 38, 41-43
Kihme 340
Kihnu 52, 53
Kiia 106, 109
Kiidjärve 227
Kiikla 161, 162
Kiisa 311
Kiiu 114, 115
Kikevere 348
Kilingi-Nõmme 50, 51
Kiltsi 40, 148
Kingissepa, see Kuressaare,
Kirbla 73
Kirikuküla 267, 275
Kirna 342
Kirumpää 240, 247, 248
Kivinõmme 170, 171
Kivi-Vigala 85, 87
Kiviõli 154, 157, 253
Klooga 106
Kloogaranna 105
Kloostri 74

Kobratu 213
Kodavere 184, 185
Koeru 148, 150, 333-336
Koguva 29
Kohala 131
Kohila 80, 81
Kohtla-Järve 157-159
Kohtla-Nõmme 158
Koidu 315
Koigi 348
Koiva River 274
Kokõmäe 252
Kolga 117
Kolga-Jaani 189, 285, 286
Kolkja 181, 199, 200
Koltsina 161
Kolu 117, 342
Koluvere 66, 67
Konnaoja 260, 270
Koogu 154
Kooljamäed 44
Koonga 54
Koorvere 225, 227
Koovi 39
Koreli stream 248
Koruste 214, 215, 262
Kose 117-119
Kose-Uuemõisa 118, 119
Kosksilla 298
Kostivere 113
Krootuse 221, 229
Kudina 191
Kuiksilla 274, 275
Kuivastu 28, 30, 34
Kukka 14
Kukruse 159
Kukulinna 201
Kullamaa 66-68, 70
Kullenga 145
Kunda 129-132, 348
Kunda River 131
Kundrussaare 189
Kuramaa 312
Kuremaa 180, 307
Kuremaa Lake 185
Kuremäe 170, 171
Kuresoo 288
Kuressaare (Viljandimaa) 315
Kuressaare 28, 36-38
Kurevere 42
Kurgja 60
Kurisoo 328
Kurkse 98
Kurnuvere 293, 294
Kuuni Lake 296
Kuusalu 115, 116
Kuusiku 91
Kuusnõmme 40, 43
Kuutsi 244
Kõinastu laid 29
Kõmsi 74, 75
Kõo 284, 293
Kõpu (Hiiumaa) 8, 20, 21, 26

Kõpu (Viljandimaa) 297
Kõrgessaare 10, 17-20, 210
Kõrkküla 154
Kõrveküla 205
Kõrvemaa 327
Käina 22, 24, 70
Käina bay 22
Käkisilma shallow 43
Kärde 176
Kärdla 10, 14-16, 109
Kärevere (Järvamaa) 345
Kärevere (Tartumaa) 204
Käravete 329
Kärkna 202, 204
Kärla 40, 41
Kärstna 262, 314, 316, 317
Käru 94
Käsmu 122, 124, 125
Käsukonna 348
Kääpa River 171, 183
Kääriku 280
Kükita 338
Külaoru 255
Küti 139
Kütioru 252

Laatre 274
Laekvere 139-141
Lagedi 114
Lahemaa 125, 127, 128, 246
Lahetaguse 40
Laimjala 31, 32
Laitse 101, 102
Laiuse 174, 179, 180
Laiusevälja 179
Lasila 144, 145
Laupa 345
Lavassaare 55, 157
Leale, see Lihula,
Leebiku 262
Leedri 40
Leerimäe 229
Leevaku 167, 232
Lehmja 110, 111
Lehtmetsa 322
Lehtse 322, 324, 325, 329
Leie 286
Leigri 16
Leisi 31, 43
Lemmakõnnu 296
Lemmatsi 206
Lepakose 289
Letipea 131
Lihula 52, 62, 73-75, 204
Liinjärv 251
Liiva 236
Livonia 174, 189, 204, 218, 225, 264, 304, 312, 317
Livonian bay 52
Lilli 304
Lindi 52
Linna 263
Linnaaluste 93

INDEX OF PLACENAMES

Linnamäe 66
Linnaru 20
Lipa 92, 93
Lohkva 205, 206
Lohu 80
Lohusuu 170
Lone, see Lohu,
Loo 113, 114
Loodi 310–312
Loodna 85
Loona 41, 42
Loosu 247
Lossiküla 274, 275
Luidja 20
Luke 213
Lutike 212
Lutsu River 229
Luua 186
Luunja 196, 206, 207
Lõmsi 309
Lõõdla Lake 242
Lämmijärv 209, 218
Läänemaa 13, 62–76, 326, 329
Lääne-Virumaa 115, 121–150, 170, 235, 273
Lääniste 208
Lüganuse 155, 156
Lüllemäe 272, 273
Lümanda 39–41
Lyckholm 65

Maardu 112
Maaritsa 221
Maarja 190
Maasilinn 31
Magari 223
Mahtra 81, 82
Maidla 156, 157
Malvaste 17
Mammaste 225
Manilaid 52
Mannare 58
Martna 68
Massiaru 50
Massu 75
Matsalu 74
Matsalu laht 62
Meeksi 258
Meenikunno (Meenikunnu) 234
Melliste 207
Meremõisa 107
Meremäe 258
Meriküla 154
Meriooni spring 230
Metsakuru 316
Metsaküla 141
Metsaääre 93
Misso 253
Moe 142, 143
Mooste 230, 232
Muhu 28–31, 53
Muraste 108
Mustjala 41, 43

Mustjärv 234, 314
Mustla (Viljandimaa) 314, 315
Mustvee 138, 181–183
Mustvee River 181
Muuga (Harjumaa) 112
Muuga (Lääne-Virumaa) 139, 140
Muuksi 116
Mõdriku 137, 138
Mõega 28
Mõhküla 186
Mõhu 186
Mõisaküla 75, 190, 301–302
Mõniste 244
Mõnspäe 22
Mädara 60
Mäejärv 247
Mäetaguse 161, 162
Mägede 322
Mägipe 20
Mägiste 299, 303
Mäkiste 273
Mäksa 207
Männamaa 22
Männikjärve 176
Männikuste 53
Mäo 338, 339, 348
Märjamaa 67, 87, 88
Määri 141
Müüsleri 332

Naelavere 199
Naha 244
Naissaar 108
Napsi 297
Narva 154, 163–167
Narva River 154, 165, 171, 172
Narva-Jõesuu 164, 165
Navesti River 49, 289
Nedrema 53, 54
Neemi 32
Neemisküla 216
Neeruti 144
Nelijärve 120
Nigula 50, 66
Niitsiku (Niidsiku) 236
Nina 199
Ninametsa 19
Nissi 101
Noarootsi 8, 15, 64, 65
Nohipalo 235
Noodasküla 252
Norra (Järvamaa) 336
Novogrodek, see Vastseliina,
Nurmsi 348
Nuustaku, see Otepää,
Nõo 212, 262
Nõuni 212
Nõva (Jõgevamaa) 184, 185
Nõva (Läänemaa) 64, 65
Nüpli Lake 278

Obinitsa 240, 256–258
Oese 86, 87, 244

Ohulepa 90
Oisu 345
Olustvere 285, 291, 293
Oostriku allikad 336
Oostriku River 336
Orava 236
Orina 330, 331
Orissaare 30, 31
Orjaku 22, 23
Ormsö, see Vormsi,
Osula 246
Otepää 211, 228, 260, 274–280, 292
Oti 31, 32
Otimägi 12, 13
Otipea (Odenpe), see Otepää,
Otissaare 190

Pada River 133, 134
Padaorg 133, 134
Padise 98–101, 204
Paduvere 177
Paide 320, 332, 338–340
Paidra 234
Paistu 294, 310, 312, 313
Paju 270, 271, 274
Pajusti 138
Paka Hill 89
Pakri 104, 105
Pala 183, 184
Palade 14
Palamuse 185, 186
Paldiski 103, 104, 105, 108, 202
Paldiski Gulf 99
Palivere (Järvamaa) 339
Palivere (Läänemaa) 66, 68
Palmse 124–127
Paluküla 14
Pamma 44
Pandivere 122, 140, 148, 198, 235, 337
Panga 43
Pangodi 211
Papisaare 42
Partsi 14
Paunküla 120
Peatskivi 196
Pedja River 141, 177
Peetri (Järvamaa) 332, 337
Peetri (Viljandimaa) 312
Peipsi 171, 172, 174, 181, 182, 184, 185, 194, 199, 209, 218, 225, 347
Penijõe 74
Peraküla 64
Peri 229
Pidula 43
Pihla 18
Pihtla 34
Piibe 150
Piiri 236, 237
Piirissaar 181, 209
Pikajärve 220

Pikasilla 262
Pikevere 148
Pilguse 40
Pilistvere 284, 285, 346, 347
Pilka 203, 207
Pinska 309
Pirita River 111, 112, 114
Piusa 94, 218, 234, 236
Plaani 254
Podmotsa 237
Polli 303
Porkuni 145, 146, 215
Prillapatsi 148
Pringi 111
Prääma 339
Pudivere 141, 142
Puhja 216, 262
Puhtaleiva 201
Puhtulaid 76
Puldre 300
Pulleritsu 293, 313
Pulli 55
Pupastvere 202
Purdi 337
Purku 88, 93
Purtsa 44
Purtse 154, 155
Purtse River 155
Purtsi 262
Puskaru 230
Puurmani 191, 192
Puutli 256
Põdrala 262
Põlgaste 223
Põltsamaa (Jõgevamaa) 174, 186–190, 285, 320
Põltsamaa (Tartumaa) 200, 201
Põlva 223–225, 229, 246
Põlvamaa 167, 217–238
Põrgamõisa 317
Pähkla 35
Päinurme 333
Pärispea 117
Pärlijõgi River 246
Pärnu 46, 48, 49, 52, 55, 59, 60, 103, 304
Pärnu River 55, 56, 58, 337, 338
Pärnumaa 46, 54, 282
Pärsama 44
Pärsti 295, 296
Päärdu 88
Päävakese 236
Pöide 31, 32, 36
Pöögle 300, 304
Pühajõe 160
Pühajõgi, see Võhandu River 246
Pühajärv 279, 280
Pühajärve 279
Pühalepa 10, 12
Pürksi 64, 65
Püssi 139, 154

Rahuoru, see Friedenthal,

INDEX OF PLACENAMES

Raikküla 78, 89, 91, 92
Raja 182
Rajaküla 161
Rakke 122, 149, 150, 333
Rakvere 122, 135–138, 198, 249, 314
Ramsi 311
Rannamõisa 96, 107
Rannapungerja 167
Rannu 154, 215
Rapla 88–91, 93
Raplamaa 78–94
Rassi 347
Rattama 295
Ravila 117, 119
Rebala 112, 113
Rebasmäe 235
Rebastemäe 20
Reigi 18, 19
Reiu River 46, 50, 55, 165
Reval, see Tallinn,
Riidaja 262, 263
Riidma 198
Riisipere 101
Risti 66
Ristimägi 17
Ristna 21
Robbers' Hill 49
Rocca al Mare 244
Roela 139
Rogerwick, see Paldiski,
Rogosi 254
Rohuküla 65
Roobe 264, 268
Roosna-Alliku 328, 336, 337
Rosma 225
Ruila 101
Rupsi 198, 199
Ruusmäe 253
Rõngu 211, 214, 215
Rõuge 245, 250–252, 256
Rõuge Suurjärv 250
Rägavere 137
Räpina 232–234
Rääbise 181
Röa 89

Saadjärv 191, 200, 201
Saarde 50
Saare (Jõgevamaa) 183, 184
Saare (Läänemaa) 65
Saaremaa 23, 25–44, 49, 75, 76, 210, 235, 279, 326, 329, 340
Saarepeedi 309
Saatse 237, 238
Saesaare 226
Sagadi 127, 128
Saku 109
Salme River 38
Salumägi 54
Sangaste 57, 260, 274, 275, 279
Sarvi 52
Sauevälja 145

Saverna 220, 221
Saxby 65
Seidla 328
Selja River 129, 134
Serga 258
Siber (Lääne-Virumaa) 132
Sihva 280
Siimusti 179
Sillamäe 152, 162–164
Sillapää 233, 234
Simuna 122, 139–141
Sindi 55, 56
Sinijärv 148, 235
Sinimäed 163, 164
Sipa 84, 85
Sonda 133, 154, 157
Soomaa 288, 294, 297
Soontagana 54, 55
Sopa spring 336
Sudiste 303
Suislepa 282, 314, 317, 318
Sulaoja 221
Surva 287
Suur Munamägi 240, 253
Suur Siniallik 311
Suur Väin 28
Suure-Jaani 282, 288–291, 295
Suure-Lähtru 68
Suuremõisa 10–13, 210
Suursadam 13, 18
Suur-Taevaskoda 226, 227
Suurupi 108, 124
Sviby 65
Sõmerpalu 246
Sõmeru 136
Sõru 22
Sõrve 38, 39, 108
Sõõru 185
Sänna 242, 244–246
Särevere 342, 344
Sääre 13
Sääre tirp 23

Taagepera 260, 264, 265
Tabivere 190, 191
Taebla 66
Tagametsa 347
Tagamõisa 42
Tahkuna 17, 18, 21, 108
Tahkuranna 48
Tallinn 31, 53, 80, 83, 88, 94, 96, 101, 103, 105, 107–111, 130, 140, 148, 160, 163, 167, 179, 187, 190, 196, 202, 204, 214, 220, 221, 230, 249, 290, 291, 301, 308, 322, 323, 326, 330, 332, 336
Tamme (Põlvamaa) 236
Tamme (Raplamaa) 89
Tamme (Tammõ) 221
Tammeküla 284
Tamsalu 94, 145, 146
Tamula Lake 248, 249, 250

INDEX OF PLACENAMES

Tapa 142, 143, 329
Tartu 39, 90, 150, 179, 181, 190, 192, 194, 199, 202, 204–206, 210, 212, 213, 214, 223, 225, 229, 230, 248, 249, 254, 255, 270, 276, 287, 292
Tartumaa 193–216, 279
Tarvastu 315, 316
Teenuse 85
Tehumardi 39
Tiheda 182
Tihemetsa 51
Tilleoru 230
Tindiorg 251
Tinnikuru 315
Tipu 297
Tobrova 258
Tohisoo 80
Toila 160, 161
Toolamaa 233
Toolse 122, 129, 130
Toolse River 130
Tooma 176
Toomja 93
Toravere 342
Tori 56–58
Torila 199
Torma 170, 179–181, 196
Tormi 191
Tornimäe (Saaremaa) 31, 32
Tornimägi (Hiiumaa) 20
Tsirguliina 274
Tsooru 242
Tubala 15
Tuderna 236
Tudulinna 152, 167, 169, 315
Tuhala 117, 169
Tuhala River 117
Tuhalaane 304
Tuhkvitsa oja 256
Tuiu 43
Turba 101
Tõhela Lake 53
Tõlluste 34
Tõnuküla 287, 304
Tõravere 212
Tõrva 264, 265, 268
Tõrvaaugu 347
Tõstamaa 52, 53
Tänassilma 285, 287
Türi 60, 320, 342–345
Türisalu 96, 107

Uhaku 156
Uhtjärv 242
Uhtna 131
Uniküla 198, 269
Unipiha 212
Urvaste 242, 243, 246
Utria 164
Utu 22
Uue-Antsla (Vahtsõ-Antsla) 243, 244
Uue-Vändra 305

Uulu 48
Uusküla 90

Vaali 333, 334
Vaemla 24
Vahastu 94
Vahtrepa 13
Vaida 348
Vaidavere 191
Vaikla 167
Vaimastvere 176, 177
Vainu 157
Vainupea 128, 129
Vaivara 154, 163, 164
Valaste 158
Valga 51, 165, 260, 268–272
Valgamaa 259–280
Valgesoo 227
Valgjärv 220, 221, 235
Valgjärve 220
Valgu 88
Valguta 215
Valipe 10
Valjala 33, 34
Valka 260, 270, 271
Valkla 114
Valli 94
Valtu 93
Vana-Antsla 243, 244
Vana-Kariste 303
Vana-Koiola 248
Vana-Kuuste 210
Vanamõisa (Läänemaa) 73
Vanamõisa (Lääne-Virumaa) 135
Vanamõisa (Tartumaa) 206
Vanamõisa (Viljandimaa) 295
Vanamõisa Lake 268
Vana-Vastseliina 254
Vana-Vigala 85, 86
Vana-Võidu 307
Vao (Harjumaa) 115
Vao (Järvamaa) 333
Vao (Lääne-Virumaa) 148
Varangu 134, 148, 149, 335
Varbla 53
Varbola 78, 82, 83, 88
Varbuse 229
Vardi 83, 84
Varnja 181, 199, 200
Vasalemma 98
Vasknarva 170–172
Vastemõisa 288, 294, 295
Vastse-Kuuste 210
Vastseliina 230, 240, 254–256
Vasula 203
Vatla 76
Vea 185
Veeru oja, see Koreli oja,
Veisjärv 317
Weissenstein, see Paide,
Velise 88
Verevi Lake 213
Verhulitsa 238

KOHANIMED

Verijärve 252
Verioja 273
Veriora 234, 235
Wesenbergh, see Rakvere,
Veskimäe 207
Vetepere 326-328
Vidva River 298
Vigala 86
Vihasoo 125
Vihi 288
Vihterpalu 98
Vihula 124, 127, 128
Viidumäe 26
Viimsi 111, 309
Viinistu 117
Viivikonna 154
Vikati 43
Viki 41
Vilimeeste 314
Vilivalla 98
Viljandi 60, 134, 264, 266, 291, 292, 296, 297, 300, 301, 304-309, 346
Viljandi Lake 307
Viljandimaa 262, 279, 281-318, 346
Vilsandi 41-43
Viluste 235
Viraksaare 320, 339
Virtsu 62, 66, 73, 74
Viru-Jaagupi 138, 139
Viru-Nigula 129, 132-134, 170, 273
Viruvere 179
Viskoosa 20, 21
Vohnja 143
Voika 212
Voltveti 51, 161
Vooreküla 229
Vooremaa 200
Vorbuse 205
Vormsi 8, 15, 62, 65, 66
Võhandu River 218, 222, 232-234, 242, 246
Võhma 284
Võhmanõmme 188
Võiküla 28
Võisiku 189
Võnnu 56, 194, 207, 208
Võpolsova 237
Võrtsjärv 194, 214, 216, 262, 313
Võru 105, 229, 230, 235, 246-250
Võrumaa 239-258, 279
Võsu 122, 124, 125
Võtikvere 183
Võuküla 232
Vööpsu 237
Vägeva 148, 150, 176
Väike Emajõgi 269
Väike Väin 29, 30
Väike-Maarja 140, 145-148, 198, 223, 329, 331
Väike-Taevaskoda 226, 227
Väimela 246, 247
Väinameri 10

Väinjärv 335
Väinjärve 334, 336
Vällamägi 240, 253
Vändra 46, 58, 59, 60, 146, 275
Värska 218, 225, 237, 238
Värska bay 237
Väägvere 205, 206
Vääna 107

Õhne River 266, 268, 318
Õisu 298, 299, 309
Õvi 204

Ähijärv 244
Äksi 170, 201-203
Äntu 148

Österby 64
Ööbikuorg 250, 251

Ühtri 22
Ülendi 20
Ülenurme 210
Ülgase 113

INDEX OF PERSONAL NAMES

Aaloe, Ago 235
Aamisepp, Julius 178
Aavik, Johannes 38
Aavik, Joosep 38
Adamson, Amandus 105, 249, 294, 329, 348
Adamson, Hendrik 282, 317
Adamson, Jaan 293, 312, 313, 314
Aderkasid 31
Adson, Artur 244, 245, 262
Ahrens, Eduard 116
Ahrens, Karl 20
Akel, Friedrich Karl 300
Albert 73, 292
Alexander I 189, 222
Alexander II 70, 125, 140, 294, 312
Alexander III 48, 70, 294
Alexy II 171
Alisch, Paul Friedrich Wilhelm 91
Alver, Betti 177, 178
Andreas, K. C. 306
Angern, Haenrich fan 81
Annist, August 286
Anrep, Reinhold von 316
Ariste, Paul 181
Arrak, Jüri 299
Arvelius, Friedrich Gustav 161
Ast-Rumor, Karl 236
Aznalin, Julai 104

Bach, Aino 335
Backhoff, Anne 289

Baer, Alexander von 333
Baer, Helene von 333
Baer, Hermann von 333
Baer, Juliana Louise von 333
Baer, Karl Ernst von 122, 145, 150, 280, 333, 334
Baer, Ludwig von 333
Baggehufwudt, Josephine von 64
Baggehufvudt, Valerian von 109
Baranov 57
Baranovski, G. 160
Barclay de Tolly, Michael Andreas 260, 268, 334
Beermann, Christoph Wilhelm 333
Beermann, Gustav Heinrich 333
Beethoven 83
Bellingshausen, Fabian Gottlieb Benjamin von 40
Benckendorff, Alexander von 106, 107
Benckendorff, Hans von 323
Benedictus 204
Benito Agirre 182
Berg, Friedrich Georg Magnus von 57, 260, 274, 275
Bezobrasov 88, 93
Birnbaum, Ernst 149
Bismarck, Otto 92
Bock, Alexander Friedrich 348
Bock, Timotheus Eberhardt von 189
Bohn, Herman Jensen von 112, 113
Bonnius, Franz 215
Borch, Simon van der 145
Bornhöhe, Eduard 135
Brandt, Friedrich 85
Brevern, Hans von 112, 113, 135
Brocmann, Reiner 144
Budberg, Otto von 73
Buhrmeister, Christopher von 191
Buxhoevden, Otto von 41
Buxhoevden (Buxhövden), Hermann, see Hermann I
Buxhövden, Reinhold von 76
Büll (Bühl), Anna Hedvig 70

Cancrin, Georg von (Kankrin, Jegor) 91
Charles IX 244
Carl XI 211
Carl XII 13, 102, 166, 180, 230
Catherine I 208
Catherine II 8, 18, 67, 104, 246, 248, 285, 336
Colongues, Peter Georg von 296
Columbus 21
Cybei, Giovanni Antonio 298

Darwin, Charles 78, 92
De la Gardie, Ebba Margaretha, see Stenbock, Ebba Margaretha
De la Gardie, Magnus Gabriel 69
Dellingshausen, Eduard von 125, 134
Demut-Malinovski, Vassili 269

Dido, Andres 263
Ditmar, Woldemar Dimitri von 265, 305
Dobrynya Nikitich 171
Dreileben, Burchard von 340

Eenpalu, Kaarel 203
Eisen, Johann Georg 170
Eisen, Matthias Johann 86, 87, 275
Elizaveta Petrovna 10, 104
Enno, Ernst 215
Erdell, Hans 264
Erdell, Mats 264
Ernesaks, Gustav 290
Ernits, Villem 184
Espenberg, Karl 332

Faehlmann, Friedrich Robert 122, 149
Fersen, Hans Axel 291
Folkvin 292
Forselius, Bengt Gottfried 96, 98, 99, 210, 211, 225, 278, 330
Forselius, Johann 99
Frederik II 187

Gailit, August 230, 260, 262, 274
Gebhardt, Eduard Karl Franz 330
Gediminas 247
Gerassimov, Mihhail 120
Glasenapp, Guido von 254
Glasenapp, Otto von 254
Glasenapp, Patrick von 254
Goethe, Johann Wolfgang 83, 184
Gorki, Maksim 323
Gortchakov, Aleksandr 72
Grünthal-Ridala, Villem 28
Gustav II Adolf 100
Gutsleff, Johan 242, 246
Göseken, Heinrich 67

Haava, Anna 184, 221
Haberlandt, Christoph von 270
Hagen, Johann August von 84
Hainsalu, Lehte 266
Handsome Villem, see Tamm, Villem
Hannibal, Abram 103
Hansen, August 327
Hansen, Leopold 214
Hansen, Peeter 327
Hansen, Robert Theodor 167
Hebbe 292
Heiberg, Marie 242, 243
Heimthal, Luise 309
Heinsalu, Ülo 117
Helffreich, Constantin von 81
Helle, Anton Thor 110, 112
Helmersen, Georg 15
Henno, Hain 314
Henry of Livonia 54, 82, 122, 190, 191, 275, 284, 292, 295, 337
Hermann I 68, 204, 276
Hermann, Karl August 188, 189, 277, 314

INDEX OF PERSONAL NAMES

Hermann, Paula 189, 277
Hilane Taarka 256, 257
Hindrey, Karl August 300, 304
Hint, Aadu 40
Hint, Johannes 40
Hippius, Otto Pius 274
Holst, Matthias von 306, 313
Hornung, Johann 216, 273
Hoyningen-Huene, Friedrich Alexander Georg von 325
Hunnius, Carl (Karl) Abraham 70
Hupel, August Wilhelm 201, 285, 305, 341
Hurt, Jakob 221, 228, 229, 263, 277, 278, 280, 294, 314
Hurt-Meyer 214
Härma, Miina 205
Häusermann 299

Ignati (Ignatsi) Jaak 210, 211, 278
Ilmjärv, Mihkel 57
Ingvar 13
Innocentius VI 254
Irv, Anton 306
Ivan III 316
Ivan IV (Terrible) 174, 187, 338

Jaaksoo, Asta 304
Jacobs, E. 273
Jaik, Juhan 245
Jakobson, Adam 180
Jakobson, Carl Robert 59, 60, 180, 181, 196, 228, 229, 263, 282, 294, 306, 307
Jakobson, Eduard Magnus 180
Jannsen, Johann Voldemar 46, 59, 228
Jannsen, Lydia Emilie Florentine, see Koidula, Lydia
Johanson, Ado 296, 297
Johanson, Friedrich 251
Jung, Jaan 284, 311
Jürgens, Hermine Elisabeth 201
Jürima, August 333
Jürisson, Johannes 288
Jürmann, Mart 333
Jürmann, Voldemar 333

Kalev 150, 201
Kalevipoeg 58, 101, 113, 137, 150, 170, 171, 181, 183, 184, 197, 200, 201, 209, 221, 249, 303, 311, 322, 326, 347
Kallas, Aino 19, 23
Kallas, Oskar 23, 287
Kangro, Bernard 244
Kangro, Tauno 136
Kapp, Artur 290, 338
Kapp, Eugen 290
Kapp, Hans 290, 291
Kapp, Joosep 290
Kapp, Villem 291
Kappel, Johannes 90

Karell, Philipp 294
Karl XVI Gustav 71
Karmin, Mati 18, 58, 250
Karupää, Mari-Ann 279
Kask, Mihkel 205
Kekkonen, Urho Kaleva 280
Kelch, Christian 329, 330
Kempe, Jonas 21
Kents, Jakob 325
Kes, Hans, see Käsu Hans
Kettler, Goddert (Gotthard) 214
Keyserling, Alexander Friedrich von 78, 91, 92
Keyserling, Arnold von 92
Keyserling, Eduard von 92
Keyserling, Hermann Alexander von 76, 92
Kihnu Jõnn, see Uuetoa, Enn
Kiiss, Aksel 197
Kingissepp, Viktor 36
Kipper, Aksel 213
Kirschten, Eduard Heinrich von 144
Kirsipuu, Tiiu 245
Kits, Elmar 214, 262
Kitzberg, August 282, 299, 300, 302, 303, 304
Klein, Valve 341
Knauf, G. 306
Knüpffer, Arnold Friedrich Johann 144
Knüpffer, Rudolf Otto von 71
Koidula, Lydia 46, 59, 105, 221, 289
Kongla Anne 132
Koort, Jaan 202, 300
Koppel, Henrik 287, 288, 304
Koppel, Karl, 287
Kotkas, Johannes 211
Kotli, Alar 302
Kotzebue, Aleksander von 84
Kotzebue, August von 83, 84, 161
Kotzebue, Otto von 84, 119
Kreek, Cyrillus 72
Kreutzwald, Friedrich Reinhold 90, 105, 122, 137, 144, 184, 221, 248, 249
Kriisa, Eduard 253
Kriisa, Hardo 253
Kriisa, Jakob 253
Kriisa, Juhan 253
Kriisa, Tannil 253
Kross, Jaan 189, 336
Krusenstern, Adam Johann von 40, 90, 146, 147, 148, 333
Krusenstern, Paul Theodor von 147
Kruszewska, Marie 308
Krusten, Erni (Ernst) 108
Krusten, Otto 108
Krusten, Pedro (Peeter) 108
Krümmer, K. 248
Kudu, Fred 280
Kuhlbars, Friedrich 269, 282
Kuld, Riho 341
Kuljus, Voldemar 168
Kunder, Juhan 312, 313, 314

Kuperjanov, Julius 57, 192, 211, 260, 270
Kurberg, Jakob 142
Kutuzov 334
Kuulbusch, Aime 299
Kuusik, Edgar Johan 220, 300, 301
Käis, Johannes 225
Käsu Hans 194, 216
Köler, Johann 23, 24, 294, 295, 306, 312
Körber, E. P. 231
Küchelbecker, Wilhelm 169
Kügelgen, Ferdinand von 139
Laidoner, Johan 111, 263, 264, 307, 308, 346
Laikmaa, Ants 66, 330
Laksi Tõnis 196
Larka, Aleksander 212
Larka, Andres 345, 346
Lattik, Jaan 273, 306
Laurits, Peeter 252
Lauw, Woldemar Johann von 187, 188
Lavretsov, S. A. 166
Leiger 23
Leinberg, Juhan 326, 336
Lembitu 284, 289, 291, 292, 295, 296
Lempelius, Paulus Andreas 19
Lepik Elisabet, see Alver, Betti
Lepik, Kalju 335
Lepp, A. 244
Liiv, Jakob 147, 197, 199
Liiv, Juhan 147, 194, 198, 199, 243, 282, 306
Liphart, Gotthard Lionel von 255
Liphart, Karl Eduard von 210
Liphart, Karl Gotthard von 210
Litke, Fjodor Petrovits, see Lütke, Friedrich Benjamin
Lohkva Taavet, see Wirkhaus, David
Loorts, Oskar 297
Luce, Johann Wilhelm Ludwig von 40
Lueder, Karl von 80
Luha, Voldemar 293
Luiga, Georg Eduard 220
Lurich, Georg 147
Luts, Oskar 185, 186
Luts, Theodor 185, 186
Luup, Rein 306
Läte, Aleksander 214, 262
Lönnrot, Elias 116, 333
Löwenwolde 233
Lütke, Friedrich Benjamin 122, 140, 141

Maasik, Elmar 262
Magnus 36, 94, 187
Maibach, Karl Ludwig 135
Maide, Jaan 342
Malm, Karl Johann 11
Manassein 312
Manitski, Jaan 117

Mannteuffel, Peter August Friedrich von 119
Manteuffel, Heinrich Otto Zoege von 139
Maran, Rein 323
Markson, Jakob 50
Marx, Karl 313
Masing, Otto Wilhelm 58, 59, 132, 133, 156, 170, 201
Masing, Uku 92, 93
Mattiisen, Alo 177, 178
Maydell, Friedrich Ludwig von 85, 224
Mellik, Tõnu 156
Mellik, Voldemar 156, 277
Mellin, Ludwig August 169
Meri, Harald 342
Mesenkampffs 316
Michelson, Johann 334, 336
Mickwitz, Dietrich Georg von 333
Middendorff, Alexander Theodor von 56, 228, 280
Middendorff, Ernst von 280
Mihkelson, Jüri 221
Miko Ode 257
Modena Wilhelm 260, 270, 292, 337
Moor, Felix 343
Moora, Harri 231
Mothander, Carl 80
Mothe 133
Mstislav Uljas 82
Muick, Jacob 126
Murrik, Ella Marie, see Wuolijoki, Hella
Murrik, Kadri 264
Mõtused 272
Mägi, Konrad 220
Mägiste, Julius 190
Mälk, August 39
Märtson, Johannes 271
Münnich, Burkhard Cristoph von 206

Napoleon 83, 268
Neff, Carl Timoleon von 139, 140, 141
Neuland, Alfred 271, 272
Nicholas I 70, 105, 106, 169
Nicholas II 70
Nikon 181, 225
Nolcken, Arved von 196
Nolcken, Georg von 206

Ohakas, Valdur 252
Okas, Evald 72, 73
Old Devil 35, 58, 101, 117, 223, 266, 298, 303
Oldekop, Gustav Adolph 222, 224
Oldenbockum, Kaspar (Jasper) von 85
Ollmann, Aksel 251, 252
Orlov, Grigori 66, 67
Osten-Sacken, Carl Magnus von 342
Otto, Johann Nicolaus 304

Pahlen, Alexander von der 126

INDEX OF PERSONAL NAMES

Pahlen, Carl Magnus von der 126
Pahlen, Gustav Wilhelm Gotthard von der 24
Pahnsch, Gerhard Alexander 84
Pakri Hansu Jüri 210
Palusalu, Kristjan 53
Pant, Valdo 220
Parijõgi, Jüri 132
Parnabas, Aleksei 88, 89
Paul I 342
Pavlov, Ivan 162
Peep, Helend 167
Peips, Leida 309
Peter I (Suur) 103, 104, 108, 255, 273
Peter III, see Pugatchov, Jemeljan
Peterson, Adam 312
Peterson, Peeter 312
Peterson-Särgava, Ernst 323
Petri, Christoph 84
Piiper, Johannes 323
Pill, Mihkel 178, 275, 315
Pinka, Friedrich Karl 317
Pinka, Herbert 317
Pirogov, Nikolai 36
Pisumaa, Darja, see Hilane Taarka
Pitka (Ansomardi), Peäro August 331
Pitka, Johan 331, 332
Poniatowski, Stanislaw August 285
Pool, Theodor Johann 58
Poska, Jaan 179
Potjomkin 336
Preobrazhenski, M. 171
Prophet Maltsvet see Leinberg, Juhan
Pugatchov, Jemeljan 104, 336
Pushkin, Aleksandr 103, 169
Pärt, Arvo 341
Päts, Konstantin 39, 48, 114, 203, 287, 308, 332, 346
Päts, Voldemar 114
Pöögelmann, Hans 312

Quandt, Johann Christian 242

Raave, Kalev 299
Rabe, Johann Valentin 159
Rand, Mihkel 32
Rastrelli, Bartolomeo 133
Ratisepp, Anne 291
Raud, Anu 309
Raud, Kristjan 138, 198, 330
Raud, Mart 309, 312
Raud, Paul 138, 330
Raudsepp, Hugo 176, 177
Raudsepp, Juhan 66, 112, 125, 333
Rehbinder, Carl Friedrich von 109
Reht, Jakob 41
Reiman, Villem 285, 286
Reinthal, Carl Gottlieb 302
Reitel, Kalju 23
Rennenkampff, Jakob Gustav von 266
Rennit, Andres 315

Resev, Madis 333
Riikoja, Heinrich 149
Rimm, Aulin 10
Rimski-Korsakov, Nikolai 288, 290, 338
Ristikivi, Karl 53
Rogosinski, Stanislaus 254
Roht, Richard 225
Roosileht, August 332
Rosen, Dorothea Augusta von 76
Rosen, Friedrich von 161
Rosen, Otto Fabian von 143, 162
Rosladen, Vassili 154
Roth, Carl August von 222
Roth, Georg Philipp August von 222
Roth, Johann Philipp von 222
Rüütel, Arnold 323

Saar, Mart 282, 288, 291, 338
Saar, Veera 323
Saareste, Andrus 323
Sabbe, August 234
Saebelmann, Friecrich August 313
Saedler, Marie Elisabeth 248
Sagrits, Richard 128, 129
Salavat Julajev 104
Salum, Vello 285
Shakhovskoi, Sergei 171
Sheremetev, Boriss 203, 206, 223, 269
Schiemann, Theodor 305
Schiller, Friedrich 76, 184, 266
Schilling, Carl von 329
Schilling, Hermann Otto 154
Schilling, Nikolai von 330, 331
Schilling, Valentin von 293
Schlippenbach, Wolmar Anton von 241, 287, 223, 269
Schmidt, Carl Friedrich 58
Schtschedrin, Apollon 269
Schultz, Hans Anton 333
Schultz, Johann 337
Schultz-Bertram, Georg Julius 181
Schwartz, Johann Georg 224
Schüdlöffel, Gustav Heinrich 113
Sedunov, Igor 171
Severjanin, Igor 161
Siimon, Abram 160, 161
Sikenberg, Jakob 326
Sillaots, Marta 149
Sirp, Ülo 16
Sisask, Urmas 324
Sivers, Peter Reinhold von 309
Skuratov, Maljuta 338
Skytte, Johan 203
Smuul, Juhan 19, 29, 53, 232, 323
Soans, Jaak 303
Sofronov, Pimen 182
Sokolovski, Ernst 60, 146
Sooster, Ülo 22
Soots, Jaan 263, 264
Soucanton, Johann Girard de 130, 131

Sprenael, Albert 277
St George 58
Stackelberg, Eduard Heinrich August 23
Stackelberg, Margarethe Victoria 176
Stackelberg, Nikolai von 154
Stackelberg, Olaf von 338
Stackelberg, Otto Friedrich von 337
Stackelberg, Otto Magnus von 107
Stackelberg, Peter von 101
Stackelberg, Viktor von 176
Stael von Holstein, Alexander Wilhelm 53
Stael von Holstein, Reinhold 48
Stahl, Heinrich 143, 144, 242, 320
Stalin, Jossif 163, 231, 240, 308
Starkopf, Anton 89, 90, 329
Stebel, Aleksander 38
Stenbock, Ebba Margarehta 10
Stenbock, Jakob Pontus 10
Stenbock, Karl Magnus 18
Stieglitz, A. 202
Stiernhielm, Georg von 203
Struve, Friedrich Georg Wilhelm 141, 212, 213
Stryk, Hugo von 263, 264
Stryk, W. v. 169
Suburg, Lilli Caroline 59, 60
Suits, Gustav 194, 208, 209
Sutor, Albrecht 211
Suuman, Aleksander 141, 168
Suur Tõll 26, 34, 35
Särgava, Ernst 59
Sööt, Karl Eduard 206
Sütiste, Juhan 204

Zakrevskaja-Benckendorff-Budberg, Maria 323

Tallents, Stephen Georg 270
Talomees, Vileomon 257
Talpak, Karl 202
Talvik, Heiti 177
Tamm, Villem 23
Tammsaare, Anton Hansen 274, 289, 320, 326, 327, 328
Taniloo, Endel 16, 132, 207, 210
Tarning, Karel 16
Taube, von 94
Teppo, Aleksander 247
Teppo, August 247, 248
Thauvon, Aino 208
Thimm, Woldemar Alexander 48
Tiedemann, Signe 125
Tief, Otto 90
Tiesenhausen, Barbara von 146, 199, 215
Tiesenhausen, Fabian von 115
Tiesenhausen, Jürgen von 215
Tiiman, Joosep 179
Tobias, Rudolf 24, 70, 338
Tode, Emil 285
Toi, Roman 290

Toll, Carl Friedrich von 334, 335
Toll, Carl von 335
Toll, Eduard 159
Toll, Nikolai von 335
Tomp, Jaan 313
Toom, Artur 42
Toom, Kusta, see Toomingas, August
Toomingas, August 214, 262
Treffner, Hugo 202
Tchaikovski, Pjotr 71
Tubin, Eduard 146, 199
Tuglas, Friedebert 221, 230, 231, 262
Tõnisson, Ilmar 287
Tõnisson, Jaan 286, 287, 300
Tõnisson, Mats 60, 304
Törs, Johannes 114
Türi, Arnold 22

Uexküll, Boris von 62, 85, 86
Uexküll, Jakob Johann von 62, 76
Uluots, Jüri 202
Under, Marie 160, 230, 245, 262
Ungern-Sternberg, Alexander Peter von 337
Ungern-Sternberg, Gustav Dietrich Otto von 19
Ungern-Sternberg, Heinrich Georg Eduard von 13, 15
Ungern-Sternberg, Johann Karl Emmanuel von 64
Ungern-Sternberg, Otto Reinhold Ludwig von 10, 11, 19, 210
Ungern-Sternberg, Peter Ludwig Konstantin von 15, 108
Ungern-Sternberg, Robert Eginhard von 16
Uthander, Matthias 242
Utuste, Marta 323
Uuetoa, Enn 53

Vabarna, Anne 218, 237
Vahtra, Jaan 224, 232
Vaik, Aarne 124
Walther, Carl 84
Vana-Rein, see Stael von Holstein, Reinhold
Vares-Barbarus, Johannes 311, 312
Vasara, Epp 310
Veeber, Renaldo 238
Weizenberg, August Ludwig 221, 222, 348
Weitzenberg, Juhan 196
Veller, Jüri 32
Wells, Herbert George 323
Veske, Mihkel 312, 313, 314
Veski, Johannes Voldemar 191
Weymarn, Heinrich von 285
White Lady 69, 266
Viies, Edgar 306
Viiralt, Eduard 148, 149, 307, 335
Vilbaste (Vilberg), Gustav 116
Wildau, Otto 264, 265

Vilde, Eduard 102, 103, 141, 142
Wilde, Peter Ernst 188, 305, 320, 341
Wilhelm 76
Villebois, A. G. de 208
Vilms, Jüri 284, 346
Virgin Mary 69, 171
Virginius (Verginius), Adrian 216, 278
Virginius (Verginius), Andreas 211, 216
Wirkhaus, David 205
Wirkhaus, David Otto 205, 206
Visnapuu, Henrik 160, 230, 262
Wolffeldt 51
Volkonski, Grigori Petrovits 107
Volkonski, Peeter 107
Wrangell, Benita von 80
Wrangell, Ferdinand von 138, 139
Wrangell, Woldemar 285
Wulff-Õis, Gustav 278
Wuolijoki, Hella 264, 304
Võerahansu, Johannes 93
Wöhrmann, J. C. 55
Württembergi Augusta Carolina 67

Äkkemäe, Rein 197

Öhmann, Thomas 284

Yelissejev, Grigori 160

PHOTOS:

Jacket:
Toomas Kokovkin

Inside:
Jaak Arro,
Endel Grenzmann
Mari Kaljuste
Toomas Kukk
Ulvi Lahesalu
Tiit Leito
Hendrik Laur
Peeter Maide
Priit Maide
Eeva Mägi
Karl Mägi
Maria Mägi-Rohtmets
Tiit Pääsuke
Aarne Randveer
Hendrik Relve
Indrek Rohtmets
Tanel Traks
Toomas Tuul

302152
285,-